Mississippi
John Hurt

Mississippi John Hurt

HIS LIFE, HIS TIMES, HIS BLUES

Philip R. Ratcliffe

UNIVERSITY PRESS OF MISSISSIPPI • JACKSON

American Made Music Series

David Evans, General Editor
Barry Jean Ancelet
Edward A. Berlin
Joyce J. Bolden
Rob Bowman
Susan C. Cook
Curtis Ellison
William Ferris

John Edward Hasse
Kip Lornell
Bill Malone
Eddie S. Meadows
Manuel H. Peña
David Sanjek
Wayne D. Shirley
Robert Walser

www.upress.state.ms.us

The University Press of Mississippi is a member of the
Association of American University Presses.

Page ii: Detail from brochure advertising Mississippi John Hurt
at the 1966 Philadelphia Folk Festival. (Tom Hoskins Archive.)

First printing 2011

∞

Library of Congress Cataloging-in-Publication Data

Ratcliffe, Philip R.
Mississippi John Hurt : his life, his times, his blues / Philip R. Ratcliffe.
p. cm. — (American made music series)
Includes bibliographical references and index.
ISBN 978-1-61703-008-6 (cloth : alk. paper) — ISBN 978-1-61703-009-3
(ebook) 1. Hurt, Mississippi John, 1894–1966. 2. Blues musicians—
United States—Biography. I. Title.
ML420.H986R37 2011
782.421643092—DC22
[B]   2010050419

British Library Cataloging-in-Publication Data available

Contents

Foreword

This book confirms what I have known and have come to accept and appreciate for most of my life: that my Daddy John[1] had a supernatural spirit that had a far greater effect on people than his music alone. I did not arrive at this personal and profound revelation based on the numerous musicians that have been inspired by him. Frankly, it was not his music, but his strong mythical spirit that has had such a resounding affect on my life!

Daddy John had many wonderful qualities that I admired and longed to mimic. His ability to speak loud without uttering a sound was so powerful and chilling. Yet, when he did infrequently verbalize his thoughts, his words were chosen carefully and delivered with such gentle wisdom and authority that one did not question or request further explanation because somehow, you just knew what he said was right!

Just watching Daddy John play his guitar was enough entertainment for me. Even the mere preparation for him to play was comical. Before every family or neighborhood performance, my father, T. C., would have in place for Daddy John his favorite straw back chair, a large dishpan of roasted peanuts, and a bottle enclosed in a too worn brown paper bag. When he arrived and saw everything in place, a smile of approval and a gentlemanly nod said it was party time!

I can still visualize Daddy John playing on the dusty circle drawn stage of our front yard, totally absorbed in his music. While the people clapped and stomped their feet in agreement with the music, Daddy John's smile would widen like a stone thrown in a pond. If it was a moonless night, to me the radiance of his smile took its place. Always on the sideline was his biggest fan, Miss Jessie, shouting sporadically with her girlish voice, "Go John Hurt, you Play that Thing!" Whenever that request was made,

Daddy John's reaction would always be the same, his shoulders would take a dip, and he would play even harder, while Miss Jessie went into a trancelike state, moving her head slowly with her eyes tightly closed and snapping her fingers in the air. It was all so funny because the songs all sounded much the same, as Daddy John never sang out loud while the younger children were around. Today, I understand why! I and my siblings do not remember hearing many of Daddy John's songs that are so popular with musicians today and we certainly didn't know the words till we were much older!

My father, T. C., had the same very distinctive physical features of Daddy John. Like Daddy John, he was short in stature, but his strong and intense character made him a giant! Comparing their personalities as they might relate to the weather, Daddy John was a perfect summer day while daddy was subzero most of the time. It is hard to describe a man like my father; he was a good provider, pious, and the most talented self-taught mechanic that I have ever known. He raised the finest livestock and produced enough vegetables to provide for his large family, give to the elders of the community, and sell at the town's market for extra cash. Besides Daddy John, the only other people that could melt that ice of a personality were my mom, the sister before me, Bobbie Jean, my brother, T. C. Jr., and my baby sister, Mary Ann.

Only God truly knows why or how a son could be so different from his father. Today, I can understand to some degree how circumstances could have altered him. After discovering some pieces of his life, it seems to me, he was born in the midst of confusion! His grandmother, Ida, married his uncle, Hardy, whose brother John married his mother, Gertrude, the daughter of Ida. For reasons unknown, his mother took him and his sister from their father, changing his last name to Conley. Two of his uncles successively married the same woman, both having children by her, and his only sister, Idella (Ida Mae), was killed by an adulterous husband. Later, his first grandchild Margaret Ann was tragically killed by her stepfather.

Additionally, Daddy was sick for all of the time I remember him. He was forever in pain with gaping recurring sores on his legs. Stuffed in his back pocket always was a bottle of Triple A, an over-the-counter medication for stomach pain. In a sense, Daddy lived his name, Hurt. It must have been painful for him to experience so much pain in his short life. However, Daddy did enjoy good times despite his hardships. He and my mother Annie Dora were two peas in a pod. For those Saturday night gatherings they worked together roasting peanuts and frying fish and laughing like newlyweds. Daddy John also helped Daddy put down those heavy bags of sadness with his music and his calmness. On some of those occasions, Daddy would play background to some of the songs with his harmonica. Daddy was a kind of closet harmonica player and wasn't that good, but whenever he joined in with Daddy John, the light of a smile would come on.

At an early age I sensed the strange magnetic or supernatural force that surrounded Daddy John. I don't know how many of my sisters and brothers felt the same, but we all had an opportunity to witness that supernatural force in action on the day of our father's funeral, en route to the cemetery in Daddy's Chevy pickup truck filled to capacity with ten of the fourteen of us, and Daddy John. We were leading the caravan of cars to the burial site, which was a one way in and out narrow road with a steep incline. Just as we got to the peak of the hill, the truck suddenly stopped. Louis, my brother-in-law, a mechanic by trade, tried with no avail to restart the truck. After some time, Louis finally threw up his hands and admitted to Daddy John that the truck was not going to start and they should think about how they were going to manually take my father's casket to the burial site. Daddy John got out of the truck without uttering a word; he simply nodded and held his finger to his lips for us to stop talking. He then moved to the center of the road, removed his hat and held it to his chest in a dignified manner. Forgetting any of us were there he looked toward the sky, cleared his throat, and began talking to Daddy as if he was standing in front of him. "T. C., son, I know this is your doing, but I want you to know that everything is going to be o.k. I gonna see to Annie and the children. Now I want you to let me take your babies here to say a proper goodbye to you." He continued to look toward the sky; suddenly a huge grin came over his face. He nodded, put back on his hat, looked up again to the sky and said, "Much obliged!" He jumped back into the truck, and shouted, "Hit it Louis!" With some hesitation, Louis turned the key and the truck roared in response and continued to its destination. We looked at each other speechless and, strangely, never talked about that day for years afterward.

Like all of my sisters and brothers, I enjoyed Daddy John's music, but it was something much more than his music that intrigued me about him. My intuitive nature kept me on the search whenever Daddy John was around to find the source of that supernatural power. Then one Sunday in church, Reverend Young, the minister of Saint James Church, centered his sermon on Samson, a biblical character whose strength was in his hair. Well, there it was, the answer to my curiosity! Daddy John did not have very much hair, but he had a battered old hat that was a permanent fixture on his head. At that time I was eight years old and had never seen him without that hat, but his guitar, which I thought had far more value than an ugly old hat, was often left alone in a corner of my parents' bedroom while he visited. So I reasoned that his power must be in his hat and I became determined to prove it! That was a difficult task! After months of stalking him when he came over and praying for a strong wind to blow his hat off or for someone to pull it off just long enough for me to put it on my head for a second, it did not happen.

Tired, but still determined, I finally asked Daddy John to allow me to put his hat on. Without hesitation, he pulled it off and plopped it on my head. He backed away at a distance and watched me as I stood as still as I could to sap as much power as I could before my Daddy came and demanded that I give it back. I was able to keep that hat on four or five minutes before Daddy appeared, but it was more than enough time to conclude that Daddy John's supernatural power, if it was in his hat, certainly was not revealed to me then or now! What I do know is that forty-four years have passed since Daddy John physically departed this world, but his spirit is still very much alive!

Over the past nine years since the establishment of the Mississippi John Hurt Foundation and the Festival and Museum, I have met or communicated with hundreds of people from various cultures across the globe who have expressed the same sentiments that I have mentioned through Daddy John's music. Foremost, every accomplishment toward the preservation of Daddy John's legacy via the Foundation or the Museum has been the result of many wonderful people that loved and respected his music or his kind spirit. I am so indebted to Mr. Bailey, Art Browning, Fred Bolden, Lost Jim, the Carroll County Board of Supervisors, Dave and Key Murphy, Neil Harpe, Mike Baytop, Attorney Linda Mensch, Attorney Jeff Glassie, and Mrs. Annie Cook.

In an effort to find photos or paintings of my grandfather for the museum, I went on a web search, which led me to a gallery that had a wonderful painting of Daddy John. I called to purchase it, but it was already sold. I guess I sounded so disappointed, that the gallery owner felt compelled to give me the direct number of the artist and gallery owner, Neil Harpe. In calling Neil, not only was I able to purchase the painting that was sold, but he also painted one for the museum. Neil Harpe also specializes in restoring old instruments and, at some point Phil Ratcliffe from Scotland, UK, called Neil seeking a Stella guitar, as he was learning to play Daddy John's music. I don't know how the conversation led to them coming to the first Mississippi John Hurt Festival, but I do know that through the spirit of Daddy John, Phil and I met. When Phil called me weeks after the festival was over and asked how I would feel if he wrote a book about

Daddy John's life, little did Phil or I know that Daddy John's spirit had already given him permission long before we met!

I am so grateful to Phil for all the hard work, travel, resources, and in-depth research, that have been applied in order to write this wonderful biography of Daddy John's life. It will be a prized resource for my family for generations to come. Phil and I would never have met in our lifetime had it not been for some divine intervention. Thank you Phil and Annie for our spiritual link forever!

MARY FRANCES HURT WRIGHT

Introduction

I was born close to Liverpool, England, in 1943. Much of the time surrounding a limited secondary education in the 1950s was swallowed up by an interest verging on obsession with New Orleans jazz and folk blues; or at least in the limited British interpretations of that music that were available in the 1950s industrial north of England. Before rock 'n' roll, swing bands and crooners dominated the charts; and apart from old records of Jelly Roll Morton, Kid Ory, Louis Armstrong's Hot Five, etc., I was enjoying the traditional jazz of Chris Barber's band. Barber's banjoist, Lonnie Donegan, was a devotee of blues and American folk music and began to perform a "skiffle" set with the Barber rhythm section. Some of these songs were recorded on a 10" LP and two were released as a single.[1] That record of "Rock Island Line" by the Lonnie Donegan Skiffle Group in 1955 had an astonishing impact on me. I had never heard anything like it. I wanted to play that song and immediately put a guitar on my Christmas wish list.

I did get that guitar and purchased every record released by Donegan until around 1960 when he drifted away from the earthy folk blues and started to do comedy and music hall material. I saw him in concert many times and had him autograph my 5-string banjo in Liverpool's famous Cavern Club, where I also saw Sonny Terry and Brownie McGhee, as well as, a year or two later, a popular group called the Beatles. By this time I had become fascinated by the fact that my hero had not actually written the songs he was performing. The phrase "Traditional arranged Donegan" appeared regularly on his records and sheet music along with names like Broonzy, Guthrie, and Ledbetter. I saw Big Bill Broonzy and Muddy Waters when they visited Britain. I had to know more about these people.

I purchased *American Ballads and Folk Songs* by John and Alan Lomax and Jerry Silverman's *Folk Blues*[2] in 1958 and, along with my rudimentary record collection, began to learn and play some of these amazing songs. There was not a great deal else available in Britain, and right up to the 1970s American blues and folk recordings were difficult to get hold of, but it was possible to find them in secondhand stores. Around 1970 in the Cob Record Center, a secondhand record store in Wales, an LP caught my eye. It was an Origin Jazz Library LP featuring the Mississippi Blues.[3] I did not recognize any of the artists' names, but it looked like something good. I bought the record, got home, put it on the turntable, and sat back and listened.

It was an incredible experience and I have not forgotten that moment to this day. The music was superb: Hambone Willie Newbern, Robert Johnson, Skip James, and Bertha Lee with Charlie Patton. I loved Mary Butler singing "Mad Dog Blues." I could not believe the atmosphere of all this music. On the first playing I was just getting used to the greatness of it all when, part way into side two, "49 Highway Blues" by Big Joe Williams came to an end and suddenly the world stood still. It was like being punched between the eyes. Mississippi John Hurt was playing "Stack O' Lee Blues." What an incredible sound! How many guitars did it take to do this? What fantastic music. I lifted the pickup arm from the record and carefully dropped it onto the beginning of track three again, and again, and again.

On the album cover the notes read:

> *Mississippi John Hurt—John Hurt was born in Teoc, Miss., in 1894 [actually 1892]. He lived in nearby Avalon all his life until his redis-covery in 1963. From then until his death in 1966 he played for audi-ences all over the country. Two other songs by him appear on OJL 5. The song on this album is a "blues ballad" well known in Negro and white tradition, especially in the areas bordering the Mississippi and Ohio rivers. Stack O' Lee (also spelled Stagolee, Stacker Lee, etc.) is a legendary gambler, variously described as Negro or white, usually said to have lived in Memphis (sometimes St Louis) around the turn of the century.*
>
> *Stack O' Lee Blues—Recorded in New York, Dec. 28 1929 [actually 1928]. Key of D.*[4]

I read this brief paragraph over, and over, and over. Was this it? One track and a vague paragraph about this incredible musician? There was mention of two other tracks on another OJL record and I wondered if anyone recorded him during the years of his rediscovery. I had to hear some more of Mississippi John Hurt. Subsequently, I purchased all of the vinyl albums available at the time. I remember being disappointed that I had been totally unaware of John Hurt's existence or his popularity in the United States between 1963–66, and now he was dead. Interestingly, over the next thirty years, I never even considered trying to play any of his music. I was flat picking in the Donegan and Woody Guthrie style, and it never even occurred to me that ordinary mortals could get close to what Mississippi John Hurt was doing.

A third of a lifetime later, I revived my latent interest in the music and began to amass a huge collection of CDs now that this music was freely available east of the Atlantic Ocean. The Stefan Grossman Guitar Workshop convinced me that maybe I could at least attempt to fingerpick the country blues, and I indulged my passion and bought a Martin OM 42 and a Stefan Grossman lesson. I began to listen, learn, and play. Having realized by now that many of the old bluesmen played prewar Stella guitars, I decided that I must have one, and to my great surprise I found a web site that specialized in old Stellas. It was owned and managed by Neil Harpe in Annapolis, Maryland. Months later, after numerous transatlantic emails that must have really tested Neil's patience and knowledge of Stella guitars, I bought one.

By this time I felt that Neil had become a friend and I announced to him that I was intending to make a tour of the southern states, visiting the haunts and gravesites of the old bluesmen. I wanted to visit Avalon, home of Mississippi John Hurt. Neil had heard that the first Mississippi John Hurt Festival was to be held in Avalon in July 2003 and that maybe I would want to tie that into my trip. I immediately decided that was for me. Within the space of a few weeks the thought of a trip across the South culminating in the Mississippi John Hurt Festival enticed Neil to accompany me and the trip was planned. I would fly into Baltimore and we would drive through Virginia, the Carolinas, Georgia, and Alabama into Mississippi.

We spent three days around Avalon and met friends and relatives of the Hurts. I met Mary Frances Hurt Wright, granddaughter of John who seemed as surprised that I had come from the U.K. to visit her festival as I was to meet her, a close relative of the great Mississippi John Hurt. I was on a cloud; I could not believe that I was here in Avalon, Mississippi, walking on hallowed ground and hanging out with the Hurts and a great bunch of kindred spirits who loved his music. I played "Got the Blues Can't be Satisfied" and "Candyman" at the festival and next day at a deeply emotional gathering at John's gravesite Mary invited me to play again. I played "My Creole Belle." My visit to that first Mississippi John Hurt Festival was the most emotional and life-changing experience in my whole life.

When I got back home, it was like a dream. I could hardly find words to express to my wife, family, and friends what had happened to me out there in deepest Mississippi. As I looked through the notes I had made of conversations with the locals in Avalon and the photos I had taken, I realized that these people possessed knowledge that the world needed to know about; remarkably, no one had told Mississippi John Hurt's story. I immediately decided that I wanted to tell that story, but I was deeply worried that Mary Frances, along with thousands of Americans, might feel that a Brit was not the one to be doing it. I talked to Neil; what did he think? He was unhesitant and simply said, "Do it." Eventually, I plucked up the courage to ask Mary. I would not go ahead without her support. I need not have worried: she was delighted with my suggestion and I was over the moon. I immediately began arranging my next visit to Mississippi. There was a huge amount of research to be done.

Over the next six years I visited Mississippi on numerous occasions and toured the eastern United States from Vermont to Georgia, tracking down the people who had known John Hurt. With every new interview the story became more complex. What an intriguing story and what a challenge I had taken on.

The unexpected spinoff from writing a book like this is meeting the many wonderful people that I have been privileged to meet, and establishing some of the most enduring and strong friendships imaginable. Even without writing this book the experience was worth it just to establish the close friendships of Mary Frances and Suzanne Hoskins Brown, elder sister of Tom Hoskins who had rediscovered Mississippi John Hurt in 1963, and their wonderful husbands Welton and Joe. I value equally my new (now old) friendships with Gene Bush, Bruce Nemerov, Max Ochs, Stefan Grossman, and their wives Linda, Mayo, Suzie, and Jo. Last but by no means least, I value deeply my long friendship with Neil Harpe and Alex. Our friendship has endured throughout this whole incredible journey and without them I would never have made that first catalytic trip to Mississippi in 2003. On numerous occasions they have allowed me to use their house as a hotel, office, and research base, lent me their car (and a guitar) to travel thousands of miles doing research, and provided me with friendship and hospitality.

In addition to the above, I am also immensely grateful to the following people who gave freely of their time and answered my many questions: John Anderson, Duck Baker, Mike Baytop, Harry Bollick, Andy and

Larkin Bryant Cohen, Louisa Spottswood Coughlin, Damien Einstein, Mark Greenberg, Holly Ann Ehrich Ochs MacNamee Henderson, Mark Hoffman, Steve LaVere, Joe Lee, John Miller, Michael Morgan, the late Jerry Ricks, Gene Rosenthal, the late Mike Seeger, Alec Silitch, Peter Silitch, Pat Sky, the late Mike Stewart (Backward Sam Firk), Bill Storck, Denise Tapp, Bill Tydings, and Dick Waterman.

In Carroll, Grenada, and Leflore Counties, Mississippi, I was helped by Mr. Floyd Bailey, Ms. Cindy Bennett, Art Browning, Billy and Carolyn Campbell, the late Charles Campbell, Steve Cheseborough, Fred Clarke, Ms. Annie Cooke, Harry and Peggy Dade, Guy Duke, Ms. Sue Duke, Giles Fuller, Ms. Nora "Bonnie" Hurt, Ms. Josephine Jackson, Lee F. Liddell, Ms. Dorothy Miller, Ms. Lillian Mitchell (Miss Kitty), Ms. Fannie Mohead, and Larry and Mary Smith.

I am also grateful to the many academics, archivists, historians, and researchers who have assisted me, including Yvonne Arnold, the University of Southern Mississippi; the late Helene Chmura, ARC, Columbia, and OKeh discographer; Paul C. Edie, specialist in Victrola phonographs; Daniel Fleck, University of Memphis; Steve Gerber, Illinois Central Railroad Historical Society; Catherine Horn and Dorothy McClure of the Mississippi Department of Transportation; Tony Howe, specialist and artist of Mississippi's historic railways; Greg Johnson, University of Mississippi, Oxford, Mississippi; Ron Johnson, researcher into Hurt immigrants to United States; Brian Ledsom for reading through early drafts and helping with graphic design; Tom Lucas, specialist on Mississippi's historic railways; Debbie McLean and Stanley "Sugar" Mullens, Old Records Room of the Courthouse, Carrollton, Mississippi; Frank Morgan, attorney for the late Tom Hoskins and his sister, Suzanne Hoskins Brown; Paul Oliver, historian and researcher; Alexandra and Guy Pate, graphic artists; Barry Lee Pearson, blues writer; David Price, specialist on Mississippi's historic railways; Tony Russell, country music discographer; Howard Rye, blues and gospel discographer; Mayo Taylor and Matt Foriest, James E. Walker Library, Middle Tennessee State University, Murfreesboro, Tennessee; Gayle Dean Wardlow, blues historian and record collector; Stefan Wirz, discographer; Laurie Wright, OKeh discographer; the library staff at the Benjamin L. Hooks Public Library, Memphis, Tennessee; and finally to Craig Gill for his enormous help, support, and goodwill during the submission and editorial process. It has been a huge pleasure to work with him and his staff at UPM.

I thank my friend Bruce Nemerov and my wife Annie for their wise counsel and patience in reading through and commenting on drafts of chapters, though any errors in the final versions are entirely my own doing. Special thanks are due to Susie James of Carrollton, Mississippi, an experienced local historian and journalist who grew up in the hill country around Valley in Carroll County. Susie has provided constant help to me in tracking down facts and documents, passing on her knowledge of local families around Avalon and Valley and helping me absorb Southern customs and culture. Special thanks are also due to Fred Bolden, the grand-nephew of Mississippi John Hurt who met with me in Boston and has, over the years, provided me with much information and many memories of his Uncle John. Special thanks are also due to historian, broadcaster, and discographer, Dick Spottswood, who has been so patient and helpful through a series of questions and discussions spread over six years. Last, but certainly not least, thanks go to Dr. David Evans, eminent music historian and editor of the American Made Music book series who has involved himself in this project at a level far in excess of that required by his editorial duties. It has been a great pleasure working with him, and this book is a whole lot better as a result of his input.

Mississippi John Hurt is one of the most influential and underrated American folk musicians. He was the youngest child of a large, poor family whose parents had been liberated from slavery. Being black and poor in Mississippi at that time did not open many doors. So how did he (along with a significant number of others from similar backgrounds) become an icon, known the world over, a century later?

This book sets out to answer that question by studying his life story and exploring the evolving social environment before and during his lifetime. A mixture of cultures and races pressured by economic and social conditions had resulted in the acceptance and development of slavery and racial oppression on a massive spatial and temporal scale. A series of historic threads evolved in concert and came together like a spider's web in the early decades of the twentieth century. Remarkably, out of these conditions came a musical heritage second to none and a genre that continues to provide the platform of much of today's popular music throughout the world.

Mississippi John Hurt is widely recognized as an important, indeed an iconic figure in the country blues. His recognition was initially stimulated by the inclusion of Hurt's 1928 recordings of "Frankie" and "Spike Driver Blues" on Harry Smith's *Anthology of American Folk Music*,[5] which presented Hurt's music to a wide audience of primarily white folk and blues enthusiasts. Following his rediscovery in 1963, he "inspired a whole new generation of acoustic guitar pickers"[6] and over the ensuing years his greatness, breadth of repertoire, and delicate stylings have been widely recognized.[7] Rolling Stone Bill Wyman describes Hurt as "one of the most revered of all the Delta players" (although Hurt did not come from the Delta), and Hurt's "Stack O'Lee Blues" as the definitive version out of over sixty recorded versions of the tune.[8] Mississippi John Hurt was inducted into the Blues Hall of Fame in 1990.

My account of John Hurt's life begins with his parents as slaves in Alabama and weaves its way through several decades of life in rural Mississippi. His story is related to the landscape and to the physical and social events and political tensions of the era. I have attempted to present a factual historic account not embellished by fiction, assumption, or supposition. However, John was a very humorous man and a great storyteller and his story is permeated with numerous anecdotes and tales. Whenever I have reported opinions, feelings, and unconfirmed events, I have clearly identified them as such.

Mississippi John Hurt's music is as fresh today as when he first recorded it in 1928. It is unlike the Delta blues; indeed much of his music was not blues at all. His repertoire included blues, spirituals, ballads, and ragtime tunes. It is lively, rhythmic and very easy to listen to, and it continues to attract new audiences. But, the biggest revelation of all while researching this book was that Mississippi John Hurt had a great deal more to offer the world than just his music.

He was an incredibly warm, friendly, and spiritual man whose personal philosophy was a model that many of us today could wisely take a lesson from. His voice and his face radiate a warmth that can still be felt. Stefan Grossman described him as "the grandfather we all wish we could have had."

Larry Hoffman expressed it as well as anyone:

> Indeed, it seems as if this gentleman was to enrich every life he touched. . . . John Hurt was a saint. For those of us who discovered the man and his music in the 1960s, none captured the heart like John Hurt. It was a stroke of genius and great luck that brought this musical icon to us for his second career. He embraced all he met as he embraced life itself. His great kindness, generosity, and gentle spirit, has made him a folk legend, and we remember and treasure him through his music—the living spirit that flows through time and the generations as does his unforgettable smile.[9]

Dick Spottswood, who knew John as well as anyone in those early years, added: "[His] music was simply an extension of the man himself and a personality that was understated, complex and, behind a convenient rural black accommodating veneer, infinitely subtle."

I have derived my impression of John Hurt from careful and objective research; but I feel as if I actually knew him—and find myself talking as if I did. This is not through any desire to mislead; it is simply as if his calm spirituality and warmth has pervaded my own personality and I genuinely feel a better person as a result of getting to "know" him. I hope that this feeling will also extend to the readers of John's story. Although this book may read as "the usual worshipful and unquestioning blues 'journalism'" that Ken Ficara contrasts with the approach used by Stephen Calt in his book about Skip James,[10] I believe that my book provides an accurate reflection of what Mississippi John Hurt was really like.

I hope that his story will interest those already touched by his music and personality, those who are interested to learn more of the social and cultural heritage of the small community in rural Mississippi from which he came, and those interested in what he gave to the world. I hope that you will enjoy reading his story as much as I have enjoyed writing it.

Mississippi
John Hurt

1. The Early Years

From Slavery to Freedom

Outside of rural Mississippi, only a small group of music aficionados had heard of Mississippi John Hurt until after he turned seventy-one years old. This knowledge was confined to the music on six 78 rpm records made in 1928. When he was rediscovered in rural Mississippi in 1963, no one knew much about him or what he had been doing since 1928, and not many cared. His early records had made him an icon, but the story of the man himself would turn out to be even more deserving of such a reputation. Mississippi John Hurt emerged from rural Mississippi in his later years to affect very many people through both his music and his deeply spiritual personal philosophy.

Mississippi John Hurt was an African American. His parents named him John Smith Hurt. His ancestors were forcibly captured and transported across the Atlantic Ocean from Africa to become slaves on the cotton and tobacco plantations of the Deep South. The European ancestors of the white Americans who would come to own the slaves also crossed the Atlantic, following a parallel course to the north. These Europeans eagerly anticipated the exciting challenges of life in the New World, while further south, in despicable and brutal conditions, the slaves had little idea of what was in store for them. They anticipated the worst and that is what they got.

The Hurts who came to own the ancestors of John Hurt's father, Isom, were probably among the hundreds of Hurt immigrants that arrived in America between 1740 and 1840. Their destinations were mainly New York, Virginia, Baltimore, and New Orleans. They came from all over Europe (the name is of Anglo-Saxon origin) with many coming from Britain, mainly Liverpool, and many from Germany.[1] The British industrial revolution was under way and the transport of cotton eastward facilitated the transport of slaves westward. In the 1790s, when much of Mississippi was impenetrable forest, most slaves were landed on the East Coast at the same places as the European immigrants and were progressively moved westward with their owners.

The introduction of the cotton gin in 1793 led to an increase in cotton production from 3,000 bales to 100,000 bales per year by 1801, leading to an enormous increase in the demand for slaves to tend the crops.[2] White families of Hurts dispersed westward and settled across the southern states, mostly in Virginia and Georgia with some in Alabama and Mississippi, where they established farms and plantations and bought slaves.[3]

Long before these immigrants settled in the Deep South, Native Americans occupied the land. The Choctaw people occupied the central portion of the present state of Mississippi,[4] which included the hill and Delta areas around what was to become Avalon in Carroll County and where John Smith Hurt was to be raised. In spite of their allegiance to the U.S. government, the Choctaw were betrayed by whites and removed from Mississippi and the southeastern United States following the Indian Removal Act of 1830.[5] Tens of thousands of Choctaw were deported from their homeland. In the winter of 1831–32, the coldest since 1776, many walked the 500-mile journey, along with the Cherokee, on the infamous "Trail of Tears" to Indian Territory in what was later to become a part of the state of Oklahoma. Many died along the way.[6]

Greenwood Leflore was chief of the Choctaws. He was an educated man and tried very hard to integrate with the whites. However, he had underestimated white determination to occupy the rich lands of Mississippi. In 1830 he signed the Treaty of Dancing Rabbit Creek in Noxubee County about a hundred miles southeast of Avalon, which ceded the Choctaw lands to the government and was made an honorary Colonel in the U.S. Army. In the territory ceded by the Choctaws he settled in an area of what, on December 23, 1833, was to become Carroll County. He established a fifty-thousand-acre plantation close to the confluence of the Tallahatchie and Yalobusha rivers, close to where John Hurt would be born almost sixty years later. Greenwood Leflore built a luxurious and stately mansion there, which he called Malmaison. He named his plantation Teoc, a Choctaw word meaning "the place of tall pines"[7] and he owned many slaves. A small settlement became established there and it was at Teoc where, after their release from slavery, John Hurt's father and mother were to raise their family, and where John Hurt was to be born before the end of the century. Malmaison burned in 1942, but the Teoc church and graveyard are still there.[8]

With the onset of the Civil War, Greenwood Leflore opposed secession and remained a Unionist throughout the war. He had lost many of his Choctaw friends over their opposition to the Treaty of Dancing Rabbit Creek, and now he lost many of his white friends over the secession issue. He died on August 31, 1865.[9]

In 1880, fifteen years after the end of the Civil War, a black family of Hurts lived in Carroll County, Mississippi. The head of the family was Isom Hurt, who was aged 27 years. He was born in Alabama, as were both of his parents. Isom was married to Mary Jane Hurt (née McCain), 26, and they had three children, James, 8, Sam, 6, and Junious, 1.[10] (The name Isom was also spelled Isome and Isham and the surname Hurt appears in the 1880 U.S. Census as Hert, which presumably reflects the written interpretations of the spoken names provided to census clerks.)

Mary Jane had been a slave on the McCain's Waverley Plantation at Teoc, where she and Isom lived before moving to Avalon, a few miles north. Teoc and Avalon were situated on the dirt roads that crisscrossed the hill country on the edge of the flat Mississippi Delta. In 1880, virgin forests, swamps, and bayous occupied much of the Delta and few people lived there. It would take several decades to clear and drain the land before it could be used for cotton plantations to supply the American and increasing European demand. The people required to do this work came from the neighboring hills.[11]

The nearest towns to Teoc were Carrollton and Greenwood to the south and Grenada to the north. At that time there was no railway joining Greenwood and Grenada through Teoc and Avalon, only dirt roads. The nearest railroad, built in 1861, connected Grenada in the north via Winona to Jackson in the south. At this time there was no railway closer to the Mississippi River.

So where in Alabama had Isom come from and under what circumstances? The 1870 U.S. Federal Census for Alabama lists a black male farm laborer named Isome Hurt who was born about 1852, aged 18, and registered in the town of North Carolina, Russell County, Alabama.[12] Isome was living with his mother, father, and siblings. The family consisted of Monroe Hurt, 53, and Patsy Hurt, 42, presumably his father and mother, and Joanna, 22, Mary A., 19, Andrew, 13, Elvira, 8, Nyley, 7, and Julia, 1. Monroe, Patsy, Joanna, and Mary A. are recorded with a birthplace in Georgia, while Isome and his younger siblings were born in Alabama. This suggests that their white owners moved the family as slaves from Georgia to Alabama in late 1851 or early 1852.

The 1860 Federal Slave Schedule lists ten white slaveholders named Hurt residing in Russell County, Alabama.[13] At this time, 77 percent of the white population of Alabama owned 333,000 slaves, largely within the cotton counties, which did not include Russell. Poorer counties less well adapted to grow cotton had a reduced economy and fewer slaves per household.[14]

The slave schedules list only the age, sex, and race of slaves. When the ages and sexes of Isome Hurt, his siblings, and parents in 1860 are matched against the slaves listed for each of these ten slaveholders, one group matches very closely. This is the slaveholder John Hurt, who was also born in Georgia.[15] The match is not perfect, but the ages of Patsy and all four children alive at that time exactly match the ages of Isome and his family in 1860, but there is no male aged 43 that matches the age of Monroe. A male slave aged 43 was listed as belonging to a Martha Hurt in the same locality. It was commonplace to separate slave families; perhaps this Monroe was Isome's father.

It seems likely, though not conclusively so, that this white John Hurt was the owner of Isome and his family and that the Hurts moved, taking their slave families with them, from Georgia to Alabama around 1852. Slaveholder John Hurt was married to Santa M. Hurt, and in 1860 they had three children, Joel E., 8, Elizabeth, 5, and Leila, 11 months.[16] In the 1850 census a John Hurt, possibly the same one, was living with the Mildman family in Muscogee County, Georgia, which shares its boundary with Russell County, Alabama.[17]

Huge numbers of white people moved into Mississippi from the east between 1830 and 1920, they and their ancestors having first settled in the Carolinas, Virginia, and Georgia. Many, like the Hurts and McCains, settled for a time in Alabama before proceeding westward to Mississippi. Many brought their slaves with them, and after the Civil War many blacks moved westward of their own volition. In 1880, of the 470,403 whites resident in Mississippi. 353,247 (75 percent) of these were born in Mississippi while 39,567 (8 percent) were born in Alabama. 61,678 (13 percent) were born in the Carolinas, Tennessee, Georgia, Virginia, or Kentucky.

Hurt historian Ron Johnson stated that there were around 230 Hurts recorded in Mississippi from 1850 to 1930. These were mostly descended from families who had settled first in Virginia and moved rather rapidly from there through the Carolinas and Georgia before heading westward. Mississippi and Louisiana were for some reason not popular destinations of the Hurt families and many of them leap-frogged those states into Texas. During slavery, slaves were not provided with family names, but following emancipation, many freed slaves adopted the family names of their previous owners. This practice was more common in Mississippi and Alabama than elsewhere.[18]

So it seems that Monroe Hurt was Isom Hurt's father and Mississippi John Hurt's grandfather. Monroe, born about 1817, and son Isom were born into slavery. At the end of the Civil War, Monroe was 48 years old and Isom 13. Isom left the family home between 1870 and 1880, by which time he had moved to Carroll County Mississippi, married Mary Jane McCain on July 29, 1876,[19] and had three children, James, Sam, and Junious. Isom also had become a trustee of the local Mitchell Springs School in Teoc.[20]

As for Mary Jane's story, slaveholder William Alexander McCain lived in Carroll County, Mississippi, in 1860. His estate was valued at $50,000 and his personal assets at $50,000. He was married with seven children and owned fifty-two slaves. One of his slaves was a seven-year-old girl (Mary Jane would have been seven years old at this time).[21] Ten years later in 1870 after the end of the Civil War, when she was 17, a Mary McCain is listed living with her two-year-old daughter, Ann, in Carroll County, Mississippi. She worked for D. M. Gordner, a white farmer who, in addition to his wife and two children, housed twenty-two black and white servants and farm laborers.[22]

In the 1860 U.S. Federal Census, William McCain's eldest child was listed as aged 17 years and born in Alabama. The McCains' next child was aged 13 and born in Mississippi. This suggests that the McCain family, along with its slaves, moved from Alabama to Mississippi between 1843 and 1847.[23]

In 1850 the family resided in Tallahatchie County, Mississippi. William A. McCain, then 36, who was born in North Carolina, had married Louisa (recorded simply with an initial L in the 1860 census), 26, and was father to son Joseph (J in the 1860 Census), 7, and daughters Mary E. (M. E. in the 1860 Census), 3, and Ann Eliza, 2. Joseph was born in Alabama, while Mary E. and Ann Eliza were born in Mississippi.[24] This supports the view that the family moved from Alabama to Mississippi between 1843 and 1847, but clearly they resided in Tallahatchie County before moving to Teoc in Carroll County. There they bought the 2000-acre Waverley plantation and became neighbors of Greenwood Leflore, the Choctaw chief who had signed away Choctaw lands to the whites in the Treaty of Dancing Rabbit Creek. In the 1880 U.S. Federal Census, Mary McCain's parents are recorded as being born in Alabama. Interestingly, the 2008 Republican presidential candidate, Senator John McCain, is a descendent of slaveholder William Alexander McCain (his great-great grandfather), who owned Mary Jane McCain, Mississippi John Hurt's mother.[25]

After the war, when slaves were liberated, it was possible to "apprentice" or take into care orphaned slaves who were under the age of eighteen. N. H. McCain, a joint owner of the Waverley Plantation along with his brother William Alexander McCain, made an application to apprentice two orphaned former slave girls, Mary Jane, 15, and Julia, 10. The petition states that he was the "former and last owner and a suitable person to cover the care and custody of said until their eighteenth birthdays."[26] This was almost certainly Mary Jane McCain, though reference to the earlier slave schedules would put her at thirteen years old in 1866, not fifteen (errors of this sort are common in census records).

Irrespective of her real age, according to this petition Mary Jane would have been freed from her ties with the McCain family in 1869, after which she lived with and worked for the Gordner family. She later met Isom Hurt, with whom she had two children, James (born 1872) and Sam (born 1874), before they married in 1876. If this is the same Mary Jane McCain as recorded in the 1870 census when she was 17, there is no further record of her daughter, Ann, who would have been 8 years old in 1876. Their next child Junious was born in 1879 and by the end of the century the other seven children had been born. The fact that Mary Jane had at least two children outside marriage did not attract a stigma in those days, and few were surprised when unmarried girls became pregnant. More importantly, perhaps, it did not appear to compel them to marry or to reduce opportunities for the girl to attract a husband at a later time.[27]

John Smith Hurt, who was to become Mississippi John Hurt, was the last of ten children born to Mary Jane. He was reportedly born on March 8, 1892 (grave marker), March 16, 1892 (Social Security Death Index), May 7, 1893 (some family members), or May 8, 1895 (draft registration). When liner notes were being written for his first Piedmont album in 1963, John told the Spottswoods that he was 69. However, a year or so later he told Louisa Spottswood, with some embarrassment, that he was actually 71 when rediscovered. Assuming that he considered himself 71 in 1963, this would make his birth year, 1892.[28] The most likely date, according to his grandnephew Fred Bolden who remembers celebrating his uncle's birthday, is March 8. Controversy remains over the accuracy of the inscription on his grave marker, but it now appears that it is correct. For the purposes of this book March 8, 1892, is assumed to be his correct birth date.

Yellow Fever

Two years after Mary Jane and Isom married, and with two young children, a frightening scourge swept through Mississippi and the Southern states. Yellow fever, an endemic disease transmitted very effectively by mosquitoes through the swampy bayous of the Deep South, suddenly became an epidemic. In late 1877 or early 1878, a sailor visiting New Orleans had died from the fever. The disease spread quickly up the Mississippi River to Memphis, which by the 1870s had become a thriving city of commerce and transport with a population of 40,000 people. A warm spring formed the backdrop to the 1878 Memphis Mardi Gras, which began on March 4, and thousands of visitors poured into the city for the parade through the streets, the highlight of Mardi Gras. Conditions for transmission of the disease were close to ideal, and by December over 5,000 people were dead in Memphis alone and around 20,000 throughout the Mississippi valley.[29]

This massive epidemic swept through the United States within the year. The disease had come from Africa with the slaves, and traders from virtually all of the slave-trading countries took the disease back home with them. The first epidemic in the West Indies occurred in 1648, and in the 1700s, with the massive increase in slave trading to America, yellow fever made inroads into the slave ports of Boston, New York, and Philadelphia. The U.S. capital was moved from Philadelphia to Washington, D.C., following a devastating yellow fever epidemic in 1793, and Greenwich Village became known as "the Village" due to its status as a refuge from the fever outside the city. Following the abolition of importation of slaves from abroad in 1808, the disease retreated from these northern cities, becoming endemic in the southern states.[30]

The newly married Hurts must have been well aware of what was happening around them and were probably frightened to travel to the neighboring towns. They must have feared catching the dreaded "Black Vomit," which at that time was a mysterious disease, the epidemiology and involvement of the mosquito as the vector being unknown. The nearby town of Grenada was badly hit, and the population was reduced from 2,000 to 200 in one week.[31] A statewide quarantine was imposed and people were prevented from entering some towns.

Early Musical Influences

The music that John began to play as a child had far-ranging origins. Slaves brought their music from Africa and white immigrants brought a wide variety of music from European countries, especially the Irish and the Scots. During slavery, music and dancing were among the only pleasures to be had by slaves, and many slaveholders encouraged their slaves to party at the Saturday night frolics. After emancipation, musicians continued to play an important part in the social life of black people, as they had done in slavery times. The slave-quarter frolic became the Saturday night fish fry.

The guitar was to become the most important instrument in the delivery of rural blues, ragtime, and old-timey music that John was to enjoy so much, but during slavery the banjo and fiddle were the instruments of choice. The banjo grew in popularity after the Civil War; by 1880 it was the most widely used fretted instrument in the South, frequently being played alongside the fiddle. However, freed slave Zack Ivey from Macon County, Alabama, recalled from slavery days, "we had guitars and blowing quills."[32] The banjo became a familiar instrument in the rhythm sections of the early jazz bands of New Orleans. But reels, jigs, ballads, and early forms of the blues were being played and guitars began to increase in popularity.[33]

Parlor music was the popular recreational music of affluent white society, and in some ways it filled a cultural niche similar to that of the back porch music that was being played in poorer households and in logging camps. The actual tunes and knowledge of musical theory were different and whites viewed parlor music as a cultural achievement, but both were intended to entertain. Parlor music was absorbed into an early mix of music involving black and white influences that evolved into the pre-blues and early blues, string band, and jug band music that John enjoyed and that began to be recorded in the 1920s.[34]

The Railways

Around Avalon and in the hill country, mule and cart would have been used for local journeys, but further afield the railways were replacing waterways as the most efficient means of long distance transport. The railways were to influence almost every aspect of people's lives for the next fifty or more years. The first passenger train on the newly built Yazoo and Mississippi Valley Railroad (Y&MVRR) rolled into Greenwood, Mississippi, a Delta town a similar distance from Avalon as Grenada, on July 1, 1886,.[35] The Y&MVRR established a network of tracks between 1886 and 1904 that linked many of the small Delta towns that have become legendary in music history and culture. The longest north-south section connected Lake Cormorant, Tutwiler, Swan Lake, Greenwood, Yazoo City, and south to North Jackson. Other spurs connected with Vance, Ruleville, Belzoni, Silver City, Lexington, and Durant (see Fig. 1.1).

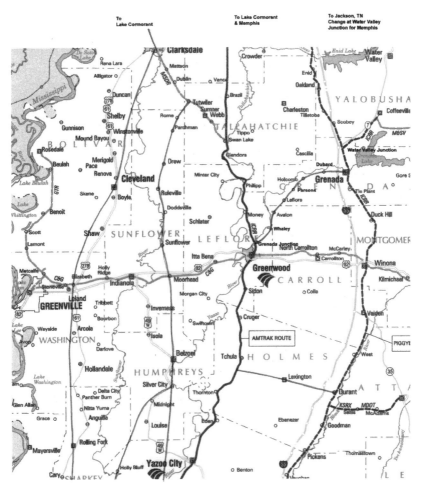

Figure 1.1 Map of railways around Avalon, Mississippi, circa 1900. Railways remaining in use are identified by letters e.g., GTR, C&G, ICRR. Present-day main highways are in pale gray. (Base map provided courtesy of Mississippi Department of Transportation. Additional artwork by Alexandra and Guy Pate.)

A spur running northeast from Greenwood through Whaley, Avalon, and Leflore to Parsons was built in 1886, providing the Hurts with rail access to Greenwood. The connecting link north from Parsons through Holcomb and Dubard to Grenada was added in 1899–1900, providing a connection to Grenada and Memphis (see Fig. 1.1), along which John Hurt was to travel on his way to record in Memphis and New York in 1928.

From east to west, the Southern Railway, later to become the Columbus and Greenville Railway Company (C&GR), linked Alabama through Winona to Greenville. It crossed the Yazoo Delta Railroad (later to be called the Yazoo and Mississippi Valley line) at Moorhead, a junction that became famous in blues history as the place, "where the Southern cross the Dog" (the Yazoo Delta Railroad, otherwise known as the Yellow Dog)[36] (see Fig. 1.1).

The Move to Avalon

Avalon, the small settlement where future generations of Hurts were to spend their lives, is located in the northeast corner of Carroll County about ten miles north of Teoc. Dr. W. A. Burkhalter bought 325 acres of wooded land from the Y&MVRR and in 1906 began to carve the original settlement out of the wilderness. He also purchased land from W. M. DuBard and was instrumental in obtaining a railroad station here. Mrs. Burkhalter named Avalon after the Avalon Valley in England. She originally submitted her own maiden name of Bondurant as the name of the place, but the railroad rejected it because of a station already located in Holmes County named Durant.[37] Dr. Burkhalter, who died in 1936, was an eye, ear, nose, and throat specialist and he practiced in Greenwood after graduation from Tulane University. In his spare time he built, or had built, a home, sawmill, gin, and cabins for his workers at Avalon. The commerce associated with the cotton gin and the railroad station would, as in other rural settlements, attract other institutions such as a U.S. Post Office, general store, and church.[38] Thus firmly established as a small town, Avalon became an important focus for the surrounding communities for the next fifty years.

Around August or September 1892, Mary Jane Hurt, along with some of her family (see Table 1.1) including baby John, just five months old, left the Teoc plantation and moved to Avalon, where she had acquired some land. Avalon lies just inside the Delta on the present Highway 7, which connects Grenada with Greenwood. A dirt road leaves Highway 7 and leads easterly up into the hill country and the small community of Valley, where John S. Hurt lived for most of his life.

The U.S. Federal Census provides a valuable series of snapshots of people living in the area with a ten-year periodicity. Unfortunately, a fire at the Commerce Department in Washington, D.C., on January 10, 1921, destroyed most of the U.S. Federal Census records for 1890, including

Table 1.1. The Hurt family in 1892		
Name	**Birth date**	**Family relationship**
Isham/ Isom	1853	Father/ husband
Mary Jane née McCain	1852/1854	Mother/wife
James	1872/1876	Son
Sam	1874	Son
Julius/Junious	1879/72	Son
Hardy	1884	Son
Ella/Louella	1884/91	Daughter
Anne	1885	Daughter
Cleveland Grover	1886	Son
Hennis	1888	Son
Paul	1889/83	Son
John Smith	1892*	Son
Source: U.S. Federal Census 1880; List of Educable Children, 1892.		
* Several dates have been recorded: March 8, 1892 (grave marker), "Man" Hurt (Son), Fred Bolden (grand-nephew); March 16, 1892 (Social Security Death Index); May 7, 1893 (some family members); May 8, 1895 (draft registration). March 8, 1892, has been assumed in this book.		

those for Mississippi.[39] This leaves an important gap in our understanding of some of the family and neighbor connections in both space and time.

The U.S. Federal Census of 1900 shows Mary Jane Hurt living in the Avalon area (Carroll County, Beat 2, District 15). With her were Julius (18), Paul (17), Hardy (16), Cleveland (14), Hennis (12), Ella (9), and John (8).[40] This is also reflected in the List of Educable Children in Carroll County for 1900, though some of the ages vary by a year either way. Isom, James, Sam, and Anne were not with them.[41] Sam had married Lizzie Johnson in 1893 and James had married Georgia Miers in 1894.[42] Anne (7) may have died, though an Annie Hurt appears in the 1920 Census (see Table 1.3).

It seems likely that Isom did not move to Avalon with his wife and family. John never remembered having a father during his childhood,[43] and the last mention of Isom is in the Carroll County List of Educable Children for 1892, where he is shown as the parent or guardian of Julius (12), Paul (10), Hardie (Hardy) (8), and Grover Cleveland (6). By 1896 the List of Educable Children shows Mary Jane as being the sole parent or guardian, so it appears that Isom disappeared from the scene between 1892 and 1896, after John was born. By 1900 the list showed the additions of Hennis, Ella (also recorded in some places as Louella), and John, who had become of school age by this time.[44]

Childhood Years

In 1900, when John was eight years old, the Avalon area was a very busy place, supporting a population of about 1,390 people,[45] not the approximate 100 as reported in numerous articles about Mississippi John Hurt. In the census records, dwellings and families are given a unique number, which relates to the order in which the census officer visited them. This usefully provides some context of neighbors in relation to one another, but unfortunately does not provide a geographic location. Mary Jane and her family were recorded as Family No. 224 in the 1900 census; exactly where they lived is not indicated. However, John's first wife, Gertrude, said that the Hurts lived along the St. James Road close to the church.[46] The census also records John's brother Cleveland Hurt (15) boarding with the Hambricks (Family No. 219), who employed him as a cook. Rosa Townsend, a white schoolteacher, 24, and Martin Boykin, 30, a black farm worker, also lodged with the Hambricks. The head of the family, J. J. Hambrick, was recorded as being a farmer and merchant,[47] and they presumably lived at the Valley Store.

Hambrick had married Minnie Lee in December 1888 and built the Valley Store in the 1880s.[48] The store became an important focus for John and the community for most of his life. Indeed, John told Tom Hoskins in 1963 that Hambrick's boys raised him from when he was around nine years old (ca. 1901) (the written transcription of John's statement states that the "Hamburg boys" raised him, but John was almost certainly referring to the Hambrick family).[49]

In those days, much as it is today in many small communities, the gathering point for local communities was the village store. The Stinson's Store in Avalon and the Valley Store were the places where people would congregate as they purchased essential groceries, cigarettes, etc. John's mother and his close family would meet friends there, discuss the news and weather, and share the local gossip. No doubt John and his brothers and their friends, including the white Hambrick boys, would play together while the older folk talked.

Among the names in the community are the Hopgoods and Joliffs, later to be associated with schools in the area, and many Kents. It was from a Mrs. Johnny Kent that Mary Jane purchased John's first guitar when he was nine (ca. 1901). Henry Hoskins (29), his wife Ida (27), their

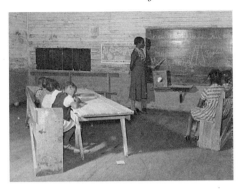

Figure 1.2. Black schoolroom
(Library of Congress, Washington,
D.C., FSA/OWI Collection.)

sons, Eddie (9) and Henry (7) and daughters Jennie (4) and Gertrude (2) lived close by. Gertrude was born in May 1898 and is almost certainly the girl who later became John Hurt's first wife. Her parents had married in 1887.[50] Gertrude lived about five miles from school,[51] and following the numbered sequence of families enumerated in the census, it appears that the Kents, Carsons, Hambricks, Moores, Hoskins, Townsends, and Hurts all lived within a five-mile radius of the school.

Around 1900, a day's earnings for many black laborers would have been less than a dollar. Coffee cost around twenty cents per pound, chewing tobacco thirty to forty cents per pound, and snuff fifty-five cents per pound. Molasses was fifty-four cents per gallon, a pair of men's work shoes $1.50, a ladies cheap day dress $2.50, and a wool fedora hat forty-five to seventy-five cents. In 1908 an enamel coffee pot cost forty-four cents, a cheap tin wash boiler $1.04, a pair of working shoes around $1.30, and a plain ladies linen dress around $3.00, available from Sears Roebuck by mail order.[52]

As the youngest child, John was almost certainly well cared for and supervised by his older siblings. Paul, Junious, Hardy, and Cleveland were sufficiently older than John to provide some of the fatherly needs that would have been otherwise absent due to the early departure of Isom and the lack of any other father figure. Junious, the oldest of Mary Jane's children still living in the family home, married Loucretia Betterton on August 7, 1903, when he was 21 years old.[53] Hennis was five years older than John and would have been of considerable support to him as a small child. John attended the St. James School, which was also known as the Joliff Line School and was situated in a fork in the road along the St. James Road north of John's home and the Church and Hurt family cemetery (see Fig. 2.4). John went as far as the fifth grade and left school when he was thirteen years old (ca. 1905).[54] Presumably his services were required to help support the family. Figure 1.2 shows a typical black schoolroom of the period.

John reckoned that when he was around thirteen or fourteen years old, he would pick three hundred pounds of cotton a day. They would start picking at seven after the dew had evaporated, and by nine o'clock he would have about a hundred and forty five pounds. "I'd get me another hundred and forty five by lunch time." He would slow down a bit after that and pick another hundred by evening; "Well, I just fool around in the evening." John would earn fifty cents a hundred pounds and so make around $1.50 a day.[55]

Black rural families were strongly matriarchal, the eldest woman in the family assuming much of the responsibility of feeding and caring for the family, and there was a huge benefit to having a large family of children that could work the land.[56] With a large family Mary Jane was in a strong position to succeed even with her husband gone. However, she must have experienced financial difficulties, perhaps struggling to repay loans to enable her to work the farm, and in 1906 she was forced to give up some of her land because of default on payment.[57] Interestingly, the land is described as being at Hamrick, Mississippi, which probably related to the name of the family that built the Valley Store. Presumably the land was close to the store.

William Henry Carson and John's First Guitar

A short distance away from Mary Jane and her family lived another African American family, the Carsons. In 1900 the Carsons consisted of Calvin Carson, 47, his second wife Ann, 27, and their children William H., 18, Diamond, 14, Millie, 6, and two daughters with illegible names, 12 and 13.[58] John said that he started playing guitar when he was nine years old (1901) and listened and learned from William Henry Carson.[59] William Henry Carson was very likely Calvin's son William H.

William Henry Carson's interest in the guitar was rivaled by his courtship with John's schoolteacher. John recalled that William Henry would visit the schoolteacher at the weekends and spend the night with them.[60] The only black female teacher in Avalon was Miss Adden Moore, who lived with her parents next door to the Hoskins'. However, in an interview with Pete Seeger on his *Rainbow Quest* TV program in the sixties, John said that the woman that William Henry was courting was named Bell Simmons.[61] There is no trace of this name in the census for 1900 in Mississippi or further away, or of any other teachers in the Valley/Avalon area. However, by 1910 William Henry had married a mulatto girl called

Bell and they had a five-year-old daughter called Roena.[62] Perhaps Bell was traveling from further afield to help out at the St. James School; apparently she knew Mary Jane, so she may have come from the Teoc area[63] and boarded close to the Hurts. Alternatively, she may have resided in the area after the census had been completed in 1900.

It is not clear whether it was William Henry, Bell, or both of them that spent nights with Mary Jane and her family. As William Henry lived so close to the Hurts, there would have been no real need for him to stay over, other than his affection for Bell and that he may have been unwilling to travel home at night. Whatever the situation, whenever young William Henry would come calling on Bell, they would meet at the Hurts and he would bring his guitar along, presumably to win her affections. The Hurt house must have been a crowded place with Mary Jane, her seven children, and Bell and William Henry.

John described Carson as a "guitar picker" and told the story that when everyone was sleeping he would creep through and try to play Carson's guitar. He was especially keen to learn to play "Hop Joint," which eventually he did.[64] John asked his mother if she would buy him a guitar, and though they were poor, she managed to acquire a secondhand instrument from Johnny Kent for $1.50.[65] John said that, "no guitar has no moore buteifuler [*sic*] sound. at the age of 14 I went to playing for country dances. Also private homes. At this time I was working very hard on a farm near Avalon Miss."[66]

As John became more proficient, he would sit and play his guitar outside the Valley Store and listen to the local gossip. He may have overheard the elders discussing the terrible storm that had hit Galveston, Texas, in 1900,[67] the end of the Spanish-American War in 1898, President McKinley's assassination, and Teddy Roosevelt's succession to the presidency in 1901. An event that was reported widely across the United States that undoubtedly became a hot topic of conversation in Mississippi was President Roosevelt's 1902 visit to Smedes Plantation in southern Sharkey County in the Delta to hunt black bear. Holt Collier, a famous bear hunter, was hired to be the President's guide. A bear was captured, clubbed, and roped so that the president could come and shoot the bear, but he refused to, stating that it would be unsportsmanlike. The press reported the story across the country in news stories and cartoons and toy bears were made. They became known as 'teddy bears."

Booker T. Washington's rise to success as a leading African American campaigner for fair treatment for blacks would have been another subject of conversation among blacks, especially after his invitation to the White

House by President Roosevelt in 1901—but only out of white earshot. Closer to home, the opening of Greenwood's streetcar line in 1907 would have created great excitement.

John referred to that first guitar as "Black Annie" and insisted to Dick Spottswood that this was the brand name of the instrument. There were many brands around at the time and some of the big manufacturers used other names to market their products, but I have been unable to track this down as a make of guitar. There was, however, a ragtime "coon" song and dance called "Black Annie" that was popular in 1897,[68] and it may be that some supplier called his guitar after this as a marketing ploy. More sinister, it was also a name (as was Black Betty) given to a leather whip used to beat prisoners on Southern prison farms.[69]

John's guitar was almost certainly a cheap instrument initially supplied by mail order to a local store, possibly the Stinson's Store in Avalon. It may have been a Stella guitar or perhaps one of the cheap guitars supplied by Sears Roebuck[70] via the rail network from Chicago to Memphis to Grenada or Greenwood, or even directly to Stinson's Store. Neil Harpe has suggested that it may have been an ebony finished Stella.[71] Whatever it was, John valued it highly as an instrument: "It was some guitar, I would put it on the bed; flies would light on the strings, and they would ring out just as if someone had been playing them."[72] Legendary blues man Charley Patton apparently preferred a Stella to a more expensive Gibson, and many other early bluesmen played Stellas including Blind Lemon Jefferson, Blind Blake, Barbeque Bob, Blind Willie McTell, Leadbelly, and probably Mississippi John Hurt.[73]

Race and Politics

Perhaps the most shocking local event that made the national news, including being reported in the *New York Times*, was the Taliferro murders.[74] A white husband and wife, the Taliferros, were murdered in their home at Carrollton, just under twenty miles from Avalon, on July 30, 1901, when John was nine. African Americans Betsie McCray, her son Belford, and daughter Ida were accused of the crime and remanded in the Carrollton jail, where a large mob gathered outside. Mississippi Governor Andrew H. Longino called Judge Stevens in Jackson asking him to catch the 2:00 p.m. train from Jackson via Winona to Carrollton so that he might calm the situation and ensure that the legal process took place. The governor also telegraphed the sheriff asking him to protect the prisoners and call for state troops if he required help, but he received no reply.

At around 4:00 p.m., before Judge Stevens arrived, District Attorney Hill reported that his committee had questioned the accused and concluded that they did not commit the murders and that the actual murderers were still at large. The committee felt that further interrogation would identify the killers. The crowd unanimously urged the committee to continue with its investigation in order to identify the real killers.[75]

However, as the crowd began to disperse, a mob of about fifty men armed with shotguns and rifles appeared and marched to the jail. Deputy Sheriff Duke immediately opened the door and let them in. Three men went up the stairs and brought out Betsie, Belford, and Ida McCray. Judge Stevens had arrived by this time and he, along with District Attorney Hill, Lynn Taliferro, the daughter of the murdered couple, and others pleaded with the mob not to kill the prisoners, as it would prevent justice being done. The crowd ignored their pleas and, intent on vengeance, took the three people about a quarter mile out of town where they were hanged and their bodies riddled with bullets. Two days later, on August 4, the governor reported that the mob had possession of the keys of the jail and the sheriff and his deputy had made no attempt to prevent them entering.[76]

The news of this must have reached Avalon quickly. Separate, guarded conversations expressing opinions within the discrete but overlapping black and white communities must have simmered on for weeks, but it is unlikely that there was much mention of it between the races for fear of upsetting the uneasy stability. The slightest indication of any support for blacks by whites could easily result in recriminations against them.

The racial situation in Mississippi was complex, and it is difficult to present an accurate summary. On one hand, the statistics speak for themselves: Blacks were consistently persecuted and intimidated. Violence against blacks by whites was common and extreme violence occurred regularly, including torture and lynchings that were planned as public spectacles. Between 1880 and 1930 at least 3,220 blacks were murdered by white mobs across the South; nearly one a week for fifty years.[77]

On the other hand, most people accepted segregation and got on with each other as best they could. Life in Avalon, and countless other rural communities throughout the South, was a hard struggle. It is easy to look back and imagine a happy country life with music and parties, but most country people, black and white, struggled from day to day to survive poverty. They did so by working hard and by mutual cooperation. Goods and chattels would be loaned and exchanged and folk, black and white, would help one another. There was a huge divide between the rich and the poor, and there were no black folk among the rich.

Immediately after Reconstruction, blacks and whites often rode together in the same railway cars, ate in the same restaurants, and used the same public facilities, but they were not permitted to interact as equals. Out in the country areas, things were settling down in an unequal but workable fashion. Blacks were subjugated and soon understood their subordinate role in society, and whites accepted it as part of the natural order. In the rural communities good relationships developed between many blacks and whites, each aware of the other's "place" in society. Few blacks owned land and most had little option but to work for white plantation owners and farmers under exploitative and frequently unfair sharecropping arrangements. On some Delta plantations the conditions of employment were little better than slavery.

The success of the Democrats in the 1875 election in Mississippi resulted from a level of intimidation that virtually prevented blacks from voting and led to an increase in violence and abuses to the black population. "Kansas fever" took hold, whereby over 30,000 blacks fled the southern states to settle in Kansas and Oklahoma.[78] White planters desperate to hold onto their cheap sources of labor attempted to check the migrations, though some whites had an opposite view: "We hope that they will better their condition, and send back so favourable a report from the land of promise that thousands will be induced to follow them; and the immigration will go on till the whites will have a numerical majority in every county in Mississippi."[79]

Jim Crow laws in the southern states provided a rigid legal and institutional basis to retain control over the black population, and by 1883 the U.S. Supreme Court had begun to strike down the foundations of the post–Civil War Reconstruction, declaring the Civil Rights Act of 1875 unconstitutional. The Court ruled that the Fourteenth Amendment prohibited state governments from discriminating against people because of race but did not restrict private organizations or individuals from doing so. Thus railroads, hotels, theaters, and the like could legally practice segregation. Eventually the Court also validated state legislation that discriminated against blacks. By 1880 it had become clear that the brief experience of black equality was over, and in 1896 the Supreme Court legitimized the principle of "separate but equal" in its ruling.[80] In January 1904 the infamous James K. Vardaman was elected Governor of Mississippi and a barbaric racism was institutionalized throughout the state.

In the early part of the twentieth century, the continuing clearance of the native forests supported a huge commercial timber industry in Mississippi, and up to 1915 it was the third largest timber-producing state behind Washington and Louisiana. Many hardwood mills operated in the Delta and many owned their own railroads to provide access to the timber. Many towns and cities, including Hattiesburg and Laurel, Mississippi, originated during the lumber boom. Many others disappeared following closure of the mills.[81]

Music Origins: A Ragtime Consciousness

John had been playing guitar for about nine years by 1910 and presumably had become quite proficient. But what kind of music was he playing? He told Dick Spottswood that he never heard a black jazz band perform when he was a young man, but he did hear musicians who passed through Avalon with minstrel bands and traveling shows. In interviews, John recalled that the first tunes he learned were "Hop Joint" and "Good Morning Miss Carrie."[82] Apparently John learned these tunes from William Henry Carson. "Good Morning Carrie" was written in 1901 by Chris Smith and Elmer Bowman with words by R. C. Cecil "Mack" McPherson, and became a big hit.[83] It was a typical ragtime or "coon" song of the time. "Hop Joint," one of the earliest blues tunes that John was aware of around 1901, has "lowdown" connotations, referring to a place were one could obtain drugs, *hop* being a colloquial name for opium.[84]

These tunes were typical of the down-home music of the day and, with their rhythmic syncopations, probably would have been classified as ragtime, if they were classified at all. John was obviously not concerned with classifying musical types. He played what he liked in the style he had partially inherited from the teachings of Carson and from his own innovations: a strong alternating pattern on the bass strings coupled with a syncopated melody picked out on the treble strings, with intricate hammer-ons and slides. Carson, himself a young man at this time, was some ten years John's senior. John also mentioned a Rufus Hanks who played a twelve-string guitar and harmonica;[85] however, there is no trace of this name in U.S. census data.

It is important to remember that most so-called pre-blues, country blues, and folk-blues went unrecorded. It was not until the 1920s when the recording companies realized the commercial value of establishing series of "race" records that some of these were recorded. Given the work of talent scouts such as H. C. Speir and Ralph Peer, we might assume that the best of these were recorded, but many may have gone undiscovered and unrecorded, and it is clear that some discoveries, including Mississippi John Hurt, were chance events. Many of the famous and revered artists of the time cite unrecorded artists from whom they learned. Charley Patton, who was born in the hill country between Edwards and Bolton, Mississippi, home of the Chatmon brothers, moved to the Delta in the early 1900s, where he learned to play guitar under the influence of a Henry Sloan.[86] Son House learned from a James McCoy from Lyon, Mississippi.[87] Like William Henry Carson, Sloan and McCoy did not record and nothing is known of their style, but like Carson they may have been pioneers of characteristic musical styles that were to influence many other musicians.

Much of John's repertoire dates back to the early 1900s or earlier, including "Stack O' Lee Blues," "Funky Butt," and "Hot Time in the Old Town Tonight" (the most popular American song in 1896). "Make Me a Pallet on Your Floor" was one of the earliest blues tunes.[88] "Creole Belles" was a cakewalk hit written in 1901 by Bodewalt Lampe with words by George Sidney (see Fig. 1.3) on which John modeled his song "My Creole Belle." However, John omitted most of Sidney's words and modified the tune considerably to suit his own style. Howard W. Odum collected many songs from Lafayette County, Mississippi and Newton County, Georgia, between 1905 and 1908, among which was, "I got de blues an' can't be satisfied." Whether this is the same song that John recorded in 1928 is not known, but there are almost certainly links between them. On April 29, 1900, John Luther "Casey" Jones took Engine 382, the Illinois Central Cannonball out of Memphis. The following morning the engine ran into the back of a freight train that was stopped at Vaughan, Mississippi, resulting in the epic crash that immortalized Casey Jones in song and tradition.[89] John played two songs on this theme, "Casey Jones" and "Talking Casey Jones."

The "Chicken Song," which amused John's audiences during the sixties, was remembered from way back. "Dat's de way to spell Chicken" became a huge coon song hit after Sydney Perrin wrote it in 1902 for *Coon's Paradise*, an operatic farce.[90] It remained popular and Riley Puckett in 1924, the McGee Brothers in 1927, and various others after that recorded "C-H-I-C-K-E-N." John blends this tune with another popular "chicken" song of the period, "You can't roost too high for me." As with much of John's repertoire, he would have learned these as amusing songs that would entertain folk.

The story of "Frankie," a folk ballad also titled "Frankie and Johnnie" and "Frankie and Albert," describes an event that is said to have taken place in a St. Louis barroom in the 1890s in which Frankie Baker shot and killed Allen (Albert) Britt, a ragtime pianist, for his infidelity with

Figure 1.3. "My Creole Belles" sheet music, 1901. (John Anderson collection.)

Alice Pryar. Bill Dooley, a prolific songwriter from St Louis, wrote the song in 1899.[91]

Several authors have addressed the story of "Stackolee" (alternate spellings include "Stack O' Lee," "Stagolee," "Stackalee" and "Staggerlee," and a variety of these have been used on John's recordings). This well-documented black-on-black murder occurred in a St. Louis barroom in 1895. However, the story has taken on the trappings of mythology, with some suggesting that Stackolee represents black solidarity against white oppression and racism in all manner of settings in all manner of places.[92] John's telling of the background of the story to Tom Hoskins in 1963, and in his introduction to the song on *Mississippi John Hurt Legend*,[93] bears little resemblance to other accounts. John insisted that both Stackolee and Billy Lyons were white men and the fight took place down in a mine where Stackolee was aiming to rob the miners who were gambling. Jesse James, who also shot one of the miners, accompanied Stackolee.[94]

"The Last Shot Got Him" was composed by Cecil Mack, Chris Smith, and Everett J. Smith and published in 1912. The Mississippi Possum

Hunters recorded the tune as a fast fiddle and string band tune in 1930, and the tune is the same as Mississippi John Hurt's recording, "First Shot Missed Him," which he recorded in 1966.[95]

The origin of the song "Louis Collins" has proved something of a mystery. Only John Hurt's version of the song is known, and he almost certainly wrote it about a real event. Jerry Ricks reckoned that it was a favorite song of John's and was about his cousin. Conversations with John, Tom Hoskins, and others during the first recording sessions for Piedmont provided confirmation from John that the murder was about a real event, but John said that it did not happen locally and did not mention a cousin. A leading question from Tom Hoskins elicited a response from John that the murder may have happened in Memphis, leaving the truth in some doubt.[96] Another source states that John made up the song from hearing people talk about the murder, which suggest that it was a well-publicized event. John added that "He [Collins] was a great man, I know that, and he was killed by two men named Bob and Louis. I got enough of the story to write the song."[97]

Searches of the U.S. Census for 1910 and 1920 indicate that a Louis Cobbins, born in 1896–97, lived in Lexington, Mississippi, in 1910 and Carroll County, Mississippi, in 1920. His mother was Laura Cobbins and he married Evaline. Another Louis Cobbins, born in 1900 lived in Leflore County, Mississippi, in 1920 with his wife Lattie and his mother Mille. Neither of these reappears in the 1930 Census. A Lewis Collins was murdered in Litwar, McDowell County, West Virginia in 1924, and the event made national news due largely to the fact that Collins was a well-respected white storekeeper in the community. He was described in the local newspapers as "one of the best beloved men of the community, counting all as his friends. He was a man of many splendid qualities, charitable and kindly disposed."[98] There is little to support the view that any of these are the Louis Collins that John sang about, but given that he was almost certainly singing about a real event, any one of them could be.

Many of the people familiar with John's repertoire have expressed an interest in why such a peaceful man sang so many songs describing violent deeds. Of the thirteen sides he recorded in 1928, six contained violent imagery: "Ain't No Tellin'," "Stack O' Lee Blues," "Louis Collins," "Frankie," "Got the Blues, Can't Be Satisfied," and "Nobody's Dirty Business." However, the ratio of violent to nonviolent subjects in his songs is much lower when his complete repertoire is considered. This may be a reflection of a reduced interest in violence as he grew older— or perhaps the OKeh Recording Company influenced the selection of violent tunes? Was he simply repeating the words of songs that he liked and had learned from other sources and not expressing anything personal? Or was there a psychological displacement of violent feelings into his songs? Whatever the case, such lines were often intended to be humorous. Elijah Wald makes the point that "it is common for white scholars to remark on the dark passions and superstitious terrors expressed in lines that in a juke joint would have produced laughter." When Robert Johnson sang the violent line, "I'm going to beat my woman until I get satisfied," it probably evoked more amusement than horror from his audience.[99]

Of course this does not explain the high proportion of violent themes in Hurt's music, nor does it rule out the possibility that he included them to amuse his audience. It is clearly possible to sing about subjects that have not been experienced personally; for example, Rube Lacy's "Mississippi Jail House Groan" was sung with great feeling and commitment and was considered by David Evans to be one of the "deepest blues ever recorded," yet Lacy never spent time in jail.[100] And many atheists appreciate and sing religious music with great feeling.

A number of writers have suggested that black music of that time, especially blues, reflected the release of frustrations due to white suppression. David Evans makes the important point that blues originated from the first generation of African Americans born outside slavery, a generation that faced enormous uncertainty and was ill equipped to cope with the traumas of discrimination, segregation, the Ku Klux Klan, unjustified jail sentences, chain gangs, lynchings, convict labor, and unfair sharecropping arrangements[101] that reached a peak in the decades on either side of 1900. Clyde Woods asserts that the blues was mainly about "cultural transmission and social explanation" from a suppressed society—almost a coded language amongst blacks.[102]

Adam Gussow in his book *Seems Like Murder Here* presents a similar case in which he considers the blues a response by blacks to dealing with white violence in an environment where direct retaliation was impossible. He suggests that lynching "was one of the prime social catalysts—even debatably, the prime social catalyst—for the emergence of blues song out of a welter of pre-blues black music." Gussow analyzes many lyrics of blues tunes, in some cases more convincingly than others, to explain their connection to white-on-black violence.[103]

John Hurt was not a violent man, and overt racial conflict was relatively low in Avalon and around Carroll County. Lynching statistics suggest no lynchings in Carroll County after 1910—though there were plenty in neighboring Leflore and Grenada Counties.[104] But of course he, along with most African Americans, had little choice but to play by the Jim

Crow rules, and using violence in song may have been a way of expressing frustration.

David Evans presents an interesting synthesis of what the blues means to its performers, concluding that it represents an emotional state usually brought on by problems; as the Reverend Rubin Lacy put it, "it boils down to worry."[105] The late Jerry Ricks, an African American musician and close friend of John's, expressed a similar view to me but in a rather more straightforward way. He considered many blues lyrics to be an expression of suppressed anger at white domination, referring to the blues as "Fuck you music."

It seems certain that by the time John was in his late teens, his style was determined and would never significantly change. I doubt the suggestions by Peter Siegel and Jon Hartley Fox[106] that white country musicians such as Jimmie Rodgers particularly influenced John, especially as he would not have heard Rodgers until after he first recorded in 1927. John did tell Lawrence Cohn that he enjoyed the music of Jimmie Rodgers, which he heard from records that one of his nieces bought in Greenwood and on the radio.[107] This would have been between 1927 and the early thirties after Rodgers had become a popular recording star and after John's style and much of his repertoire had become firmly established.

Even when John wrote new songs (e.g., "Candy Man," "Louis Collins," "Avalon Blues"), put the words of others to his own music ("Richland Women Blues," "Waiting for You"), covered other artists' songs ("Waiting for a Train," "Goodnight Irene"), played established traditional tunes ("Pallet on the Floor," "Oh Mary Don't You Weep," "Nearer My God to Thee") or copied popular songs of the time ("Good Morning Carrie"), his own style was dominant. The heavy, pounding alternating bass notes coupled with the intricate hammer-ons and slides picked on the treble strings were forever his trademark. Perhaps the only evidence of a significantly different style in his repertoire was when he used a knife to play slide guitar in "Talking Casey Jones," which he performed and recorded after his rediscovery in the 1960s.

It is possible and to some extent likely that some of the songs that are only known from Hurt's repertoire and assumed to have been composed by him were actually learned from others or at least derived from other tunes he had heard. For example, W. C. Handy published and recorded a tune written by Memphis bandleader Douglas Williams called "The Hooking Cow Blues" in 1917. Handy's tune bears no resemblance to John's "Cow Hookin' Blues," but did John pick up the tune or the title from another version that he had heard somewhere else? The inspiration for John's song, "Trouble, trouble, I had it all my days" may have come from a verse in "Down Hearted Blues" by Alberta Hunter recorded in 1922.[108] "Monday Morning Blues" was a tune performed by the Norfolk Jazz Quartet in 1921,[109] but that recording bears no resemblance to Hurt's song of the same name.

Daniel Fleck's detailed study of the repertoire of Mississippi John Hurt[110] indicates that Hurt varied his songs rather less than other artists did with theirs, but John's delivery nevertheless did frequently change. Sometimes John Hurt's performances of the same songs showed little variation even when songs were performed thirty-five years apart (compare "Stack O' Lee Blues," recorded in 1928, and again as "Stackolee," "Stagolee," "Stack-O-Lee," and "Staggerlee" between 1963 and 1966). Conversely, his version of "Candy Man" recorded in 1928 was much simpler than when he played and recorded the song in the 1960s and did not include the bridge: "You and the Candy Man you're getting mighty thick / You must be stuck on the Candy Man's stick."

The alternating bass pattern played with the thumb, so characteristic of John Hurt's style, has been considered by many to be a typically eastern or Piedmont style characteristic of musicians such as Elizabeth Cotten (North Carolina), Etta Baker (North Carolina), Archie Edwards (Virginia), Frank Hovington (Delaware), and John Cephas (Virginia). Other musicians employing this style, but not exclusively so, include Reverend Gary Davis (South Carolina), Blind Boy Fuller, (North Carolina), and Willie Trice (North Carolina). But Jerry Ricks, who knew John very well, reckoned that John had never heard of these musicians, and even if he had his style was established long before he had access to their records and before he traveled to the eastern states after his rediscovery in 1963.

Andy Cohen analyzes regional blues guitar styles based on his studies into the hand positions adopted by different musicians.[111] Assuming that those born after 1915 in Cohen's sample may have been much influenced by recordings and other outside influences, I have examined a sub-sample of sixty-one born before 1915 from Cohen's sample of ninety-four black guitar players. Of these, six played exclusively in the alternating thumb style and used an extended thumb position that is strongly related to this style. Four of the six (Jim Jackson, born 1890, Hernando), Mississippi John Hurt, Robert Wilkins (born 1892, Hernando) and Babe Stovall (born 1907, Tylertown) were from Mississippi, and all of these were from the hill country and the Piney Hills area, not the Delta.

However, although these musicians played in a similar style they did not necessarily produce a similar sound. Robert Wilkins, although using a similar playing style, sounds more like the Delta musicians and does not play on the guitar a simultaneous version of the vocal melody, as Mississippi John Hurt does most of the time. These Mississippi hill country musicians were from distant locations. Wilkins and Jackson were from Hernando in the loess sandy hills of the northern part of the state; John was also from the same hills but about eighty miles south; and Babe Stovall was from the Piney Hills a further 180 miles away in the extreme south of the state close to the Louisiana border. Given the poor transportation systems prior to the 1920s, it seems unlikely that these musicians overlapped in their ranging. But it is possible that medicine shows (and before them the minstrel shows) would have spread the foundations of this music around the South and into the hill country of Mississippi,[112] resulting in a very wide-ranging Deep South regional blues style.

John was clearly influenced by the popularity of blues music, which was reflected in his and OKeh's choice of tunes for his 1928 recordings. However, OKeh initially marked the file cards for his Memphis recordings as "Old Time Music," suggesting that they intended to issue them in their Hillbilly series before changing their minds and placing them in the "Race" series.[113] Adding to the confusion, many of John's recordings were marketed as blues, presumably to boost sales, but were actually not blues at all, including "Candy Man Blues" and "Stack O'Lee Blues."

Much of the music in John's repertoire preceded the development of the blues and was dispersed far and wide by traveling minstrel, circus, and medicine shows in rural areas and in the developing black vaudeville circuit in the larger towns and cities. Newman I. White, author of *American Negro Folk Songs*,[114] suggested much interchange of songs between blacks and whites up until the twenties, and in a sample of 680 tunes sung by African Americans, over 27 percent were of white origin.[115] Ragtime music encompassed a wide variety of genres including coon, minstrel, and vaudeville songs. Paul Oliver suggests that many of the songs of the early songsters were in circulation long before recording existed.[116] The traveling shows were an important route by which coon songs, ragtime, and subsequently blues and jazz spread around the country and provided good access to small backcountry towns and villages.[117] Although the shows were segregated, the main stage being for whites, sideshows would often be staged for black audiences enabling people in the smallest townships and rural settlements to keep up with the popular tunes of the day and the old favorites of the minstrel tradition and ragtime era.[118] By 1928 the phonograph had become the source of much of the songster's material. And as the blues evolved and became the popular music of the time, the old-timey music continued to be popular alongside it. John Hurt, among others, continued to apply the style to whatever he played.

I find the term *pre-blues* unhelpful in that it encompasses music that predates, was contemporaneous with, and postdates blues. Suffice it to say that John played what he liked; this comprised traditional secular and sacred music, popular tunes, ragtime, and blues. As for his particular treatment of the tunes, when John's boss during the 1950s and early 1960s, A. R. Perkins, asked him how he constructed his melodies, John answered "Well sir, I just make it sound like I think it ought to."

Daniel Fleck provides a detailed analysis of Hurt's repertoire describing his use of a range of forms of American folk music including blues, ballads, spirituals, rags, and folk and popular songs, including some tunes that demonstrated a white influence. In keeping with many ragtime musicians, John mainly played in the keys of C and G, but would sometimes use D, E, and A and open tunings. He often used the guitar as a "second voice," dropping the vocals unexpectedly and permitting the guitar to complete a vocal phrase.[119]

In summary, it appears that William Henry Carson was the main direct influence on John's guitar playing when he was only around nine or ten years old. There were a few other musicians around at the time, but they were mostly fiddlers. The old timey music that Carson probably played had developed from the minstrel and medicine shows and was what continued to influence John. When asked about hearing local blues musicians, John recalled that, "they rarely passed near home."[120] His style became embedded in his consciousness and he applied it unwaveringly to the tunes he liked, including ballads and blues, and the tunes that he wrote himself. Most folk musicians played in a style they liked and become proficient at, and which in most cases was well developed by their late teens. The will and ability to make big changes after that were probably rather limited, and few folk musicians managed or wanted to do it.

Teenage Years, Family, and Marriage

John soon began to be asked to play at parties, and by age 12 or 13 (1904–5) had left school to help out on his mother's farm while playing at local small gatherings in his spare time. John remembered working for a local black farmer, Felix Ivans (Evans), who owned the place next door to John's,[121] around this time; but census data indicate that the Ivans did not move next door to John until between 1910 and 1920.[122]

Ida Hoskins married Hardy Hurt, John's older brother, in 1907, and John would come by to visit his brother. That is most likely how John met and began to court Gertrude, Ida's daughter. Gertrude was born in

May 1898 to Harry and Ida Hoskins[123] and presumably Harry left or died between then and 1907. John and Gertrude would chop cotton for his mother Mary Jane. According to Gertrude, John and Hardy were half brothers, having the same mother but different fathers. Given that Hardy was eight years older than John, it seems likely that Isom was Hardy's father rather than John's, and so it appears that Isom may not have been John's father after all. In fact, Gertrude later recalled that Mary Jane had said to her, "If you want my John, go ahead. He's not a Hurt; he's a Boykin."[124] But, whatever his biological parentage, John was a firm member of the Hurt family and used the name all of his life. So who was Boykin, and was he John's father?

In 1880, at Teoc, when Isom and Mary Jane Hurt were married and supporting their new family of James, Sam, and Junious, a Clay Boykin, 30, was boarding with the Porter family who lived close by. In 1900 a Henry Boykin, 40, lived near Avalon with his 65-year-old mother Rachael and 72-year-old father Alec along with his daughter Rosa and sons Van and Joseph. There was no wife residing with him at that time. She had presumably left or died during the three years since the birth of her son Joseph. They lived in Carroll County. A Charles Boykin, 46, also lived close to Mary Jane in 1900. He was married to Varney and had two sons Park and Walter. Martin Boykin, a thirty-year-old black farm laborer, who was also a cook, boarded with the Hambricks. In 1910, another Henry Boykin, 32, lived with his wife Agnes and children Louie and Earnest next door to John's guitar mentor, William Henry Carson and his family.[125] There are no links connecting any of these Boykins with Mary Jane, though one of them could have been John's father. However, all of Mary Jane's children including John were conceived and born while she was in Teoc, so it is tempting to speculate that Clay Boykin had a relationship with Mary Jane in Teoc either before or after Isom had left. As discussed earlier, Isom was still with Mary Jane in 1892, the presumed year of John's birth.

Gertrude began dating a boy named Robert Lee Hayne when she was 13 years old. She stayed at school until the ninth grade. Assuming that Gertrude began to date John a little later than this, she may have been around 15 and he 18 (ca. 1910). Gertrude recalled that John would drive her and the other children the five miles to and from school in a mule and buggy. The mule's name was Ada, and a long-legged dog would follow along. John would come to the school to play his music for parties and everyone would dance to the music. Gertrude recalled that there was a fiddle player named Anison Lang in the Avalon area around 1910.[126]

Several black families of Langs lived in the area in 1910, but none with the name Anison or anything similar.

The population of the area changed little in size between 1900, when there were approximately 1,390 people, and 1910, when there were about 1,464.[127] Strangely, Mary Jane and her remaining family of Julius, Cleveland, Hennis, Ella, and John do not appear in the 1910 U.S. Federal Census, and neither do Hardy Hurt and his new wife Ida. However, next-to-youngest son Paul appears, and he had married Daisy and they had daughters Letesia (Teatsie) and Hearline. James parted from Georgia Miers or she died and he married Oza (Osie/Onilla) on June 11, 1907. By 1910 they had a son James.[128] Hardy, although not located in the 1910 census, had married Ida Hoskins on April 7, 1907.[129] A search throughout the entire U.S. census data for 1910 failed to locate Mary Jane or the other children still living with her, or their families, and it can only be assumed that the census somehow overlooked them.

John's older brother Cleveland married Lillie Meeks on June 16, 1907. They divorced on June 26, 1915,[130] and, it seems, the very same day Lillie married their other brother Hennis![131] Lillie apparently took her children Lorenzo and Teddy R. with her to live with Hennis and later they had two children of their own, J. T./I. T. (1919) and Norama (1921). Nellie (Neilza) (1923) is shown in the 1930 census as a third child, but she also appears in the Census as the daughter of Lorenzo, Lillie's first child with Cleveland (see Fig. 1.5).[132] By 1930 Teddy R., I. T., and Norama were living with them. Lorenzo was living close by with her daughter Nellie (who may have moved between her mother and her grandmother, causing the double recording in the census), and four boarders, one black and three white.

Lorenzo was born in 1905, two years before Lillie married Cleveland, and Teddy R. was born during the period that Lillie and Cleveland were married. Lorenzo and I. T. later moved to Philadelphia using the name Meeks, their mother's maiden name. Following his rediscovery in 1963, John visited them while touring with fellow rediscovery Skip James. Skip and Lorenzo were introduced and later entered into a common-law marriage. Cleveland went on to marry Fannie Clark and was with her from 1916 to 1924, during which time they had three children, Catherine, Everlene, and Lorenza.

The Stinson's Store in Avalon opened in 1908 and became an important focal point for the community for many years to come. The Stinson family in 1910 consisted of W. J. Stinson, 35, from Tennessee, his wife Edna, and daughter Rebecca. Stinson was listed in the census as a store merchant. William Henry Carson lived nearby with his wife Bell and daughter Roena.[133]

In 1910 J. J. Hambrick was again listed as a merchant and still owned the Valley Store, by which time he and Minnie had four children, three sons, Ward, Flowers, and J. W., and a daughter Norma.[134] John stated that he grew up there with Hambrick's boys and that they practically raised him,[135] although given their respective ages it is more likely that John shared his time as an equal with Ward Hambrick and that J. J. may have become something of a father figure to him. So John spent much of his early teens hanging out with these white children around the Valley area, apparently with little racial complication.

John was 18 years old in 1910, courting Gertrude and therefore presumably spending less time with his buddies at the Valley Store. In 1912 J. J. Hambrick went broke and sold the store to C. J. Kerr.[136] The Hambricks moved to Greenwood, where Hambrick became a clerk in a large department store. They were still in Greenwood in 1930.[137] The boys John had played with at Valley as a child started up a car sales business in Greenwood that was still there in 1963, and John would go and visit them when he went into town.[138] Kerr sold the Valley Store to S. K. Witzel in 1918. After a brief period, he sold it to D. B. and Blanche McDonald on November 21, 1918, who then sold it to Jessie Arnold Kent on December 20, 1921.[139]

Mary Jane's sharecropping arrangement was probably based on the common model whereby the landowner would agree to rent a house and some land with a part payment towards tools, seeds, mules, and other supplies to the sharecropper. In return the owner would get a half or two-thirds share of the value of the sharecropper's harvest and he would pay the sharecropper to cultivate and harvest his own crop.[140] The sharecropper could draw credit for food and clothing against the owner, who frequently would run the local store and cotton gin, thus controlling the sharecropper's credit and the price paid for his cotton. After harvest the owner would calculate the sharecropper's share of the profit, less his accumulated debt. While sharecropping seemed fair and attractive, plantation owners and farmers often cheated their tenants by lying about the income from the cotton harvest, overcharging for items and charging exorbitant rates of interest on loans.[141] Although it was common for the farmer or plantation owner to own the store, the gin, and the cotton crop, this was not the case with the Stinson's and Valley stores.

John and Gertrude secretly courted for about a year and then eloped. John had obtained a marriage license on July 14, 1916, from Circuit Clerk J. C. Allen, witnessed by John's neighbor, Felix Evans. Gertrude recalled

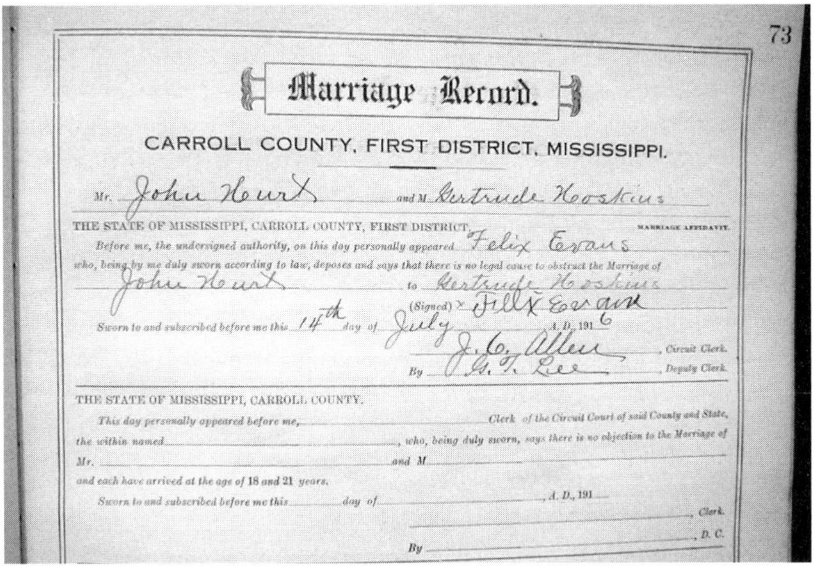

73

Marriage Record.

CARROLL COUNTY, FIRST DISTRICT, MISSISSIPPI.

Mr. John Hurt and M Gertrude Hoskins

THE STATE OF MISSISSIPPI, CARROLL COUNTY, FIRST DISTRICT. MARRIAGE AFFIDAVIT.

Before me, the undersigned authority, on this day personally appeared Felix Evans who, being by me duly sworn according to law, deposes and says that there is no legal cause to obstruct the Marriage of John Hurt to Gertrude Hoskins

(Signed) x Felix Evans

Sworn to and subscribed before me this 14th day of July A. D., 1916

J. C. Allen, Circuit Clerk.

By G. T. Lee, Deputy Clerk.

THE STATE OF MISSISSIPPI, CARROLL COUNTY.

This day personally appeared before me, ______ Clerk of the Circuit Court of said County and State, the within named ______, who, being duly sworn, says there is no objection to the Marriage of Mr. ______ and M ______ and each have arrived at the age of 18 and 21 years.

Sworn to and subscribed before me this ______ day of ______, A. D., 191__

______, Clerk.

______, D. C.

By ______

Figure 1.4. Marriage Record of John Hurt and Gertrude Hoskins, 14 July 1916. (County Records, Carroll County Court House, Carrollton Mississippi.)

that they went to a preacher that they knew named Tom Willis, who married them in church, but it was actually the Reverend G. W. Miller who married them on August 20, 1916. Ida, Hardy's wife and Gertrude's mother, became John's sister-in-law and his mother-in-law at the stroke of a pen! The newlyweds stayed in the preacher's house for about a week, then moved to Mrs. Williams/Wilkins's place near Avalon, where they stayed for a long time. Gertrude did not visit her home for about a month because her mother was upset about their marriage. Later Gertrude cooked and cleaned for "old man Taylor."[142]

Homemade music, local dances, and parties provided entertainment for the hill country folk, but by the second decade of the twentieth century the wind-up phonograph was beginning to appear. By 1909, 15,000 Victrola wind-up phonographs were in homes across America. Tabletop models were introduced in 1910 and sold for between $75 and $105, and by 1911 lower-priced models had been introduced and the price had dropped to $15–50.[143] Although even these would have remained beyond the means of many black people in rural Mississippi, some in the neighborhood would have had access to a Victrola by the 1920s. An article in 1916 in the black newspaper the *Chicago Defender* informed its readers that "Records of the Race's great artists will be placed on the market" once the major record companies realize how many black homes own a Victrola. By 1921 this became a reality and race record labels became popular.[144]

However, few sharecroppers would have had money to spend on records or a Victrola, and only those with access to more affluent neighbors would have had access to a phonograph. Of the blacks who did buy records most were women, but a lot were bought; Jackson record store-owner H. C. Speir stated that he might sell between 300 and 600 records on a good day in the 1920s when poor country folk came to town. Speir would stock 3,000 records, and most of these were race records sold to blacks.[145] In the absence of electricity the spring-motor phonograph was able to carry the latest music trends into some rural homes, and from these initial sources the tunes would spread around and musicians would have opportunities to learn and copy what they heard and pass it along to others.

The United States entered World War I by declaring war on Germany on April 6, 1917. Six weeks later, on May 18, 1917, the Selective Service Act was passed and every male living within the United States between the ages of 18 and 45 was required to register for the draft. The draft included all of Mary Jane's sons except James, who at age 50 was too old. Sam was 43 years old, but does not appear to have been registered and may have died by this time.

The remaining six sons all registered, but it is not clear how many of them, if any, actually served in the military. Their draft registration cards are available and provide useful information on birth dates, employers, and next of kin. Cliff Mullen, the employer of Paul and Junious Hurt (see Table 1.2), was the white plantation manager based in Avalon next door to M. M. Mullen, who managed the Avalon cotton gin (see Table 1.3). On the draft cards for Hennis and John it is stated, "No exemption is claimed." The registration card had the corner torn off if the person was of African descent. On the reverse of the card the registrar provided a brief physical description and judged John to be of medium height and medium stature with black eyes and black hair. John signed the form on June 5, 1917, when he was recorded as being 22 years old and born on May 4, 1895 (He was actually 25, born on March 8, 1892).[146] Relatively few of the men registered in the draft actually served in the war. The census record for 1930 and John's death certificate[147] indicate that he did not serve in the military.

John's nephew Fred Bolden told me that John actually met bluesman Skip James in Jackson, Mississippi, during World War I and that John and Skip both recalled their earlier meeting when they toured together during 1963–66. One source has suggested that John began to play at

Table 1.2. World War 1 draft registration data for the Hurt Brothers			
Name	**Date of birth**	**Next of kin**	**Employer**
Paul	September 4, 1878	Teatsie Hurt	Cliff Mullen
Junious	January 12, 1880	Lucrecia Hurt	C. M. Mullen
Hardy	March 10, 1881	Ida Hurt	Sam Timmous
Cleveland	November 25, 1885	Fannie Hurt	J. H. Williams
Hennis	June 4, 1887	Wife, child, mother	None given
John	May 5, 1895	Wife, 1 child	None given

local dances and parties around Jackson in 1912,[148] but I have been unable to verify this and the original sources cited do not support this view, although John did state that he played for country dances back home before he made his records in 1928. It seems unlikely that James was a musician during the war as he was only 15 when America declared war. Perhaps they met sometime later when John was playing a little further afield? Local man Charles Campbell remembered someone driving up from Louise, twelve miles south of Belzoni, a round trip of about 120 miles, to collect John and take him to perform in a "joint" down there. This probably occurred during the 1930s or 1940s.

On September 26, 1917, the famous Silas Green From New Orleans show company played Grenada, Mississippi, and the next night was in Greenwood. The route from Grenada to Greenwood would have taken them through Avalon. The Sun Bros. Circus played Grenada on October 8, and the Barnum Circus was in Greenwood on the eleventh. There were thirty-one shows playing in the Delta in 1917 following a good cotton harvest with cotton selling for thirty cents a pound.[149] The shows sometimes stopped in Avalon, probably just to collect some refreshments or tobacco at Stinson's Store, and John recalled that "one of them wanted me, but I said no because I just never wanted to get away from home."[150] This means that John must have been playing there, probably to his friends outside the store. The procession of vehicles would have raised a comment or two from the locals hanging around the store.

All of the Hurt boys had married by 1917, and Paul, Cleveland, Hennis, and John all had children. Divorce was relatively uncommon,[151] and although Cleveland had been legally divorced from Lillie, it appears that his second separation, from Fannie, was not subject to a legal divorce. However, Paul and Daisy divorced on January 11, 1916,[152] and Paul named Teatsie, their eldest child, as his next of kin on his draft registration.

After the Hurt children married, they continued to live close to one another and almost certainly helped each other out when harvesting crops, killing hogs, etc. Even outside the close family ties, the common need to survive and desire to have fun would have brought neighbors together. This commonality was at its strongest within the separate races; intimate mixing between blacks and whites was not outwardly tolerated. However, as long as the basic rules of segregation—laid down and strongly enforced in some areas by local politicians, police, and vigilantes—were adhered to, considerable cohesion, collaboration, and cooperation between blacks and whites were possible.

In Avalon and Valley, and presumably many other rural communities, it seems that race was a less immediate problem than poverty. People frequently enjoyed the company of their neighbors whatever their race, although blacks and whites mixed under rather less relaxed conditions. The tensions between blacks and whites were less in the hill country where the perceived social, economic, and political threats to white class structure and the economic disparities between the races were less than in the Delta. White Delta planters were constantly in fear of blacks and poor whites forming coalitions aimed at social justice and undermining their economic and social superiority.[153]

Segregation clearly did not stand in the way of a close relationship between John and the Hambricks. They clearly enjoyed each other's company. John recalled a tale from his teenage years when he and one of the Hambrick boys, Ward, went off on horses to buy a "yellin" (yearling cow). They rode for about twelve miles through the hills, and their horses had Texas saddles. When they arrived to buy the yearling, a problem arose because the seller would not sell it without its mother. John takes up the story: "the man wasn't sellin the yellin without he bought the cow. So he had to buy the cow to get the yellin." So they put a rope on the cow and started back home with the yearling following behind.

Understandably, given the tedium of the long journey home, thoughts ran to spicing up the day and so John said: "Hey Warren [*sic*].[154] He says, 'Yeah.' 'Hey man,' I says, 'What about you leadin' my horse?' He says, 'Leadin' your horse?' 'Yeah,' I says, 'I'm gonna take the saddle off my horse and ride that cow.'" After putting the saddle on the cow, Ward suggested keeping hold of the rope in case the cow would not be guided, and John reluctantly agreed. John mounted the cow but it would not budge so he applied his spurs: "I kicked him with that spur and she come up then I bet you. Right over I went too. Horns were just about that long. I come right down on my head, heels up because she threw me away. Those horns caught me right along, fit me just like this, built, just good and tight, nice fit you know. She went runnin' down the hillside towin' the rope you know and my head hangin' down just plowin' those hills, heels up, I rollin' and swingin' on the rope, that stopped her. When I got up, he says, 'she hurt you,' I says 'no.' He says, 'you want to get back on.' I says, 'no, I want to get on my horse, like I should've been.'"[155] The fact that Ward had hold of a rope to the cow saved the day and this and the deep layer of leaves on the ground probably saved John from serious injury. Apparently John gave up riding cows after that.

This seems typical of the man that people remember with a mischievous sense of humor and a twinkle in his eye. Throughout his life John was known for his sense of humor, and he was polite and helpful, cheerful and pleasant, and warm and spiritual. Through all of the research on this book I have not encountered a single contrary opinion to this view. This was clearly his natural demeanor, but he also knew how to play by the Jim Crow rules to ensure his and his family's personal survival.

In the twilight of his teenage years or his early twenties, John settled down to married life with Gertrude. In 1917 their first child T. C. was born, followed in 1920 by daughter Ida Mae. John worked for his neighbor Felix Ivans (Evans) and for his mother Mary Jane raising cotton and corn. When John was around 22 years old in 1914, he worked for about five months for the Y&MVRR (later to become the Illinois Central Railroad [ICR]), which operated the track from Greenwood through Avalon connecting north to Grenada and on to Memphis. He worked "lining track," which involved working in a gang and relining the railroad tracks where they had become bowed. John explained: "Well, the railroad bowed see, we would run railroad jack, the track was kind of hoppin' like wire you know. Even get out of sight, he'd holler out, 'Hey, joint ahead.' Somethin' like that. They would jack up the line and then lever it back into line before dropping it back down and they would have someone 'Callin' track' or singing a song to keep all the track lining gang moving the line over together." John explained that only one man would sing and everyone would keep in time. Different people would take turns doing the calling.[156]

Tom Hoskins asked John if he could remember any of the songs. John replied, "Well I wouldn't know the names, just the verses that I was singing a while ago? 'Ida when you marry, I want you to marry me, Like a flower held, baby you never see,' you know like that."[157] With a little prompting John recalled that he learned "Spike Driver Blues" from a railroad hand called Walter Jackson. Walter Jackson appears in the 1920 U.S. Federal Census as a section man on the railroad and probably lived in the Delta at Avalon (see Table 1.3). John told Tom Hoskins that he would play at Saturday night parties when he did not have to get up early in the morning to go to work on the railroad. John probably would have walked the three miles from his house to the railroad and was required to report for work at seven o'clock.[158]

John learned "Casey Jones" from his cousin who also worked on the railroad. He added, "Of course some of them verses I didn't get them from him, I got 'em all together by hearin' people talk about what happened." John himself became a section boss where they would pay off every two weeks, making $50, but he left to help his mother out on the farm. When asked about people singing while they picked the cotton and whether they had special cotton-picking songs, John replied, "Well, they sing religious song. Maybe some would sing an old, no I wouldn't say it's a cotton pickin' song, but it's along the cotton pickin' line, be a regular old farm song. Sometime they sing together and sometimes . . . it's like I said, maybe some over there start a song and maybe somebody else join in and help, sometimes they wouldn't. They'd be singin' by themselves."[159]

Into the Twenties

According to John's conversation with Tom Hoskins, Mary Jane still owned some land until he was 27 years old (1919). John suggested that she moved away and began doing domestic work. The final loss of her land at this time may have caused her to move away from the area or she may have died. Mary Jane would have been 65 to 67 at this time. A widowed Mary Hurt appears in the 1920 Census living next door to Hennis (see Table 1.3), but she is recorded as being aged 57, when she would have actually been 66 to 68. A Mary Jane McCain died somewhere in Mississippi in 1918.[160]

John spent some time making crossties for the railroad around 1920. Cypress, oak, pine, and sweet gum trees were used for making crossties. John would fell the trees with a crosscut saw and split the logs with wedges, a sledgehammer and a broad axe. The ties were sold to the Y&MVRR. John explains: "these ties would have to be inspected you see. He'd inspect these ties and put them on the railroad, stack 'em up on the side of the railroad. Well when you got enough ties made that you want to call this inspector, well he would come out, I'd say twice a month and he'd inspect them. He would inspect those ties; he was real picky on those ties. They had to be flat and smooth, you know, eight feet long and six inches wide." John would get a dollar to a dollar and a quarter for each tie and it took him about an hour to make one, but the price included hauling them to the railroad. "Then you have to haul them to the railroad, you see. Get someone with a truck or get some mules and a wagon. I towed many a crossties I made across my shoulder."[161]

By 1920 the population of the area had increased to about 2,045 from 1,464 in 1910.[162] The 1920 U.S. Census lists all of the Hurt children except Paul, and their families. A number of Hurts had settled close together. Ella had married Ned Moore and was living next door to Cleveland, Fannie, and daughters Catherine and Everlene. A little further away were Hardy and Ida, who gave birth to their daughter Iris that year. John, now 28, and Gertrude along with their new family of T. C. (2) and Ida Mae (4 months) lived a short distance away. Felix Ivans, who John had worked for when he was younger, and whom he probably still helped, and his family still lived next door (see Table 1.3).[163] J. W. Stinson was recorded as the postmaster and his wife Edna[164] as a general store merchant, presumably in Avalon (see Table 1.3).

John did some sharecropping and would purchase provisions on credit from one of the stores and accumulate debt, which he would repay with interest at harvest time from his share of the cotton crop he had worked to produce. Tom Hoskins asked John, "If you didn't like the interest there wasn't much you could do?" John replied, "There wasn't much I could do about it, that's right. I wouldn't say it wasn't fair, but to him, all right, he was making out all right."[165] John, true to form, was not keen to criticize. Given the close relationship John had with the succession of owners of the Valley Store, it seems likely that he got a reasonably fair deal from them. Perhaps in the hills life was a little less harsh and confrontational than down in the Delta, where the economics of cotton production made a few people very rich and a lot of people destitute.

While it has proved impossible to accurately map the locations of family homes, Table 1.3 provides some geographical context that, used alongside the maps (see Figs. 2.4 and 2.5), provides a picture of the community as it was in 1920.[166] Figure 1.5 presents a simplified family tree of the Hurts at this time.

Of the 440 families in the area, those numbered from 1 through 134 appear to have lived in the Hills. Three hundred and one families almost certainly lived on the flat Delta land around Avalon.[167] The number of families divided by the number of "same race" family clusters suggests that clusters were larger in the Delta (average of 5.4 families) and families were 81 percent segregated (where two clusters, one black and one white, equals 100 percent segregation and 440 alternate black and white families equals 0 percent segregation). In the hills clusters were slightly smaller (average of 4.8 families) and segregation slightly less at 80

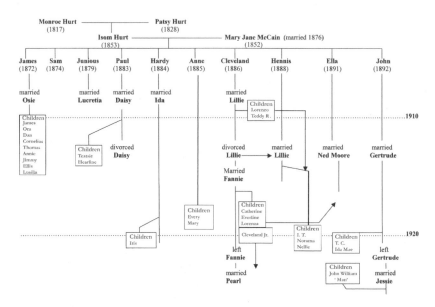

Figure 1.5. Simplified family tree of Hurt family relationships 1920-1930. (Artwork by author.)

percent. Individual cluster sizes were higher in the Delta than in the hills. In the Delta eight clusters contained more than ten families, the largest being forty-seven families; in the hills only four clusters contained more than ten families, the largest being seventeen families. This demonstrates greater segregation in the Delta compared with the hills.

In the area as a whole, the grouping of black and white families (see Table 1.3) demonstrates that there were 89 clusters of "same-race" families and 440 families in total providing a figure of 80 percent segregation. This shows that there is a much higher probability of a family living next to another family of the same race than of a different race. John and his family lived in a cluster of eleven black families, which included the families of his brothers Cleveland and Hardy, his sister Ella, William Henry Carson's daughter Roena, and Felix Evans. Of course, these bare statistics do not display the close daily interactions that were evident between many black and white families.

Cleveland left second wife Fannie and married Pearl in 1924, and the three girls went to live with their aunt Ella (Cleveland and John's sister) and Ned Moore, who lived next door.[168] In 1925–26, John's brother Hennis was a trustee of the local Joliff school, which had sixty-five pupils.[169] Cleveland and Pearl looked after newborn Cleveland Jr. who, according to John's grandnephew Fred Bolden, was Cleveland's child with Fannie and born the same year that they separated. Cleveland's social behavior may appear rather unusual. Lillie had taken Lorenzo and Teddy R. with her when she left Cleveland to marry Hennis; Catherine, Everlene, and Lorenza, the children from Cleveland's second marriage to Fannie, had been left with his sister Ella and Ned Moore (see Fig. 1.5). But the adoption of family members within an extended family following a family break up was relatively common, suited the participants, and probably benefited everyone concerned. In fact, John and his second wife Jessie would later adopt this procedure when they raised their grandchildren following the breakdown of their son John William's marriage. Children of common-law relationships were not considered illegitimate, as they were similar in their stability to legally sanctioned marriages. Indeed, many women exercised a great deal of control over getting the children they needed to strengthen their family for the years ahead by selecting a father without the unwanted constraints of a marriage or a permanent relationship with a husband. Such children, along with those resulting from promiscuous relationships, were called "stolen children," while those procured by women already with children, from a second relationship, were termed "children by the way."[170]

The talk at the Valley Store around this time probably included the opening of Woolworth's 5 & 10 Cent store in Greenwood on January 20, 1923. And it probably also covered the Ku Klux Klan march through the streets of Greenwood on October 14, 1924, which ended at the ballpark at the end of Mississippi Avenue. Dr. R. J. Stephenson, Grand Titan of the Realm of Mississippi, introduced the speaker, Dr. William J. MacDougal, a former Scottish Rite lecturer and a Presbyterian minister. They both were introduced by the master of ceremonies, the Honorable Means Johnston.[171]

During the time that John was in his teens and into his twenties, the Avalon and Valley areas were densely populated. The hill areas, though heavily wooded today, were probably much more open then due to forest clearance and the grazing impact of high numbers of livestock. Cows, hogs, and chickens would have been numerous due to their importance in contributing to the subsistence farming that many families were dependent on. Trees would have been regularly felled to provide domestic construction timber and firewood as well as to supply crossties to the rapidly expanding rail network. There were no paved highways in Mississippi at this time, only dirt roads that would become muddy and difficult to travel on during wet seasons.[172]

On the edge of Avalon, across the flat cotton fields to the east, the division between the hill country and the Delta is so abrupt that it is almost possible with a single step to move from one to the other. Down in the flat area of the Delta a more exploitative use of land existed than did in the hills. The drier, naturally drained areas supported large expanses of cotton crops, while the wetter wooded breaks and cypress groves were systematically cleared and drained to provide timber and to allow the remaining land to be reclaimed to grow more and more cotton.

It appears that John would take whatever work was going, and he did casual work for several of his neighbors. One such man was Paul West, a mulatto who lived down in the Delta not far from John's home. John was clearly a very practical man who could turn his hand to anything. As we have seen, he could ride and he could work on the railroad. He could also work a mule, and on one occasion while plowing a crop for Paul West he encountered a rattlesnake. John tells the story:

"I was plowin' for him, plowin' his crop. Whenever I would go for lunch, why I would be ridin' the mule. I be sittin' on the mule, sittin' sideways like this, takin' it easy." There was a single peach tree there and John being partial to peaches decided to pick one: "Oh I want me a peach. This mule was awful gentle. So I lookin' up in the peach tree had my eye on the peaches. I pull me down one or two peaches, sittin' down on the mule, peelin' my peaches, eatin' my peaches. The mule just kind of drop his head down and Hooooo. I looked down see what she's looking at, man there's a great big long rattlesnake stretched out there, had his head up you know."

John decided to take action. Gus Barnes's house was on the way to Paul West's house and John could see Gus Barnes sitting eating his lunch. John shouted to Gus to bring his shotgun and kill the snake. But before he got there a grasshopper jumped onto the snake and the snake slid away into a brush pile on the edge of a dry bayou. Gus handed John the gun while he began removing brush. John continued the story: "After while I saw him. I saw that head come out. I clipped it off, just smooth as you take a knife whack it off. Gus says, 'You got him?' Yeah I got him."

In the 1920s before the woods were cleared, the wildlife of the area included coyotes, wolves, bears, and panthers. John related an amusing story to Tom Hoskins about his cousin John T. being attacked by a wolf. He ran away and climbed a tree, leaving the wolf circling below and scratching at the tree. "Well, John T. played a mouth harp that he carried in his pocket and so he got that harp and started blowin' that harp." The wolf did not like the music and ran off allowing him to get out of the tree and make his way home.[173]

Family No.	Name	Race	Number of "same-race" families	Employment	Probable Location
			Table 1.3.		
		Avalon and surrounding area in 1920. Summary of families, employment, and distribution.			
1-9		Black	10	Farming	Hills
10	Florence Liddell	Black		Teacher	Hills
11-14		White	4	Farming	Hills
15-16		Black	2	Farming	Hills
17-19		White	4	Farming	Hills
20	Fannie Sabin	White		Teacher	Hills
21-26		Black	6	Farming	Hills
27-36		White	10	Farming	Hills
37-40		Black	4	Farming	Hills
41-43		White	3	Farming	Hills
44		Black	1	Farming	Hills
45		White	1	Farming	Hills
46		Black	1	Farming	Hills
47		White	1	Farming	Hills
48		Black	1	Farming	Hills
49-51		White	3	Farming	Hills
52		Black	1	Farming	Hills
53-56		White	4	Farming	Hills
57-62		Black	15	Farming	Hills
63	George Wilson	Black		Tie maker (railroad crossties)	Hills
64-71		Black		Farming	Hills
72		White	1	Farming	Hills
73-86		Black	14	Farming	Hills
87		White	1	Farming	Hills
88-104		Black	17	Farming	Hills
105-108		White	4	Farming	Hills
109		Black	1	Farming	Hills
110-111		White	2	Farming	Hills
112-113		Black	2	Farming	Hills
114-121		White	8	Farming	Hills
122	Cleveland Hurt (John's brother)	Black	11	Farming	Hills
123	Ned & Ella (John's sister) Moore	Black		Farming	Hills

124		Black		Farming	Hills
125	J. C. Simmons plus grandchild Roena Carson, daughter of William Henry Carson, John's guitar mentor	Black		Farming	Hills
126		Black		Farming	Hills
127	Hardy Hurt (John's brother)	Black		Farming	Hills
128		Black		Farming	Hills
129	Felix Ivans (Evans) (for whom John worked when in his teens)	Black		Farming	Hills
130	John Hurt	Black		Farming	Hills
131-132		Black		Farming	Hills
133	T. J. Hatley	White	3	Blacksmith	Hills
134	3 men	White		Logging	Hills
135	C. C. Maddox	White		General store	
136		Black	1	Farming	
137	Edgar Giles	White	1	General Practitioner	
138		Black	1	Farming	
139		White	1	Farming	
140	George Williams	Black	1	Public ferryman	Delta
141	J. W. Stinson (owner of Stinson Store in Avalon)	White	1	Postmaster & Store merchant	Delta
142	George and Nettie Travit	Black	1	Laborer around store and Cook	Delta
143	William O'Reilly	White	1	Salesman Country Store	Delta
144-147		Black	4	Farming	Delta
148		White	2	Farming	Delta
149	B. D. Beloff	White		Fisherman on river	Delta
150-151		Black	3	Farming	Delta
152	Annie Hurt (possibly John's oldest sister, widowed with two daughters)	Black		Farming	Delta

153	E. D. Mills	White	1	Sawmill machinist	Delta
154		Black	1	Farming	Delta
155		White	1	Farming	Delta
156-159		Black	4	Farming	Delta
160-161		White	2	Farming	Delta
162		Black	4	Farming	Delta
163	Junious Hurt (John's brother)	Black		Farming	Delta
164-165		Black		Farming	Delta
166		White	1	Farming	Delta
167		Black	1	Farming	Delta
168	G. C. Stubblefield	White	1	Bookkeeper at Country Store	Avalon, Delta
168	Rosa Townsend (boarder and schoolteacher in 1900)	White		clerk at Country Store	Avalon, Delta
169-177		Black	28	Farming	Delta
178	John Gulledge	Black		Logging	Delta
179-181		Black		Farming	Delta
182	Lissem Clarke Jr.	Black		Railroad Section Head	Delta
183-196		Black		Farming	Delta
197-199		White	3	Farming	Delta
200-210		Black	11	Farming	Delta
211		White	1	Farming	Delta
212-232		Black	21	Farming	Delta
233		White	1	Farming	Delta
234-245		Black	12	Farming	Delta
246	Shelley Smith (guitarist with fiddler Willie Narmour, who resided close by in Enumeration District 29)	White	1	public road controller	Delta
247		Black	1	Farming	Delta
248		White	1	Farming	
249-250		Black	2	Farming	
251	C. S. Christoferson (Norwegian immigrant)	White	2	Blacksmith	Delta

252		White		Farming	Delta
253	Hennis Hurt (John's brother)	Black	7	Farming	Delta
254	Mary Hurt (widow, living alone, possibly Mary Jane, John's mother)	Black		Farming	Delta
255-258		Black		Farming	Delta
259	Paul West (John worked for him plowing)	Mulatto		Farming	Delta
260		White	1	Farming	Delta
261		Black	1	Farming	Delta
262	S. J. Brunson, local farmer referred to by John	White	2	Farming	Delta
263	Russell Brunson (local farmer referred to by John)	White		Farming	Delta
264-273		Black	10	Farming	Delta
274	Katie Chatham (John worked for her)	White	1	Farming	Delta
275-276		Black	2	Farming	Delta
277-281		White	5	Farming	Delta
282-285		Black	4	Farming	Delta
286-291		White	6	Farming	Delta
292	Will Hoskins	Black	6	Section Head, railroad	Delta
293-297		Black		Farming	Delta
298-299		White	2	Farming	Delta
300-302		Black	3	Farming	Delta
303	Charles B. Turner	White	1	Salesman, General Store	Delta
303	E. L. Mabry	White		GP Physician	Delta
304-313		Black	10	Farming	Delta
314		White	1	Farming	Delta
315-316		Black	18	Farming	Delta
317	Jim Hurt (John's brother)	Black		Farming	Delta
318-332		Black		Farming	Delta
333		White	1	Farming	Delta
334-353		Black	20	Farming	Delta

354-362		White	9	Farming	Delta
363		Black	1	Farming	Delta
364-365		White	2	Farming	Delta
366-392		Black	47	Farming	Delta
393	G. W. Thomson	Black		General Store Merchant	Delta
394-412		Black		Farming	Delta
413	Clifton Mullen	White	1	Plantation Manager	Delta
413	M. M. Mullen	White		Ginner Avalon Gin	Delta
414		Black	7	Farming	Delta
415	Casey Filman	Black		Section Head Railroad	Delta
416-420		Black		Farming	Delta
421	Terry Proctor	White	1	Railroad Section Journeyman	Delta
422	Walter Jackson (from whom John learned Spike Driver Blues while working on the Y&MV Railroad)	Black	4	Railroad Section Man	Delta
423-425		Black		Railroad Workers	Delta
426	Paul Dix	White	1	Plantation Manager	Delta
427-431		Black	14	Farming	
432	George Burton (John worked for him or his neighbor John Burton (433)	Black		Farming	Delta
433	John Burton	Black		Farming	Delta
434-440		Black		Farming	

Other than those with a direct connection with John Hurt, only people with occupations other than farming have been included, for brevity and to indicate the range of occupations and skills within the community. Location provides a suggested location from the family number relative to neighbors and from those businesses known to be at Avalon. "Hills" refers to locations around Valley and the St. James Road area, while "Delta" refers to locations on the flatland around Avalon. The column headed "Number of 'Same-Race' Families" provides the number of families which have the same race as a neighbor, thus providing an indication of the degree of intermixing of races within the community.

Source: U.S. Federal Census 1920, Carroll County, Mississippi (Township 20, Beat 2, Enumeration District 28).

John and John T. would play music together to entertain local people. "We go along to people's private homes, way in the night, midnight, twelve, one o'clock. Serenadin' we call, just like we knew you well, you know, we tip up on the porch and we'd wake you up with music." Sometimes they would be invited in to play, and sometimes folks would just lie there and listen.[174] Presumably they would pick up some money for their performances.

On one occasion, at around one thirty in the morning with the moon shining brightly, the twosome were heading home through the woods after doing some serenadin'. John takes up the story:

Somethin' attacked us, didn't know what it was. I was walkin' along behind him, I walkin' along with my head down, I was a little pace behind. He had seen this thing and he had stopped. I bumped into him, I thought oh boy. He said, "What is that, John? What's that there, he standin' there." Well, I tell you what it looked like to me, I don't know what it was, it looked like a panther to me. We standin' there talking to one another and he says, "give me your guitar." I hand him my guitar and he just walkin' along goin' "Rmmmm Rmmmm." He didn't run, he just got out of the path and let him by. God almighty, I jumped in front of him and I lit out man. I went runnin' you know, he takin' off right behind. Oh I was runnin' and he fell, he fell. I thought the thing had him, whatever it was. I couldn't stop, I had to keep goin'. That's the funny part about it, anybody prayin' and cursin' too. He was yellin' and kickin' Lord almighty. Goddamn off. I thought he got him. He was cursin' and prayin' all the way. Oh Lordy, Oh Goddamn, yeah. I swear I got way up on top of the hill. He got over his scare I reckon. When he got up he says he didn't see nothin'. He's rappin' on the old guitar, when we got inside I saw him looking back. I say, "Hey John T., that thing get a hold of you." He says, "Devil, what do you want to know about it, you run off." I says, "I couldn't come back out." He says, "why didn't you come back and shoot, you heard me holler." I says "Oh boy," I turned around, I thought, I'm goin' in while he's eatin' you.[175]

So, wonderful man, world class songster, and musician though he was, it seems that John was not the guy to be with in the face of danger!

Wild animals including bears and panthers were common in the area during the early decades of the century, and around 1913 to 1915, during an organized Thanksgiving Dinner turkey shoot near Avalon, the hunters' dogs surprised a bear. The bear immediately attacked the dogs, and Dr. Charles C. Mattox, the owner of the dogs, shot the bear to prevent it

Figure 1.6. Bear killed during turkey shoot, Avalon, Mississippi, circa 1913. (Lee Mattox, Carrollton, Mississippi.)

killing his dogs. This exciting event was photographed and recorded for posterity, and Rosa Townsend, the white schoolteacher who had lodged with the Hambricks and later worked at the Valley store, was photographed there (see Fig. 1.6).[176]

Musical influences traveled the country through circuses, medicine shows, and tent shows. These would tour rural areas stopping in any small community where paying audiences could be attracted. Billy Terrell's Comedians was such a group that in the mid-1920s made several tours of the Mississippi Valley. During one of these tours a young Jimmie Rodgers introduced himself to Terrell when the group was playing Meridian, Mississippi, and became a performer in his troupe.[177]

Many blues musicians frequented jook joints and worked in a violent environment. Some served time in prison, like Bukka White, Son House, and Leadbelly, and many others including Memphis Minnie, Skip James, Charley Patton, and his wife Bertha Lee had a record of violence. Clearly, John avoided much of this lifestyle, preferring to stay at home with his family.

Production of Victrolas had risen to 560,000 by 1920. Technological innovation and development progressed rapidly during the mid-1920s with the appearance of radio, microphones, and electric phonographs. Following depressed sales during and following WWI, the Orthophonic Victrola was introduced in 1925. This state-of-the-art machine provided much higher quality sound reproduction than previous phonographs and sounded better than most radios of the time. A Silvertone tabletop phonograph, the Valencia, sold in the 1927 Sears Roebuck catalog for just $36, and there were portable models for as little as $14.95. Although this was still a lot of money for a sharecropper or farm laborer, it did mean that records were within reach of a lot of people through parties and house visits. The introduction of the Orthophonic model also led to large numbers of the older obsolete machines being available at very low prices, sometimes for as little as $5. A 1928 monograph on nutrition in the Mississippi Delta contains a photograph of a room in a tenant farmers home with a phonograph. Apparently around 12 percent of black families had a phonograph in the 1920s. In 1929, the onset of the depression reduced sales and the Victor Company was purchased by RCA, creating RCA Victor. This company continued to manufacture phonographs into the 1930s.[178]

By 1923 Sears Roebuck were only selling their own make of guitars, Supertone. In the 1927 catalogue the cheapest of these was an imitation mahogany instrument with decalcomania patterning (transfers of ornamental designs) and a metal tailpiece costing $4.79. The high end model was made from koa wood with a mahogany neck and rosewood and holly inlay and a fixed ebonized bridge. The standard size cost $19.75 and the Grand Concert, $23.45.[179]

Blind Lemon Jefferson was the most successful and well known of the early recorded blues musicians and is known to have played in the Delta, probably in 1926 following the popularity of his first recordings released that year.[180] Although it is unlikely that John would have met such musicians, it seems equally unlikely that he would have been unaware of their music. Jefferson's popularity and the subsequent success in marketing rural blues coincided with the invention of the electric recording process and was largely responsible for the rapid increase in field recording excursions by the major record companies which led to the enormous amount of recorded music within this genre that is available today, including that of Mississippi John Hurt.

Records could be purchased by mail order by responding to black newspaper advertisements and from furniture stores and local plantation stores. Stinson's Store in Avalon may have stocked some of the more popular titles. Jeff Todd Titon researched the behavior of the record-buying public in the 1920s, shedding some light on how people chose records and how and where they came to hear new material.[181] Many of the people Titon interviewed bought records that they heard played in their local record store. They were also interested in records of their favorite artists. Unfortunately, he does not give any indication of the social status or color of his interviewees, but it seems unlikely that black farmhands and sharecroppers spent much time in record stores, especially those who lived far from towns with record stores. However, Titon did learn that neighbors would invite friends and relatives around to listen and dance to records on their Victrola. It seems likely that John would have

Figure 1.7. Stinson Store, Avalon, Mississippi, circa 1920. (Josephine Jackson, Carrollton, Mississippi.)

participated in such gatherings. Maybe the various owners of the Valley Store would have had a Victrola and they would certainly have made trips into Carrollton, Greenwood, and Grenada to buy stock for their store.

Blues musician John Jackson told Bruce Nemerov that his family bought a record player and records from a peddler on a monthly installment plan, and each month the peddler would return on his route to collect payment and sell them the latest records. This is how, in rural Virginia in the late 1920s and early 1930s, Jackson heard Blind Blake, Jimmie Rodgers, Uncle Dave Macon, and other favorites. The family could audition the new records and buy the ones they wanted. Musician Fred McDowell recalled listening to the records of Blind Lemon Jefferson and Charley Patton on a Victrola when he stopped by at a friend's house. McDowell added, "Those people who had a Victrola really had something y' understand."[182]

Musical acts were touring provincial theatres, though these were segregated and beyond the access of most rural blacks. By the 1920s Greenville had become a cosmopolitan city with French and Italian restaurants, coffee shops, pool halls, movie theatres, and twelve miles of paved streets. It attracted well-known entertainers including W. C. Handy. Greenwood and Moorhead had theatres where Blind Lemon Jefferson and Rubin Lacy played together in 1928 or 1929 shortly before Jefferson died. Tent shows appeared regularly in the Delta towns.[183]

Alcoholic drinks played an important role in musical gatherings, and moonshine was accessible to most people long before Prohibition came to Mississippi in 1908 as a result of efforts by the Women's Christian Temperance Union.[184] Twelve years later, on January 16, 1920, the Eighteenth Amendment to the U.S. Constitution went into effect, prohibiting the making, selling, possession, and consumption of alcoholic beverages throughout the United States. Huge black-market businesses were quickly established by gangsters and bootleggers as well as corrupt law enforcement officers and politicians.[185] Although the Federal government repealed Prohibition with the Twenty-First Amendment to the U.S. Constitution in 1933, it continued in Mississippi until 1966.

Amongst rural blacks in Mississippi, Prohibition probably had a limited impact, as branded liquor would have been a seldom-indulged luxury for them compared with the homemade variety. Techniques for making bootleg whisky were perfected by the time Prohibition arrived, after which it became the only available liquor. John's brother Hennis became well known for his production of fine-quality homemade whiskey, but it is not known exactly when he began to brew and distill liquor; suffice it to say that his whiskey earned a reputation far and wide.

Mary Frances Hurt Wright stated that John and Gertrude parted when Mary's father, T. C., was 5 years old, which would be in 1922. John later took up with Jessie Lee Cole and he told the Spottswoods that he married Jessie on December 4, 1927. His memory was accurate and confirmed by the marriage record in the Leflore County courthouse, but Jessie's name was registered there as Nelson, not Cole.[186] Apparently Jessie had previously been married, changing her name from Cole to Nelson. Why John and Gertrude parted is not known, but in 1997 she told the Greenwood *Commonwealth*'s managing editor, Tom Miller, "Never was much for listening to the blues. Had too much God in me." However, she liked to dance and party later in life and was no prude. Some later accounts suggested that his marriage to Gertrude was short-lived, but he began courting Gertrude around 1910, married her in 1916, and stayed with her for a further six years.

That the blues is the devil's music is of course a common concept, and many blues singers felt that one either sang blues or religious music, but not both. As Gayle Dean Wardlow put it: "You were either serving the Lord or you were serving the devil. And if you played blues and lived that lifestyle, you served the devil and you were going to hell. Good church people didn't have anything to do with blues singers."[187]

Of course many blues men switched allegiances, or at least hedged their bets, especially if they thought they were approaching death. John Hurt clearly did not believe that the two types need be mutually exclusive, and he played an eclectic mix of blues, bawdy, and religious songs, and his deep religious belief was a strong foundation to his life, at least in later years. Blues were played in jooks where gambling and drinking occurred and fighting and womanizing was common, so perhaps the clue is in the quote from Wardlow above: singing the songs was acceptable as long as you weren't living "that lifestyle."

Although John believed that he had been divorced from Gertrude, no evidence of this has been found, and this was to become the subject of legal proceedings some seventy years later when John's will was contested. His brothers Cleveland and Paul had both gone through legal divorces, and so he would have been aware of how to go about it. In any case, divorces were relatively uncommon and voluntary separation was generally accepted and considered the same as a divorce without the cost. Consequently, remarriage often occurred with no regard for the status of the previous marriage, and some people believed that crossing a county line or crossing the Mason-Dixon line extinguished previous marriages.[188] Gertrude met and settled down with Will Conley, and they along with John and Jessie shared the parental responsibilities of T. C. and Ida Mae until Gertrude and Will moved away to Bolivar County in the Delta between 1927 and 1930, taking the two children with them.[189]

Jessie was born in Hattiesburg, about 200 miles south of Avalon, and according to John's grandnephew Fred Bolden was a first cousin to Nat King Cole. In 1910, at the age of 16, she was living with her mother Susie Cole, father William Cole, and siblings in Hattiesburg. They lived close to a family of Nelsons with a son Willie. In 1920 a Jessie Nelson was married to a William Nelson, an oil mill worker, and they were living with Scott and Mattie Cole in the same locality.[190] It seems likely therefore, that Jessie had married William Nelson in Hattiesburg and that they shared a dwelling with her relatives Scott and Mattie Cole, but that she parted from him later and then moved north to Avalon.

During his teens and twenties John played at local dances. John explains: "We called them square dances. Hands up four. Ten gallons, Oh I don't know what you call these little dances, where they two steppin'."[191] And, in another interview: "They danced the two-step, shimmie-shamwabble, breakaways and the slow drag. I remember the dance they called the camel walk. They also did some sort of trot they called 'takin' a trip.'"[192]

John began playing with white fiddle player Willie Narmour sometime around 1923; Narmour was aged 29 in 1920 and lived in the area (in Enumeration District 29 adjacent to District 28, which forms the basis for Table 1.3).[193] Shell Smith, Narmour's guitar accompanist, lived close to John and some of his brothers. John played with Narmour when Shell Smith was not available: "Well, Mr. Smith was Mr. Narmour's second and lots of time when he couldn't be with him, well he would get me." John told how he backed Narmour by strumming with a flat pick rather than playing melody as he did when playing alone, and "that was all Shell Smith could do." They played the popular songs of the day like "Rubber

Dolly" and the fiddle tune "Carroll County Blues" made locally popular
by Narmour. They never played as a threesome and John never sang with
Narmour, though he did do so later when he played with Bea Anderson.
In spite of the racial tensions of the time, black and white musicians often
played together.[194]

The Mississippi Flood

Early in 1927, prolonged heavy rain poured unprecedented volumes of
water onto the catchment of the Mississippi River and its tributaries, from
Oklahoma and Kansas in the west to Illinois and Kentucky in the east. At
Greenville in the heart of the Delta, it rained heavily for several months
and by April the river was higher than ever before and reached the top
of the levee. On top of all this, on Good Friday, April 15, a widespread
storm hit Missouri, Illinois, Arkansas, Mississippi, Texas, and Louisiana.
In New Orleans fifteen inches of rain fell in eighteen hours.[195]

The heavy rains must have affected Avalon and the Valley area. The
torrential rain would have hampered farming activities and John would
have had to pick his way carefully through the mud and ruts on his way
to the store. The rains continued and every small watercourse was full to
overflowing. Groups of locals would have sheltered under the front porch
of the Valley Store watching the unrelenting rains. Potacocowa Creek,
which swept down from the hills onto the Delta at Avalon, would be
carrying a huge volume of water toward its meeting with the Yalobusha
River and eventually into the great Mississippi River. On April 16 a levee
burst thirty miles south of Cairo, Illinois, flooding 175,000 acres. The
Great Mississippi River Flood had begun. As the torrent made its way
south, levees failed in 120 places along the river, flooding over 27,000
square miles and rendering around 930,000 people homeless.[196]

In Mississippi, the levees at Miller Bend and Mound Landing were
of most concern. Both were north of the town of Greenville, where a
break at either levee would flood the town and threaten its population of
about 15,000 people. At Mound Landing in lower Bolivar County, levee
guards pushed the folk hard to maintain the height of sandbags ahead of
the rising water when, on the morning of April 21, 1927, a massive crevasse opened up, pouring a huge volume of water onto the surrounding
countryside. Within ten days, ten feet of water covered nearly one million acres. The force of water bursting through the crevasse collapsed
buildings, uprooted trees, and left tens of thousands of people clinging to
rooftops and trees.[197]

Greenville, sixty miles west of Avalon, was one of the hardest-hit cities with its downtown covered by ten feet of water. White landowners, scared that they might lose their laborers, forced hundreds of black families to stay behind in temporary camps. They were crowded onto the eight-foot-wide crown of Greenville's levee and forced to maintain the levees from further danger of crevasse by using sandbags to stem the flow of water.[198]

Families, mostly African American, slept in makeshift tents of quilts and materials brought along in their escape from their homes. Eventually the Red Cross provided tents, kitchens, and sanitary facilities and organized a refugee camp at the end of Washington Avenue that extended northward along the levee for seven miles. Typhoid shots and other immunizations were given to prevent the spread of disease. The relief effort and supplies were predictably prioritized to whites, and hundreds of blacks were treated like animals being forced under conditions similar to slavery to work on the levees. Local officials directed by William Alexander Percy's Relief Committee called in the National Guard to keep order.[199]

The decision not to let African Americans evacuate and to work them without pay soon brought an eruption of racial tensions. The squalid living conditions and work requirements of African Americans were first reported through the Associated Negro Press, and by the end of May the news had spread to the white press. Famous musician Lonnie Johnson was responsible for the most overt protest song about the treatment of black labor with his "Broken Levee Blues," recorded in March 1928, nearly a year after the flood. David Evans suggests that the defiance against white direction expressed in the song would have brought Johnson serious harm had the record been released at the time.[200]

Almost 300,000 people fled the flooded areas. Many blacks managed to escape the flooded areas around Greenville and move to higher ground that, although still part of the Delta, included Greenwood. The huge area from Greenville toward Greenwood and south to Yazoo City and Vicksburg was the largest part of the Mississippi Delta to be affected, along with another large area west of the river in Arkansas and Louisiana. The National Safety Council estimated that a thousand people died in the Yazoo-Mississippi Delta.[201] Although many sought refuge in and around Greenwood, many kept going and sought refuge in the hill country. In his "High Water Everywhere, Part 1," Charley Patton states his intention to move away from the flood zone but that he was prevented from moving to the hill country: "I would go to the hill country, but they got me barred."[202]

The Columbus and Greenville line carried the last trainload of refugees from the city of Greenville to the safety of the hills.[203] Avalon, like Greenwood, was sufficiently high to escape the worst of the flood, but complete safety was available up in the hills around Valley. An elderly resident of Valley, Charles Campbell (b. 1916), remembered a refugee camp at Valley; "Across the road from my Uncle Sid Smith's place, there was a tent city nearly two years after the 1927 flood. There were twenty-nine tents and the folk took their baths in pond water, and they rationed water for them to drink and cook with." John was 35 at the time of the flood and must have met many of these refugees as they went about their business, probably making purchases from the Valley Store.

The Mississippi River Flood of 1927 was, at that time, the nation's greatest natural disaster. Thousands of animals drowned and an entire crop year was lost.[204] It was certainly the greatest natural disaster to hit Mississippi, and conversation at the Valley Store must have focused on the topic for many months and continued sporadically for years.

By 1930 Gertrude and Will Conley, along with John and Gertrude's children T. C. and Ida Mae, had moved to Bolivar County in the Delta alongside the Mississippi River.[205] The lower part of Bolivar County had been badly affected by the flood but it is not known whether Will, Gertrude, and family had moved there before the flood or if they were directly affected by it. If they were there, they would almost certainly have suffered hardship as a result. However, no interviewees who knew Gertrude, including her granddaughter Dorothy, recall her mentioning any personal experience of the 1927 flood, which strongly suggests that they were not there at the time.

The Discovery of Mississippi John Hurt

John told Tom Hoskins the story of how Willie Narmour, who was driving the school bus at the time, won a fiddling contest. The contest at Winona, Mississippi, was held in 1927, when John was 35 and was organized by Doc Bailey, a local veterinarian who also ran a furniture store that sold Victrolas. He acted as the local agent for the Victor recording label and ran a local radio station. Doc Bailey also had a hand in establishing the Mississippi Possum Hunters, a local string band that recorded for Victor in 1930 in Memphis, and booked Jimmie Rodgers to play the Winona Auditorium. There is no record of Jimmie Rodgers actually appearing in Winona in Nolan Porterfield's biography of Rodgers, but the list of appearances is incomplete, and Rodgers did tour Mississippi in

January and February 1929, appearing at Jackson, Vicksburg, Meridian, and Hattiesburg. It is possible that Rodgers made a Winona appearance at this time. It was at the Winona fiddle contest, as John recalled, "some folks from New York heard Narmour." These included. Brockman and Stevenson of the OKeh Recording Company.[206]

Narmour and Smith played breakdowns, blues, ragtime, shuffles, fox-trots, and waltzes, and many recordings made them famous. Their biggest hit was "Carroll County Blues No. 1." Although Narmour was the fiddler in the duo, Shell Smith did play the fiddle, and they recorded one tune, "Rose Waltz," in this reversal of roles. They also recorded a tune called "Avalon Quick Step" in 1930 and an "Avalon Blues" in 1934; it bears no resemblance to John's tune of the same name recorded some six years earlier.[207]

Later, Tommy G. Rockwell, the recording director for OKeh, asked Narmour if he knew of anyone in his neighborhood that could play music. Willie Narmour told them about John. John takes up the story:

"He brought them through here. One o'clock that night. . . . Said, 'Get up—some fellows from New York want to hear you play.' I had an old guitar—played them a piece and they said, 'that'll do, can you come up to Memphis and put out some records?'" Apparently the piece John played for Tommy Rockwell that won him the opportunity to record in Memphis was "Monday Morning Blues."[208] "Thirteenth of February I come to Memphis. Got me a place to stay. Made three records—Can't remember what I played." Jessie interjected in the conversation, "'Stackolee' and 'Candy Man.'" It is unlikely that John performed "Candy Man" in Memphis, as he has said he wrote that later, around the time he traveled to New York.[209] If John did perform "Stackolee" and "Candy Man" at the Memphis session, no record of this has survived.

In another version of the story John told Pete Seeger around 1963–64, Rockwell asked John: "What about getting you to come to Memphis?" John replied, "I ain't never did anythin' like that." Rockwell responded, "That's not the question." John answered, "Well, I guess I will." Rockwell asked, "you ever been to Memphis?" John told him, "Once or twice." Rockwell left the train fare with Willie Narmour. Rockwell asked Willie, "Will you promise me you'll get him to the train?"[210]

John did take the train to Memphis. The passenger train running through Avalon only ran between Grenada and Greenwood and in or-der to get to Memphis, it would be necessary to change trains at either Grenada or Greenwood. There were trains through both of these towns that ran to Memphis, but according to railroad historian Tony Howe, there were probably more trains on the line through Grenada. It seems

Figure 1.8. Advertisement for musicians to record by T. G. Rockwell of the OKeh Recording Corporation, *Memphis Commercial Appeal*, February 10, 1928. (James E. Walker Library, Middle Tennessee State University, Murfreesboro, Tennessee.)

likely that John took the Grenada route, which necessitated a further change of trains at Water Valley Junction (see Fig. 1.1).

On their field trips, OKeh used hotels or office buildings as temporary recording studios, and on February 10, 1928, Tommy Rockwell placed an advertisement in the *Memphis Commercial Appeal*—WE WANT FIDDLERS—requesting that musicians, who "must be in groups of two or more" and who thought they could make phonograph records, apply to him at the Artophone Corporation, McCall Building, Memphis, Tennessee (see Fig. 1.8).[211] The emphasis on fiddlers and groups made a clear case that, on that occasion, they were not actively seeking solo blues guitarists but instead string bands and country (hillbilly) music. The eleven-story McCall Building, at 75 McCall Street west of Main Street, where John made those historic recordings, was also used by Victor for location recordings and was a downtown landmark for over sixty years (it was demolished in 1975 to make room for the Beale Street urban renewal project).[212]

Of course John had been pre-booked for the session by Rockwell when he visited Avalon, and Rockwell was clearly thinking of placing John's music in the hillbilly series before later changing his mind.[213] John must have been feeling very nervous as he walked to the McCall Building from the train station that day. He remembered the recording session: "great big hall with three of us in it, me, the man (T. G. Rockwell), and the engineer. It was really something. I sat on a chair, and they pushed the microphone right up close to my mouth and told me that I couldn't move after they had found the right position. I had to keep my head absolutely still. Oh, I was nervous, and my neck was sore for days after."[214]

On Tuesday, February 14, 1928, he recorded the following:

Monday Morning Blues (400219-B)

Shiverlie Red Blues (400220-B)

Frankie (400221-B)

Casey Jones (400222-B)

Nobody's Dirty Business (400223-B)

Blessed Be The Name (400224-B)

Meeting On The Old Camp Ground (400225-B)

Sliding Delta (400226-B)[215]

On Monday, February 13, 1928, the day before John began his first recording session, Jim Mooch Richardson accompanied by Lonnie Johnson recorded "Rag Keep Time" (Matrix No. 400218B) backed with "Frisco Rag."[216] The Arkansas Barefoot Boys followed John's session on February 14 with "Benton County Hog Thief" (400227), "I Love Somebody" (400228), "Eighth of January" (400229), and "The Prisoner At The Bar" (400230).[217] The next day W. T. Narmour and S. W. Smith recorded "Captain George Has Your Money Come?" (4000231), "Whistling Coon" (4000232), "The Sunny Waltz" (4000233), "Who's Been Giving You Corn" (400234), "Heel And Toe" (4000235), and "Little Star" (400236),[218] and Nap Hayes and Matthew Prater with Lonnie Johnson recorded "Let Me Call You Sweetheart" (400237), "Memphis Stomp" (400238), "Violin Blues" (400239), "I'm Drifting Back To Dreamland" (400240), "Somethin' Doin'" (400241), "Easy Winner" (400242), "Nothin'Doin'" (400243), and "Prater Blues" (400244).[219]

The OKeh field trip to Memphis lasted from February 13–28. The following artists were recorded: Jim "Mooch" Richardson with Lonnie Johnson (February 13), Mississippi John Hurt, the Arkansas Barefoot Boys (14), Narmour and Smith, Nap Hayes, Matthew Prater, and Lonnie Johnson (15), Rust College Quartette, T. C. Johnson and 'Blue Coat' Tom Nelson (16 and 17), I. C. Glee Club (16), Mumford Bean and his Itawambians, Keghouse and Jaybird, Johnson (T. C.), Nelson and Porkchop (17), Dick Parman, Blind Andy (20), Lonnie Johnson, Raggedy

---

Okeh Electric Records

Shipped to Any Part of the U. S. C. O. D. We pay postage on orders for Two or More. C. O. D. 15c.

You Should Have These Hot Numbers

Mississippi John Hart	WALTER BEASLEY
(Vocal with Guitar)	8564------Southern Man Blues
8560------Frankie	75c Sore Feet Blues
75c Nobody's Dirty Business	
VICTORIA SPIVEY	**HATTIE McDANIEL**
(Vocal with Guitar)	8569---------Just One Sorrowing Heart
8565------Your Worries Ain't Like	75c I Thought I'd Do It
Mine	**Louis Armstrong's Orch.**
75c A Good Man is Hard to Find	(Fox Trot)
8550------Jelly Look What You Done	8566--------Struttin' With Some Bar-
Done	becue
75c Red Lantern Blues	75c Once In a While

Figure 1.9. Advert for "Frankie"/"Nobody's Dirty Business" by Mississippi John Hurt, released April–May 1928 (OKeh 8560). Note misspelling of Hurt. Source: (Liner notes, Columbia Legacy CD, CK64986). The original source of this advertisement is not known.

Ann's Melody Makers (21), Fiddlin' Bob Larkin and His Music Makers, Trenton Melody Makers, Rev J. M. Gates (22–23), Friendship Quartette (23), Mintons Ozark String Band, Sherman Teddes, Chas. Winters and Elond Autry, Mississippi Juvenile Quartette (25), Tom Dickson (27), and Elder Richard Bryant's Sanctified Singers (28).

John's recollection, thirty-four years later, of making three records was not quite accurate; he actually recorded material for four records (eight sides). Only one was released, "Frankie" backed with "Nobody's Dirty Business" (OKeh 8560). An advertisement for this record appeared in an unknown newspaper (see Fig. 1.9).[220]

The date the Hurt record was released is not known, but Lonnie Johnson's "Life Saver Blues"/"Blue Ghost Blues" (OKeh 8557) was advertised in the *Baltimore Afro-American* and *Pittsburgh Courier* on April 14, 1928, and "Tiger Flowers' Last Fight"/"The Ball Game Of Life" by the Reverend J. M. Gates and his Congregation (OKeh 8562) on May 12, 1928, in the *Baltimore Afro-American* and *Chicago Defender*. As these releases were respectively before and after "Frankie"/"Nobody's Dirty Business," it suggests that John's first record was released between mid-April and mid-May 1928. Columbia pressed around seven thousand copies of blues and gospel releases in late 1928. It is impossible to say just how many copies of "Frankie" entered the market but, since Columbia owned OKeh at the time, it seems likely that around seven thousand copies may have been pressed.[221]

"Frankie" must have sold very well because Rockwell wrote John asking if he would travel to New York to make more records:

November 8 1928

Dear John
We have been trying to get ahold of you for sometime in order that we might make arrangements for you to come to New York for some more recordings.
The first record that you made sold fairly well, but we did not obtain satisfactory masters on the balance of your recordings.
If it is possible for you to make arrangements to get away from Avalon for a week and come to New York for recording, we will pay you $20 per accepted selections and all your expenses to New York and return for this work.
We would like to have you get together about eight selections at least four of them to be old time tunes similar to selections "Frankie" and "Nobody's Business." There are a great many tunes like these that are known throughout the south.
We have written to Mr. Hughs Smith, manager of the James K Polk Inc., 3rd floor of the McCall Building, Memphis, Tenn., regarding you and if you will call on him he will buy you a ticket and give you some expense money to come to New York.
Please advise me by wire, collect, when you can leave for New York. I am sure that you will enjoy the trip and we will see that you are well taken care of when you are here.

Very truly yours
(signed)
T. G. Rockwell
Director of Recording[222]

John told Pete Seeger that he got the letter asking if he would go to New York to record about a week after returning from Memphis, but John's memory of events was flawed. The letter from Rockwell was dated November 8, 1928, and clearly references sales of John's first record during the summer and fall of 1928. Artists would only be asked to record in New York if they were considered to be a highly saleable commodity by the record company. Gayle Dean Wardlow knew of only two other artists from Mississippi who were summoned to New York to record: Charley Patton and the Mississippi Sheiks. However, that was much later. Patton recorded in 1934. The Mississippi Sheiks did not record as a band in New York, but Bo Carter, who frequently played with the Sheiks, recorded in New York in 1931. The practice was in use elsewhere: OKeh summoned Victoria Spivey to New York after recording her in St. Louis in 1926, and did the same for Lucille Bogan after a trip to Atlanta in 1923.[223]

John set off for New York and met Tommy Rockwell in Memphis: "Rockwell met me in Memphis." John said he was happy to see him as he did not want to go to New York on his own. But, "Rockwell said, 'I'm going to Dallas, Texas.'" So he gave John his tickets and he had to travel to New York alone. The cost was $49 one-way and he traveled via Alabama.[224]

It must have been a lonely trip and an even lonelier stay in New York for John. He traveled on either Wednesday, December 19, or Thursday, 20, and probably returned on Saturday, 29, having spent Christmas away from his family in a strange big city. Perhaps nostalgia and loneliness prompted him to write "Avalon Blues," which was responsible for his being rediscovered over thirty years later. Whatever the reason, he did not have long between experiencing New York and getting the song ready for recording on Friday.

John also remembered pleasant times in New York. OKeh had given him $10 a day to stay in a hotel in New York, but he struck up a friendship with Johnson Bennett, the janitor in the OKeh building, who offered him an unlimited stay at his house sharing his wife's cooking, for $10. John figured it was a good deal and clearly made a profit out of it. After riding on the streetcar and visiting a barbershop they arrived at the man's home. John remembered the meal they were served: "she had some fish and some good country sausage. And she had the fish baked, ooh man did I eat."[225]

OKeh's New York offices and studio were originally at 145 West 45th Street, where Mamie Smith made her famous recording of "Crazy Blues" in 1920; but by 1928 they had established studios near Times Square at 25 West 45th Street, and at 11 Union Square West. At one of these studios, on Friday, December 21, 1928, Mississippi John Hurt recorded:

Ain't No Tellin' (401471-A)
Louis Collins (401472-A)
Avalon Blues (401473-A)
Big Leg Blues (401474-A)

Seven days later on Friday, December 28, 1928, he recorded:

Stack O'lee Blues (401481-B)
Window Light Blues (401482-B)
Candy Man Blues (401483-B)
Got The Blues Can't Be Satisfied (401484-B)
Blessed Be The Name (401485-B)
Praying On The Old Camp Ground (401486-B)
Blue Harvest Blues (401487-B)
Spike Driver Blues (401488-B)

The matrix numbers prior to John's first New York session tells us that Eva Taylor backed by the Clarence Williams Orchestra recorded "Happy Days and Lonely Nights" (Matrix No. 401469) backed with "If You Want The Rainbow (You Must Have The Rain)" (Matrix No. 401470) on Thursday, December 20, 1928.[226] Six recordings were laid down between John's first and second New York sessions. These were by Vaughn de Leath singing "Me and the Man In The Moon" (Matrix No. 401475) and "I'll Never Ask For More" (Matrix No. 401476) following John's sessions on December 21, and Charles W. Hamp (The California Blue Boy) with "The Spell Of The Blues" (Matrix No. 401477), "My Kinda Love" (Matrix No. 401478), "Sitting On The Stairs" (Matrix No. 401479) and "Avalon Town" (Matrix No. 401480) on Saturday, December 22.[227]

Recording resumed on December 28, with John's "Stack O'lee Blues" (Matrix No. 401481-B). No recordings were made immediately after John's last New York session until the New Year, when on January 3, 1929, recording resumed with an Italian tenor, Alfredo Bascetta (Matrix Numbers 401489-401490) and the Italian Orchestra Ferraro (Matrix Numbers 401491 –401492).

On the occasion of John's "re-discovery" in March 1963, as he responded to questions from Tom Hoskins about his recording experiences, John recalled meeting Lonnie Johnson: "[I met] Lonnie Johnson, didn't remember anyone else." In a later interview with Tom Hoskins in Washington, D.C., in 1963, John recounted his experiences in Memphis and New York to Tom and Nick Perls.[228] John remembered meeting with Lonnie Johnson, but spoke of someone else calling himself Lonnie Johnson being in Memphis and meeting the real Lonnie Johnson in New York. He went on to say that Lonnie recorded ahead of him and that was how he knew it was the real Lonnie Johnson. Given that documented records of the OKeh sessions show that Lonnie Johnson was in Memphis on February 13 and 15, 1928, on either side of John's recording,[229] it seems likely that John actually met Johnson in Memphis. There is no record of Johnson being in New York in December 1928.

Figure 1.10. "Candy Man" by
Mississippi John Hurt. (Author's
collection.)

However, there is an unexplained problem with this theory. John told
of Johnson actually being present at the time he recorded in New York:

Me and Lonnie, we was in the recordin' room there so I had just writ-
ten this "Candy Man." I forget some of the verses so they typed them on
the chart, look and sing, so I was singin' and so Lonnie, he says, see I
was practicin' on it while they was gone. And Lonnie says, "ain't a little
too high." I say "yeah," he says "gotta be low. Gotta let it down son.
High," I says, "high right." I'll never forget the manager, T. J. Rockwell
come in, he says, "whose been messin' with that chart." Lonnie says, "I
did." "And what are you?" "I didn't think it would do any harm, it was
too high." "Ah well," he looked at me and says, "is it too high for you," I
says, "yeah, it was a little too high, I couldn't sing good, kinda playin' it
on the front and sing some." That's how I know it was for sure Lonnie
Johnson, but the other guy in Memphis, he was black, I didn't know, I
never met Lonnie, thought, yeah this was him.[230]

According to this version, John had not yet written "Candy Man" when
he was in Memphis, telling Tom Hoskins, "Oh, well, you know I got the
verses while I went home. While I went to New York." Tom asked, "Just
been recently" and John replied, "Recently, I had it written in pencil
and I gotta tell you they typed it for me. Sure. I could just put it out just
right."[231] This confirms that the man who helped John with the chart
showing the words of "Candy Man" did so in New York. John's reference

to the man in Memphis being black infers that the man in New York was white, suggesting that John was unaware of Johnson's race and virtually confirms that he actually met Johnson in Memphis.

John could not recall any other musicians he had met until prompted by Hoskins that when he met Victoria Spivey at the Newport Folk Festival in 1963, she had remembered meeting John in New York. John remembered meeting her in the hallway of the recording studio. Spivey recorded at the OKeh studio with Clarence Williams and Lonnie Johnson in October 1928 and must have been visiting for some other purpose in December. John then went on to say that he met Bessie Smith. He did not speak to her, but recalls that she and the gentleman with her were both carrying guitars.[232] There is no evidence that Bessie Smith ever played guitar and it seems unlikely that she would have been carrying one. She was a Columbia recording artist but, following the merger between Columbia and OKeh in 1926, she may well have visited the New York OKeh studio. She did not record there in December 1928.[233]

From the twenty recordings laid down in the three 1928 sessions twelve sides were issued:

Frankie/Nobody's Dirty Business OKeh 8560

Stack O'Lee Blues/Candy Man Blues OKeh 8654

Blessed Be The Name/Praying On The Old Camp ground OKeh 8666

Blue Harvest Blues/Spike Driver Blues OKeh 8692

Got the Blues Can't Be Satisfied/Louis Collins OKeh 8724

Avalon Blues/Ain't No Tellin' OKeh 8759

John was paid $20 for each issued side, $240, a lot of money for a Mississippi farmhand at that time. Only "Frankie"/"Nobody's Dirty Business" had been issued from the Memphis sessions, but all except "Window Light Blues" and "Big Leg Blues" were issued from the New York sessions. Of the unissued titles, "Blessed Be The Name" and "Meeting On The Old Camp Ground" from the Memphis sessions were recorded again in New York and subsequently released (the latter with a slight change of title). "Big Leg Blues" survived as a test pressing from the Columbia vaults and was issued later on Yazoo L1009. "Monday Morning Blues," "Casey Jones," and "Sliding Delta" were well established in John's repertoire and became firm favorites with audiences following his rediscovery in the 1960s. These titles were recorded on many occasions after 1963. The remaining unissued titles, "Shiverlie Red Blues" and "Window Light Blues," apparently did not survive. John did not remember the tunes following his rediscovery, and the songs appear to be lost forever.

John could not remember "Big Leg Blues" after his rediscovery and probably never had an opportunity to hear his early recording of it. The test pressing of this performance was first issued commercially on an LP on the Yazoo label two years after Hurt's death.[234] However, among the outtakes of his original Piedmont 1963 recordings[235] is an almost identical melody along with the words, "I love you baby," and on the recording Tom Hoskins made in Avalon, "Woke up in the morning, didn't know right from wrong."[236] Likewise, his "Trouble, I've had it all my days" is rather similar to "Big Leg Blues."

The selection of songs that were issued by record companies from those actually recorded may simply reflect the sides that survived the recording process best. However, marketing potential was probably the main reason behind the selection. Given the popularity of blues at the time, artists were asked to play blues, and as we have seen, record companies would often add the word *blues* to a title in order to promote its sales. This process effectively presented a biased view of the repertoire of many performers toward blues tunes. Elijah Wald has suggested that the concept of a blues musician was an artificial one promoted by record companies and that many artists played a much more varied repertoire than their recordings suggest.[237] The variety of music in Mississippi John Hurt's 1928 output and his 1960s repertoire adds considerable support to this thesis. It is of interest that "Monday Morning Blues" was the tune that initially encouraged Rockwell to record Hurt, but eventually OKeh chose not to release this title.

In his liner notes to the reissue of the original OKeh recordings, Lawrence Cohn reports that John was paid $240 for the Memphis recordings and that John told him that he met "Lonnie Johnson, Blind Lemon Jefferson, Bessie Smith and lots, lots more. We were all seated outside the hall, each waiting for our turn." The payment of $240 was actually for all twelve recorded sides from all of the sessions. Although Jefferson did record eight sides for OKeh in Atlanta in March 1927 (only two were issued, "Black Snake Moan" and "Matchbox Blues"), he primarily recorded on Paramount Records, and it seems unlikely that he would have been around the OKeh recording sessions in Memphis or New York when John attended. Cohn's interview with John took place at John's apartment in Washington, D.C., in 1965, but sadly he forgot to take along the power cord for his tape recorder and could not tape the interview.[238]

And so at the age of 35, John Hurt had become a recording artist and acquired a prefix to his name.[239] Mississippi John Hurt had been born. What would the future hold for him?

2. The Middle Years, 1929–1962

Return to Avalon and the Depression

Mississippi John Hurt returned from New York to Avalon to await further developments in his new career as a musician. He had more money in his pocket than he had seen for a long time and must have been full of hope. But he had a long wait for the fame he was due. He was to achieve recognition and fame but he was going to have to wait thirty-four years for it. As for fortune, that was never to be.

Although there is no advertising or sales information available relating to the five records released from the New York sessions, other OKeh recordings issued around the same time were advertised and the dates of these can be used to estimate release dates of the Mississippi John Hurt titles. For instance, Victoria Spivey and Lonnie Johnson's recording of "Furniture Man Blues Parts 1 and 2" (OKeh 8652) was advertised on February 9, 1929, in the *Baltimore Afro-American* and the *Chicago Defender* newspapers. The Silver Leaf Quartette of Norfolk recording of "When Jesus Comes"/"My Soul Is A Witness For The Lord" (8655) was advertised on February 16, 1929, in the same newspapers. The release number of Mississippi John Hurt's recording of "Stack O'Lee Blues"/"Candy Man Blues" (8654) falls between these two releases, suggesting that it was issued in early February 1929. Lonnie Johnson and Spencer Williams's record of "It Feels So Good, Parts 1 and 2" was advertised on March 16, 1929, and "You Better Let That Liar Alone"/"That's What's The Matter With The Church Today" by the Silver Leaf Quartette of Norfolk on March 30, 1929. This suggests that Mississippi John Hurt's "Blessed Be The Name"/"Praying On The Old Camp Ground" (8666) was issued in late March. Similarly, Louis Armstrong and His Orchestra with "No"/"Basin Street Blues" (8690), Mississippi John Hurt's "Blue Harvest Blues"/"Spike Driver Blues" (8692) and Hambone Willie

Newbern's "Way Down in Arkansas"/"Hambone Willie's Dreamy-Eyed Woman's Blues" (8693) were released in succession. The Armstrong record was advertised on June 22, 1929, and the Newbern one on July 6, 1929. Lonnie Johnson with "You Can't Give A Woman Everything She Needs"/"From Now On Make Your Whoopee At Home" (8722) was advertised on October 19, 1929, and the Little Chocolate Dandies with "That's How I Feel Today"/"Six Or Seven Times" (8728) on November 9, 1928. "Louis Collins"/"Got The Blues Can't Be Satisfied" by Mississippi John Hurt (8724) would have been released between these dates. John's final release, "Ain't No Tellin'"/"Avalon Blues" (8759) came between Louis Armstrong's "I Ain't Got Nobody"/"Rockin' Chair" (8756) advertised on February 2, 1930 and "Monkey And The Baboon"/"Wipe It Off" by Lonnie Johnson with Spencer Williams and Clarence Williams respectively (8762) on March 22, 1930.[1]

Using this information provides these approximate release dates:

"Stack O'Lee Blues"/"Candy Man Blues" (OKeh 8654): February 9–16, 1929

"Blessed Be The Name"/"Praying On The Old Camp Ground" (OKeh 8666): March 16–30, 1929

"Blue Harvest Blues"/"Spike Driver Blues" (OKeh 8692): June 22–July 6, 1929

"Got the Blues Can't Be Satisfied"/"Louis Collins" (OKeh 8724): October 19–November 9, 1929

"Avalon Blues"/"Ain't No Tellin'" (OKeh 8759): February 2–March 22, 1930[2]

Not all record releases were advertised in newspapers, sales probably being most dependent upon point-of-sale publicity. Presumably, records with high sales expectations—such as female vaudeville singers, well-known jazz bands, and guaranteed good sellers like Lonnie Johnson—were allocated much of the available advertising budget.

Whether OKeh maintained contact with John about his record sales is not known, but seems unlikely. In any case, they never called on Mississippi John Hurt to record again, and it seemed as if his short-lived recording career was over. John must have been disappointed, especially with local musicians Narmour and Smith continuing to do well through the early thirties, but his resilient nature and calm acceptance of his destiny would have helped him deal with his disappointment. The lack of interest from OKeh and the relative scarcity of the 78 rpm records from his New York sessions suggest that his records did not sell well. Mississippi John Hurt 78s were often found in white homes by collectors in the 1950s,[3] suggesting that unlike the Delta blues, John's music appealed to a wider audience. It also suggests that had OKeh marketed John's records outside the confines of the race label, as they initially intended to do,[4] they might have experienced larger sales.

John's white neighbors Willie Narmour and Shell Smith, who first recorded in Memphis in February 1928 at the same sessions as John, recorded again in 1929, 1930, and 1934.[5] Popular African American musicians the Mississippi Sheiks, a fiddle and guitar duo, first had been recorded at a similar OKeh field session in Shreveport, Louisiana, on February 17, 1930. The Mississippi Sheiks were so popular that they were called back to record in San Antonio in June 1930, where they recorded fourteen sides, and again to Jackson, Mississippi, in December to record another ten. The Sheiks' popularity continued and they recorded again in 1930, 1931, 1933, 1934, and 1935; under their own names, Sheiks members Bo Carter and Walter Jacobs continued to record until 1940.[6]

Some hope of further recording work for John came along, probably in late 1929 or early 1930, when he received a letter from W. E. Myer who owned his own record company, The Lonesome Ace. Dock Boggs had already recorded for the Virginia label.[7] Myer wrote to Dock Boggs on June 10, 1930, acknowledging receipt of some records and informing Boggs that he had written to the OKeh Company "About the compositions that John Hurt, Colored, has on hands and they might want to use you on some also, and if they made a trade with me on his playing, I might work you in on some."[8]

Myer had heard John's 1928 recordings and decided that he was the right man to provide the melody and record some songs that he had written. Myer sent John the words to twenty-two songs and John put his own melodies to two of them, "Waiting for You" and "Richlands Women Blues," a song about Myer's home town of Richlands, Virginia. Myer sent the Jimmie Rodgers record "Waiting For A Train" to John, asking him to make use of the melody; John applied it to Myer's song "Let the Mermaids Flirt with Me."[9] These three songs became mainstays of John's future performances.

Although Myer had asked John to write something in the style of Jimmie Rodgers, America's Blue Yodeler, who had become a household name in the South by this time, Myer did not care for yodeling, and on his record label under the company name was a promise: "Without a Yodel."[10] Given that Rodgers made his reputation yodeling, one wonders whether Myer presented this caveat to John. Myer fell ill and wrote to John saying that when he was well he wanted John to record some songs for a company in Port Washington, Wisconsin. The company was the New York Recording Laboratories (NYRL), a company inaugurated by the Wisconsin Chair Company that had become involved in the manufacture

of phonographs. NYRL owned the Paramount label that Myer commis-
sioned to produce his The Lonesome Ace records.[11] After a while, John
had not heard any more and wrote to Myer. He received a reply saying
that Myer was still sick. John never heard from him again. Boggs had returned 141 of his records to Myer because he could not sell them and enclosed in the letter from Myer he received payment of $70.50 for them.
After that, Boggs never heard from Myer again and he began searching
for other recording opportunities. The Lonesome Ace, like many other
record companies, was a casualty of the Depression. Had Myer not fallen
ill, John may well have released further records on The Lonesome Ace,
OKeh, or Paramount, and his future may have been very different. In
1963, after his rediscovery, John wrote again to Myer, receiving a reply
from his wife saying that he had passed away.[12]

Some of John's tunes present lyrics that are difficult to interpret today,
and "Richlands Women Blues" is a good example:

> *Gimme red lipstick and a bright poppy rouge,*
> *A shingle-bob haircut and a shot of good booze;*
> *I'm rarin' to go, got red shoes on my feet.*
> *My minds sittin' right for Tin Lizzies seat;*
> *Dress skirt cut high, then they cut low,*
> *Don't think I'm a sport, keep on watchin' me go;*
> *With rosy red garters, pink hose on my feet,*
> *Turkey red bloomers in a rumble seat.*

The song contains details of fashion accessories that were current in
the late 1920s such as the "shingle-bob haircut," rouge, red garters, and
pink hose. A "sport" is a playboy or party girl. "Tin Lizzie's Seat" was a
seat in a Model T Ford, known as Tin Lizzie, and a rumble seat was a
seat that could be folded out of the trunk of some models of cars at the
time. The theme of the song, sung from a female perspective—"Hurry
down, sweet daddy, come blowin' your horn / If you're comin' too late,
sweet mama will be gone"—underlines the importance of an automobile
in attracting the opposite sex, a principle that appears to be just as valid
today.

Following the affluent times of the 1920s, for middle-class and many
wealthy Americans the 1930s brought economic collapse and the great
Depression. The crash of the stock market in Wall Street, New York, in
October 1929 caused a collapse of financial institutions. In Greenwood,
Mississippi, five of the six banks closed.[13] Although poor folk in Mississippi
had not really benefited from the good times, they were certainly

affected by the bad. The effect of the Depression and a major drought in Mississippi in the summer of 1930 seriously affected the cotton crop. The mainstay of the rural economy, cotton's value dropped to around five cents per pound, down by more than 50 percent from its previous peak.

Everything was affected. Record sales slumped in spite of a drop in prices from around seventy-five to thirty-five cents. Sales of race records dropped from around 5 percent of total record sales in 1927 to only 1 percent by 1931. By May 1930 Columbia, one of the biggest record companies, had reduced its output to around 2,000 copies of each new race recording, down from about 11,000 in 1927, and 5,000 at the end of 1929. Sales of John's records, especially "Got the Blues Can't Be Satisfied"/"Louis Collins" (OKeh 8724), issued in the fall of 1929, and "Avalon Blues"/"Ain't No Tellin'" (OKeh 8759) in the spring of 1930, must have suffered badly. This may be reflected in their rarity compared to his earlier releases. Every major record company except Victor and Columbia (which by now included OKeh) went out of business in the early 1930s.[14]

Following its takeover of OKeh, Columbia continued to operate the two companies independently and market the two labels separately. They managed to stay in business, but with drastically reduced sales. Blind Willie Johnson, who had become enormously popular, was selling only around 5,000 copies of his titles, while Bessie Smith managed only 3,000 in 1929. By 1931, these artists, along with Blind Willie McTell, were selling only a few hundred. OKeh fared better than most and, with the popular Mississippi Sheiks, and the solo releases of Sheiks artist Bo Carter, did rather well in 1931. There was clearly no appetite for risk among record companies, and Mississippi John Hurt apparently disappeared from the radar. Although the record industry had slumped and the A&R men had lost interest in the country blues, the popularity of live music remained, especially in the small Mississippi towns.

Republican president Herbert Hoover presided over the Wall Street crash without doing much to prevent it. New Democratic president Franklin D. Roosevelt came into office in 1933, bringing hope to a disillusioned nation. Roosevelt introduced his New Deal, a suite of reforms aimed at guiding the country to recovery. The New Deal included programs aimed at subsidizing farmers, replanting deforested landscapes of Mississippi and elsewhere, and getting people back to work. The Works Progress Administration (WPA) ran from 1935 to 1943 and set out to provide jobs for the unemployed on a variety of public projects, including road building, rural rehabilitation, and reforestation.[15]

With the onset of the Depression, John worked hard to make a living and would take on anything he could get, "anything 'cept robbin' and stealin'. I'd fool around, raisin' a pretty good patch. Work for this man for just what I could get." John worked on a WPA program putting gravel on the roads, clearing trees from roadsides, and building dams and levees for three dollars a day. The WPA provided work in seven-day stretches: "you work seven, then you stop seven, then you go back to work and you work seven, then you stop seven."[16] The WPA built the Carrollton Community Hall in John's local town of Carrollton, which became an important focus for community functions in the years to come and where, sixty years later, the Mississippi John Hurt Foundation annual Gala would be held.

With things just getting back to normal after the 1927 flood, heavier than normal rainfall again fell on the Delta in late 1931. The Potacocowa Creek again channeled huge volumes of water from the hills through Avalon, into the Yalobusha River, and on into the Yazoo. The constant winter rains began to ease by February, but by this time the Yazoo was overflowing and there was high water everywhere. Just five years after the great flood of 1927, refugees headed for the hills to escape the ravages of the worst known flood of the Yazoo, adding to the misery created by the Depression.[17]

The Red Cross was mobilized to Greenwood, where levees were maintained and constructed, saving the main part of the town from inundation. Levee building had changed dramatically since the early days when these massive structures had been built by black and Irish hands using wheelbarrows and shovels, to the thirties with tractors and earth moving equipment.[18] However, large parts of the town were under water and people used boats to get around. In north Greenwood the streets had become rivers. Some folk improvised by making "flood buggies" from their cars by jacking up the body four or five feet above the axles.

Although John commented that the boll weevil had not reached Mississippi at this time,[19] this hugely important pest of the cotton crop had originally spread from Mexico through Texas and Louisiana early in the century and arrived in Mississippi by 1907. It affected virtually all of Mississippi by 1910, causing financial ruin. After this initial infestation there were several fluctuations in the impact of the boll weevil, a very heavy and damaging infestation occurring in Mississippi in 1923.[20] Perhaps John's comment reflected a period of low weevil activity around 1930, or possibly it actually had not previously affected the area around Avalon. A number of songs relating the impact of the boll weevil appeared, as it continued to spread through southern states, reflecting the enormous social and economic impact it was having. Delta bluesman Charley Patton recorded a song about the boll weevil in 1929.[21] One method of reducing the numbers of boll weevil was to alternate the cotton crop with peanuts, which became an important crop in Mississippi. During the 1960s, John told Tom Hoskins about the alternation of peanuts and cotton: "Well, I say, you have a field of peanuts this year, well you might get smart and put cotton here where I had the peanuts." John went on to describe how they would harvest the corn in the fall to provide winter feed for stock: "You have what you call a corn crib, you know a house for the corn. This month, what's this October, regular corn gatherin' month, you see harvestin' corn. Have 'em cured, hard dry, put it away, house it up. You feed your stock off it you know, mules and cows."[22] Peanuts were a favorite snack of John's; granddaughter Mary Frances said that Daddy John (an affectionate name for John used by his grandchildren) could always produce a handful of peanuts from his pocket.

Asked about picking cotton, John said that he could pick over three hundred pounds a day but recalled two men from Duck Hill—who came to the Brunson plantation in Avalon—who could pick a whole bale a day between them: "Just like goin' to a show, lots of people went down to Mr. Brunson's field to see these men pick this bale of cotton a day, just two men."[23] Fifteen or sixteen hundred pounds of cotton would need to be picked from the fields to yield the 500 pounds of cotton required to make up a bale, once the seeds had been discarded.[24]

Conditions were hard for plantation workers, and some writers have suggested that it was worse than slavery.[25] Delta musician Sam Chatmon recalled conditions on the plantation where he had lived in Mississippi: "Old colored ladies would always be the ones to look after the young kids. And they had a trough to mix bread and stuff up in so the children could eat. . . . Yeah, a trough! Just like pigs."[26]

As the effects of the Depression eventually eased and federal programs helped recovery, things improved for Mississippi farmers. New arrangements for agricultural credit ended the accumulation of debt, and loans from the Department of Agriculture came to the assistance of farmers. The introduction of the mechanical cotton picker raised the possibility to harvest as much cotton in an hour as a man could pick in a week. The first public demonstration in 1936 at Leland, Mississippi, in the Delta had increased optimism by planters, but many feared a collapse of the sharecropping system and huge unemployment, adding to the effects of the Depression. However, it was the 1950s before mechanized picking became widespread.[27]

Music around Carroll County

Around 1930 John met black fiddlers Bea Anderson, who had come to Avalon from Louisiana after the boll weevil had ruined the cotton crop there, and George Hanks from Duck Hill, about twenty miles east of Avalon. Following John's meeting with Anderson, and presumably helped by his local fame as a recording artist, he began to play more dances for both black and white audiences, and they would perform the tunes that John had recorded. In such a duo the fiddle usually took the lead with the guitar providing chorded rhythms and occasional bass runs. John said, "Oh I used to play the guitar, I never did try to learn the pickin'."[28] It seems that John was quite focused on what he liked to play and although he might play along as an accompanist, he did not bother to learn the detailed picking of the melody for tunes that were not part of his repertoire. John remembered them playing a tune that went, "Bumble Bee, Bumble Bee, Bee buzzin' around my hive," that Anderson taught to John.[29]

John gave his white neighbor Fred Clarke one of his records and, after listening to it, Fred's folks ordered a Victrola from the Sears Roebuck catalogue and purchased several of John's records. "We would sit up until midnight playing the Victrola, 'Candy Man,' 'Stackolee,' 'Some of these days gonna wake up boozy, get my gun, kill old Susie'" (a reference to a line from "Nobody's Dirty Business"). Annie Cook remembers her father returning from Carrollton with a Victrola and a copy of "Carroll County Blues," but she told me that it was the older people that liked John's music; she and her friends preferred big bands, jazz, and swing.

Fred also recalled house parties and country dances where John would play with "a colored fella, Bea Anderson, picked a mandolin and played a fiddle, long tall colored boy, his nickname was 'Coon.'" John's wife Jessie did not care for Anderson's music and would say, "I'm sick of hearing that box." Ms. Kitty, a black friend of John and Jessie, who now lives in Grenada, also remembered hearing Bea Anderson, saying he played a banjo. Two local residents Fred Clarke and Josephine Jackson independently referred to Anderson playing a mandolin,[30] a common alternative to a fiddle sharing the same tuning.

Willie Narmour was a contemporary of John's, born in 1889. He died from a stroke in 1961. Shell Smith was born in 1895 and died in 1968. Coleman Narmour, Willie's son, told local journalist and historian Susie James in 1997 that country dances were held frequently, especially before World War II. He told Susie about life in those days: "You plowed with a middle buster. We didn't have no jet planes. We got 'T' models and 'A' models and didn't have no roads to put those on. I used to ride a horse from Valley to Carrollton to the gristmill." Arnie Watson told Susie James that 1930s Carroll County was a wild place and in the Valley area "there was a bootlegger in every hollow."[31] Of course, John's brother Hennis would have been one of them!

Arnie told how the local musicians played for his party: "Willie and Shell played at an all-night party on my twenty-first birthday and John Hurt spelled them. The cultures, black and white, didn't mix, but John Hurt had his style and they had theirs."[32] But Arnie Watson presumably had his own reasons for wanting to reinforce and perpetuate this separation: he was, at one time, an officer of the Council of Conservative Citizens (C of CC), an organization rising from the remains of the previous White Citizens Council.[33] The C of CC believes that the United States is "a European country . . . we [also] oppose all efforts to mix the races of mankind, to promote non-white races over the European-American people through so-called 'affirmative action' and similar measures to destroy or denigrate the European-American heritage, including the heritage of the southern people, and to force the integration of the races."[34]

Willie Narmour's daughter, Hazel Wiggins, at the age of 79 told Susie James that her grandfather, Willie's father, also played fiddle and made his young son learn on a homemade cigar-box instrument before he would buy him a real one. She also remembered her uncle Henry Narmour playing fiddle or beating straws and buck dancing.[35] Narmour and Smith played the Alice Café in Greenwood and continued to play locally long after their recording careers were over.[36]

The record that firmly established the careers of Narmour and Smith was "Carroll County Blues." There is some disagreement about who actually composed the tune, some attributing it to Willie Narmour and Shell Smith, some saying that Narmour heard a black farm hand humming the tune, and others saying that Doc Bailey, the Winona veterinarian who had organized the Winona fiddle contest that first established Narmour and established the Mississippi Possum Hunters, had taken Willie Narmour to hear a white farmer play the tune. However, folks around Avalon believe that Gene Clardy (43 years old in the 1930 census) wrote it. Clardy, a Carroll County fiddler who was one of Willie Narmour's mentors, recorded four sides, though "Carroll County Blues" was not one of them.[37] Perhaps the tune was a well-known traditional tune in the area, which Narmour and Smith arranged and recorded. Clardy was stabbed to death at a local dance in the mid-1930s.[38] John apparently did not often accompany Willie Narmour after 1930.[39]

In the 1930s John and Jessie lived on St. James Road and in 1932 their only child, John William "Man" Hurt was born. Around that time, John and Bea Anderson played at the home of Josephine Jackson, now a retired schoolteacher who recalled how, when she was a child, her father had invited John and Bea Anderson to play at their home: "On a Saturday night Daddy might get John to play. Another black man, Bea Anderson, might come too. We'd sit in one of the rooms; we didn't have separate living rooms in those days. Daddy would invite other neighbors. Bea Anderson would play the mandolin and John would sing and play the guitar. Daddy'd pay them a dollar or two." John said that Bea Anderson died in Mississippi in 1938.[40]

The polarity between religious and secular music was much in evidence throughout the Deep South; many musicians experienced the tension of being pulled in different directions with regard to their musical preferences. John W. Work III, in his essay "Secular Music," suggested that secular music "grows and thrives in ratio to its distance from the influence of the church," and provided several references of the mutual exclusion of sacred and secular music from interviewees. One man told how "They [the church] make like they going to turn you out if you dance, and you have to beg pardon to get back. They have a group of critics and they gives you a sixty-day lay-off. All you do is tell them that you wants to beg the church's pardon for your evil ways, and that you're not going to do it no more. Of course, you know you are!"

Similarly, a 19-year-old schoolboy told Work: "Yes sir! I think blues is wrong to sing, especially for a Christian. No folks around here who calls themselves Christians sing the blues. Dancing is all right if it's just a sociable thing, but it ain't right if it's like at the juke." Work considered that this meant group dancing such as round and square dancing being acceptable, but not close dancing by couples such as the slow drag, which was popular at the jukes; however, the boy may have been contrasting dancing at home to dancing in a juke. Work also stated that "Muddy Water," who had recently been discovered by Work and his co-workers, "would like to join the church, but to do so would mean abandoning his guitar—a sacrifice too dear to make now."[41] Some forms of secular music were acceptable. For example, much popular written music was considered respectable, but the blues had become associated with brothels and jukes and was therefore considered wicked.[42]

John appears always to have been at ease playing both kinds of music and continued to do so during his rediscovery years in the sixties, when, as Holly Ochs Henderson recalled, he would frequently begin a performance with a religious song saying, "Got to put the Lord out front." The local acceptance of John's repertoire containing such a variety of sacred and secular music is all the more surprising considering the stricter hold of the church in the hills as opposed to the Delta, where the church was less in control of community life and secular music flourished. This is clearly articulated by an elderly Sunday school teacher in the Delta who was interviewed by Professor Work:

I done been here, and lived around here [Coahoma County, Mississippi], and have seen most of it. That's not all neither. I done been all up around in the Hills. Up there things are not like they are down here. Well, I tell you. Up in the hills, folks don't get around as much as they do down here. And the Negroes on the plantations up around in there, I don't know what they do now, but they didn't used to move around as much as they do down here. Folks get to living in a cabin on the plantation and they lives there for years and years. Everybody, all their neighbors knowed them. And the devil didn't seem to have much of a chance up in the Hills.

Up in the hills community sanctions influence almost all that you find anybody doing. The folks up there, as I told you, lived in one place longer than they do down here. The man, his wife, and his children feel a closer kinship to the land. A few of them own, and those who don't own still get along fair. They just been there on the land, and it's just a part of them. They have seen it for many years—when it's been good to them and when it's been bad.[43]

Perhaps these words explain a great deal about John's personal philosophy and the way things were in the hill country communities. And perhaps it explains a lot about why the blues was able to develop so effectively in the Mississippi delta, away from many of the social constraints found elsewhere.

In the late 1930s Carroll County was "wet" (alcoholic drinks were legally available), while neighboring Montgomery and Grenada Counties were dry, and so the county line juke joints were popular places. Chambley's was one such juke in "Little Texas" between Avalon and Grenada.[44] Young folk would go and dance there, but no one recalls John ever playing there; probably the jukebox had taken over from live music by that time. John Work reported of Clarksdale in 1941: "The music to which Clarksdalians now dance is furnished chiefly by the juke boxes, which are called 'Sea Birds'—a corruption of the name Seeburg, one of the makers of Nickelodeons. The 'Sea Birds' have practically eliminated the folk performers and music from the Clarksdale dancing scene. The guitarists, harmonica and mandolin players now perform on street corners or in barber shops for pure entertainment purposes for which they collect small gratuities from appreciative passersby."[45]

During the 1930s and 1940s the Delta was an incredibly fertile area for musical development, and the blues was being played everywhere. One of the first tunes the young Muddy Waters learned was "Walkin' Blues," and he said, perhaps with some hyperbole, "That was the theme in Mississippi, most every guitar player was playin' that."[46] Another favorite tune was "Catfish Blues," which was first recorded by Robert Petway in March 1941 and in September 1941 by Tommy McClennan as "Deep Blue Sea Blues."[47] Petway and McClennan were popular musicians around the Greenwood area in 1941.[48]

In 1932, Robert Johnson returned from his birthplace in Hazlehurst, south of Jackson, to the Delta community of Robinsonville where he had been raised, with incredible guitar-playing and performing skills. According to legend he had traded his soul to the devil in return for his proficiency, but more likely he had spent the time practicing hard. He caught up with old acquaintances Willie Brown and Son House, who were amazed at his progress. Johnson's first recordings in 1936 included "Terraplane Blues," "I Believe I'll Dust My Broom," "Sweet Home Chicago," and "Ramblin' On My Mind." "Terraplane Blues" was immediately popular, and the others would become so in the 1960s when white blues enthusiasts got to hear them.[49]

"Honeyboy" Edwards's girlfriend recalled seeing Robert Johnson playing on Johnson Street in Greenwood in the spring of 1937, where she paid him fifteen cents to play "Terraplane Blues."[50] Honeyboy himself recalled the event, saying that a woman asked Johnson to play the tune for a dime when he was playing outside of Emma Collins, a "good-timing house" (presumably a brothel) in Greenwood that also sold whiskey.[51]

In August 1938 Johnson played at a house party at Three Forks near Quito outside Greenwood, where he was poisoned and later died.[52] Johnson's grave is variously reported to be at the Zion Church near Morgan City south of Greenwood on Highway 7, the same road that runs through Avalon to the north of Greenwood; at the Payne Chapel M. B. Church at Quito; or at another location north of Greenwood.[53] Johnson was about eighteen years younger than John and it is not known whether John was aware of his music, though he may well have heard some of his tunes, especially the popular "Terraplane Blues."

Helena, on the Arkansas side of the Mississippi River, was one of the main centers of blues in the Delta in the 1930s. Musicians would cross on the ferry to play there and travel up and down Highway 61 to Memphis. Helena became the home of the King Biscuit radio show on station KFFA in 1941, and after 1944 Avalon fell within the eighty-mile broadcasting range of the station. Sonny Boy Williamson II (Rice Miller) and Robert Lockwood Jr. were the mainstay performers and they attracted a large number of guest artists. Broadcasts featured the Delta blues.[54] It seems likely that John would have heard these at some time, probably in the houses of his white neighbors.

John must have been familiar with the surge of music coming from the Delta, especially in the Greenwood area, and he may well have heard some of the Delta bluesmen performing in the area. Whatever the case, John was clearly not sufficiently taken with the modern Delta blues to include it in his repertoire, sticking to the old timey tunes and his ragtime interpretation of other tunes that he liked.

Closer to Avalon, Mack Allen Smith, a white musician from Little Texas, Mississippi, and distant cousin of Shell Smith, recalled seeing Mississippi John Hurt performing along with his uncle Herbert at the school bus shop in North Carrollton.[55] Mack Allen Smith was born at Hickory Grove, Little Texas, in 1940. He grew up at Carrollton hearing his mother play guitar and sing Jimmie Rodgers tunes. Her brothers played guitar, fiddle and bass and sang many of the popular country songs of the day. Mack described how in North Carrollton he could hear country and western music coming from the white cafés and rhythm and blues on the other side of the tracks from the black community . Mack preferred the black music and naively thought that that whites and blacks frequented different cafés because they liked different kinds of music.[56]

Mack led a number of bands that played locally, traveled to England, and made many records. In 1962 Mack's band the Flames included a young lead guitarist named Art Browning who later returned to Avalon to become the curator of the Mississippi John Hurt Museum. In 1959, when Mack first formed the Flames, Keith Worrell played lead guitar. Keith like Art was a big fan of Mississippi John Hurt and Keith actually knew John and learned from him. The band played regularly at the Carrollton Community Hall, built during the WPA project.

Keith Worrell grew up in the Valley area during the 1950s and 1960s. His father was principal of the Valley school and knew John, Willie Narmour, and Shell Smith well. John and Willie Narmour played at Keith's eighteenth birthday party on March 16, 1961. John and Keith would also trade guitars and Art Browning remembers a couple of old Harmony Stellas, possibly the one that John was photographed with outside the Stinson's Store (see Figs. 2.1, 2.2).

Not only country music was played in the area. Dardanelle Hadley was a local white girl and a gifted musician who became famous in the 1940s and 1950s. She was born on the Mullen plantation in Avalon and told how

Figure 2.1. Mississippi John Hurt with Harmony guitar outside Stinson's Store, Avalon, Mississippi, ca. 1950. (Tom Hoskins Archive.)

traveling black musicians would come through Avalon and always play on the porch of "Daddy's Country Store" there. Her father was a ragtime pianist. "My daddy would hold me up on his shoulders and get such a kick from my response to the music." One band played Dixieland jazz: "The leader was a man called 'Big Boy' who played a tuba and they also had trombones."[57]

So throughout the 1930–1960 period there were many local musicians, and many responded to changing musical fashions as electric rhythm and blues, country and western, rockabilly, and rock 'n' roll swept the nation. Interestingly, the young musicians who listened to John appear to have adapted their music to the style of the day, while John himself never changed, staying true to the style he had established from the early guidance of William Henry Carson.

In the first half of the thirties Memphis Minnie, Buddy Moss, Josh White, and Bo Carter were some of the big names in the country blues. After 1934 the urban blues became established, with artists such as Big Bill Broonzy and Tampa Red working with a pianist or a small combo introducing the early beginnings of the Chicago sound. By 1937 the industry was booming, and guitar-accompanied blues music continued to

Figure 2.2. Mississippi John Hurt with friends playing Harmony guitar outside Stinson's Store, Avalon, Mississippi, ca. 1950. (Tom Hoskins Archive.)

be popular. Blind Boy Fuller first recorded in 1935 and by 1938 was one of the most prolific of blues performers. By the late 1930s Broonzy and Fuller had become the best-selling blues artists; after Fuller's death in 1942, Big Bill, Tampa Red, and Washboard Sam were the biggest names. Lonnie Johnson, who had recorded at the same Memphis session as John in 1928, survived in the business longer than anyone and was still going strong up to his death in 1970.[58]

Tough times hit the record industry again, when in 1942 the U.S. government restricted the use of shellac in the recording industry to support the war effort. Later the same year J. C. Petrillo, the head of the American Federation of Musicians, announced a ban on all recording to safeguard live music against the increasing use of records on radio and jukeboxes and to gain increases in musicians' wages. All commercial recording studios were closed down for nearly two years and the output of the race labels was hit very hard, with only previously recorded material from sure-selling artists like Broonzy and Fuller being released.[59]

However, the Library of Congress was not a commercial outlet. Alan Lomax, having taken over supervision of its Archive of Folk Song, continued to record at penitentiaries, prison farms, and in the rural countryside through the 1930s and early 1940s. Lomax, John Wesley Work III (a black professor of music at the Fisk University at Nashville, Tennessee), and Lewis Jones (a Fisk assistant professor of sociology) conducted a groundbreaking study of a black community in Coahoma County, Mississippi, in 1941 and 1942. The study focused on Clarksdale, including the Stovall Plantation, and recorded church services, spiritual singing, oral histories, and secular music, including blues. Their study extended outside of Coahoma County to other rural locations in Mississippi including Mound Bayou in Bolivar County and Money in Leflore County.[60]

They recorded the music at a Baptist church service in Money on September 1, 1941, just six miles west of Avalon. How close they were to the home of Mississippi John Hurt—a chance meeting could have resulted in Hurt's gift to the world being recognized twenty-two years earlier than it eventually was. Sadly, they did not meet him, but their prize from the expedition was nonetheless a big one. They were introduced to the young McKinley Morganfield at the Stovall Plantation near Clarksdale, Mississippi.[61] He became known as Muddy Waters, one of the first musicians to make the complete transition from rural acoustic country blues to urban electric blues and rhythm and blues.[62] David "Honeyboy" Edwards, Son House, and Sid Hemphill were also discovered during these trips. By the time the Petrillo ban ended in 1944, the electric blues was becoming established and the heyday of rural blues was over. Throughout all this, Mississippi John Hurt stayed true to the style and music he enjoyed and continued to play for appreciative local audiences.

Apparently John played some paying gigs. Local man Charles Campbell remembered someone driving up from Louise twelve miles south of Belzoni to collect John and take him to perform in a "joint" down there, a round trip of 120 miles. "He would play there for black audiences. There was no mixed audiences back then." Annie Cook recalled hearing John playing on a local Grenada radio station in 1941, and John mentioned this during his conversation with Tom Hoskins in 1963, referring to the "Jubilee outfit."[63] Jubilee groups were singers who performed in the style of the popular Golden Gate Jubilee Singers and commonly performed on weekly radio programs in the South. This was practically the only live black broadcasting at that time and it may be that John appeared on such programs.

Ishmon Bracey told of his meeting with Mississippi John Hurt in a juke joint in Greenwood: "In this juke in Greenwood, I walked in and heard this little guy playin'. I took out my guitar and started playin' when he finished and I had the crowd and he wouldn't play no more. He come up to me later and says, 'How you tuned?' and I shows him. We got to be friends after that, but he didn't ever get over (on) me."[64] Like John, Bracey had recorded first in 1928 in Memphis. Bracey was in Memphis just ten days before John: he recorded two sides for Victor on February 4, 1928 with Charlie McCoy on second guitar.[65] Like John he was rediscovered in 1963 (by Gayle Dean Wardlow).

Blind Lemon Jefferson apparently played in Greenwood in 1928 and 1929, the same year of his reported death in Chicago, and Bracey may have played there up till around 1935, after which he did not play very much until his ordination as a minister in 1951 and his subsequent rediscovery in 1963.[66] It is possible that John may have met Bracey in Greenwood, probably before 1935 when Bracey was regularly in Greenwood. It may even have been earlier, when Bracey was working with Jefferson in Greenwood[67]—which introduces the possibility that John may have met or heard Jefferson playing in Greenwood around the time of his own recording experiences in Memphis and New York in 1928. However, as far as I can discover, John never mentioned knowing either Bracey or Jefferson.

John traveled as far south as Louise near Yazoo City to play and appeared on radio in Grenada. Unfortunately, it is not known how frequently such opportunities arose. However, although he preferred to stay close to his family, and the Avalon/Valley area was rural and relatively isolated, John undoubtedly came into contact with the popular music of the day both through hearing music on his travels, listening to traveling shows, on shopping trips to Greenwood and Grenada, and from the radio and phonograph records played on the Victrolas of his friends.

The Hurts and the Avalon/Valley Community

The population of the Avalon/Valley area declined by about 12 percent between 1900 and 1910, but by 1920 it had risen again and changed very little between 1920 and 1930 (see Table 2.1), continuing to be a busy and relatively densely populated community.

Table 2.1. Population changes in the Avalon/Valley area 1900-1930			
1900	**1910**	**1920**	**1930**
1,830 (District 15)	1,419 (District 29)	2,045 (District 28)	2,029 (District 2)
1,656 (District 16)	1,649 (District 30)	1,476 (District 29)	1,504 (District 3)
3,486 (Total Beat 2)	3,068 (Total Beat 2)	3,521 (Total Beat 2)	3,533 (Total Beat 2)

Note: Districts 15, 29, 28, and 2 (second line) reflect different terminology applied in the different censuses, but the areas are geographically identical and include all territory in townships 20 and 21 in Range 2 East and that portion of Township 20 in Range 3 East lying north of the Potacocowa Creek. Geographically, it includes Avalon and the western part of the Valley hill country.

Districts 16, 30, 29, and 3 (third line) reflect different terminology in the different censuses but are geographically identical and include all territory in Township 20 in Range 3 East lying south of the Potacocowa Creek. Geographically, it covers the eastward extension of the Valley hill country.

The Lynn Gravel Company (and later the Harleston Construction Company) opened up a large gravel pit below St. James Road in the 1920s to provide gravel for the upgrading of Mississippi's roads; many of the roads in Mississippi were surfaced from there. It was a large operation and created a lot of local employment. While many of his friends and neighbors worked there, John made crossties for the railroad spur that connected the gravel pit with the Yazoo & Mississippi Valley Railroad (Y&MVRR) at Avalon. This line was a standard gauge railway called the Avalon & Southeastern Railroad, and Tony Howe discovered that one of the engines (see Fig. 2.3) was purchased from a company in Georgia.

John was living along St. James Road near the church that stood across the road from the Hurt cemetery. Charles Campbell told me: "there were four houses along that road; John lived in a log house about halfway up the road toward the church. John had helped Hennis build his new house above the gravel pit." Interestingly, Hennis was the only family member who owned his own house, valued at $700,[68] no doubt on the proceeds of his illicit whiskey business. Charles Campbell also recalls mention of a murder in the St. James schoolhouse in the 1920s.

The 1930 census shows John living next door to his brother's family Cleveland and Pearl, who lived next to Hennis and Lillie. Next door to them were their white neighbors Andy Organ and his family, and then Hilman Moreland, his wife Norma, and daughter Sylvia (see Table 2.2).[69] Hilman Moreland was farming in 1930, but was later to own the Valley Store during the 1960s. Larry Smith, the current owner of the Valley Store, informed me that there was also another store directly opposite the Valley Store, which the Fullers owned in the 1930s.

It appears that Hennis and Lillie came on hard times when, in 1931, they sold a parcel of land for $687.04 to Mrs. Edna Stinson, who, with

Figure 2.3. Avalon & Southeastern Railroad 2-4-0 locomotive bought for use on the Avalon Gravel Pit line in 1925 from the Southern Iron & Equipment Co. in Atlanta, Ga. (David Price Collection.)

her husband, owned and ran Stinson's Store in Avalon. The land is in the Valley area west of the Hobgood Road and west of the land previously held by Hennis's mother Mary Jane. The sale value is close to that of the valuation of Hennis and Lillie's house at the 1930 census and may represent the sale of their house; however, the odd amount may involve a settlement at the store or another debt.[70]

Much enthused by my questions and interest in Mississippi John Hurt, Charles Campbell volunteered to make a rare excursion from his house to show me where John had lived and so, on a hot and humid July morning in 2005, we walked along St. James Road to view the overgrown wooded area that had replaced a community. It appears that in 1930 John and Jessie lived closest to the church and next to his brothers, Cleveland and Hennis, who lived further south closer to the road connecting Valley and Avalon. Hardy, Jim, Paul, and Ella (married to Ned Moore and caring for Cleveland's children from his previous marriage to Fannie Clarke) all lived in the Valley/Avalon area (see Table 2.2, Fig. 2.4). The Kents were still running the Valley Store, a major focus for the community and a place to chat and pass on news and gossip.

Table 2.2 provides details of some of the people known to the Hurts in the Avalon/Valley area and the relative locations of important tradesmen and professionals. (Most families occupied in farming are omitted for brevity.) Dardanelle Hadley (born Marcia Marie Mullen),[71] reflecting on

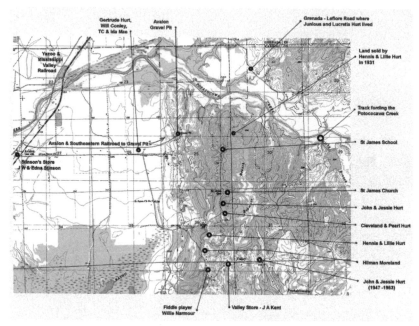

Figure 2.4. Map of Valley and Avalon, Mississippi, circa 1935. (Base map provided courtesy of Mytopo, Billings, Montana. Additional artwork by Alexandra and Guy Pate.)

her childhood in Avalon, provides interesting anecdotes of life in Avalon.[72] She talks of "Daddy's Country Store" where she along with her friends would take Coca-Colas and fizzy drinks from the icebox in the store. They would walk or ride from their house to Avalon passing a house that was used to store the cotton before it was taken to the Avalon gin. It was built on a raised Choctaw mound and as children they had found Indian arrowheads around there; her grandpa (Mullen), who had purchased land from Greenwood Leflore, had a wooden cigar box that contained arrow heads he had collected. This land became the Mullen Brothers plantation, where John's brothers Paul and Junious had worked in 1917.[73]

Some of the old sharecroppers shacks in the Delta had old discarded signs advertising Coca Cola, BC Headache Powder, Garrett Snuff, and Red Man Chewing Tobacco nailed on to the outside to keep out the weather. Dardanelle would listen to Fats Waller records on the jukebox at the gas station at Avalon. She went on bullfrog hunts with her brother Robert; they would bring back pockets full of frogs and their momma would cook the frog legs.[74]

Dardanelle relates that Avalon was a big town and provides some clues to the locations of some families. She does not provide dates, but it seems

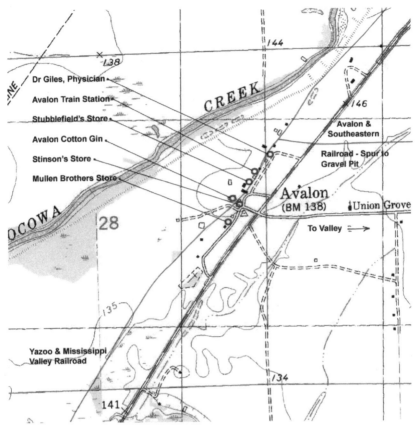

Figure 2.5. Map of Avalon, Mississippi, town center circa 1935 (Base map provided courtesy of Mytopo, Billings, Montana. Additional artwork by Alexandra and Guy Pate.)

likely from her descriptions that her account relates to the 1930s, when she was between 12 and 22 years old. Her descriptions largely tie in with some of the census data for 1930 and help locate various families from the census record (see Table 2.2).[75]

There were at least four stores in Avalon. The Mullen brothers' land extended into Avalon and they owned a store there. Her Uncle Dick and Aunt Juntie lived near "Daddy's Country Store," and along the road from the Mullen Brothers store was the Stinsons' brick store and another store run by a Mrs. Stubblefield. Close by were the Stinsons' home and the Avalon cotton gin, which, along with the railroad station, is the only one of the original buildings remaining today. At the end of the row lived Dr. Edgar, Giles the local physician (see Table 2.2, Fig. 2.5).[76]

Table 2.2. Avalon and Valley Area in 1930. Carroll County, Beat 2, Enumeration District 2. Summary of families, employment, and location.

Note: No families allocated to numbers 1-2.

Family No.	Name	Race	Number of "same-race" families	Employment	Probable Location
3	J. A. Kent	White	3	Merchant	Valley (Hills)
4	W. T. Narmour (musician)	White		Driver - School travel	Valley (Hills)
5		White		Farming	
6		Black	4	Farming	
7	Henry Greer	Black		Railroad	Avalon
8		Black		Farming	
9	Hardy Hurt (John's brother)	Black		Farming	Avalon
10-14		White	5	Farming	
15		Black	3	Farming	
16	Felix Evans Jr.	Black		Farming	Avalon
17		Black		Farming	
18-19		White	2	Farming	
20-24		Black	6	Farming	
25	Lillie Sanders	Black		Cook-Boarding House	Avalon
26	W. L. Nash	White	8	Manager-Gravel Pit	Avalon
27	T. J. Stevens	White		General Manager-Gravel Pit	Avalon
28	W. Hendrix	White		Boiler welder-Gravel Pit	Avalon
29	Henry Hall	White		Engineer-Gravel Pit	Avalon
	Henry Wood	White		Gravel washer-Gravel Pit	Avalon
30-32		White		Farming	
33	J. W. Stinson	White		General Store	Avalon
	Eden E. Stinson	White		Manager General Store	Avalon
	C. Worthey (boarder)	White		Clerk Store	Avalon
	L. B. Chatham (boarder)	White		Clerk Store	Avalon

	Harry Worthey (boarder)	White		Clerk Store	Avalon
	Neal Cannon (boarder)	White		Clerk Filling Station	Avalon
34-45		Black	12	Farming	Avalon
46	Ardena Baker	White	2	Salesman General Store	Avalon
47	Marcus Mullen (father of jazz pianist Dardanelle Hadley)	White		State Highway Patrolman	Avalon
48-50		Black	3	Farming	Avalon
51	Terry Proctor	White	1	Section foreman Railroad	Avalon
52-58		Black	12	Farming	Avalon
59	Ron Miller	Black		Gravel Shovel	Avalon
60		Black			
61	Lorenzo Meeks (brother Hennis's widowed daughter)	Black		Cook Board Camp (Gravel Pit)	Avalon
	Cleophus Parkes (boarder)	Black		Gravel Pit-laborer	Avalon
	John E. Bynum (boarder)	White		Locomotive engineer (Gravel Pit)	Avalon
	James A. Sisson (boarder)	White		Gravel Pit-bookkeeper	Avalon
	Carol H. Craig (boarder)	White		Gravel Pit-Shipping clerk	Avalon
62	Robert Stansbery	Black		Brakeman-Railroad train	Avalon
63	Ned and Ella Moore (John's sister) with Catherine, Everline, and Lorenza (John and Ella's nieces; Cleveland's daughters)	Black		Gravel Pit-Night watchman	Avalon
64	Henry E. May	White	1	Locomotive engineer	Avalon
	Thomas E. May	White		Locomotive engineer	Avalon
65	Clemey Avant	Black	11	Brakeman-Railroad train	Avalon
66	Bussie Gore	Black		Brakeman-Railroad train	Avalon

	James Moore	Black		Laborer-Gravel Pit	Avalon
67-75		Black		Farm and rail-road laborers	Avalon
76	Sam J. Brunson (Employer of some Hurt brothers and founder of black school near Gravel Pit; Father of Annie Cook, interviewee)	White	1	Farmer Plantation owner	Avalon
77-81		Black	19	Farming	Avalon
82	Edgar E. Mills	Black		Fisherman-Setting Nets	Avalon
83-87		Black		Farming	Avalon
88	Paul Hurt (John's brother)	Black		Farming	Avalon
89	Elija Green	Black		Laborer-Gravel Pit	Avalon
90	Luther Moore	Black		Laborer-Gravel Pit	Avalon
91-93		Black		Farming	Avalon
94	Jim Askew	Black		Laborer-Railroad track	Avalon
	Lou Sanders	Black		Fireman Engine	Avalon
95		Black		Farm	Avalon
96	Edgar Giles	White	1	Physician-County Practitioner	Avalon
97	John E. Sanders	Black	9	Brakeman Train	Avalon
98-105		Black		Farming	Avalon
106	Frank Bennett	White	1	Log cutting-Woods	Avalon
107-109		Black	3	Farming	Avalon
110	George C. Stubblefield	White	2	Merchant-General Store	Avalon
111		White		Farming	
112-120		Black	13	Farming and Gravel Pit laborer	Avalon
121	Cara Prone	Black		School teacher	
122	William Smith	Black		Laborer-Store	
123-124		Black		Farming	
125	Frank Carethers	White	1	Carpenter-General building house	

126		Black	25	Farming	
127	Neal Rogers	Black		Carpenter-General building house	
128	Sam Glover	Black		Laborer-logging	
129-136		Black		Farming	
137	Thomas Green	Black		Blacksmith shop	
138-150		Black		Farming	
151	Mary R. Long	White	1	Teacher-School	
	Edwin L. Mabray	White		Physician-County Practitioner	
152	Jennie Long	Black	1	Cook in private home	
153	William Waters	White	2	Logging Timber man	
154	T. L. Cale	White		Skidder (timber)	
155-156		Black	2	Farming	
157-158		White	2	Farming	
159-168		Black	10	Farming	
169		White	1	Farming	
170-171		Black	2	Farming	
172		White	1	Farming	
173-177		Black	41	Farming	
178	Frank Williamson	Black		Laborer-Sawmill	
179-213		Black		Farming	
214-215		White	2	Farming	
216-217		Black	6	Farming	
218	Herman McNeil	Black		Fireman-Engine	Delta
219-221		Black		Farming	
222		White	1	Farming	
223-225		Black	3	Farming	
226		White	1	Farming	
227-228		Black	11	Farming	
229	George Kimble	Black		Log loader-woods	
230-237		Black		Farming	
238	Clyde Carlisle	White	1	School teacher	
239-241		Black	3	Farming	
242		White	1	Farming	
243-249		Black	7	Farming	

250	Monroe Welch	White	1	Fisherman-River works	
251-275		Black	99	Farming	
276	Sylvia Cox	Black		School teacher	
277-307		Black		Farming	
308	Jim Hurt (John's eldest sibling)	Black		Farming	
309-312		Black		Farming	
313	Joe Hudson	Black		Carpenter—House Building	
314	Alonzo McCurty	Black		Proprietor-Auto Repair Shop	
315-349		Black		Farming	
350-352		White	7	Farming	
353	Ruth Long	White		Teacher	
354-356		White		Farming	
357-359		Black	3	Farming	
360	Hinds Long	White	1	Book keeper-Cotton Association	
361-378		Black	18	Farming	
379		White	1	Farming	
380-399		Black	20	Farming	
400		White	1	Farming	
401-417		Black	21	Farming	
418	John Hurt and Jessie	Black		Farming	Hills. St. James Road
419	Cleveland (John's brother)	Black		Farming	Hills. St. James Road
420	Hennis (John's brother)	Black		Farming	Hills. St. James Road
421	Andy Organ	Black		Farming	Hills. St. James Road
422	Hilman Moreland	White	1	Farming	Hills. St. James Road
423-425		Black	3	Farming	
426	Jessie Carroll	White	7	Laborer-shop	
427-429		White		Farming	
430	Shell Smith (musician)	White		Farming	
431-432		White		Farming	
433-437		Black	5	Farming	

438-439		White	2	Farming	
440		Black	1	Farming	
441		White	1	Farming	
442-468		Black	27	Farming	

Source: U.S. Federal Census, 1930, Carroll County, Mississippi, Enumeration District 2.
Note: Enumeration District 2 includes all territory in townships 20 and 21 in Range 2 East and that portion of Township 20 in Range 3 East lying north of the Potacocowa Creek. It is adjacent to Enumeration District 3, which includes the remainder of Beat 2, and covers all of the territory in Township 20 in Range 3 East lying south of the Potacocowa Creek. Geographically, this places Avalon within District 2 with the Valley hill country extending eastward through District 2 and into District 3.
   Only families connected with the Hurts or having specialist skills other than farming are included. See also Figure 2.4.

Of the 466 families in the area, those numbered 3, 4 and 418–422 (7) lived in the hill country around the Valley area and families 7–120 (114) lived in Avalon. It is impossible to assess where the other 345 families lived and therefore it is not possible to compare levels of segregation between the Delta and the hills as in 1920 (shown in ch. 1). With the establishment of the gravel industry and associated infrastructure, including the railway, Avalon appears to have increased in size and supported more families than in 1920. In 1930, sixty-three white and four hundred and three black families shared the area. John and his family lived in a cluster of twenty-one black families, which included the families of his brothers Cleveland and Hennis.

   The dispersion of families in the area demonstrates a relatively close geographical mix of the races, with blacks and whites living close to one another in spite of social and cultural boundaries. There are sixty-three separate clusters of "same-race" families and 466 families in total providing a figure of 87 percent segregation (where 2 clusters of families, one black and one white, equals 100 percent segregation and 466 alternate black and white families equals 0 percent segregation). Segregation increased from 80 percent in 1920. Even at this relatively high level of segregation, it contrasts significantly with the situation in many small towns where races were more strongly segregated by neighborhood and blacks often lived literally on the other side of the tracks in ghettoes. Perhaps the racial mix, and the fact that there were so few racially motivated crimes in and around Avalon, provided a psychological platform that enabled John to be so comfortable with white audiences both pre- and post-rediscovery.

   In 1930 2029 people were living in the Avalon area (Enumeration District 2), but the whole community Avalon/Valley (Census Beat 2) also included Enumeration District 3, which listed an additional 1,504 people, making a total of 3,533 in the whole Avalon/Valley area (see Table 2.2). Additional notes scribbled in the margins of the census returns indicate that some families in District 3 lived along the Grenada and Leflore Road and Greenwood and Duckhill Road. Some noteworthy families and individuals lived on the Grenada and Leflore Road, including John's brother Junious and his wife Lucretia, the Joliffs, and the Hobgoods, who had played such an influential role in the provision of schools in the locality, living next door to one another.[77] Next door to the Joliffs lived the Liddells, who later built the shotgun house on the Perkins place in which John and Jessie lived from 1947 to 1963 (see Fig. 2.4).[78]

Jesse N. Hobgood, the head of the family, was the local registrar and recorded the birth of John and Jessie's son John William Hurt in 1932. The midwife, a Lillie Javis or Travis,[79] does not appear in the 1930 census. The birth certificate states that Jessie's maiden name was Nelson, referring to her previous marriage and not her original family name of Cole, and that she had four other children, all of whom died by 1932. Presumably they had died before 1922 when she and John met.

A family of Talisferros (Taliferro), the head of the family being a Lynn Talisferro, were recorded in District 3. This was the unusual family name of the white couple that had been murdered near Carrollton in 1901 (discussed in chapter 1), a surviving child of the murdered couple being Lynn Taliferro, and this family may be the surviving family members from that event.

Gertrude and Will Conley, with T. C. and Ida Mae, lived in Bolivar County along with a lodger, Pete Barney, in 1930[80] but by 1935 had returned to Avalon, where they settled on Delta land close to the gravel pit alongside family. Will Conley is recorded as the guardian of T. C. and Idella (Ida Mae) in the Black Donley School list for 1935.[81] Ida Mae married "Doc" Johnson in the late 1930s and they had two children, Dorothy, born in 1939, and Jesse, born in 1948. Dorothy remembered that their shotgun house was close to her grandmother Gertrude's house.

Census records are not available for 1940 or more recently, so it is not currently possible to reconstruct the population at that time. However, in 1940 the total population in the Delta was around 508,000 about 362,000 (72 percent) of which were African Americans. More than 87 percent of adult male African Americans were employed in agriculture, predominantly in tenant farming or sharecropping, and most were illiterate.[82]

Little information is available on the local towns of Grenada and Greenwood at this time, but Samuel C. Adams provided valuable insight into life in Clarksdale, the largest of the Delta towns in 1941. It is likely that Greenwood, and to a lesser extent Grenada, would have offered similar facilities to John Hurt. In Clarksdale there were many businesses, schools, and churches. There were fifty-one food stores, twenty-four clothing stores, twenty-two eating places, twenty general merchandise stores, eleven automobile dealers and garages, eight furniture, radio, and electrical appliance stores, five major lumber yards, nine Negro juke joints, and nine drug stores. The town was strongly segregated, with poor black, poor white, residential black, white, and black business sections, as well as Jewish, Italian, and Chinese sections identified by Adams.[83]

The area mostly frequented by blacks coming into Clarksdale from nearby plantations centered on Issaquena, Sunflower, and Fourth Streets, where one could wander around with little intention of buying much except for cigarettes, beer, and candies. Music would emanate from "vendors" (black vernacular for juke boxes) in restaurants and poolrooms. The Dipsie Doodle was a café and beer tavern popular with blacks; in 1941 its juke box played tunes by Fats Waller, Count Basie, Art Tatum, Sister Rosetta Tharpe, Louis Jordan, and Earl Hines, "Key to the Highway" by Jazz Gillum, "Beer Drinking Woman" by Memphis Minnie, and "Yes, I Got Your Man" by Washboard Sam. Tommy's Place on Sunflower Street was the only place where teenage blacks were permitted to dance.[84] It is not known to what extent Clarksdale was similar to Greenwood or Grenada, but it is likely that there were similarities including the popular music.

Although the jukebox had become popular by the mid-1930s, they were mainly found in towns and highway joints. Live music remained very popular, and many traveling bluesmen continued to make a living playing in Delta jukes.[85] Honeyboy Edwards recalled his experiences of playing the small Delta towns: "On Saturday, somebody like me or Robert Johnson would go into one of these little towns, play for nickels and dimes." Sometimes musicians would need to obtain permission from the authorities, but mostly they were able to play and often drew big crowds. Edwards added:

Then sometimes the man who owned the country store would give us something like a couple of dollars to play Saturday afternoon. We'd sit in the back of the store on some oat sacks or corn sacks and play while they sold groceries and whiskey and beer up front, and the people would come in and listen to us and pitch in. In the afternoon or maybe in the evenin' we'd go to the movie theater and play before or between the movies. Then people would start leavin' town. About eight or nine o'clock at night they'd go out in the country where they could make all the noise they wanted, drink that corn, dance all night long. The people that was givin' a dance, they would put coal oil in a bottle, put a wick in it, and hang it up in a tree. We'd follow that light goin' to the dance. Maybe the man giving the dance would see you in town that afternoon and hire you to come out and play there that night. Wasn't too much money, but we'd play, eat, drink, have a good time. They would cook fish, sell fish sandwiches and white whiskey. Some outside gambling on a old table, bad lights, way out in the country, you know. We'd play inside, sit down in a chair and relax.

Sometimes they'd give a big picnic out in the country, dig a deep hole in the ground, put charcoal down that hole, put an iron grate across it, and lay a whole hog on that grate. They'd let that hog steam, mop it with that hot barbecue sauce, and keep it turnin' all night long. In the mornin' it would be so tender, you could take a fork and just cut the meat right off the bone. They'd have barrels of lemonade sitting out there, some guy got four or five gallons of corn whiskey. Sometimes they'd get a wagon, two mules, three or four men, and rent a piano in town, haul it out there, have a platform built with a brush arbor over it, have piano and guitar playin' under there.[86]

Blacks from the towns and cities would also visit rural areas, where they could enjoy freedom from curfews and regulations on liquor. Outside of Clarksdale on the neighboring King and Anderson plantation were share-croppers' "shotgun" houses, mostly with two rooms and a wall covering of newspaper. They would have an iron stove, and some had a separate kitchen area.[87] Such houses were the common type of dwelling for black sharecroppers and farm workers throughout Mississippi. John and Jessie's home in Valley—which survived the massive clearances of these build-ings in the 1960s and 1970s and now houses the Mississippi John Hurt Museum—is similar. Already in 1940, tractors, flame weeders, and crop-dusting airplanes were making an appearance, and black labor became less in demand, encouraging a shift from rural to urban locations. For the first time, plantation blacks had time on their hands, and the advantage of a large family was no more.

Of course, rural Mississippi had seen many changes during the 1930s. By the end of the decade the automobile had become a relatively com-mon sight, the WPA had provided many miles of paved and gravel roads, and electric lights appeared in the towns. However, country blacks contin-ued to use mules and wagons well into the fifties and sixties. Phonograph records were common, and jukeboxes increased rapidly in the 1940s. Electric guitars and amplifiers began to appear.[88]

In 1940, women's dresses cost two or three dollars and a woman's jacket and skirt five or six. Men's corduroy trousers were around two dollars, a man's fedora cost the same, and men's and women's shoes two to three dollars. You could buy a pair of denim overalls for under a dollar. A Silvertone radio phonograph with electric motor cost $24.95, and wind-up portable phonographs were available for around ten dollars. Acoustic flat-top guitars were available from Sears Roebuck for $4.45 to $12; the Gene Autry model, with spruce top and maple back and sides, including one book on songwriting and another titled *Gene Autry's Deluxe Collection of Over 80 Songs*, could be had for $11.95. A hardwood-bodied resonator guitar with nickel-plated resonator cost $13.95. Electrically amplified guitars with an amplifier included were available from $54.50 to $150. Cigarette packs cost fifty cents to a dollar, depending on the brand.[89]

The Valley Store changed hands again when the Spencer-McCain Chevrolet Company sold it to V. A. Watson for $500 on February 4, 1941. The Watsons, who also owned the whites-only barber shop opposite the Valley Store, ran the store until they sold it to D. H. Moreland on June 17, 1952.[90] The house that was destined to become home for John and Jessie and that now houses the Mississippi John Hurt Museum owes its existence to a devastating tornado that struck the Valley area in 1942. Net Jackson was living in a house on the site, along with her son Whit. The Brunsons lived opposite. On March 16, 1942, Annie Brunson (Cook) walked outside with her father, who looked up at the sky out toward the west, saying, "We better get into the potato cellar, there's a storm coming." The potato cellar was an underground bunker used for storing potatoes and other foodstuffs away from the frosts, and was covered in railroad crossties and earth. The family climbed down into the cellar and a violent tornado swept through Valley. The earth and cross ties were blown off the cellar and Annie's daddy's hat was sucked out by the wind. Annie Cook remembered her and her family emerging later to find the Jackson's house had gone. Whit had been lifted up and dropped some way away relatively unharmed while Net was found lying among the debris and later died from her injuries.

A government emergency aid program provided funds to rebuild a small house on the site for Whit and W. B. Vance, who owned the land and had the house built. He subsequently sold the house to a Ward Smith, who later swapped it for some land with A. R. Perkins, the man that John and Jessie were later to work for.[91] Vance asked his neighbor, Charles Liddell, to build the house for him and was satisfied with the building, except that he complained that the porch was too wide. Liddell answered that he was sorry, "but if I had made it any smaller, a man and

Figure 2.6. Yazoo & Mississippi Valley passenger train running between Greenwood and Grenada at Avalon, Mississippi, ca. 1920. (Josephine Jackson, Carrollton, Mississippi.)

his wife could not sit out there together." John and Jessie moved into the house when they began to work for Perkins[92] and undoubtedly spent many happy hours sitting together on that porch!

John and Jessie had moved from their house on St. James Road in the 1930s. Annie Cook remembers them living on the Banham place close to Highway 7 where it crosses the Potacocowa Creek, before moving onto the Perkins place in 1947[93] where they remained until 1963. Jessie also worked for Perkins and she would take in washing. Perkins was seldom seen without John accompanying him.

Local white residents Charles Campbell and Fred Clarke worked with John at different times. In 1947 Charles remembered driving mules to pull crossties out of the forest: "We would make around twenty a day and deliver them to a Columbus and Greenville Railway (C&GR) boxcar at Avalon. We would be paid $1.20 a tie, a lot of money in those days." The railroad that ran through Avalon at this time was the Illinois Central, which had taken over the Y&MVRR, but it may have used C&GR rolling stock. Fred Clarke helped John collect the branch wood for firewood, while Jessie worked as a cook providing food for the workers at the gravel pit. The train from Greenwood to Grenada made two round trips each day, calling at Avalon and other small towns along the way. Annie Cook and her friends called the train the "Doodle-Bug."

Annie Cook recalled a huge deluge sweeping down the Potacocowa Creek and flooding Avalon in 1946, causing serious damage to the rail-road tracks and flooding the three stores in Avalon at that time, Stinson's being the biggest. The Illinois Central Railroad abandoned the line from Greenwood to Grenada in 1947 after the flood damage. Railroad histo-rian Tom Lucas stated that the former I.C. depot in Avalon was used as a private residence from 1949 until around 1980, and the derelict build-ing partially collapsed in 2008 still carrying its AVALON sign. In 1949 the Avalon gravel pit closed and the rail spur was removed.

John and Jessie's son "Man" began playing guitar when he was 16 (1948), and he remembers asking his daddy to teach him to play.

I asked him one time, I say, "Daddy, why don't you show me how to play the guitar?" He wouldn't say too much on it. Then I kept asking him; I kept worrying him on it. I say "Daddy, why don't you show me how to play the guitar, daddy?" Mama say, "Man, stop worrying your daddy so much!" He say, "that's alright, Jessie, I'm gonna show him." He showed me one time! That was it. You know what he told me? He said, "Son, it's just like riding a bicycle." I could not understand what he was saying. He said, "Once you learn it you never forget it."[94]

Man also recalled from his childhood the parties that John would play at and how they would barbecue a goat. People would pass a hat around and John would make five or ten dollars a night.

Daddy would play all night long. And he had a song he played called "Lovin' Spoonful." And every time he would play it, someone would get to fighting. I don't know why, but every time he say, "I just got to have my lovin' spoonful . . ." white or black . . . someone would get to fight-ing. Yes, man! They'd be side steppin' too, you know, and the younger ladies were about 20-some years old. They had fly-tailed skirts . . . the dudes'd be jealous, you know. They couldn't stand the fly-tailed skirts went around them legs and stuff. They get to fightin' man. One time, they were playing and it got so rough 'til my daddy run out . . . run through the cotton field . . . and the bolls of cotton were just whooping on the strings, you know . . . you'd try to get out the way. There was a shooting going on! There sure was."[95]

Man also recalled a man named Willie Hill who was around Avalon when he was about eight years old (ca. 1940). Hill referred to John as "'Hurt,' he would say, 'Hurt, come play for me,' and daddy would play all night long." Hill would say, "Hurt gonna put the little party in the big one." Man remembered John coming home next day from parties and having to feed Perkins's cows. Jessie would get mad and shout at him and he would say, "Hush hollering, Jessie." John's peaceful dignified presence was noteworthy. However, Shell Smith's son Sonny recalled how he once saw John get angry with Jessie. "He [John Hurt] was a very calm man [but I saw him] angry one time. Chased his wife into the house. She locked the door, he was shouting at her, trying to get in. Very angry. Someone asked him why. The reply was, 'She called me out of my name.'" Meaning that she cussed John.[96]

Olin Goss remembered Man Hurt as a childhood playmate, and that one time they were going down to the river to fish when Gertrude hollered, "Ain't no fish goin' to bite now, they got their heads down." "We'd say we would put those hooks down deeper then, where they would have to see them," said Goss.[97] Interestingly, this illustrates an interaction between Man and Gertrude in spite of him later saying that he did not know her. It is possible, but seems unlikely, that he was unaware of Gertrude's early marriage to his father.

Man would sometimes be left with John's brother Paul, who was blind. Man did not want to stay there because Paul liked cheese and crackers and Man did not. He would say, "Daddy don't leave me here," and start to cry. John replied, "Boy, if you don't shut up that I'll get on you and tear you up fine as cat hair," and so he would have to stay the night. On one occasion Man told of a party at their house when a man named Molasses dropped by. "Daddy would play, 'My baby loves shortnin' bread' and Molasses would dance, he loved that song."[98] Molasses's real name was James Isaac, who was married to Lillie Belle and possibly the father of the three Isaac boys photographed at the Valley Store in 1963 by Tom Hoskins (see ch. 3).

Fannie Mohead (Mary Frances's aunt and sister of her mother, Annie) lives in the Valley area close to the Mississippi John Hurt Museum. She was born in 1935 and remembers the forties and fifties well. She remembers hearing John play. "John would come and play the guitar at Sunday school, 'Good Morning Little Schoolgirl' and religious songs. He was a very nice man. When I was in school in the 1940s we would dance to his music. He would also come and play at Saturday night school dances. It was a one-room school house on the Hobgood Road."

Hobgood Road is one of the dirt roads up in the Valley hills along which many families lived in the forties, including Cleveland and Pearl and Fannie's parents. Fannie told me that John once lived on Hobgood Road before moving to St. James Road. She remembers the St. James church, but not the school, suggesting that the school was removed before 1945. The church was removed during the 1950s.

Fannie could hear the trains from where she lived on Hobgood Road and recalled that her family would take the train from Avalon to Greenwood or Grenada, usually Greenwood. The trains were segregated. In addition to shopping trips to Greenwood and Grenada, the family shopped at the Valley Store, owned by Hillman Moreland, or Stinson's Store. In Avalon, at that time, the bus station, juke joint, and gas station were housed in the same building. Fannie was not permitted to frequent the juke joint. The family would sometimes visit Carrollton: "We would ride in a wagon to Carrollton. When we got tired of ridin' we would get out and walk a while. It took many hours."

John was a natural storyteller with a large repertoire of tales about the wildlife of rural Mississippi. He harbored a deep fear of snakes and local lore had clearly labeled them as undesirables. John told Tom Hoskins in 1963 about the coach whip snake: "I never heard of one bitin'. But what he does, the coach whip, he whip you to death." John went on to tell the story of Joe Watts sitting on the steps near his house. "This old coach whip come out of that hole and ease up and had him tied up before he knew anything. When he discovered he was tied up by a snake why he jumped you know and he was strikin' at him." Joe grabbed his knife and began cutting the snake until it let go and disappeared down the hole. Coach whips are patterned in a way that resembles a plaited whip and myths suggest that they chase people and whip them. Tom Hoskins recalled meeting Joe Watts on one of his visits to Avalon in 1963.[99]

And there was the stinging worm. John described this animal as a green or black worm with a sting like a needle. He and some workmates saw one sting a tree; two hours later the leaves withered and the tree died. Similar stories of snakes stinging trees, causing them to wilt and die, are recorded in Southern folklore. In Alabama a man named Eddie Vice stated that when he was a boy he was playing with some pals when they came across a stinging snake. "We got some sticks and started playing with it. Well, this snake started stinging the sticks. Then it got so mad that it started stinging everything around. Two or three times it struck a big twelve inch pine that was standing by." They killed the snake, which had a half-inch-long "stinger" that looked like a black needle. He continued: "Well, the next day we went back down the field to see what had happened to the big pine tree, and sure enough it was wilting and dying."[100]

On another occasion John was clearing some wetland with Jesse Carter. They were cutting trees and briars with axes and long-handled cutting tools when they spotted a snake. John said, "Man that's a stingin' snake that's what he is" and immediately refused to work there anymore. Carter tried to persuade John to continue, saying that they would kill any snakes and that they should wear boots: "the snake can't bite you through boots." But John was having none of it. "No, you're right, that's all right, but he don't bite that's the thing. He stings that's what he does! My boots not as hard as a tree, I'm just stayin' out of this new grass and I did."[101] (Jesse Carter does not appear in the US. census for 1910, 1920, or 1930, so this event presumably happened sometime later than 1930.)

Beliefs about the capabilities of snakes were common folklore motifs in the South, and stories of their incredible feats pervade folk culture.[102] Even in the blues Memphis Minnie sang about the Stinging Snake, but according to her lyrics it seems that the snake represented something a good deal different to her from what it did to John:

> *Hmmmm, I wonder where my Stinging snake gone?*
> *Hmmmm, I wonder where my Stinging snake gone?*
> *I can't see no peace since my stinging snake left me home,*
> *I got a Stinging snake, I love sometimes better than I do myself,*
> *I got a Stinging snake, I love sometimes better than I do myself,*
> *If the Lord has to take him, I won't be stung by nobody else.*[103]

The stinging snake was probably a harmless mud snake, a large aquatic snake that has a spinelike tip to its tail. Southern folklore also suggests that this snake can take its tail in its mouth forming a hoop, and roll like a wheel to chase its prey, giving rise to its other name, the hoop snake.[104]

Charles Campbell, one-time sheriff of Carroll County, recalled John coming to his house to play the guitar. "I remember he would sit on the porch playing a song 'bout a rooster and 'Blessed be the name of the Lord.'" Campbell also recalled how he and his wife were once picking cotton when she said, "Taking me for a fool, I smell liquor cooking." She thought her husband was involved in the illicit activity. He claimed innocence and began walking, his nose picking up the telltale vinegary smell. They followed the smell and came to a still near where the Potacocowa Creek forks. "Toward Wes Hobgood's place I came upon it. Boys from Tallahatchie County was cooking it."[105]

Campbell also remembered a still along St. James Road near St. James Church and cemetery: "Me and Shell Smith found this one, we got about 27 gallons of whiskey." It is likely that this was Hennis Hurt's still, as he lived in this area and was known to brew the best moonshine in this area. Charles told me: "Hennis once gave us a half-gallon, it was so strong that you put it in your mouth and it would evaporate through your nose!"

When I asked if it tasted good he replied, "the more you drink, the better it gets!"[106] Asked the same question, Man's wife Bonnie Hurt replied, "Best this side of Tennessee."

John always enjoyed hunting. Fred Clarke told me about going hunting with John in the late 1930s when Fred was in his mid-teens. John had two slim brown pointer bird dogs and Fred would say to John, "You need to feed them dogs." John would reply, "Oh, no, no, no, you don't want to let 'em get fat."

Fred had his own bird dog named Major that would point rabbits. John was not interested in rabbits, and he would let them go and concentrate on quail. John had his dogs very well trained. He would put down a biscuit for each of them and they would sit and wait till he said they could eat it. "When the dogs pointed some birds, he would just talk quietly to them dogs until he was ready and then he would let the dogs flush them." He'd say to me, "You take the first shot and I'll take the strays (birds that broke back over your head). He would turn around and let both barrels go. John was a very good shot. He would hold the dogs and then say, 'Dead, Dead' and the dogs would go and pick up the birds. They would run back with a bird each and John would hold his jacket open and the dogs would drop the birds into his two inside pockets!" Campbell also recalled hunting and fishing trips with John. John had an old ten-gauge shotgun. He also remembered John catching fish by hand; "He [John] would grab 'em by hand and put 'em in a sack."

Campbell stated: "A lot of people kept hogs and cows in those days and many families would keep a milk cow or two and maybe a beef cow and two or three hogs. All this would be for family use, not commercial. Meat was 10–15 cents a pound in the 1950s." Fred Clarke remembers John's brothers Hardy, Cleveland, and Hennis. Presumably the others had left the area by the time Fred was around in the late 1930s.

Cleveland, who was still married to Pearl and had Cleveland Jr. (born 1924), began keeping hogs and Fred would help him out. They would kill some before Christmas and they would boil and salt down the hams and put them in a smokehouse. Cleveland and John would kill five or six hogs at one time and Dennis Richardson would help them. The womenfolk would also help with the all-day process. John would also fish for trout and catfish in the lake, and Hennis had a still down there. Hennis's wife Lillie and Pearl helped care for Fred's mother when she was disabled with rheumatism; they would boil water day and night for her to put her hands and feet in, and they would wash her clothes.

At Christmastime in 1947, 86-year-old Hines Moore, probably Ned Moore's cousin,[107] visited Will Conley and Gertrude, and on December

26, he set off through the gravel pit for his home a mile away. He never arrived at his home and around 4:00 p.m. on January 3, John Hurt discovered his body in a fifty-foot gully. John reported this to Carter at the store in Avalon, who then called the Carroll County sheriff. Hines Moore had apparently got lost on his way home and suffered a stroke. He had pulled off his shoes, stockings, and coat before he died. John said, "I reckon he thought he was home and was goin' to bed."

Later, toward nightfall, a reporter and photographer, Jerry Yocuma and Jack Hairston, raced to Avalon to get a story. They got hopelessly lost among the creeks, gullies, and cliffs of the seemingly endless gravel workings. Eventually they heard voices and came upon a group of men standing around the body. After getting some information and photographing the body, they set off. John yelled, "Hey, wait a minute boss man, that ain't the way out of here." John took charge and with his flashlight, led the men out of the area. The reporters commented: "he led us out of the eerie place like a flock of sheep." John told them, "I have been huntin' and workin' in these pits for a long time, but the other night I got lost in these gullies and stayed all night befo' I found my way out. This is the easiest place to get lost in this part of the country."[108] Some folk reckon that John might have been on the way to Hennis's still when he discovered the body!

In spite of the closure of the gravel pit, Avalon continued to be a thriving community. Annie Cook remembered that in the 1950s it supported a population of over 300 people in the immediate vicinity of the center, qualifying it as a small town. The Stinsons' Store sold clothes, housed the U.S. Post Office, and operated the gas pumps outside. There were a corn mill, a cotton gin, and the Illinois Central railway station. About a hundred yards toward Greenwood from the Stinsons' Store was the Hole in the Wall juke joint. John and Gertrude's son and daughter T. C. and Ida Mae, along with their spouses Annie and Doc, and Man Hurt all frequented the juke during the forties. Dorothy remembered her mom and dad doing the swing to the jukebox. White and black folks used the juke. She did not remember any live music being played at the juke, but Daddy John would play on the steps of the store. Ida Mae had her portrait painted around that time and Dorothy still has the painting on the wall of her house in Greenwood (see Fig. 2.7).

One night in 1950 Ida Mae, then 31, spent the night with her mother Gertrude, and next morning she rose early to go over to her house to collect some flour to bake a cake for the church. She arrived at the house to find her husband Doc in bed with another woman. Ida Mae was a small but feisty lady described by her daughter Dorothy "as mean as she was

Figure 2.7. Painting of Mississippi John Hurt's daughter, Ida Mae Johnson (Dorothy Hurt Miller, Greenwood, Mississippi.)

pretty" and "a tough little cookie. She would take him on and he would have been afraid of her." In the altercation that followed, Ida Mae ran out of the house toward Gertrude's house with Doc running after her with a gun. He shot Ida Mae twice in the back, killing her. She was buried in the Teoc cemetery. John had tragically lost his only daughter. Doc Johnson was not tried for the crime, and local hearsay has it that he was kept out of prison by a white farmer who applied the threat of a prison term to persuade Doc to work and support his children. Allegedly he did not do this and left the area for Illinois where he died in 2006.

T. C. and his wife Anne Dora Richardson had fourteen children, including Mary Frances Hurt. Mary remembers that as a little girl, when her mother was angry at her she would call her "You little Ida," and Mary grew up thinking that Ida was a swear word. It was many years before she realized the potential connection with the death of her aunt.

Fred Clarke remembered attending country dances at Leflore, a small township on Highway 7 toward Holcomb and Grenada, and watching people dancing to John's music as he played on the porch of the Stinsons' Store in Avalon. Annie Cook (née Brunson) remembers that she was not allowed to go, nor was she permitted to frequent such a place as the Hole in the Wall. She remembered a shooting there in the 1940s, when she would have been in her mid- to late twenties. "Avalon was real active for nightlife and up towards Holcomb was real active. People would come here and get into trouble. Some people got shot and somebody shot the mule from under a man."

On another occasion Belle, the wife of a man named Hookerman, who worked for Nash, the son-in-law of Stinson who owned the store, got mad at her husband and stabbed him five times. Annie Cook's grandfather told Belle, "You'd better not do that again." The husband jumped to his wife's defense, saying: "She didn't mean it; if she'd meant it she would have stabbed me six times!" The place was still a juke joint in the 1950s. Avalon was the hub of the surrounding area, with many houses scattered across the now open and empty fields.

During the 1950s and 60s, John's grandchildren would play together and buy marbles and candy from the Stinsons' Store, and Mrs. Stinson was very nice to them. Dorothy and Mary Frances remember watching Daddy John playing his guitar when they visited him and Jessie at their house up the hill past the Valley Store on the Perkins place, and sometimes Dorothy and Mary Frances would stay over. They would sit around the Valley Store drinking pop. Larry Smith, the current owner of the Valley Store, remembers his uncle, Theo Joiner, and his daddy playing music with John in the early fifties. "They would go over and get John to come over and play. Afterwards they would get drunk and dance." Theo is recorded in the 1930 census aged 15 (Family No. 105), which would put him at 35 years old in 1950.

Dorothy attended the Brunson School (presumably linked to the Brunson plantation in Avalon) until 1952, when the school closed. It was a one-room schoolhouse close to the gravel pit, teaching black children up to the seventh grade. After the closure, she would walk to Money, some six miles west of Avalon across the Potocowa Creek, to attend school. The younger grandchildren later attended the school at Money.

Mary Frances recalled that many of John's siblings moved away from Avalon, but up until the 1960s Hennis and Cleveland lived in the Valley area. "Hennis was very different from John. He was tall with light skin and did not do any physical work. He made a living from making moonshine whiskey, which was the best available in the area, and he was always well dressed and well off." Everyone around, black and white, would come for Hennis's corn and rye whiskey, but his bootlegging activities once got him arrested. He was sent to a federal prison in Atlanta, where he made whiskey for the prison staff![109] A local resident from North Carrollton, Arnie Watson, said, "They'd arrest him every now and then, but the big shots in Greenwood would go bail him out."[110]

Olin Goss, a white resident of Carroll County, remembered visiting John and Jessie at their house in the late forties or early fifties. "We'd set [sic] up near all night. John would pick and sing, and we'd talk, then Jessie would cook scrambled eggs for us." When asked if there was any drinking, Goss replied, "You haven't ever seen a bunch of Carroll County rednecks gathered who weren't drinking, have you? They'd be drinking corn liquor most of the time from wherever we could get it. John would also drink moonshine; He'd get high enough so he could really play that guitar. John Hurt wasn't popular just because of his musicianship. He was one of the best colored people in the area, not just for his picking and singing. He was just a good fella."[111] It was likely that the whiskey came from Hennis's still.

Jessie liked to drink as well, and Dorothy remembers that she would be quiet until she started drinking. "Jessie would start off quiet and then get drunk and loud. She would carry a bottle in her bag. She would urge John to play bawdy songs like 'Candy Man,' and she also liked 'Richland Women Blues.' She was a nice lady and there was always a lot of laughter, but I never heard her sing." But of course she did sing and had a good voice. She sings along with John on the Avalon recordings.[112]

Gertrude remained close to the family and continued to live behind Mary Frances's house until after Mary's father T. C. died in 1966. She moved to Greenwood long after T. C. and John had died. Fred Bolden recalled his mother, Cleveland's daughter, telling him that they had visited John and Jessie in Avalon in 1948. Presumably, they also visited Cleveland and his wife Pearl, and possibly other family members.

John and Jessie's son Man attended the Hobgood School in Valley, where he remembers John's brother Cleveland playing Santa Claus. Bonnie Lott also attended the Hobgood School where she first met Man; they married in 1954, when Man was 22, and moved into a little two-room house on Chatham Hill, just above the end of St. James Road. In late 1954 Man left to work on a fruit farm in Florida and never returned to live with Bonnie. Bonnie's first child, Ella Mae, was born there on Chatham Hill on November 27, 1956. Bonnie and Ella Mae moved to Greenwood where, in 1959, Bonnie's second child Andrew was born on March 18.

In 1960 Bonnie and the two children moved to Birmingham, Alabama, and she remained there until moving to Indiana in 1971. The two children moved back to Avalon to live with their grandparents, John and Jessie, in 1962. Bonnie moved from Indiana to Phillip, Mississippi, north of Money, in 1974, but her house burned down and she moved to Greenwood. In 1963 Man was living in Holcomb, north of Avalon, and later moved to live in Minnesota.[113]

Fannie Mohead remembered Hardy, Hennis, Julius, Cleveland, and John, and presumably these were the members of the family that continued to live around Avalon/Valley. Julius also lived on Hobgood Road. Fannie said he died young, but he was aged 50 in Beat 2 District 3 at the time of the 1930 census . She confirmed that Hennis dressed well and did not do manual work, presumably relying on his whiskey to provide a living. She never knew where his still was, but did get to taste his whiskey.

In the 1950s John worked a while for Kate Chatham, a white widow who lived and owned land close to the hill leading up to Valley from Avalon, known as Chatham's Hill. The Chathams had moved away to reside in Sunflower County and had two teenage daughters in 1930.[114] Presumably Kate returned to Avalon after her husband died, possibly in the 1950s.

Ms. Kitty (Mrs. Lillian Mitchell), a black friend of John and Jessie, who was to find John and Jessie a place to live in Grenada in 1966, had known them from the days when she and her husband lived in Avalon and her grandfather lived "above the gravel pit near the old church" (on St. James Road). While living in Avalon she remembered parties where they would stay up all night playing cards and drinking and John would play guitar while folks danced. "John would play my favorite songs, 'Nearer My God to Thee' and 'Jesus Keep Me Near the Cross. Oh, I did enjoy it."

John's son from his marriage to Gertrude, T. C. Hurt, and his wife Annie lived on the flat Delta land near Avalon, where he sharecropped. T. C. had an old "A" model car for a long time and Olin Goss recalled that he would put thirty-five cents' worth of gasoline in the car and take folks to Greenwood or Carrollton: "He burned the motor out of that car because he tried to speed it up. The car went so slow a highway patrolman stopped him, complained because he was driving so slow, and followed him all the way into town."[115]

Annie Cook remembered how folks would hire T. C. to take them places, and one time he took a black man somewhere and when they reached the destination he asked T. C. how much he owed. T. C. replied, "Just give me what you got." The man attacked T. C. with a knife or a razor and slit his throat. He managed to drive the car back home and knocked on the door of Annie Cook's house. Son Virgil answered the door, and seeing T. C. standing there bleeding, got him inside and bandaged him up. They took him to the doctor at Money and got his throat stitched up.

T. C.'s son Lonnie recalled that he and his thirteen siblings would pick two bales of cotton a day, getting from sixteen to twenty bales off a little over twenty acres. He added, "we'd still come out short", referring to the settlement deal.[116] Tales of the injustices of the sharecropping system have entered folklore, like the story from the Yazoo Delta of the shrewd black sharecropper who listened to the plantation owner at settling time tell him that the books exactly balanced. The sharecropper said, "Then I don't owe you nuthin' Cap'n?" "No you don't owe me a cent." "An' you don't owe me nuthin'?" "You saw the books." "Then what's I gonna do with them two bales I ain't done hauled in yet?" "Well, what do you know, just look at that. Here's two pages stuck together, I'll have to add up the whole account again."[117] Annie Cook commented, "Most people were honest, but some weren't and would brag about it. At that time white folks were poor too, there just wasn't any money."

T. C.'s daughter Mary Frances was born on July 4, 1956. She was the ninth of fourteen children and provided her perspective on life in Avalon in the 1950s and 1960s:

In many ways my life was much like any other African American child born in rural Avalon, Mississippi in the mid-1950s. I, like many other children in and around the community, was from a large family. Our parents were sharecroppers or farm laborers. All the families were poor, yet they shared a richness that far outweighed the lack of financial resources. There were genuine concerns for one another that reached across generations. If there was a family crisis, the community swooped in like bees to assist. They came together to celebrate each other's victories. Every adult took on the responsibility of raising every child in the community properly. In essence, I and every other child belonged to the community! So I and my thirteen brothers and sisters belonging to T. C. and Annie Dora were just pieces of a community quilt that begun long before any of us came into existence.

One humid evening, after the folks attending the first Mississippi John Hurt festival in Avalon in 2003 had drifted away to their homes, a few musicians, led by Mary Frances, visited the Hurts' family cemetery to pay their respects at Mississippi John Hurt's gravesite in the wooded glade along St. James Road. It was a deeply emotional occasion. We gathered around John's grave, some of us paying our own tributes with one of John's tunes. Mary was not alone in shedding a few tears and I had noticed her kneeling by her daddy T. C.'s grave. We returned to the festival ground, and groups of folk sat around chatting, some playing guitars and sharing songs. Mary and I sat together on the front porch of John and Jessie's old house. I asked Mary about her recollections of Daddy John and about life in rural Mississippi. She told a story that tells so much about the life of a sharecropper family, as recently as the 1960s, that I include it here just as she told it.

It was the Christmas Eve before my sixth birthday [1961]. In the morning everyone around the house was in a very joyful mood. The wonderful presence of Christmas was everywhere! The smell of cakes, peppermint candies, and fruit lingered in the air. Clouds of misty smoke curled from the neighbors' houses, creating a halo over the community. Even our neighbor Mr. Davis was in an unusually cheerful mood. He shouted a brisk "Merry Christmas" to daddy and mama as they stood motionless on the rickety old porch. Though my parents seemed unmoved by Mr. Davis's greeting, it kind of sealed my heart and mind into thinking that this was going to be the best Christmas ever! Plus, I had overheard my daddy earlier waking my mama to get dressed for the anticipated shopping spree. He reminded her that everyone in Avalon would have all the stores in Greenwood packed doing their one-day shopping trip. "Remember Ann, to put the children's shoe sizes in your pocketbook right now, so when Mr. Glaser give me my check, we can rush on to the stores and get back here before dark," daddy reminded her. I was so exited at the prospect of new shoes.

When I could no longer hear my mama and daddy's movement on the porch, I tiptoed to a large crack in the door and watched them standing ever so still looking down the old dusty road leading from our house. It was confusing watching them stand there when there was so much stuff to be done for our Christmas celebration. Although mama had been busy every evening after work baking pies and cakes, there was still much cooking and baking to be done. I wanted so badly to ask mama how come they hadn't left yet. But I dared not, because I knew the consequences of getting into grown folks' business. It seemed like a lifetime before daddy's cough broke the silence and he turned to face mama. I watched my daddy's mouth form words that seemed to cause him physical pain. "Ann, if Mr. Glaser don't come soon, we won't be able to make it to town before the stores close and our children won't have nothing for Christmas," he stated painfully. My mama did not respond, instead her finger stabbed the air pointing toward a funnel-like cloud of dust coming down the road. With an immediate smile daddy beamed, "That must be Mr. Glaser!"

Sure enough, within minutes Mr. Glaser's big white truck roared up to the house in a cloud of dust and came to a sudden stop. My daddy stepped off the porch and disappeared into the cloud of dust. Daddy greeted Mr. Glaser with a tilt of his head. Mr. Glaser responded with a robust, "Morning T. C." Quickly looking at his watch, he corrected himself, "I mean afternoon." Daddy nodded his head in acceptance of the correction. Mr. Glaser took out a thick tattered black book and began flipping through the pages while daddy waited patiently. Frequently Mr. Glaser's tongue licked his paper-thin lips as he searched. Finally, the pages stopped turning and Mr. Glaser removed his hat as if this would help my daddy to hear better. My mama eased closer to the edge of the porch and quickly regained her stature. "T. C., you know this has been a real bad year for everybody," Mr. Glaser reminded. Daddy nodded in agreement. "Yes sir, I know it was pretty bad." Seemingly happy with daddy's agreement, Mr. Glaser's tone turned a little more cheerful: "Well let me finish up this business so you folk can get on with Christmas," he bubbled. He then began to read from his notebook and the longer he read, the lower my daddy's shoulders fell. Finally, he was done and handed my daddy a piece of paper. He put his hat on and drove away in the same dust cloud that brought him there just minutes before.

Long after the dust settled my daddy stood in the road staring at the piece of paper. My mama called out, "T. C., T. C., come on let's go." Daddy slowly turned around revealing a dusty tear-stained face. Mama stepped back as if pushed with the shock of seeing him this way. I froze in confusion and pain. I had never seen my daddy cry! "Ann, we don't have enough money to get our children nothing for Christmas," daddy stated painfully. I don't remember what mama said, but I do remember that it was the worst pain I had ever felt. I did not understand what could be so bad that could cause my daddy, a man who was afraid of nothing and could fix anything, to cry! I knew that Christmas would never be the same again. It was like a light had been turned off in my heart seeing my father cry.

On Christmas morning I could hear the rattling of paper bags and smelled the familiar scents of peppermint and fruit. Daddy and mama had been up for hours putting together our Christmas bags. There had been hours of restlessness and whispers of anticipation of gifts around the crowded bedroom. Bets had been thrown around the living room the night before of who would or would not get their favorite requested *toy. Finally, mama summoned us to get our Christmas bag. Before the words were barely from her lips, there was a stampede to the fireplace where the bags had been placed in birth order. I peered inside my bag, I couldn't believe my eyes! I reached into my bag and pulled out the most beautiful doll I had ever seen or imagined. She was dark brown like me with big soft brown eyes that closed when I held her back. She had long silky black curls that bounced back in place when I pulled them. Her dress outmatched anything that I had ever seen in the Avalon store or the Sears catalogue. It was pink with a lacy white collar peppered with tiny flowers that matched her ruffled socks and panties. I fell in love with her instantly. I cuddled her and rocked her gently in my arms as her beautiful brown eyes closed for a nap in her new mama's arms.*

As I lost myself in my new baby, I looked across the room and met my daddy's eyes as he smiled at me. Suddenly, the image of my daddy's tear-stained face washed over me! I quickly stuffed the doll back in the bag and walked over to my daddy laying the doll gently in his lap and told him, "Daddy, I don't like this doll! Go and get your money back!" Within seconds, a wave of anger swept over daddy's face and he grabbed me by my shoulders and shook me, "You selfish ungrateful little girl," he hissed. His bloodshot eyes spoke volumes of the disappointment and anger he felt. Suddenly he released his vice-like grip and left me and the doll in a heap on the floor. He stumbled from the room with the same fallen shoulders as I had witnessed the day before. But this time it was not Mr. Glaser that had caused it, it was me!

As the day cooled, I watched Mary's troubled expression and finally broke the long emotional silence, asking, "Didn't you ever explain to your daddy why you had done that?" She answered slowly: "All my life I have regretted not telling him how much that doll really meant to me and how much I appreciated the incredible sacrifices he had made to give it to me. Even more I regretted that I never told him how much I loved and respected him before he passed away just a few years later. What Daddy John did with his guitar, my daddy could do with machines, and like Daddy John, he taught himself too." After a long pause she added, "But today, at his grave, I told him."

Sharecropping continued for a while longer as smaller farms continued to need people to hand pick and to weed or "chop" the cotton. Eventually, however, with the wider use of the cotton picker and the development of herbicides, sharecropping virtually ceased. Widespread unemployment continued to reinforce the migration of blacks from rural Mississippi to cities such as Memphis, Chicago, and St Louis.[118]

Race Issues

Vehement oppression of blacks continued throughout Mississippi and the South, and around Avalon black folk went about their business keeping their heads down. But in 1937, news quickly spread that two black men had been tortured and murdered at the nearby town of Duck Hill after being accused of the murder of a local storekeeper. A mob gathered and over 500 people are reported to have witnessed the executions of Roosevelt Townes and "Bootjack" McDaniels, who had previously been taken from the sheriff in Winona as they were being led from the courtroom to the jail to await trial.[119]

Segregation kept abreast of technology and innovation. Taxis were segregated in Mississippi in 1922, and separate waiting rooms were required at airports by the 1940s.[120] By this time just about everything was segregated, from public water fountains to graveyards, and segregation was so complete that little contact was made between blacks and whites outside of formal interactions, although during the thirties the situation had eased temporarily as people struggled through the Depression.

In Mississippi a state law was passed requiring separate textbooks for black schools, in which "all references to voting, elections, civic responsibilities and democracy will be excluded. Thus Negro children will not be informed as to their theoretical rights or duties under the democratic system of government."[121] As a result, in April 1940 the National Association for the Advancement of Colored People (NAACP) published an article in their journal stating: "Down in Mississippi they are afraid of democracy."

By the end of the 1940s attitudes were changing in some places. The NAACP, the social gospel movement, and pressure from north of the Mason-Dixon line influenced a growing awareness and sympathy for the plight of southern blacks. The number of bills favoring civil rights increased: in the 81st Congress (1949–50) seventy-two such bills were introduced. President Harry S. Truman began to take action, providing the stimulus to end segregation in education, outlawing the poll tax and lynching and, in 1948, ending segregation in the military.[122] But little changed in Mississippi.

The Supreme Court, in the famous decision *Oliver Brown et al. v. Board of Education of Topeka, Kansas*, ruled that segregation in schools had a detrimental effect on black children and that the doctrine of "separate but equal" established in 1896 (*Plessey v. Ferguson*) was invalid.

This decision initiated a sequence of major improvements over the next ten years, but not without an enormous struggle, continuing racism, and heightened violence against blacks. *Brown* laid down no time scale for compliance and allowed flexibility for local interpretation, which allowed segregationists an opportunity to thwart change. Mississippi declared the *Brown* decision unconstitutional and created a State Sovereignty Committee to resist desegregation. Loopholes in the law were sought and found. Federal law prohibiting segregation on the grounds of race and color did not prohibit segregation based on illegitimacy, morals, or welfare, and in the Deep South segregation continued. In Mississippi, resistance hardened into paranoia; after three years without lynchings, four black men were lynched in 1955. At least another ten were killed under mysterious circumstances between 1956 and 1959, bringing back all the fear and repression of the past.[123] Random violence against blacks had the intended effect of instilling fear and intimidation in many blacks.

Just six miles away from Avalon, across the county line close to Money in Leflore County, 14-year-old Emmett Louis Till was lynched for disrespecting a white woman. On August 24, 1955, Till and some of his friends congregated outside a store in Money, the small Delta town where John's granddaughter Dorothy attended school. Emmett is said to have wolf-whistled or "talked back" to Carolyn Bryant, the white woman who, with her husband Roy, owned the store. Word got around about this "outrage," and in the early hours of Sunday morning, August 28, 1955, Roy Bryant, his half brother J. W. Milam, Carolyn Bryant, and Johnnie B. Washington abducted Emmett from his great uncle Mose Wright's cabin near Money. Roy Bryant and Milam took Emmett to a barn on the Shurden Plantation near Drew, Sunflower County, where they beat him before shooting him and throwing his body into the Tallahatchie River, weighted down with a cotton gin mill fan. Robert Hodges, a local fisherman, found Emmett's body at Peca Point near Philipp on the boundary of Tallahatchie and Leflore Counties on August 31. The body was taken to the Central Burial Association in Greenwood.[124] The news of this atrocity spread around the world. One wonders how news of this circulated at the Valley Store? Bryant and Milam were brought to trial and acquitted, defense attorney John Whitten directing the all-white jury to follow their Anglo-Saxon duty and acquit the accused. Later, protected by double jeopardy legislation, Bryant and Milam confessed to the crimes and were paid $3,500 for their story.

Guy Duke, a white friend of John and the Smiths and Narmours, told of Grover Duke, a fiddle player who lived in Money during the 1950s, playing fiddle with John at the Valley store. Grover Duke testified as a character witness for Roy Bryant at his trial for the murder of Emmett Till. It seems that he was able to apply double standards, having fun and making music with his black neighbors but doing his "duty" when called upon to uphold white supremacy.[125]

An uneasy quiet, punctuated by continuing terrorism-fuelled intimidation, descended on Mississippi—until September 1962, when James Meredith, the son of a Mississippi sharecropper, applied to enroll as the first black student at the University of Mississippi ("Ole Miss"), in Oxford, less than 80 miles from Avalon. The university refused his admission, with strong support from the Democrat-led state government. Governor Ross Barnett, a vehement racist and segregationist, appeared on television encouraging the white people of Mississippi not to yield to tyranny from the federal government. The university board of trustees surrendered their authority to Barnett and a peaceful solution seemed impossible.[126]

Supreme Court Justice Hugo Black, following a number of appeals, ruled that Meredith should be enrolled. This reinforced the substantial resistance from the university, the white community of Oxford, and the governor. As a result, President John F. Kennedy ordered federal marshals to ensure Meredith's right to enroll and to protect him as he moved to the campus. On Sunday, September 30, one hundred and seventy federal marshals accompanying Meredith flew into Oxford, the Highway Patrol withdrew, and a riot began. Simultaneously, President Kennedy was speaking to the nation on television, but it was too late. The riot continued through the night, leaving over 300 people injured and two dead. Civil rights problems in the American southern states had again been brought to the attention of the whole world.[127]

Integration began to occur, but not in Mississippi and Alabama. In 1962, only 6.7 percent of African Americans in Mississippi were registered to vote and around Avalon nothing changed. But, the constructive, if contrived, relationship between many blacks and whites continued and, as Ms. Annie Cook put it: "Everybody struggled and worked hard, there was no time to waste on that [racism]." Fannie Mohead had no recollection of any civil rights activity around Avalon. "We got on fine with the white folks when I was growin' up." Fred Clarke told me, "We mixed with the black folks, never had no problems. There was mixed picnics. They would dance separately, but watch one another and chat." Art Browning had a similar recollection. "There was no trouble here, it was just separate. Most folks were gentle and friendly. They had common values and would swap corn for a wagon wheel, etc." Larry Smith added: "Never were any racial problems. Every white church had benches up the back for blacks." John's grandson, Lonnie Conley Hurt, considered that John's boss, Perkins, was far kinder than most white landowners and that he protected his workers from the Klan.[128]

Although there were relatively good relations between blacks and whites in Avalon, it was different in Greenwood. Larry Smith worked in Greenwood and recalls having to close the store where he worked during a civil rights march in the early 1960s. He asked the police outside why they had German Shepherd dogs. An officer replied, "Gonna turn 'em loose on these niggers." Greenwood was a center of civil rights activity from 1961 to 1963, which gathered strength with the Greenwood Voter Registration project that started in August 1962. An account of some of the activities there is presented in the recording produced by Guy Carawan for the Student Non-Violent Coordinating Committee (SNCC) in 1965. Leflore County had a population of about 50,000 people in 1960, approximately two-thirds of whom were black. Whites owned 90 percent of the land and held all of the political offices. Of 168 hospital beds available, 131 were reserved for whites. Ninety-five percent of whites of voting age were registered to vote and only two percent of blacks.[129]

African American Clarence Jordan, who lived his entire life around Greenwood, told how he worked hard for whites all of his life and pleaded for equality. "We know that the procedures that are being taken now to qualify people to register and vote is not pleasing to our white neighbors, but the law has been passed that we have rights to go to the court house and apply for registration, and we are goin' without any weapon at all." He continued, "Why do they hate us so bad, and we've been workin' for 'um all of our lives? They go on ridin' in fine cars while our children goin' to school barefoot and never get no automobile and we're not able to pay for one. Why do they try to just keep us down? We're not wantin' to stay down now, and we're ready to fight." "Amen."

Winters in the towns of Mississippi were always lean. Many people depended on the provision of food by the government. Fannie Lou Hamer told of people standing in line waiting for food while plantation owners rode by calling out their names and telling them to go back to the plantations. Two African Americans, Sam Block and Willie Peacock, risked life and limb in their courageous efforts to persuade blacks to register. White brutality continued, but increasing numbers of blacks registered to vote. Greenwood became a testing ground for democracy.[130]

The civil rights movement in general, and the increasing tensions and tragedies that had played out across the surrounding landscape in Duck Hill, Money, Oxford, and Greenwood, must have been discussed within the confines of the separate black and white communities around Avalon. John Hurt and his African American friends who congregated on the porch of the Valley store must have discussed the events that were unfolding in the wider world. But these conversations no doubt were abruptly curtailed at the appearance of a white face.

An Increase of White Interest in Black Music

The recordings of and writings about American folk music by John and Alan Lomax—including their landmark songbook collection, *American Ballads and Folk Songs*, published in 1934[131]—initially attracted only small audiences of specialists. By the early 1950s interest in the subject had increased, and in 1952 Harry Smith's *Anthology of American Folk Music* was published.[132] This three-volume presentation of six long-playing discs, drawn from Smith's collection of old 78 rpm records, raised the profile of this musical genre enormously, attracting folk revivalist musicians such as Dave van Ronk, Eric von Schmidt, and Jim Rooney. White collectors and folk music enthusiasts discovered Mississippi John Hurt, whose "Frankie" and "Spike Driver Blues" were included on Smith's anthology.

While some white college students were becoming strongly involved in supporting civil rights issues, others were developing an interest in American folk blues, work songs, and spirituals. In 1960 Robert Zimmerman, who was to metamorphose into Bob Dylan, was contemplating a move east to find his hero, Woody Guthrie. He arrived in New York City in 1961 and, like some others, began to take an interest in civil rights as well as folk music. Dylan successfully combined the two with his song "Oxford Town" about the riots surrounding the enrollment of James Meredith at Ole Miss.[133]

A group of young white hippies around Washington, D.C., spurred on by Harry Smith's *Anthology*, developed an obsession with the old blues and ragtime music of the Deep South and particularly of the Mississippi Delta. This obsession led to a record collecting frenzy, and the likes of Joe Bussard, Dick Spottswood, and the late Mike Stewart (a.k.a. Backward Sam Firk) began to scour used record stores and thrift stores in southern towns in the hunt for old race records of the 1920s and 1930s. Records of Robert Johnson, Charley Patton, Son House, Furry Lewis, the Mississippi Sheiks, Mississippi John Hurt, and many others were found.

In Britain the skiffle craze initiated by the release of Lonnie Donegan's "Rock Island Line" in 1955 eventually led to a realization that songs like "Rock Island Line," "John Henry," "Stewball," "Stackolee," and "Midnight Special" had been recycled many times in the past from African American work songs, field hollers, spirituals, ballads, and blues, and that the big hit for Nancy Whiskey and the Chas. McDevitt Skiffle Group, "Freight Train," was actually the work of Libba Cotten, an African American.

The End of an Era

Between 1958 and 1960 there were around 300 families living in the Valley area and over 200 houses in Avalon. Hilman Moreland, a friend of John and Jessie's, owned the Valley Store, which had been a hub of community activity for over half a century. Annie Cook had married and left Avalon in 1938 when her husband served in the military; the family returned to Avalon in 1946. John would often be invited to play at local schools and parties, and local folk were aware of his prowess on guitar. Mississippi John Hurt Museum curator Art Browning remembers many of John's friends from the fifties and sixties. Archie Herbert, the fiddle-playing school bus supervisor, would put on a big squirrel stew and invite John to come and play. The McCrorys, who lived in the Valley area, would invite John over and get him to teach the kids guitar. Art never did meet John; he and his friends once invited him to come down and play but he could not make it. At that time, Art was getting involved with a rock 'n' roll band and girls, and he left Avalon to live in Jackson. He returned to Avalon in 1995 because of his interest in Mississippi John Hurt and his music, met Mary Frances, and became curator of the Mississippi John Hurt Museum (see ch. 5).

Mary Frances remembers Daddy John having two black-and-white bird dogs in the early 1960s, indicating that John had maintained his interest in hunting. Mary's mother Annie would insist that the children all attend church on a Sunday. Often John, Jessie, and Gertrude would join them, Gertrude being noted for her beautiful voice. "We would have preachin' once a month and Sunday school for the other Sundays," Mary recalls.

So, in 1962, John and Jessie, along with Ella Mae and Andrew, were living close to the Valley Store. Gertrude and Will Conley lived down on the Delta land in Avalon close to Annie Cook's house and John's son T. C. Hurt, along with his wife Annie and their large family including six-year-old Mary Frances. All the families that young Mary knew were sharecroppers. Life was hard and there was little time for play. Most folk, including the young children, were at work in the fields before first light. Mary's duties, at the age of six, involved cooking, cleaning, and looking after children for most of the daylight hours. "Why were things so bad and why weren't they ever going to be any better?" she wondered.

John did not own a guitar but would still play whenever he got an opportunity. His day was occupied by tending Perkins's cows, while Jessie did some housekeeping for the Perkins family. The cows were fed around late afternoon and before that the day would be punctuated with a walk along to the Valley Store where he would buy a packet of Camel cigarettes and chat with his neighbors and Hilman Moreland, the storekeeper. As the year drew to a close he could not possibly have conceived of the upheaval that was about to unfold early in the new year.

3. Rediscovery and Sweet Success

As 1962 came to an end, John Hurt probably anticipated a new year much like the last one and much like those of the three or so decades before. He was 70 years old, looking after Perkins's cattle, and keeping a few hogs and chickens to help sustain his wife Jessie and grandchildren Ella Mae and Andrew Lee. Jessie helped out in the Perkins's house. They were poor but appeared contented. Meanwhile, the world outside Avalon was jumping.

The civil rights movement was gathering strength. Young whites from the North and East were taking a personal interest in the status and treatment of blacks in Mississippi and other southern states. Older generations were becoming jaundiced about the alleged threat of communism, and the focus on race relations was intensifying. Black students and their white supporters were raising their hopes on the back of the increasing popularity of Martin Luther King Jr. and the young president from Massachusetts.

Back east, white folkies had been aware of Mississippi John Hurt, largely through the Harry Smith *Anthology* in the 1950s, and Hurt's music became an obsession with a few of them. In particular, around Washington, D.C., and Annapolis, Maryland, Mike Stewart (a.k.a. Backward Sam Firk), Max Ochs, and Tom Hoskins (Fang) spent a lot of time trying to re-create Hurt's music, with a high degree of success. Around Greenwich Village in New York, Dave Van Ronk, John Sebastian, a young Stefan Grossman (Kid Future), an even younger Rory Block (Sunshine Kate), and others were doing the same thing. Mark Greenberg remembers hearing Mike Seeger playing "Frankie" and Tom Paley playing "Stackolee," with both attributing the songs to Mississippi John Hurt.

None of them really considered what had happened to Hurt until, in late 1962 or early 1963, Dick Spottswood acquired some tape recordings of some of Hurt's other 1928 OKeh records from Peter Kuykendall, who in turn got them from John Edwards, an Australian record collector.[1] The tapes included "Avalon Blues."

Thomas B. Hoskins

From here on, this story needs to follow the twin tracks of Mississippi John Hurt and Tom Hoskins, the man who rediscovered him. Hoskins was a likable hippie with no permanent job, and a fondness for girls, alcohol, and drugs in no particular order. He and his friends indulged in the hippie lifestyle and some of them spent a considerable time polishing their skills on the guitar. Hoskins was passionately interested in the rural blues.

His sister Suzanne speaks fondly of her little brother Tommy as a warm, friendly, and loving brother, but even she got frustrated with him. She recalled the rehearsal for her wedding at which Tommy was to be an usher. Tommy was a motorcycle courier around D.C. at the time and had left things late to travel down to Charlottesville, Virginia. With the rehearsal dinner in full swing, Tommy walked in wearing his motorcycle clothes. "I was mad as hell with him, but I just ran up and hugged him and started to cry." Suzanne's husband Joe, a military medical doctor, was hardly Tommy's type, but always enjoyed his company and always looked forward to seeing him. On one occasion when Tommy stayed with them at the officers' quarters of the army barracks in Germany, they returned to their apartment to find that Tommy had hung his wash out of the apartment window to dry, much to the consternation of their neighbors!

Tommy's close friend Denise Tapp provides what I think is a fairly accurate description of the man:

By now, you probably understand that Tom Hoskins suffered from some form of arrested development, which was not helped by his massive consumption of drugs and alcohol. He could be a real pain in the ass and was kicked out of just about every place he attempted to visit for any length. The constant pranks and disruptions got to everyone. I myself made a number of death threats to him and I absolutely swore never to take him to a restaurant again after the first try. But, still he was lovable and friends always forgave him. He could see and hear things that others couldn't and he pointed out thousands of little treasures that we had overlooked. It will be difficult to capture that kind of personality in print.

Louisa Spottswood stated: "He was a very ingratiating young man with southern country manners. We became aware as time went on that he was very unreliable, often being late for appointments, etc., but he had a certain charm and I always had a soft spot in my heart for him. I didn't get as mad at him as Dick. He was led astray by others."

Max Ochs liked Tom but, after being let down on a couple of occasions, stopped trusting him. He likened him to the confidence tricksters the Duke and the Dauphine from *Huckleberry Finn*. In Max's words: "He burned his way through everybody. He was a carpetbagger. He had a million little scams and schemes. He was a consummate actor and could talk his way into and out of anything."

Dick Spottswood commented in 1964:

> *Tom is a rather good left-handed guitar player whose origins are Southern. He was born and reared in Charlottesville, Virginia. He played guitar for a number of years and he started out as a rock 'n' roller. He played in a number of bands down there before he moved to Washington a couple of years ago. He started listening to the old blues, but his relationship was between the old Negro country blues and rock 'n' roll. Tom began to listen to the old records and he became interested in the old blues artists themselves.*[2]

Tom described himself as "an aspiring young guitar player in the early 1960s" who was, "interested in early country, blues and gospel music. My main source of material was 78 rpm records of the 1920s and 1930s, which could only be found in junk shops and by canvassing door to door in neighborhoods throughout the southern states."[3] Philadelphia Jerry Ricks reckoned "for a white kid, he could play black with remarkable ease" and rated him as the best of the white kid guitar players in those days, saying that his music had black soul and emotion. Hoskins took his nickname Fang from the record by Nervous Norvus (Jimmy Drake), "The Fang."[4]

The Search for Mississippi John Hurt

It was Tom Hoskins's fascination with the old musicians that led to him finding Mississippi John Hurt. He wrote:

> *My friends and I often wondered, who were these marvelous musicians whose mysterious and colorful sounding names appeared on the worn*

*record labels: names like Peg Leg Howell, Little Hat Jones, Blind Lemon
Jefferson, Cripple Clarence Lofton, Sleepy John Estes and the Masked
Marvel. Once while listening to the often badly scratched and cracked
discs, trying to understand the words of "another voice from another
time," or trying to figure out how a particular passage was played on
the guitar, a friend remarked, "It's too bad we don't have these guys
here to show us how it's done. I wonder where they are?" I began to
wonder too, especially about the singer with the gentle sounding voice
and the unique complex, finger style guitar style, who was known only
by the name on a couple of rare, old, battered 78s, "Mississippi John
Hurt." Of all those old musicians he had impressed me the most so,
when a friend [Dick Spottswood] got a tape, from Australia of all places, that included a previously unheard cut by John Hurt, I hurried over
to listen.*[5]

Following the acquisition of these tapes, Tom Hoskins and Dick
Spottswood developed a nagging and increasing obsession to find out
what happened to Mississippi John Hurt. Apart from the Mississippi tag
there had been no clues. But now they had more recordings from the
1928 sessions. Among these was the recording of "Avalon Blues" made
in New York City in which John sounded homesick, referring to Avalon
as "my home town." Hoskins remarked, "The words in the opening verse
set off flashing lights in my head, 'Avalon's my hometown, always on my
mind.' I thought, 'He's telling me where he lives!'"[6] Searching maps of the
southern states they could only find an Avalon in Georgia, which seemed
an unlikely home for someone with a Mississippi prefix! However, Tommy
did travel to Avalon, Georgia, looking in vain for Mississippi John Hurt.[7]

Sometime later, in Leland Talbot's house in Sherwood Forest outside
Annapolis, Maryland,[8] Hoskins was looking through an old Rand McNally
atlas of Mississippi, and there between Grenada and Greenwood was the
small railway stop of Avalon, Mississippi. Could this be the place that
Mississippi John Hurt called home?[9]

There are three distinctly different accounts of what happened next
and who actually traveled to Avalon on that first memorable trip. In addition, there are many variations of these three main themes.

The first account comes from handwritten corrections by Tom Hoskins
to an article called "Avalon to Eternity," published in 1976 and found
among Hoskins's possessions in 2005, and a letter written by Hoskins
to Alex Haley on February 12, 1982.[10] With encouragement from
Spottswood and Stewart, Hoskins headed south with a tape recorder and
some cautious optimism.

Several days later, I had borrowed a car and $200, and was on my
way to Mississippi, where on a chilly March Friday evening, in the
Mississippi hills overlooking the infamous flatlands of the Delta coun-
try, I was to knock on the door of a three room country shack and ask,
"Is this where Mississippi John Hurt lives?"

It was and he did, simple as that, and late Sunday evening, after
spending the day with John, his wife Jessie and several friends, I was
driving north again through the Mississippi darkness with a two hour
tape recording of a living, breathing, treasure of a young old gentleman
of about 70 years, who until that day had been only a shadowy figure
from an unknown past and presumed dead.

These tapes have recently come to light. They are labeled "Recorded in
Avalon, Mississippi by Thomas Hoskins, 3/3/63."[11] This firmly documents
the date of John's rediscovery. On the journey home Hoskins recalls: "I
kept touching the tape box to make sure it was real, and that I still had it,
knowing that I would not be believed without it. The dizzying excitement
that I felt that night is difficult to describe."

This word-for-word account of the event by Hoskins himself was written in 1982, nineteen years after the event, but he recounted various
other versions to his friends both before and later. These close friends
swear that their accounts are correct, and maybe they are, but the facts
remain that most of them were not actually around at the time and that
Hoskins himself did purvey several versions of the event.

The second and perhaps most familiar version is that in February 1963
Tom Hoskins was at a party at American University in D.C., where he
met an attractive young woman named Janet Rodd.[12] Undoubtedly under
the influence of at least one social drug of the time, Fang invited her to
accompany him on a trip to the New Orleans Mardi Gras. Whether he
mentioned to her his intention to call in at Avalon in an effort to trace
Mississippi John Hurt is not known, but that was his intention.[13] The
young woman contributed the news that she had a new Dodge with a
slant-6 engine that they could use, which really clinched the deal, and
they set off for New Orleans.

In a slightly different account of events, Dick Spottswood recalled:
"Tom Hoskins left Washington late in February when he went south to
attend the New Orleans Mardi Gras. When Tom was in Mississippi, he
happened to get a state map and discovered Avalon, Mississippi. He drove
over 200 miles out of his way to get to this little town"—suggesting that
Hoskins had not decided on the quest to find Hurt before going to the
Mardi Gras.[14] This account is unlikely, as the information that Hoskins set

out to find Hurt, having found Avalon in an Atlas in Washington, D.C., appears to be reliable.

Having crossed the Virginia state line on the first day of their trip, the couple pulled into a motel and booked a room for the night. They settled in and Hoskins, intending to cash in on all his good fortune, came on to Miss Rodd upon which she rapidly decided that maybe this trip was not such a great idea. She rebuffed his advances, announcing that she was a virgin and not ready to sacrifice her maiden status to the Fang, and added, "by the way I am only 15 years old and this is my daddy's car!" Being a good-natured hippie, he was able to control the testosterone coursing through his veins and recall the behavior of the southern gentleman that was omnipresent behind the often bizarre behavior and sometimes criminal events that he indulged in. He calmed the girl down and slept on the floor.[15]

However, this was the least of his worries. He had crossed a state line with an underage girl. This amounted to statutory rape under the Mann Act, which makes it illegal to transport females across state lines for immoral purposes and provides for enhanced penalties for transporting minors. Chuck Berry was imprisoned in 1959 under this act after bringing a fourteen-year-old girl from Mexico to his nightclub in St Louis.[16]

Next morning things had calmed down and, in spite of police across several states issuing APBs, the couple, oblivious to the furor they had caused, got to New Orleans and enjoyed the Mardi Gras, which was held on February 26 that year. After four or five days in New Orleans they headed north through Jackson to Greenwood and onto Highway 7 to Avalon.

In a third account of events, the late Mike Stewart, who certainly was around at the time, recalled: "Fang called me up and says, 'Hey, we found Avalon, Mississippi and I'm gonna go and find Mississippi John Hurt. Do you want to come along?'" Unhesitatingly, Mike was up for this adventure and he and Fang set out for Mississippi. According to Stewart, the car they used for this trip was possibly Fang's old Volkswagen Beetle, Firk's Borgward, or a friend's (Hugh Claudy) Volvo or Peugeot.[17]

A number of Hoskins's friends, including Joe Lee and Denise Tapp, have argued that Fang and the girl went to Avalon that first time[18] and that Mike Stewart went on a subsequent trip, but they did not meet up with Hoskins until much later and could have been influenced by more recent accounts from Hoskins and by repeated written accounts. However, it is virtually certain that Stewart was not there on the first trip to Avalon, but that he did go down there later.

The sequence of events in Avalon is more or less undisputed. At Avalon, he/they pulled into the gas station at the Stinson Store on Highway 7 and enquired as to the whereabouts of Mississippi John Hurt. Unhesitatingly the attendant replied, "Take the dirt road opposite, third mailbox up the hill is John's place." Mike Stewart told me that he clearly remembered asking for directions, persuading me that he may have been present on this first visit. They drove up the hill past the Valley Store to find John's shotgun house. Mike recalls that the door was open but John was not around. They met Jessie, who was very suspicious of the strangers and their interest in John, and the two grandchildren. They decided to wait. Mike remembers up on the wall in the living room was a calendar advertising Black Draught, a cure for constipation and various other ills. Later, a small black man wearing a fedora showed up. They asked if he was Mississippi John Hurt. He answered, "Sure, that's me."

A photograph, dated March 1963, (see Fig. 3.1) of a Volkswagen outside the Valley Store, suggests that this was not the trip that the Fang was accompanied by the girl with the Dodge, and there is no photographic evidence of a white girl being present, nor is there any indication on the recordings made on that day of a second visitor being present. The conversation on the tape that Hoskins recorded in John's house provides the kind of breakthrough that all historical researchers dream of. Tom Hoskins says to John, "I just wish a friend of mine, Backward Sam Firk [Mike Stewart] were here to listen to you. He sure does like you. To which John answers questioningly, "He does?" Hoskins continued: "He can't get your records but he has got a couple of tapes he made of your records. He just sits and listens to them hour after hour." Thus, Mike Stewart did not accompany Hoskins on that first trip to Avalon.[19]

Ed Ward's account tells of Hoskins and Stewart finding Hurt driving a tractor in a field close to his house,[20] but as far as I am aware John never learned to drive a tractor or anything else. In the second version, Hoskins left the girl in the car, knocked on the door, and John answered it. Mike Stewart remembers Hoskins making the trip to New Orleans with the girl but reckons that this was on a different occasion and not connected with John Hurt's rediscovery.

Mike Stewart recalled to me his memory of traveling back through Tennessee with Hoskins driving and John Hurt in the middle seat asleep with Hurt's head on his shoulder, in awe of the fact that he was sitting "with Mississippi John Hurt's head on my shoulder." The facts that John did not return to D.C. on the occasion of his rediscovery and that a VW Beetle would not seat three people across the front seats suggest that this was not the first visit, adding support for the absence of Stewart on the first trip. The fact that Dick Spottswood recalls going down there to collect John, and that John remembered traveling back via Birmingham, Alabama, suggests that this was a third or subsequent visit when perhaps both Hoskins and Stewart went to collect John and bring him to Washington.

John himself told his own story of how it all happened, some of the detail obviously obtained from some of the locals and from Hoskins.

Well, Mr. Hoskins goes to a little store right in the center of town. Dick Switzel owns the store. He asked Mr. Switzel, "Does Mississippi John Hurt live around here?" Mr. Switzel answered, "Why, yes! He lives probably five miles east. You go right across that road until you hit that gravel road and you go east. You go right up that hill until you come to a little country store on the right. Just on the other side of that store, on the left, is Mississippi John's employer's house. You keep on going and the next house on the left, sitting out there in the pasture, is where Mississippi John Hurt lives.[21]

These instructions are accurate and remain easy to follow to this day. The store that Hoskins first called at on Highway 7 was always known, and is still referred to today, as the Stinson's Store, though it no longer exists. The "little country store" is the Valley Store (see Figs. 3.1, 3.4, 3.5); this building is still there and there are plans by its current owner, Larry Smith, to restore it. John's employer Perkins's house is still there, but is no longer owned by the Perkins family. A historic marker was placed alongside the Valley Store in 2008 that identifies the site as being frequented by Mississippi John Hurt. The site of John's house can easily be found today, but the house has been moved from its original site to another site close by where it now houses the Mississippi John Hurt Museum (see ch. 5).

John continues:

About nine o'clock that night, Mr. Hoskins knocked on my door. I asked, "Who is that?" He said, "Is this where Mississippi John Hurt lives?" I thought it was someone nearby so I said, "Yeah," and I opened the door and he walked in. He looks at me and said, "John, have you got a guitar?" I told him I didn't have one and he said, "No sweat." He walked right out to his car and came back with a guitar and he said, "John, I want you to play this."

I thought the man was a sheriff or the FBI and I was thinking to myself, "What have I done?" I hadn't done anything mean and I knew he was after the wrong man and he wasn't looking for me. Then he said,

*"John, we have been lookin' for you for a long time. I want you to come
to Washington with me and make some records. Will you go?" I said,
"Yeah, I'll go. But, first I'd like to talk to my employer a little bit." He
told me okay. The next day Mr. Hoskins came back with his recorder
and I did some tunes.*

John had not played a guitar for about two years, but when handed
Hoskins's Gibson J-45 (customized with stars and moons in mother-of-
pearl inlay by Bill Tydings) it soon was obvious that, although a little rusty,
this was indeed the famous man himself. This account by John also suggests that Hoskins was alone and fits in with information from the Avalon
recordings.

Yet another variation on the story also came from John when he attended a workshop at the University of Cincinnati in 1966. When asked
by Dick Waterman to talk about the blues, John replied, "I will let my
music speak for itself tonight." Waterman, wondering how to proceed,
asked John to tell people about his rediscovery in 1963. John described
Tom Hoskins approaching a guy at the Stinson Store and asking where
he could find John Hurt's burial site. The man answered, "If he ain't died
since, he went that way with two sacks of groceries at eleven o'clock this
morning." The rest of his story was more or less according to that described earlier.

Photographs (see Figs. 3.1–3.6), including some previously unpublished, discovered among Tom Hoskins's possessions in 2006, record ele-
ments of that first trip to Avalon (the photos were developed in March
1963). They show an unidentified white person (possibly Hoskins) standing alongside a Volkswagen Beetle outside the Valley Store. Bill Tydings,
a auto repairman and close friend of Tom Hoskins who was around at the
time, recalls, "Fang went down there in a 1957 Volkswagen." There was
no sign of a girl or a new Dodge car. Other photos show a group of John's
friends outside the Valley Store and John with some of his friends. Again,
this suggests that Hoskins was alone, although it is unknown who took the
pictures in which Hoskins appears.

Tom Hoskins recorded two consecutive one-hour tapes on that Sunday
afternoon of March 3, 1963. It is likely that as well as John and Jessie
and the grandchildren, Ella Mae and Andrew, Gertrude, John's first wife
and her elder sister Jennie Simms were also present. They all appear together on the photograph taken outside John's house that same day (see
Fig. 3.6), and the recording certainly indicates a party mood with several
participants.

Figure 3.1. The Valley Store with (probably) Tom Hoskins and his car in 1963 with Tom Hoskins's handwritten caption. Printed March 1963. (Tom Hoskins, March 1963, Tom Hoskins Archive.)

That these tapes have survived is incredible. They represent a most valuable and important part of the history of Mississippi John Hurt, and they record the details of his rediscovery. The tape begins with John playing "Cow Hooking Blues" and Jessie adding, "John, you make the most of this." This is followed by a conversation in which Tom Hoskins asks about John's childhood and his 1928 recordings. Jessie helps John with his answers. John goes on to play "Nobody's Dirty Business" and "Stack O'Lee Blues," and in spite of some people reporting that John was rather rusty immediately following his rediscovery, this version of "Stack O'Lee Blues" is superb. Later, John launches into a great performance of "Candy Man," but partway through gets a little lost and the guitar break merges into "Salty Dog"—fabulous material and a great insight into how John sounded at that time, having not owned a guitar for a considerable time and being relatively unpracticed.

The whole event becomes a regular hootenanny, and the second tape begins with a bright version of "Frankie." John is suffering from a cold and has some difficulty singing, and there is some discussion about his condition. Next, John is accompanied by Jessie (and others?) on "Waiting for You." They forget some of the words, but are clearly enjoying themselves

Figure 3.2. John's house photographed in 1963 with handwritten caption by Tom Hoskins. Printed March 1963. (Tom Hoskins, March 1963, Tom Hoskins Archive.)

and the recording represents an absolute gem of a regular Mississippi family singalong, albeit with an exceptionally talented guitarist. There is a real party atmosphere with children calling out and roosters crowing outside, and as the tape is coming to an end, John announces that, "It's getting close to feedin' time. Mr. Perkins's cows get fed around three or three-thirty."

As the events surrounding his rediscovery are such an important part of John Hurt's story, I have presented all of the facts as far as I have been able to collect them, and readers are invited to interpret them as they wish. What follows is my deduction of what probably happened. Tom Hoskins drove alone to Avalon directly from Washington, D.C., in his Volkswagen, inquired at the Stinson's Store, and was directed to John's house. He arrived there at around nine in the evening of March 2, 1963, six days before John's seventy-first birthday. After introducing himself to John and Jessie, Tom left his guitar with John and drove to Grenada where he stayed overnight (he mentions this on the recording).

He returned next day around midday, took some photos at the Valley Store and at John's house, and began recording the conversations and music that followed over the next two hours. The available recording tape ran out around three o'clock, when it was about time for John to go and

Figure 3.3. Mississippi John Hurt on his front porch in 1963. (Tom Hoskins, March 1963, Tom Hoskins Archive.)

feed Perkins's cows. He packed his guitar, tape recorder, and tapes into his car, said his farewells, and headed back to Washington.

Mike Stewart almost certainly did visit Avalon with Tom Hoskins on a subsequent visit to collect John. Fang certainly drove with Janet Rodd in her father's car to the New Orleans Mardi Gras and perhaps they visited John and Jessie in Avalon on the way home.[22]

Mississippi John Hurt Visits Washington, D.C.

Tom Hoskins returned to the Spottswoods' home in Arlington, Virginia, where John would be given the use of their spare room. Dick Spottswood takes up the story.[23] "When we heard the tape we were almost hysterical with joy but we didn't want the news to leak out. We knew as soon as someone in New York heard about it there would be a plane with someone going down there and beating us to it. We had no signed contract. So we waited about a week and we started back to Mississippi in my car. The three of us returned to Washington in early March." John recalled to

Figure 3.4. Locals outside the Valley Store in March 1963. Later identified by Mary Frances Hurt Wright as (left to right) three Isaac brothers, Lawrence Pickett, Shack Pryor, unknown, and Rosetta Magic. (Tom Hoskins, March 1963, Tom Hoskins Archive.)

Pete Seeger that they traveled back via Birmingham, Alabama, and that was the first time that John had ever been there.[24]

Before John left Avalon, some of his friends warned him, "You ain't going to get nothin' out of it." John replied, "I'm going to get the trip." This attitude of not having high expectations and taking things as they come was built on his earlier experience with OKeh in 1928 and epitomized the gentle man who was about to take the folk world by storm.[25]

Max Ochs was awakened by the telephone one morning in his New York City apartment. "Max, we've found Mississippi John Hurt," the voice said. Max could hardly contain himself. He dressed quickly and caught the train to D.C. In Spottswood's living room he saw a circle of young white folk, some with guitars. Partially hidden in the center of the ring was a little black man wearing a fedora. It was Mississippi John Hurt. Waves of emotion engulfed Max. One surprise was that the artist's impression of John Hurt that Max had previously drawn of a tall white guy with a straw in his mouth was so far from the reality. Why had Max assumed this music to be the work of a white man? Well, white and black musicians were both playing some of this music in the 1920s, as opposed to the Delta blues, which was exclusively produced by blacks, and Max would have been unaware of John's musical sources. John had drawn from many white musicians such as Jimmie Rodgers and of course he had played with Willie Narmour and Shell Smith, two white musicians from Avalon. Harry Smith refused to identify performers by race on his *Anthology* recordings (assuming that he was aware of their race), and Max's mistaken impression served to reinforce the fact that these folk were interested in the music and not the racial origins of the artists.

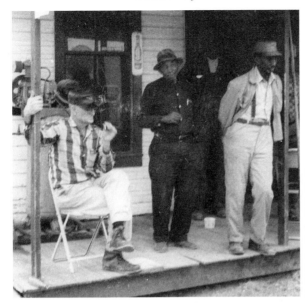

Figure 3.5. John with friends on the front porch of the Valley Store in March 1963. Later identified by Annie Cook as (left to right) Hilman Moreland, John's brother Hennis, and Mac House. (Tom Hoskins, March 1963, Tom Hoskins Archive.)

Max picks up the story of what he observed that day in Dick Spottswood's house.

In the living room sat a little man on a chair. Around him, in a circle, were all these disciples, including probably the best white blues guitar player alive, Mike "Backward Sam Firk" Stewart. Firk said to John, "Why don't you play something?" I think John played "Nobody's Dirty Business," but he was rusty—in those 35 years he had lost some of his sharpness. Firk interjected, 'Wait a minute John, on the record you made in 1928 didn't you play it like this?' and he began to play. John's eyebrows lifted and his eyes were wide. He realized that Wow! These guys mean business. John must have been surprised to see and hear a young white man playing his style and sensed adoration from these disciples. He soon picked up where he had left off and over the course of the next few months became better than he had ever been.

Although Max's account summarizes the events that took place, the detail that John's guitar playing may have been rusty seems suspect, because his rendition of "Nobody's Dirty Business" and other songs that he played on the day of his rediscovery in Avalon was typical Hurt-style intricate finger picking.[26]

In spite of an imposing and magnetic stage presence that would become familiar to his followers, John was a small man, around 5' feet 4"

Figure 3.6. Outside the Hurt family home 1963. Left to right: Jessie, Gertrude Conley Hurt (John's first wife), Jennie Simms (Gertrude's older sister), John, and grandchildren Ella Mae and Andrew Lee. This grouping of John and Jessie along with first wife Gertrude and her sister Jennie Simms is important as it provides evidence that, in spite of contrary views, Gertrude remained close to John and his new family. Mary Frances and other grandchildren who have many fond memories of Mama Dear (Gertrude) at various family gatherings support this view, which was to become important after John's death when inheritances were questioned (see ch. 5). (Tom Hoskins, March 1963, Tom Hoskins Archive.)

and weighing about 130 pounds. With age he had become a little stooped, but he carried himself erectly and with dignity. A long lifetime of hard work and country living had given him a heavily muscled neck, biceps, and chest. Bill Givens reckoned that he was an ideal subject for a bronze sculpture.[27]

Bill Tydings was a non-playing member of the group. He remembers when Hoskins arrived back in Maryland with John Hurt. "John thought he was under arrest when Fang found him—he had never known a white man that didn't lie to him." Soon after he arrived a group of them were sitting having a meal together when John said to Bill, "I never sat down to a meal with white people or slept in a white man's bed before." "He had never dreamed that this would be possible. But he came into a group of people that were different," said Tydings.

Holly Ann Ehrich Ochs MacNamee Henderson was married to Max Ochs during the early 1960s. She spent time with John during his redis-covery years. She recalls John adding to the story of his rediscovery, say-ing that he did not initially believe that people from Washington, D.C., were interested in his music. He did however, know where D.C. was: it was the seat of government, and for some reason he figured he was in trouble with the government. He assumed, therefore, that if he resisted he would be forced to go. He did not want to go. But, he knew he had done nothing wrong and he knew that God would protect him. And so, this good man, bordering on elderly, who had been out of the Deep South only once, got into the car and went with them. In common with just about everyone who ever met John Hurt, Holly was deeply moved in his presence: "The depth and quality of that faith was so powerful that it would touch thousands of people in the few remaining years of his life. I was one of them."

The Contract with Music Research Incorporated

Hastily a contract was drawn up between Mississippi John Hurt and Music Research Incorporated (MRI). The contract covered management and recording and was signed on March 15, 1963, in attorney B. J. Powell's (an old friend and guardian of Hoskins during his teens) office in Washington. MRI manufactured Piedmont Records. The contract was signed by John S. Hurt as artist, Richard K. Spottswood as manager and president, Thos. B. Hoskins as manager and vice president, and Louisa C. H. Spottswood as secretary (see Fig. 3.7). Interestingly, on a number of duplicates of this same contract, Hoskins's name has been erased from the copies.

The contract is printed in full in Appendix 2. It was intended to promote the professional welfare and career of the artist to the mutual profit of both manager and artist. It gave MRI sole and exclusive rights worldwide to represent the artist and covered all types of performances and recordings. The artist agreed to refer to the manager all requests for appearances and services and agreed not to engage any other persons to act in the capacity of manager, representative, or advisor.

The contract stipulates: "As compensation for Manager's services herein, Artist agrees to pay Manager a sum equal to Fifty percent (50%) of all gross compensation received by artist from all sources as the result of Artist's professional activities . . ." It continues: "Artist hereby further agrees to reimburse Manager with respect to any and all expenses Manager may incur on Artist's behalf, but only to the extent of royalties received by Artist." Record sales were to provide $0.15 per record sold to the artist, with the Manager bearing all expenses of the production of records. The contract covered a five-year period from the date of signing with an automatic extension for a further five years, if, at the end of the first term, "the Artist shall have earned a gross aggregate sum in excess of five hundred Dollars, ($500.00)" during the first term. This contract appears to reflect similar terms and conditions to those employed generally in the music industry at that time. However, it was to be seriously questioned in subsequent years.

Attorney B. J. Powell and Tom Hoskins on separate occasions told Denise Tapp that John Hurt had insisted on the fifty-fifty arrangement because he would never have seen any extra money without Tom's help, and all of Tom's friends at that time are adamant that Tom spent most of his share of the proceeds helping John and his family. Tommy also told his sister Suzanne that he had originally suggested that John receive 90 percent while Tommy took 10 percent, but that John insisted on a fifty-fifty split.[28] Stefan Grossman told me that Tom Hoskins really loved John and that he was therefore surprised to see the conditions of the contract. Dick Spottswood said that the terms of the contract were never applied.

An important development in addition to the signing of the MRI contract was the agreement established with Pete Kuykendall of Wynwood Records. Hoskins later testified: "It was an arrangement whereby we could use Wynwood's recording facilities free of charge in exchange for giving the publishing rights of John Hurt's music to Wynwood." The agreement gave publishing rights to Wynwood and provided for 50 percent of publishing royalties to go to MRI.[29] This meant that John would receive only 25 percent of the money made from the sale of his compositions.

The First Piedmont Recordings

With some urgency a recording session was planned, and a long series of tapes were recorded. These tapes were recorded at Sandy Fisher's house in Annapolis by Peter Silitch, Peter Kuykendall, and Sandy Fisher on March 24, 26, 29, and April 2, 1963. Peter remembers John applying kerosene to his fingers because they were sore, having not played guitar for a time. Because of John's nervousness, the tapes were left running during long periods of playing and conversation. Selections from these masters were used for the first Piedmont album, *Folk Songs and Blues* (PLP 13157).[30] On this first visit he also played at the Showboat and the Brick Cellar, two clubs in D.C.

Dick Spottswood described John's reaction to lodging with the Spottswoods in a "lily-white" section of Arlington, Virginia. "He felt quite frightened when he first came here. John was the only Negro for several

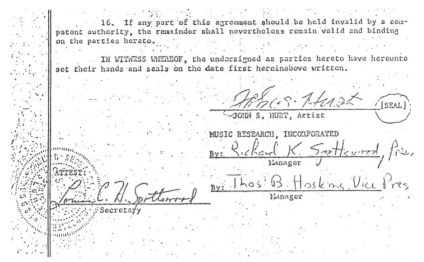

Figure 3.7. Final page of contract between Mississippi John Hurt and Music Research Incorporated, dated 15 March 1963, showing signatures. (Tom Hoskins Archive.)

blocks, but it worked out pleasantly. No one bothered him, so he gradually became accustomed to his new surroundings. He was afraid at first to be seen with Louisa in public places, because down there there's a strict code against that. In Mississippi, the most horrible thing they can imagine is a Negro man and a white woman." Dick went on to describe how John loved parties and how he would play for hours at the drop of a hat.[31]

On March 27, 1963, just over three weeks after Tom Hoskins had rediscovered Mississippi John Hurt in Avalon, and during the period he was recording his first Piedmont tracks, a civil rights march in Greenwood began as a response to the burning down of the Student Non-Violent Coordinating Committee (SNCC) voter registration office and a shooting at the home of George Greene, a SNCC worker. On the march to the county courthouse several African Americans were arrested. As the protesters approached the courthouse, police appeared wearing yellow helmets, carrying riot sticks, and leading police dogs. Some protesters were attacked and bitten by the dogs.[32]

Around this time John was encouraged to write down a summary of his life story, which details some of the events documented in earlier chapters. The document was labeled "Life Record Letter" in John's handwriting (see Fig. 3.8). There is no date or address. It reads as follows, with all writing errors preserved:

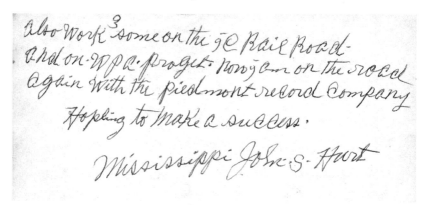

Figure 3.8. Final page of Life Record Letter written by Mississippi John Hurt in early 1966. (Tom Hoskins Archive.)

I was born and raised in the state of Mississippi Born at teoc Miss My mother moved 5 miles north off teoc when I was a 2 or three month old baby still this is in the carroll county Mississippi there is where i grew up to man hood. When I become school age my mother send me to saint James school. Later William H. Carson stardid coating my teacher. he was a guitar picker he would spend the week in night at my mothers home I wasent Alowed to bother with his guitar. I would wait untill he go to sleep. Then I would slip his guitar into my room try to play it.

there I learn to play Guitar at the age of 9 year old. a week after that My Mother Bought Me a second hand Guitar at the price off. $1.50cts. No Guitar has No Moore Buteifuler sound. at the age off 14 I went to playing for Country Dances. Also private homes. at this time I was working very hard on a farm near Avalon Miss. In the years off 28. and 29. I recorded for the OkeH. Recording Company at Memphis tenn. in 28. New York in 29—after that i came back to my home in Mississippi worked hard on a farm. for my licking [?] work on the River with the U.S. Ingnurs [Engineers?]

also work some on the I C Railroad. and on. WPA. project. Now i am on the road again with the piedmont record company

Hoping to make a success.

Mississippi John S. Hurt

The late Jerry Ricks, an African American musician who was very close to John, questioned the validity of this letter, feeling that a black farmer from Mississippi would not use this type of language. While this may be true, it is clear that the letter is in John's own handwriting; perhaps it was dictated or drafted for him? However, from what I have learned about John, I think that this is just what he himself would have written. John says that he is now "on the road again with the Piedmont Record Company" and ends on an incredible note of modesty: "Hoping to make a success"!

John stayed around D.C. for about three weeks. After he finished the tapes Hugh Claudy drove him back to Avalon, probably during the first weeks of April. He was certainly back there by April 22, 1963, when John wrote to Tom Hoskins.

Carrollton Miss. R2 box 60
 April the 22th 1963
 Dear Mr Hoskins i recieve your kind and welcome letter was glad very glad to hear from you it found me ok. hope this will find you the same. Mr Spottswood. Miss Louisa Miss Mariann. Also i hope all is well. Hugh Claudy was a good traveling companion to travell with he was just like a brother. he put me right to my Door. before he left me he was a realy a nice man. I miss you all. i am hoping to be back with you all as soon as i can. Everything is going pretty smooth so far. good to no that the people in Washington likes my music thanks for the compliments Jessie says Hellow to you all. tell bill Hellow Hellow may god be with us all till we meat again.
 By. sincerely
 yours
 Mississippi John S. Hurt[33]

He offers his good wishes to Spottswood, Louisa (Dick's wife at that time), and Marianne (probably Marianne Chandler, who was Fang's girl-friend at the time and who worked for the Spottswoods). She may have become the wife of Phil Lynch, the emcee of the Ontario Place coffee-house in the Adams Morgan section of Washington where John was to become the resident artist.[34] When John asked Tom to "tell Bill Hellow [*sic*]," he was probably referring to Bill Tydings, whom he had met on his visit to D.C.

In an undated recorded interview, Hoskins recalls a visit to Mississippi when he had given John a lift into Greenwood. John rode in the front seat with Tom and was dropped off in town. Tom told John that he would collect him later. As he was about to drive away, a grey car pulled over. "A typical redneck got out and says, 'What do you think your doin' down here drivin' about with a goddamn nigger in the front seat of your car?'

I thought Uh! Uh! I drove off, but they followed me around the town." The four men in the car pursued him. At some traffic lights they tried to get out of the car, but the lights changed and Hoskins again drove off with the men in pursuit. "I thought there's no way I'm gonna handle these four guys." He pulled up at the police station and ran inside, running past the sergeant's desk and into a courtroom. "I went into the courtroom, over benches and chairs, these guys right behind me. They cornered me; all four were right in front of me. They's [*sic*] all slinging punches and I'm getting hit. If this is what's gonna happen, I'm gonna get mine; I saw this one guy's face and Pow! Blood and teeth were flyin.' About that time, the cops came in." The police separated them and sent the four assailants away. The police chief said to Hoskins, "We don't want no trouble." "He lectured me a bit and said, 'You can't go around here doin' this stuff,' and then let me outta the side door." Hoskins drove to where he had left John. "John was waiting. I said, 'get in the car John.' They drove out of town and up the first dirt road they came to. They drove around for a while to make sure no one was following. John knew what was happening."[35]

Mike Stewart recalled that on record-collecting trips with Hoskins they were frequently harassed by the police, on one occasion being told, "Well, Stewart, we don't like your kind around here and if I see you around here again I'm gonna put you in jail and throw away the key." Conversely, black folks were always friendly and Hoskins recalls many incidents of warmth and hospitality offered to him and Mike Stewart in Greenwood when canvassing for old 78 records. They were offered iced tea or lemonade and often stayed awhile chatting. Folks would say, "You boys come in, Ya'll be hungry."[36]

At the time of the intense activity to get John settled into the Washington scene, civil rights events continued to escalate. In Birmingham, Alabama, Martin Luther King and the Southern Christian Leadership Conference (SCLC) were confronting segregation through peaceful demonstrations, rallies, boycotts, and appeals to justice aimed at attracting national attention and encouraging public sympathy. Civil rights leaders anticipated a violent response from Birmingham Police Commissioner Bull Connor to suppress the demonstrations.

They were correct in their assumptions. Police dogs and fire hoses were used to disperse the demonstrators. Martin Luther King was arrested by Birmingham police on Good Friday, April 12, 1963, and thrown into jail. During his stay, white ministers of Birmingham churches urged King to call off the demonstrations and boycotts. This provoked King to write his "Letter from Birmingham Jail," among his best-known writings. On May 3 Birmingham police used dogs and fire hoses on student protesters organized by the SCLC; and 250 were arrested. Within five days 2,500 had been arrested and Birmingham, Alabama, was on the world stage again. The initiative for the Civil Rights Bill emerged from a very worried presidential administration.[37]

On May 4, 1963, John wrote again to Tom Hoskins addressing his letter to Mr. Hoskins and Miss Marianne.

Carrolton Miss Rt2 box60
　May the 4th 1963.
Hellow Mr Hoskins and Miss Marianne hope you all is ok. i am ok Jessie is ok. i am trying to get fix every day to see you all soon as I can I miss you Mr Spottswood Miss Louisa. and Miss Marianne. hope to be back with you all in Washington soon Jessie says she will be willing to live there but wants me to make one moore trip and get everything fix for living there. i would like to live as clost to you all as i could i very glad to no that the Brickskellar and Showboat. wants me back for return engagements. so Kinder look out for me a good place as clost to you all as possible hope to hear from you soon by from yours sincere
　John. S. Hurt[38]
　P.S. havent latch on to a guitar yet but have had the boys Guitar everyday since I got back home
　　Give my love to all

On his visits to Washington during 1963, John stayed with the Spottswoods, and they have many happy memories of the time John spent with them. Louisa recalls teaching John how to use the telephone and how both he and Jessie took to it; when they moved back to Mississippi in 1966, they had two phones installed in their house in Grenada.

On May 27 John wrote again:

Carrollton Miss. May the. 27th. 1963.
Dear Mr Hoskins I recieve your kind and welcome letter was glad very glad to hear from you and Mr Spottswood. i was overwhelome with joy glad off the invitation. to the folk festivals so I will try to be redy so send for me the 15th if I live I will try and be redy so when you send be right there to meat me. Everybody here, both white and black wants some of my records asks me everyday when will they be able to get some of them. i was very glad to hear about the guitars i was just fixing to try to get one from the music house on installment i got a letter from Mr Claudy a few days ago ask me when was i going back to Washington tell all i say Hellow Miss Marrianne Mr Spottswood Miss Louisa. i got

my glasses the next week after i got home they are nice but hevent heard how my chest EXray. Mr tommie please send me your forn No. Might want to call you sometime before i get off to Washington Jessie sends Hellow to all.
Yours sincere. JohnS Hurt PS tell bill Hellow.

John mentions that he is pleased with his new glasses but he has not heard about his chest X-ray. I know of no photographs of, or reference to, John wearing glasses. His reference to the folk festivals was a response to his invitation to the Newport and Philadelphia folk festivals in 1963. The reference to guitars followed being told that the organizers of the Newport festival had decided to buy him a guitar.

Dick Spottswood recalled: "John returned in June [his second trip to D.C. and presumably rather late in June] and we scheduled him into the Ontario Place as the folk musician in residence. We had to have some means of guaranteeing John some sort of steady income in Washington where living costs are much higher."[39] It was probably this trip about which Mike Stewart recalls borrowing Hugh Claudy's large Peugeot car to go and collect John in, and in which John traveled back and slept with his head on Firk's shoulder. Mike recalls that it was a large comfortable car with reclining seats.

The Ontario Place was one of many coffeehouses that had become the in-places to relax, meet girls, listen to music, and presumably drink coffee. The Spottswoods knew Phil Lynch, the emcee there, which presumably provided the opportunity to get John some work. Coffeehouses had provided meeting places for liberals and intellectuals since Café Society opened at 2 Sheridan Square in Greenwich Village, New York, on December 28, 1938. Café Society was a nightclub rather than a coffeehouse; its companion club, Café Society Uptown opened on East 58th Street in October 1940.[40] The proprietor, Barney Joseph, loved jazz and was disgusted by the racism that occurred at nightclubs in 1930s New York City. Café Society was one of the first public places to break down the color barrier.[41]

John Meets Archie Edwards

Archie Edwards, an African American from Virginia, grew up in a musical family and had listened to Mississippi John Hurt records in the 1930s. Archie enlisted in the army in 1941, just prior to the United States' involvement in World War II. He learned to play the guitar in his teens; his father played guitar and had records of various blues singers, including Mississippi John Hurt. Archie recalled that at that time in the thirties, Blind Boy Fuller was really big on the East Coast, and that he would also listen to Mississippi John Hurt records.[42]

Around 1943–44 Archie was stationed at Camp Van Dorn in the Homochitto National Forest near Centreville, Mississippi, on the border of Wilkinson and Amite Counties just north of the Louisiana state line. While there he enquired about Mississippi John Hurt. "In the back of my mind, I knew I would meet Mississippi John Hurt, so I kept picking the guitar." He asked a lot of local people if they knew Mississippi John Hurt, but they didn't know where he was. "Well, some of the old-timers around there knew him, but they didn't know where he was. He has kinda faded out. So I stayed in Mississippi about two, three years, and didn't find John Hurt. I didn't find John Hurt but, I always had it in my mind that I would meet him."[43] It seems unlikely that any of the locals in and around Centreville actually knew John. Possibly they knew of him from his records.

Archie relocated to Washington in the 1950s and bought a barbershop on Bunker Hill Road in northeast D.C. In 1963, having bought a Sunday paper, unread until the following Thursday, Archie saw a picture of a man with a guitar and an article saying that Mississippi John Hurt was playing nightly at the Ontario Place. Archie could not believe that this really was *the* Mississippi John Hurt and called the Ontario Place to ask if it was true. "Well I didn't find him in Mississippi, but I found him in Washington."[44]

Archie told his wife the news and two days later, Archie, who was suffering from laryngitis at the time, went down to the Ontario Place and met John. They hit it off really well and John said, "Well brother Arch, I'll tell you what, we'll get together sometime and when you get so you can talk, we'll play and sing some." Archie and John became great friends and had some good times together. Archie would collect John and bring him to his barbershop. John would sit around and play the guitar while Archie cut a few heads of hair. They played together a lot: "we didn't have to practice together. Anything he could play I could back him on. And whatever I could play, he could back me up on. So we just made a good team."[45]

John frequently offered Archie advice. He told him: "Always keep your hat on. You know back in those days there was quite a lot of jealous guys in the audience and sometimes you have to run. But, if you got your hat on your head and you have to run, you know you left the house with it." Judging by all the photographs and film clips of John, he always stuck by that. Once when Archie had told John that he had an electric guitar and played some rock 'n' roll, John had said, "Brother Archie, rock-and-roll players are gonna be ten cents a dozen pretty soon, so you stay where you are."[46]

Archie Edwards told Barry Lee Pearson that he reckoned Mississippi John Hurt was responsible for much of the folk boom in the sixties. "You could see people coming out of music stores with guitars. You'd say, Uh! Uh! John has done spread an epidemic, you know." Archie suggested that John brought a lot of people out. "John brought out John Jackson, Elizabeth Cotten, Flora Molton, and Ester Mae Scott."[47] Later John was to ask Archie to keep his music alive: "Brother Arch, whatever you do, teach my music to other people." He said, "Don't make no difference what color they are, teach it to them. Because I don't want to die and you don't want to die. Teach them my music and teach them your music."[48] After John's death Archie committed himself to do John's will; his barbershop became a regular hangout for musicians, and it remains so to this day. Archie Edwards passed away in June 1998.

John appeared at the Berkeley Folk Festival in June 1963, along with Joan Baez, the New Lost City Ramblers, Doc Watson, and Almeda Riddle.[49] ED Denson (he uses double capitals in his first name), cofounder of Kicking Mule Records with Stefan Grossman, was a friend of Hoskins and later helped road manage John Hurt. He wrote to Holly Ochs about a phone call he received from Tom Hoskins. The voice said, "Hello ED this is the Fang." ED continues: "so i drive mississippi john and fang to sacramento that afternoon, top down and hot brown hills, furnace, back killing me and offwego [*sic*] spent week with fang and mjh at the folk festival, really dig john hurt."

At this or a subsequent Berkeley festival, Stefan Grossman, who was living in California at the time, remembers driving John down to Los Angeles with Steve Katz to play the Ashgrove. At one Berkeley festival, John was introduced to Lightnin' Hopkins at ED Denson's house. Lightnin' was dressed in a red jacket, yellow pants, and black and white shoes. After they had politely addressed each other as Mr. Hurt and Mr. Hopkins, Lightnin' told John that there was a Mr. Daniels would like to meet him, opening his jacket to reveal a pint bottle of Jack Daniels whiskey. John said that he would be pleased to meet Mr. Daniels and the two of them walked off into the garden and were not seen again for several hours.[50]

While John was getting accustomed to life as a professional musician and establishing himself with his mostly white audiences, racial unrest gathered momentum. On June 11, 1963, John F. Kennedy submitted his civil rights bill to Congress; the next day Medgar Evers, field secretary for the NAACP, was shot in Jackson, Mississippi.[51] John Hurt and thousands like him kept their heads down, having no interest in getting personally involved in the national challenge to white supremacy.

In mid-July, Pete Seeger and a number of other musicians visited Greenwood, Mississippi, supporting the registration of black voters. While in Mississippi they sang at a Baptist church, an NAACP meeting in Jackson, and a large festival outside Greenwood (close to Avalon) at which Bob Dylan and Theodore Bikel appeared.[52] This was an enormously dangerous and courageous activity.

On July 15 and 23, 1963, John recorded the bulk of his entire repertoire for the Library of Congress at Coolidge Auditorium. Most tunes were released and are now available on the double CD, *D.C. Blues*.[53] A few tunes were left out, such as "Lazy Blues," "Nobody Cares for Me," and "I've been Cryin' Since You Been Gone," but these were recorded on the second Piedmont LP, *Worried Blues*,[54] in March 1964. At that time John had not yet learned "Goodnight Irene" from Leadbelly's recording, nor had he written "Boys You're Welcome." Dick Spottswood had commented, "My thought at the time was, Look, this guy could keel over tomorrow. And if he does, it will be a sad and tragic thing. But, it will be a lot less sad and tragic if we have definitive recordings of these songs in place. I was thinking preservation."[55]

Being a shy man, John was always reluctant to sing bawdy material to people he did not know, especially ladies. This is demonstrated at the end of the recording of "Funky Butt." John performs the song, leaving out many of the risqué lyrics and allowing his guitar to fill in the tune. At the end Joe Hickerson, head of the Library's Archive of Folk Song, comments, "I don't think you were singing the whole thing there, John," to which John agrees, with a knowing chuckle.[56] There was another take of the tune in which John did fill in many of the words. When asked to perform Jimmie Rodgers's "Waiting for a Train" John again responds with a chuckle, saying "But I can't yodel," before he plays the tune.[57] He was clearly enjoying the experience.

After a spell at the Ontario Place's Café Gallerie, John appeared at the Newport Folk Festival (July 26–28, 1963) held at Freebody Park in Newport, Rhode Island. Dick Spottswood tells the story. "We stayed in Newport for three days. The funny part of the whole thing was that none of the directors at Newport, aside from Bill Clifton, had ever heard of John Hurt. The critics and writers gave John tremendously favorable reviews at his Newport engagement. When it was all over and we were leaving, Bill Clifton said to John, 'You know, you were the jack-in-the-box of this whole affair.'"[58]

That third Newport Festival was the biggest so far, with reports variously suggesting between 37,000 and 46,000 people attended the four concerts and twenty workshops. Mississippi John Hurt was in good company, sharing the bill with Peter, Paul and Mary, Pete Seeger, Jean Ritchie, Ramblin' Jack Elliott, Joan Baez, and the young newcomer Bob Dylan. Bill Monroe, Doc Watson, Clarence Ashley, the Georgia Sea Island Singers, John Lee Hooker, and Dave Van Ronk also appeared. John's young grandnephew Fred Bolden went along to one of the workshops in the Newport Casino with his Uncle John and Tom Hoskins. "Uncle John played 'Spike Driver Blues' and Joan Baez came over and BAM!!! I fell in love with her right on the spot. Man, the way I looked at her would have gotten me lynched had we been in the South."

John's performances at the 1963 Newport festival were recorded, with agreement, by Vanguard,[59] but not before some wrangling. Maynard Solomon of Vanguard Records had prepared a contract (see Appendix 3), which John signed, agreeing to pay John $50.00 or the going rate of the American Federation of Musicians (AFM) union scale, whichever was greater, for each solo performance released. The contract gave Vanguard exclusive rights to record and sell recordings of all John's performances at Newport 1963 and includes a statement that, "I [Mississippi John Hurt] am free to give you this right and that no prior agreement or performance interfere therewith." A copy of the contract, signed by Maynard Solomon and Mississippi John Hurt, is annotated with notes by Tom Hoskins suggesting that the contract contradicts earlier statements made by Music Research Inc. and that it (wrongly) indicates that John is free to make deals on his own (i.e., without prior agreement with MRI).

John's recorded performances of "See, See Rider," "Stagolee," "Spike Driver Blues," and "Coffee Blues" appear on the Newport album. "Candy Man," "Trouble, I've Had It All My Days," and "Frankie" were also released on the *Blues at Newport* album in 1964.[60]

A host of country blues enthusiasts were at Newport 1963, including Phil Spiro and Eric von Schmidt. John's rediscovery and his appearance at Newport generated a huge wave of interest and excitement. Blues enthusiasts started to seek out more of the old bluesmen. John Fahey and ED Denson sought out and found Bukka White. Fahey, Bill Barth, and Henry Vestine (later of the group Canned Heat) located Skip James. In July 1964, Nick Perls, Phil Spiro, and Dick Waterman located Son House.[61]

These enthusiasts, who would become known as the Blues Mafia, were almost entirely young hippie types, but Stephen Calt cynically claims that they became driven by monetary gain, to some degree based on the knowledge that Mississippi John Hurt was making $200 a week. Calt goes on to recount that Skip James became "enmeshed in business transactions that were quite shameful, thanks to the shamelessness of his assorted sponsors." He refers to John Fahey and other discoverers as mentors "disguised by an aura of pious altruism," criticizing Fahey for calling himself an ethnomusicologist.[62]

The late Philadelphia Jerry Ricks remembered first meeting John at Newport. "Tommy Hoskins introduced us, Tommy was really cool and left us alone talking a while. An audience of over 15,000 people was waiting to hear this new discovery from Mississippi. John walked onstage and said, 'Hi, how ya doin'.' There was a 40 second silence and then a roar. It was like he was saying welcome to my gig." The recording provides the detailed facts of that event. Pete Seeger introduced John, who walked on stage saying, "Good evening people, glad to be with y'all. First little number I'm gonna do ya is 'See, See Rider.'" After the applause died down, John did "See, See Rider" and then introduced "Stagolee": "Do you a little number now, Stagolee, desperado." "Spike Driver Blues" followed, and he finished his set with "Coffee Blues," introducing it with his usual "Maxwell House, good to the last drop." By this time the audience were eating out of his hand and the applause was huge.[63]

John played a vintage Emory twelve-fret guitar with a slotted peg head that was built around 1900. Tom Hoskins initially acquired this guitar from Mike Stewart. Tom then loaned it to John for his Newport appearance. This guitar stayed with Tom for the rest of his life, and he always valued it highly.

It was around the time of the 1963 Newport Festival that the festival directors took John to Marc Silber's store Fretted Instruments adjacent to Israel (Izzy) Young's Folklore Center in New York, to buy him a guitar. Marc Silber, and others including Tom Hoskins and Stefan Grossman, encouraged John to choose an expensive, high-quality instrument and suggested a Martin OM-45. John quietly declined and chose a sunburst Guild F-30 NT. John provided Gene Bush with an interesting account of the time he was offered the new guitar from the Newport festival committee. The Guild was priced at $180 and the Martin at $200; John told Gene that he chose the Guild because he was getting it free and did not want to take advantage.[64]

Sometime between the end of July and August 29, John returned to Mississippi. On August 28 an historic march on Washington occurred. Over 250,000 people participated in the peaceful demonstration aimed at pressuring the Federal government to advance the civil rights agenda. The demonstration culminated in the famous "I Have a Dream" speech by the Reverend Martin Luther King Jr.[65] Tens of millions watched on television.

On August 29, the day after the march on Washington, John wrote again to Tom Hoskins.

> *Carrollton Miss. Rt. 2 box 60*
> *August the 29th 1963*
> *Mr Thomas B. Hoskins. Hellow My friend how are you ok i hope. This leaves me and family all well hope you and family is well and enjoying life. i receive your welcome letter was glad to hear from you but sorrie to hear business aint so good but just as you said in your letter Less stick with it. i haven't told the man that i am fixing to move yet but i will tell him sunday morning. I am making redy every day to get moved. So if i don't get up there I am moving just the same. but i am still looking forward to get up there*
> *O yes should I still be looking to meat my invertation to the folk festival in Philadelphia pa the 6 7 8th of September. let me no by anser soon. yours truly*
> *Mississippi John Hurt*
> *P.S. i got a package here was sent to Backyard sam firk they sent it to MD. in his name. then mail it on to me in my care i tore it open by it being my mail before i noticed his name on it so please get him word for me so i will no what to do about it its 2 oil filter bran new*

The P.S. regarding the delivery of an oil filter to Avalon addressed to Backward Sam Firk c/o John Hurt, reinforces the fact that Mike Stewart had in fact been down there. Why the oil filter was forwarded from Maryland to Avalon is a mystery that even Mike himself could not solve!

Perhaps Stewart and Hoskins went down to collect John? Perhaps this was the trip when Mike Stewart recalls the story of John falling asleep with his head on Mike's shoulder? Whatever happened, John was back to perform at the Philadelphia Folk Festival on September 6–8. He shared the bill with Elizabeth Cotten, Dave Van Ronk, and the Jim Kweskin Jug Band.

The next time Jerry Ricks met John was at this Philadelphia festival. He spotted John and Tommy and thought he would go and say hello. He walked over ready to introduce himself and say that they had met earlier in the year at Newport, when John's eyes lit up and he shouted over, "Hey man, remember me," completely turning the tables. Of course, Jerry Ricks and Archie Edwards were probably the only African American musicians around in John's new circle of friends.

Figure 3.9. Brochure advertising Mississippi John Hurt at the 1966 Philadelphia Folk Festival. (Tom Hoskins Archive.)

Musician John Miller recalls seeing John Hurt perform in the Saturday evening concert at the Philadelphia Folk Festival. The concert starred Mike Seeger, Elizabeth Cotten, Hobart Smith, Dave Van Ronk, and Jimmy Martin and the Sunny Mountain Boys, as well as Mississippi John Hurt. John went on to play at the 1964, 1965, and 1966 Philadelphia festivals. In 1965 Jerry Ricks joined John on stage and played several numbers with him. John Miller recalled how much John had improved during that year.

John, Jessie, Ella Mae, and Andrew Move to Washington D.C.

By September 1963 John and Jessie had agreed to move permanently to Washington. In his letter of May 4 John had said that he and Jessie were willing to move and that he hoped to live as close to Tom and the Spottswoods as possible, and in his letter of August 29 said that he was "making redy evry day to get moved." Dick was unwell at the time and it was decided that his wife Louisa would drive down to Mississippi to collect Jessie, the family, and their belongings. The Spottswoods' home help, an African American lady named Rosalee Coles, expressed a desire to accompany Louisa "to see some history" and they set off together on September 13, 1963. Rosalee had her hair done for the occasion and they sat side by side in Louisa's mother's Chevrolet, pulling a U-Haul trailer in which to transport the Hurts' possessions.

They took the southern route through Virginia, Atlanta and Birmingham, and along U.S. 82 through Columbus and Winona to Greenwood, Mississippi. They were acutely aware of the attention that their companionship might provoke, so during the drive down through Virginia, they ate together in some public places, mainly in Howard Johnson's restaurants, which had recently integrated, but in Alabama and Mississippi they did not go into any public places together. They ordered their food to carry out in some places. Louisa recalled to me the feeling of tension and anxiety while traveling in Alabama.

In Birmingham their anxiety was justified when a local person told them that the folks in these parts did not approve of black and white women traveling in the same car together and warned them of "bad repercussions." Louisa asked, "You mean they would harm women in broad daylight?" He replied in the affirmative, saying, "the women in Alabama are with us on this," or some similar threatening statement. Surprisingly, on crossing into Mississippi, Louisa noted a calmer, friendlier atmosphere.

Following directions furnished by Dick and Tom Hoskins, they arrived at the Hurts' house beyond the Valley Store at around sunset on September 14, 1963. Perkins, the landowner and boss of John and Jessie, appeared. Louisa spoke with Perkins while Jessie and friends loaded the trailer with the Hurts' belongings including Jessie's treadle sewing machine.

Perkins handed Louisa a bill for $89 and some cents saying that the Hurts owed him this money and that he had been to a magistrate who had confirmed that this was a valid debt and that the Hurts could not leave the area until the bill was paid. The bill was for sundry items, but included a $10 payment on a refrigerator, which he had paid when John was sick. The bill included interest charges at 6 percent since the loan had been given. Louisa observed that Perkins actually had a bright red neck, contrary to her previous understanding that this was simply a metaphor for such a person!

Louisa had around $120 in cash and immediately paid the owed amount to Perkins, who looked astonished. She interpreted this gesture as disbelief on his part that anyone could think that John Hurt or his family were worth $89! Louisa had a distinct sense that she was buying them off the land: "Mr. Perkins, I believe viewed it that way as he said that he would never have collected the debt if the Hurts had stayed." Rosalee later told Louisa that Jessie had been so enraged that Perkins confronted Louisa with the bill that she had picked up a shotgun with intent to kill Perkins. Fortunately, Rosalee had disarmed her! John was also enraged when he heard that Perkins had demanded payment of the debt and told Dick Spottswood that Mississippi is "the asshole of the world!"

John had sent gifts of autographed copies of his first Piedmont LP (see Fig. 3.10) for Perkins and Watkins, who worked at the Stinsons' Store. Louisa passed on the gifts. Watkins accepted his, but Perkins would not accept it as a gift and insisted on paying $5 for it. Louisa observed that Perkins did not appear to be angry or hostile, but he seemed determined not to be in debt to the Hurts. He may also have been disappointed in losing reliable workers in John and Jessie. He had been getting John's services for $1 a day as a herdsman and Jessie's for $4.50 per three-day week. The Hurts were also getting $40 per month each from Social Security. That night, Rosalee stayed with a friend of Jessie's while Louisa stayed in a motel in a nearby town, probably Greenwood.

Next morning, Sunday, September 15, 1963, Louisa arose early, breakfasted around 6:00 a.m., and was in Avalon at 7:00 a.m. She arrived to find Rosalee pacing back and forward in front of the little cabin. Rosalee began to laugh when she saw Louisa arriving. She had been told that she would not see Louisa again, but not to worry as they could get Rosalee out of Mississippi! This may have been because Louisa had given a lift to a black teenage boy who wanted to go into town. The youth sat in the back seat and did not speak to Louisa on the journey. It was after dark and no one saw them. Louisa, Rosalee, Jessie, and the two grandchildren were quickly on their way. They drove north toward Memphis, wanting to avoid Alabama on the return journey.

That same day, in Birmingham four young African American girls, Addie May Collins, Carole Robertson, Cynthia Wesley, and Denise McNair were getting ready to attend the Sixteenth Street Baptist church. The girls were dressed in their Sunday best and were preparing to attend Sunday school and appear at the 11:00 a.m. adult service. At 10:22 a.m. that morning, as Louisa and Rosalee with Jessie, Ella Mae, and Andrew traveled east through Tennessee, a bomb blew apart the Sixteenth Street Baptist Church killing the four black children and injuring another twenty people.[66] Since 1911, this church had served as the center of life for Birmingham's African American community. The bomb attack was the work of the Ku Klux Klan. By the end of the day, riots and fires had broken out in Birmingham and another two teenagers were dead. These events shocked the nation and strengthened the civil rights movement.

Figure 3.10. Autographed cover of the first Piedmont album as sent to Mr. Perkins by John and delivered by Louisa Spottswood when she visited Avalon to collect Jessie and grandchildren Ella Mae and Andrew in September 1963. Cover photo is of John playing Tom Hoskins's Gibson J-45. (Author's collection.)

Louisa called home and arranged to have some money forwarded to Knoxville, Tennessee, and Dick informed her of a hotel in Knoxville that accepted black and white groups. The group stayed there that night and was informed that the money was awaiting them at the Western Union office. They collected the money next morning and continued on their way to Washington. Louisa's mother's old Chevrolet struggled through the mountains of east Tennessee and they had to stop every fifty miles or so to put water in the leaking radiator.

Jessie was a little nervous as they drove through the mountains of east Tennessee and Virginia. Neither she nor John had previously traveled out of their home patch in Mississippi (apart from John's recording trips to Memphis and New York in 1928). Rosalee chatted to Jessie, Ella Mae, and Andrew to comfort them on the long journey, as Louisa concentrated on keeping the car going and getting them all to D.C. safely. The party arrived in Washington without further incident. John was quickly reunited with Jessie, Ella Mae, and Andrew (a.k.a. Brother), and within a few days the Hurts moved into an apartment at 30 Rhode Island Avenue NE. The Spottswoods had looked around for a while for somewhere for them to stay before the Hurts selected this one. Dick Spottswood commented: "It was a little run down, but it was clean, roomy, and the lights and plumbing worked. I don't remember how much the rent was, but I recall that it was reasonable." Mike Stewart helped them move in and while moving some furniture into the apartment some of the movers stole some items. Fang retorted, "We'll go after the sons-of-bitches," but John just said, "Well its alright, some folks is just like that."

Fred Bolden's account of the move suggests a lack of concern about the family's welfare.

Moving into that derelict dwelling was a culture shock for him. That neighborhood was infested with murder, robberies, rapes, drugs—you name it. Aunt Jessie gave me a clearer description during the summer of '65, but we had heard Uncle John complain long before that. Personally, I feel better accommodations could have been made. It's true that Uncle John never felt at home with white folks, but if this was someone's idea of placing him among his own kind so as to make him more comfortable, well, it only brought the opposite effect. Already, they were pining again for Mississippi.

Tom Hoskins later said that Dick Spottswood had moved John and his family into this "crime-ridden inner city neighborhood in Washington, D.C." Hoskins had wanted them to live in Takoma Park, Maryland, an integrated, bohemian suburb. "He was miserable being stuck there," said Hoskins, and this added to the rift that was to develop later between Spottswood and Hoskins.[67] In his letter to Hoskins of May 4, 1963, John had asked Hoskins to try to find them a house close to him and the Spottswoods.[68]

Back in Avalon, John's new Piedmont LP was being sold at Stinson's Store. *Mississippi Magazine* reporter Sean Ambrose reported: "A man at the Stinson and Company Store in Avalon had this to say about Mississippi John's long-play album, 'We didn't have any trouble selling them, but I've been listening to him holler for twenty years now, and the $5 looks better to me in my pocket.'"[69]

The family settled into their new home in Washington and maintained a friendship with Tom Hoskins and the Spottswoods. John would sit and talk with Louisa and had mentioned to her that he had been previously married, but little mention appears to have been made of the other side of the family prior to John's death in 1966. The Spottswoods were keen to provide John with a reasonable quality of life and offered to help him attend to his teeth, of which he had very few. They helped him contact a competent black dentist in order to get some dentures fitted. After several visits, the dentist made up drawings and prepared to attend to John. But, eventually John declined to have the work done and Louisa was astonished to hear from John that "the D.C. dentists don't understand that you will bleed to death if you have the work done in the wrong phase of the moon. In Mississippi, such work is done when the blood is in the feet." John never did have his teeth attended to or have dentures fitted.

When interviewed about his past life in Mississippi, John often talked of cutting crossties for the railroad.[70] After he moved to D.C. he became anxious to locate the long-handled axe that had been his longtime companion in the venture. Eventually, after much persuasion, Tom Hoskins called someone in Avalon to find John's axe and ship it to Washington. This they did, and thereafter that axe occupied a prominent position in John's house, presumably reminding him of days gone by.[71]

Civil rights pressures continued. On November 22, 1963, President John F. Kennedy was assassinated in Dallas, Texas. Lyndon B. Johnson, the vice president, assumed office and ensured the passage of the Civil Rights Act on July 2, 1964. This legislation decisively provided an end to any legal support for segregation. By the close of 1963, southern whites were so touchy that any white stranger, especially if carrying a guitar, was suspected of being involved in civil rights activity or at least being pro-black. When John Phillips, later to become leader and songwriter of the Mamas and the Papas," led a Hootenanny Tour into Alabama, he mentioned Josh White and the audience erupted with shouts of "nigger." The tour continued through Mississippi and was associated with riots and violence for much of the time.[72]

Increasing Popularity

During the winter of 1963–64 John's popularity increased enormously, and he was kept busy playing a host of venues including New York's Columbia University, Hunter College, the Gaslight Café in Greenwich

Village, the Second Fret in Philadelphia, Boston's Café Yana, and the Ontario Place in D.C.[73] Artist John Gerakis owned the Ontario Place until it closed temporarily in early 1964, and it was the main focus of John's activities while he lived in Washington. The club reopened later in the year under the management of Bill Givens, founder of the Origin Jazz Library. John continued to perform there for at least one long weekend each month. Eric Park summed up the situation in Washington:

From the moment John was brought to Washington he had been appreciatively taken up by the entire extensive membership of the District of Columbia Folk Song Society who turned out en masse wherever John performed in the area and to whose sponsorship and generous financial support both John Hurt and the Ontario Place management were considerably indebted. John established a close rapport and intimacy with the Ontario Place and its staff and regulars and it was common to see John surrounded by a group of admirers chatting well into the early morning hours.[74]

Ed Ward was at Antioch College in Yellow Springs, Ohio, and heard of a Mississippi John Hurt concert being held a couple of hundred miles away. He and a bunch of his folky pals piled into a car to go and see the show. Ward reports:

We were rewarded by a typically spellbinding show. During the intermission I saw him sitting over to one side, alone, so I walked over to him to tell him how happy I was to have seen him. I guess I startled him: a silver flask was half way to his lips. But he heard me out, and grinned in a way that still warms me when I remember it. Taking the shot glass-shaped cap off the flask, he poured some whiskey into it. "Now, I know you're not old enough," he told me with a wink. "But don't you tell nobody. I'm too old to be getting into trouble." The whiskey burned its way down my throat but I knew better than to refuse. It wasn't an old man giving alcohol to a teenager, it was a communion. And I've kept my promise to him until now. Somehow, I don't think he'd mind.[75]

In February 1964 Dick Waterman, having met John briefly at the previous year's Newport festival, booked him for a week at the Café Yana in Boston. John packed the place for six consecutive nights.[76] Alan Wilson, later to become an important figure in the blues-rock band Canned Heat, was born and raised in Boston and occasionally accompanied John on harmonica at his Boston gigs.[77] Fred Bolden remembers the two of them jamming in his living room in Boston in February 1964, after John had completed a five-day engagement at the Café Yana.[78]

The Second Fret in Philadelphia was well known and booked many famous people in the acoustic blues genre including Mike Seeger, Libba Cotten, Lightnin' Hopkins, Jessie Fuller, Josh White, and Brownie McGhee and Sonny Terry. The late Philadelphia Jerry Ricks booked many of the acts for the Second Fret and recalled that when Brownie McGhee introduced "Backwater Blues," he would always say, "this is a great song about the Mississippi flood.[79] A lot of great things came out of that flood including the great musician, Mississippi John Hurt."

One of the people influenced by John was Dave Van Ronk, who first met John after watching his performance at the Café Yana. After the show they all went back to where John was staying with his relatives at Roxbury (probably grandnephew Fred Bolden's family home) to attend a party aimed at celebrating Uncle John's birthday (probably March 1965). Van Ronk takes up the story. "The family was anxious to make sure Uncle John was shown a good time. I had a good time myself, and much of the evening is a blur, but the last thing I remember is a snowball fight in a graveyard. John was seventy that year [he was actually seventy-two], but he had a high, hard pitch that you would not believe—I think I still have the lump on my head."[80]

Like almost everyone who ever met John, Van Ronk saw John as

The sweetest, gentlest man that ever came down the pike. To get an idea of his personality, you just have to listen to his records, because that is exactly the kind of man he was. In life as in music, he was an understater and a minimalist. Most blues artists deal in intensity, but he dealt in subtlety and nuance. The beat was always there, rock solid, but there was also a lyricism and deftness, and he was very, very easy on the nerves.

John spent a lot of time around the village and seemed to genuinely enjoy hanging out with us. I remember one time somebody was passing around a joint, and it came to John. He looked at it for a moment, and said, "Oh Yeah, I remember this. We used to call it poor man's whiskey." And he just passed it on. He was a delight. One of the odd things about him was that he did not like beds; he preferred a good comfortable armchair. He was the easiest man to put up overnight: "Here John we have a couch." "Oh, I don't need a couch. Say that looks like a great chair . . ."[81]

Maybe John's preference for an armchair gave him some relief from the bronchial condition from which he suffered, probably brought on by a lifetime of smoking.

Dick Spottswood recalled that rediscovered Mississippi bluesman Skip James was an unusual and at times very bitter man and, unlike most people, was contemptuous about John and many other musicians. Much of this contempt was probably because he was much less popular than John. He expressed his views to Stephen Calt: "Guys like John Hurt, and Son [House], you know, they're just shaky. A white could tell 'em, 'Go ahead and put your head in that hole nigger.'" James certainly didn't care for most whites, although he believed them to be more honest than blacks. Like John, he had little interest in the civil rights movement or voting.[82] John seldom showed much interest in politics or bothered to read a newspaper, but Jessie would talk about things. Fred Bolden remembers Jessie talking about Emmett Till's murder, saying that it had happened close to where they lived.

Grandnephew Fred Bolden is the son of Everlene Hurt, the daughter of John's brother Cleveland and his wife at the time, Fannie. Everlene grew up with her aunt Ella and Ned Moore after Cleveland and Fannie parted. Fred was in his early teens in 1963 and his mother had often talked of Uncle John from Mississippi. Everlene had moved from Mississippi to Boston in 1939. John's first visit to Boston following his rediscovery was a time for celebration, a family reunion, and Fred remembers this and many subsequent visits to their home:

"It was in 1963 and Tom Hoskins called us from the Hotel Statler where they were staying. Tom didn't know how to get to our house, so my dad went and picked them up. I'll never forget that moment when he walked through our door. At that point my mom and dad hadn't seen him since 1948 when they had gone down to Mississippi for a weeklong visit. Anyway, I think he must have picked that guitar until around midnight that first night." Fred also remembered his uncle John playing the harp. "He would lounge around our home, he'd take out the harp and blow 'Liza Jane.' Those other harp numbers escape my memory. He used a D harmonica. The thing was very small."

John enjoyed female company and was a huge flirt. Fred Bolden remembers him flirting with Jessie Martin, a friend of Fred's mother. And of course, there are David Gahr's photographs of John clearly flirting with Elizabeth Cotten at the Newport Folk Festival in 1964. Jerry Ricks recalled that Libba enjoyed John's company.

Fred would give up his bed for Uncle John when he stayed and John would teach Fred chords and finger picking techniques on the guitar.

Fred remembers the first songs that his Uncle John taught him were "Chicago Bound" and "Oh Mary Don't You Weep." John played many songs that he did not record, such as "Just a Closer Walk With Thee," "Milky White Way," and "Midnight Special." For breakfast John loved eggs and thick bacon. He enjoyed southern food such as pork, chitlins, and cornbread.

Tom Hoskins brought John to Boston that first time and many times after that, but Jessie never came. "Tom was a nice guy—the family liked him," Fred declared. Later, Dick Waterman also visited their home at the time that he was booking appearances for John Hurt and Skip James. Although Fred's mother knew Gertrude and her side of the family, Fred does not recall her talking about them. His mother Everlene's stepsister Lorenzo (who later married Skip James) and cousin I. T. lived close by, also having moved from Mississippi in the late 1940s.[83] Lorenzo was Cleveland's daughter and I. T. was Hennis's daughter from their marriages to Lillie. Both had grown up with Hennis and Lillie. They would have known all the Hurts living around Avalon.

Apparently John did not often visit Avalon after moving to Washington and was happy with his new lifestyle. His brother Hennis reported in 1964: "Brother John stays gone now, he don't ever be at home. . . . Brother John likes it fine now, he'll never come home again 'cept to visit. He likes it both ways, you know; there's difference in the money and the treatment."[84]

On December 13, 1963, Mississippi John Hurt headlined with Dock Boggs at the Friends of Old Time Music (FOTM) concert held at the NYU School of Medicine Alumni Hall at First Avenue and 32nd Street in New York. Ralph Rinzler, John Cohen, and "Izzy" Young organized and directed the FOTM with much support from Mike Seeger, Alan Lomax, Jean Ritchie, and Sam Charters. FOTM had a major effect in bringing traditional music to a wider audience through the concerts. FOTM organized fourteen concerts of traditional music, including bluegrass, old time and religious music, in New York. These concerts provided exposure for older traditional musicians such as Clarence Ashley, Doc Watson, Maybelle Carter, Fred McDowell, Jesse Fuller, Roscoe Holcomb, and Dock Boggs as well as Mississippi John Hurt.[85]

Stefan Grossman remembers attending this concert. It was the first time that he saw Mississippi John Hurt. "Dock [Boggs] was a tall straight white man—he performed first. John played his set and then Dock came on again. John did 'Funky Butt' and they looked great together—a tall white man and a little black man, both from the South." Stefan was a friend of Tom Hoskins and they (with Rory Block and Marc Silber) went backstage to meet John. "I was playing for them and they were cordial and very friendly. It was a magic concert."

Peter Siegel writes:

The concert by Dock Boggs and John Hurt was an extraordinary event. Mike Seeger, who had recently rediscovered Dock Boggs in Norton, Virginia, hosted the show and accompanied Dock gracefully on guitar. The evening highlighted some striking parallels and contrasts in the careers of Boggs and Hurt. Each had visited New York once before, Boggs to record for Brunswick in 1927, Hurt to record for OKeh in 1928. Each of them was back in New York for the first time in over three decades. When John walked onstage he announced, "So I'm back with y'all once again. And the reason why I say that [is that] in '28 and '29, I recorded for the OKeh Company. And I haven't had the chance of being back to New York until tonight. And I feel kind of like I'm at home." He followed by playing "My Creole Belle."[86]

Interestingly, John frequently referred to recording his OKeh tunes in 1928 and 1929 when they actually were all made in 1928, February in Memphis and December in New York.

Hurt was a black musician influenced by white country artists such as Jimmie Rodgers. Boggs was a white musician influenced by blues artists. Decades earlier, both men had been contacted by W. E. Myer, a Richlands, Virginia, businessman and songwriter who sent song poems to each (see ch. 2). Myer eventually signed Boggs to his The Lonesome Ace record label. Boggs recorded for The Lonesome Ace in Chicago in 1929. The final tune of the evening saw Boggs and Hurt collaborating on "Banjo Clog," in which Dock played banjo and John danced![87]

The huge importance of the Harry Smith *Anthology* and the enormous influence of Mississippi John Hurt prior to his rediscovery comes over strongly as Dave Van Ronk reminisces about the time that he played "Spike Driver's Blues" to John.

I had been playing John's "Spike Driver's Blues" ever since the mid 1950s, and it wasn't until I met him that I realized I had got the basses backward. John and I were sitting around with a guitar one evening down at the Gaslight, and I was playing my version for him, and this puzzled look came over his face. He started watching my right hand, and he said, "You've got those basses backward." And he played me a few measures of the way he did it. It was just like on the record and by god he was right. I said, "Oh, shit, back to the old drawing board." And

he says, "No, no, no. You really ought to keep it that way. I like that."
That's the folk process for you: some people call it creativity, but them
who knows calls it mistakes.[88]

The other Hurt track from the *Anthology* was "Frankie," and similarly, enthusiasts were keen to play it. It was fast and difficult. Van Ronk tells of their efforts to learn it.

It was incredibly fast, though, and after a week or two I dropped by
the wayside. A few persisted, and my friend Barry Kornfield, for one,
disappeared into his chambers and emerged six weeks later, blinking
like a mole, and he had it. Note for note, just as clean and fast as on the
record. When I first saw John at the Café Yana, there he was playing
"Frankie's Blues." However, I noticed that it was a lot slower than on
the record. Of course, he was a good deal older, but it struck me that
it sounded better at that tempo. I wanted to ask him about it, but I
wanted to be as diplomatic as possible—I didn't just want to say, "So,
Pops, can't cut it any more, eh?" Apparently, I was not the first person
to have asked, because John intervened and saved me from further em-
barrassment. He just smiled and said, "Oh, you want to know why it's
so much slower than on the record." I said, "Yeah . . ." He said, "Well,
you know, that song was so long that they had to speed it up to get it all
on one side of a 78." All I could think of was Barry, sidelined with acute
carpal tunnel syndrome.[89]

Mike Stewart reckoned that the tune actually speeds up due to a mechanical problem during the recording.

New York Times music reviewer Robert Shelton provided glowing accounts of John's performances at the Gaslight and elsewhere and undoubtedly contributed to John's success, ensuring packed venues wherever he appeared.[90] Musician Happy Traum recalled seeing John perform at the Gaslight.

After each set (there was usually three a night), a few of us would ven-
ture back to the room that was euphemistically called "backstage" but
was really a corner of the kitchen where the ice cream was kept. We
perched on the freezer or stood elbow to elbow in the tiny space, duck-
ing the steam pipes that traversed the low ceiling. John would sit in a
straight-backed chair, his guitar in his lap and his brown fedora firmly
on his head, amiably chatting and showing us the licks and songs we
asked him about. Always polite and soft spoken, tolerant of the barrage

of questions and seemingly pleased with all the attention he was get-
ting from all these white kids, John Hurt won our hearts. His smile was
warm and encouraging, and his soft brown eyes made us feel an instant
kinship with a man whose life and background we could hardly imag-
ine, much less understand.[91]

Stefan Grossman described him as, the grandfather we all wish we
could have had." Fred Bolden remembers that John would always finish
his performance with a singalong, usually to "Goodnight Irene" or "You
Are My Sunshine." He would then rush down to the exit to thank his audience, shake their hands, and offer autographs.

By February 1964 John had been playing regularly and his compe-
tence had increased enormously. Dick Spottswood commented;

I would like to add something that I know John would never say about
himself. Since the recordings for Piedmont last March, John's fingers
have grown very, very nimble and much less hesitant than the music
you hear on the record. The point of the record was to get something
out quick, and we didn't know John's ability. Each time he has come
back to Washington he has played better and better. Now he is a musi-
cian who is quite superior to the man who made those OKeh records 35
years ago. In this case, age has mellowed and improved the man rather
than taken away. Every time I hear him I want to throw away all the
material in the can and start all over again. Mississippi John Hurt is
rather special in many ways.[92]

Unfortunately, John was forced to withdraw from a tour of Britain
and France with George Wein's Blues and Gospel Caravan in May 1964
due to illness.[93] His withdrawal was too late to change the publicity and
Mississippi John Hurt's name appeared on posters (see Fig. 3.11). Tom
Hoskins recalls that John was given polio injections prior to the trip, and
had a bad reaction to them.[94] Dick Spottswood stated that John had had
a "slight seizure, which prevented him going." The second Piedmont LP,
Worried Blues, was released in May 1964. It was recorded at the Ontario
Place, John's regular venue in Washington, on March 14, 15, and 21,
1964. Mike Stewart remembered a fantastic performance there when
John Hurt and Robert Wilkins duetted. Mike also played the Ontario
Place and accompanied John a few times.

Mike Stewart remembered staying for about a week with the Hurts in
Washington. "I got to eat Jessie's short bread and we drank beer. Jessie
was drunk a lot of the time. John drank 'Old Granddad' whiskey." No

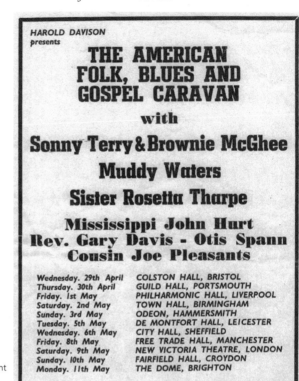

HAROLD DAVISON
presents

THE AMERICAN FOLK, BLUES AND GOSPEL CARAVAN

with

Sonny Terry & Brownie McGhee

Muddy Waters

Sister Rosetta Tharpe

Mississippi John Hurt
Rev. Gary Davis - Otis Spann
Cousin Joe Pleasants

Wednesday. 29th April	COLSTON HALL, BRISTOL
Thursday. 30th April	GUILD HALL, PORTSMOUTH
Friday. 1st May	PHILHARMONIC HALL, LIVERPOOL
Saturday. 2nd May	TOWN HALL, BIRMINGHAM
Sunday. 3rd May	ODEON, HAMMERSMITH
Tuesday. 5th May	DE MONTFORT HALL, LEICESTER
Wednesday. 6th May	CITY HALL, SHEFFIELD
Friday. 8th May	FREE TRADE HALL, MANCHESTER
Saturday. 9th May	NEW VICTORIA THEATRE, LONDON
Sunday. 10th May	FAIRFIELD HALL, CROYDON
Monday. 11th May	THE DOME, BRIGHTON

Figure 3.11. Advertisement for European tour. (Tom Hoskins Archive.)

one ever seems to remember John ever being the worse for drink. Mike remembered that John and Jessie used to frequently indulge in domestic squabbles and Jessie once shot John in the foot. Fred Bolden told me that Jessie would sometimes get very angry with John, especially if she had been drinking. "Uncle John would get on her nerves and she would shout at him, 'If you don't shut up John, I'm gonna put this pan across your you-know-what.' John always backed down." But Jerry Ricks told me that John would whisper, "What's it gotta do with you," out of earshot of course!

Although Archie Edwards and John played a lot together at his barbershop in D.C., Archie's first appearance in front of a public audience was in 1964 when Dick Spottswood had booked him to play along with John Hurt and Skip James. They played at the National Institutes for Health. Skip played first, then Archie, and finally John. John played Archie's Gibson 150.[95] Later, Archie was to acquire a Gretsch resonator guitar for $22.50, which was his pride and joy, and there is a photograph of John playing this guitar at the Ontario Place.

In the fall of 1964, Skip James and John Hurt appeared on a WTBS radio show hosted by Phil Spiro in Cambridge. ED Denson was present and Al Wilson played harmonica.[96] That evening John and Skip were booked to play at the Unicorn Coffeehouse in Boston. Fred Bolden remembers that John was staying with them at the time and was

decked out in a starched white shirt and dark trousers. That was the first time I ever really saw him dressed. It was well known in our family that he didn't care much for dressing up and that trying to persuade him was like trying to corral a circus monkey. Of course he didn't require a tuxedo to play for those that came to see him. Having gone to concerts with him, I can tell you first hand that the hippies in those coffee houses usually came attired in beads, fringes and bell-bottom pants while the beatniks wore those dark turtle neck sweaters along with sunglasses and drank espresso coffee.[97]

At Philadelphia's Second Fret in 1964, John Miller attended a Mississippi John Hurt performance with his brother Allan and a friend. John played two sets and included "Ain't No Tellin'," "Avalon Blues," "My Creole Belle," "Spike Driver's Blues," "Louis Collins," and "I Shall Not Be Moved." Miller remembers being so impressed with John's performance that the trio decided to wait outside the green room to try to tell him how much they had enjoyed his music. John came out; he was gracious and friendly and offered them a cigarette, to which the young John Miller responded that he didn't smoke and was only thirteen years old. Miller later visited a club in Bryn Mawr, Pennsylvania, to see John again. The last time he saw Hurt was at the Main Point in 1965 or 1966 and he remembers thinking that he did not look well and lacked his previous energy.

In mid-1964 the Mississippi Freedom Schools Summer Project, aimed at encouraging the teaching of black history and the philosophy of the civil rights movement to African Americans, was gaining momentum. Folksingers such as Pete Seeger, Phil Ochs, and Judy Collins became involved and traveled through the state singing and holding workshops. The Klan was targeting the Freedom Schools with a firebombing campaign, and the performers were constantly in a state of fright. In spite of over 150 cases of violence and intimidation against black civil rights workers and their white supporters, the federal government did little to stop it until two white civil rights workers disappeared near Meridian, Mississippi. Andrew Goodman and Michael Schwerner, along with James Chaney, a black Mississippian, had investigated the firebombing of the

Mt. Zion Methodist Church in nearby Longdale, which had been identified for use as a Freedom School. The search led to widespread national media attention and huge numbers of federal troops and FBI officers were drafted in to search for the missing boys. Their bodies were found on August 4. The Klan had murdered them on Sunday June 21.[98]

By the fall, the presidential election campaign was in full swing with President Lyndon Johnson running against Barry Goldwater. African Americans had cause for concern as Senator Goldwater of Arizona, who had nationally supported the Civil Rights Acts of 1957 and 1960, opposed the much more comprehensive Civil Rights Act of 1964. Goldwater's opposition, in which he was joined by only four other non-Southern Republican senators, strongly boosted his standing among white Southerners who opposed such federal legislation.[99] In 1964 Goldwater had fought and won a bitterly contested, multi-candidate race for the Republican presidential nomination.

Even with this threat to social progress for African Americans, John was not interested. When Louisa Spottswood asked John if was going to vote in the presidential elections of 1964, he replied, "If I vote for Mr. Johnson, Mr. Goldwater will be mad at me, and if I vote for Mr. Goldwater, Mr. Johnson will be mad at me." Louisa had an impression that John figured that secret ballots were just a rumor designed to get folks into trouble. There seems little doubt as to which side John would have supported and the good grace he offered in not wanting to offend the candidates almost certainly reflected the oppression that had seeped into the souls of southern blacks over a lifetime of white intimidation.

Another grave concern to African Americans was the momentum of the Alabama governor George C. Wallace's campaign for the Democratic party's presidential nomination. In 1962 he had been elected governor on a pro-segregation, "states' rights" platform in a landslide victory. He took the oath of office standing on the gold star where, 102 years prior, Jefferson Davis had been sworn in as president of the Confederate States of America. In his inaugural speech in January 1963, Wallace used the line for which he is best known. "In the name of the greatest people that have ever trod this earth, I draw the line in the dust and toss the gauntlet before the feet of tyranny, and I say segregation now, segregation tomorrow, segregation forever."[100] He lost the battle for the Democratic nomination to Johnson, who won the presidential election in a landslide victory over Senator Barry Goldwater.

If any racism arose or if the subject of civil rights came up, John would register some recognition, but would never get involved in any discussion. Max Ochs reminisced that everyone within the circle of friends seemed to be comfortable in the view that their relationship did not require it. By 1965 it would become apparent that the 1964 legislation was not successfully enabling African Americans to vote. Violence against civil rights activists continued, and the murder of three voting-rights activists in Philadelphia, Mississippi, had gained national attention. On March 7, 1965, peaceful demonstrators were heading for the state capitol in Montgomery, Alabama, when Alabama state troopers attacked them near Selma. The President and Congress were finally persuaded that existing federal anti-discrimination laws were not enabling enforcement of the 15th Amendment, and the Voting Rights Act was enacted on August 6.[101]

John always appeared to be comfortable among black and white people and, as earlier in his dealings with the white folk around Avalon, John was a respected figure even within the constraints of the Jim Crow South. In the North he could get along with anyone. Bill Givens observed that there was nothing, "in John's manner seeming in the least deferential or complaisant [*sic*], nothing beyond the simple country courtesy [that] John extended [to] everyone on sight."[102]

At a later date in New York City, John again exercised his strong commitment to avoid offending people. John was playing at the Gaslight and Dick Waterman informed John that a rival club in the Village was offering to pay double the Gaslight's rate to book John. Dick explained the position, telling him that Clarence Hood, the owner of the Gaslight, was aware of the offer and was keen for John to take it up and earn the extra money. Waterman told John, "It's your decision." John thought for a while and said, "Well, if I was to play this other club and business was poor and Mr. Hood's club was crowded, I would feel badly for my new boss. And if business was good when I was playing and business was poor at Mr. Hood's club . . ." His sentence petered out as he looked at Dick. John stayed at the Gaslight.[103]

Of course, John's old fedora hat became his trademark, and he was seldom seen without it. One such occasion can be witnessed on the silent black-and-white film footage shown at the end of John Miller's video lesson in Stefan Grossman's Guitar Workshop series. John sits playing and singing without his hat on. Grandchildren Ella Mae and Andrew enter the room and sit and watch while Ella Mae plays "air guitar" on the arm of the chair. Later Jessie joins them and Ella Mae does the twist to John's music. Eventually she decides that John should be wearing his hat and brings it to John who pops it on his head and continues to play.[104] John's grandnephew Fred Bolden recalls that Jessie often scolded John for wearing the old battered hat and that he later bought himself a new coal black Stetson, which he wore at the Club 47.

The University of Chicago Folklore Center held its fifth annual three-day festival Friday through Sunday, January 29–31, 1965. The festival was packed with lectures, workshops, and concerts. Mississippi John Hurt appeared in concert on Saturday afternoon along with Robert Pete Williams from Louisiana, Doctor Ross, a one-man blues band from Detroit who was originally from Mississippi, and Avery Brady from Chicago, also originally a Mississippian. The four of them held a blues guitar workshop at 10:00 a.m. Saturday. John also performed at the Friday evening concert beginning at 8:00 p.m. with Robert Pete Williams, the Stanley Brothers with their bluegrass band the Clinch Mountain Boys, cowboy singer Glenn Ohrlin, Nashville comedian and banjo picker Stringbean, and Sarah Gunning, a miner's union organizer specializing in labor songs. John and Doctor Ross appeared again at the Saturday evening concert along with Stringbean, Ohrlin, the Phipps family (Carter family tradition), and the Beers Family, who specialized in pioneer music. The concerts were in the Mandel Hall at 57th Street and University and lectures were in the Noyes Hall on East 59th Street. Admission was $1.50 to the Saturday afternoon concert, $2.50 for the evening concerts.[105]

John continued to play at the Ontario Place and at the Gaslight and he would often hang out at the Kettle of Fish bar above the Gaslight. In his book *The Mayor of MacDougal Street*, Dave Van Ronk provides a tale of John's prowess at arm wrestling at the club, following the consumption of a large quantity of John's favorite drink of Old Grand-Dad Kentucky bourbon whiskey. Sam Hood, Rambling Jack Elliott, and Van Ronk were present. All three were big strong guys and began arm wrestling much to John's amusement. Eventually someone asked,

Come on John, give us a shot. Now, John was a little guy, and damned near as old as the three of us put together, but he plants his elbow on the table, and blam! blam! blam! He throws all three of us. This did not sit well with me. I do not have a sporting drop of blood in my body, and I was damned if this superannuated sharecropper was going to make us look like idiots. But, I figured, look, he just threw these three bohrans; his arm must be tired by now. So, I said, "John, that was just a fluke. We weren't ready. Let's try it again." And, blam! blam! blam! He threw us again. As I remember, he even did it a third time, just to put us in our places.[106]

Dick Waterman tells of another amusing event that apparently happened regularly in the Kettle of Fish. John had established himself as a regular in the bar and whenever John would come in the young waiter,

Tommy Sullivan, would see John and shout to the bartender, "Bourbon, water on the side." Tommy would bring the drink across and put it on the table in front of John. "What is this?" John would say. "That's your usual, John, shot of bourbon with water on the side." John would announce, "my usual eh? Now suppose in the time since I was last here that I was to have taken to drinking something else. That would make that 'something else' my 'usual' wouldn't it?" Tommy was forced to agree and would pick up the drink and ask politely, "Well, Mr. Hurt, What are you going to have?" John would chuckle and say, "Bourbon, water on the side, that's my usual you know."[107]

John Sebastian whose band the Lovin' Spoonful was named after a line in Hurt's "Coffee Blues," recounted the time that he and the Spoonful were playing at the Night Owl Café in Greenwich Village. "We'd be playing to maybe six beatniks. Then I'd go to see John at the Gaslight and the place would be full of those beautiful college girls that we couldn't get down to our little club. All the girls were nuts for John Hurt."[108] John also liked to flirt with the ladies and an entry on the Second Fret website, which aims to collect memories about the Philadelphia club, says it all: "I can't even list all the performers I met while I was there, but the ones I enjoyed the most were—Uncle John—Mississippi John Hurt. He was such a sweet unassuming gentle man and yet he had a twinkle in his eyes for a pretty girl too." It is signed, "Sam the blonde waitress 1963–1967."[109]

Max Ochs was living with his new wife Holly in their apartment on the Lower East Side of Manhattan. John stayed with them twice for a total of around five or six weeks. Firk and Fang had said that John needed somewhere to stay in New York City and asked Max if he could stay with him. Max asked Holly, "Is it OK?" She said, "Sure." Max had played at the Ontario Place himself and had opened there for Elizabeth Cotten. He and Holly had seen John play there and were in the audience when John and Libba shared the billing. John flirted with Libba and Max remembers it being a fantastic evening. They also saw John at the Gaslight in Greenwich Village. Max felt he was becoming a friend of John's. John came to stay.

One night at home, Max, a big fan of Blind Willie Johnson, was playing his own rendition of Johnson's "The Soul of a Man." John sat intently listening. After Max had finished, John said, "Max, I have been thinking about that question you asked, 'what is the soul of a man?' To me the soul is the whole man, it is the body, the soul and the spirit." Max, having never really considered the words of the song he had so frequently sung, was quick to dismiss all this. "Oh yeah, whatever you say John." But this

Figure 3.12. Mississippi John Hurt playing at Ontario Place. (Tom Hoskins Archive.)

had made the lasting impression that John Hurt was a deep thinking and spiritual man.

Holly recalls that when John was staying with them, "No matter how early we woke on a Sunday, John was up earlier, sitting in a chair by the window, dressed in his Sunday best, reading the Bible." Another occasion she remembers:

> *One morning, when I got up to go to work, I wrote a little doggerel verse for him, and left it with his breakfast.*
> *"Just a little bit of sausage—*
> *And a little bit of eggs—*
> *Will fill up*
> *Those hollow legs . . ."*
> *I signed it with a heart. When I came home, he had set it to music, and sang it for me. He had added a chorus all his own:*
> *"Here's my heart—*
> *It's thissaway—*
> *You're just as welcome*
> *As the flowers in May."*

The happiness and relief this brought me was very great. Despite our thoughtlessness, and our failings as hosts, he nonetheless knew how truly welcome he was. Years later, I would discover that he had recorded this song in his Last Sessions album.[110] *He had named it, "Boys, You're Welcome." Tears streamed down my face as I listened to it. After so many decades, his love still touched my soul. There was a special bond between us because he had brought a certainty of God into my life. Whenever he left, he said, "Miz Holly, I hope I'll see you soon. But if I don't see you here, I'll see you there. And I'll say, Wo, Miz Holly, you made it too!!" And we would beam at each other. Then he would head for home, taking for Jessie the gift she had requested. Black stockings. Size Four.*

Tom Hoskins had been present in Max and Holly's apartment when this happened and he recounted the same story during a recorded interview that has only recently (2007) come to light. After Holly had gone off to work, John showed Holly's note to Tom Hoskins and said, "I feel at home now. I'm not worried about anything." Tom added, "He then set it to music and called it his 'Welcome Address.'" John would color his hair with a little hair-black occasionally and during the same interview Tom Hoskins mentioned that when John went to bed he would always put a small towel on the pillow so as not to soil it.[111]

John was always happy to teach people and Max learned many songs from John including "Frankie" and "Pallet on the Floor." "He would slow things down and exercise the utmost patience," Max recalls. One night when Max and John had been up late talking and playing music, Max's last joint was about finished and John's last drop of bourbon was almost gone and they decided it was time for bed. At the top of the stair as John was about to go into his room, he jabbed Max very sharply in the ribs, saying, "Max, did you feel that?" Max replied, "Well sure I felt it." John asked again, "Do you have any doubt that I just touched you?" Again Max replied that he was in no doubt that John had touched him. John answered, "Well, just as sure as you felt that, I can feel the presence of God right here with us in this room. I have no doubt at all that he is here with us." Max thought a lot about this event, realizing that John was concerned for him. He was not preaching religion, but was genuinely concerned that Max was alone without faith or belief.[112]

During John's stay in New York in 1965, Max remembers taking John to appear on the Merv Griffin talk show. John was very nervous about appearing on television. This is perhaps not surprising, as he had never even owned a TV set. Before walking out on the set, he said to Max, "I've forgot all my songs." Max said, "Sing 'Spike Driver,'" the first thing that came into his head, and that's what John did.[113] John also appeared on the Johnny Carson *Tonight Show* where he performed "You Are My Sunshine." Dick Spottswood stated that the event did not go well and that the staff was poorly prepared to work with a performer not experienced at appearing on television. Viewers witnessed a conversation between Carson and Hurt which made it clear that neither understood the other, and the performance was marred by blinding spotlights and an awkward exit.[114] Some years later Stefan Grossman approached NBC in an effort to locate the tapes to find that they had been destroyed to make room in their storage facility. Stefan also tried to track down an appearance on Canadian television to be told that CBC have no record of it.

Holly learned from John that at least one of the men booking his gigs was stealing from him. "John didn't find out about this until he was questioned by the IRS about undeclared income. 'I declared it,' he said, puzzled; 'I declared everything I made last year—all $2,000 of it.' When it became clear what had happened, John simply shook his head and made only one soft comment: 'That one, he's young and wild.' That was all he ever said about it." Sometimes John's agents and managers would also stay with Max and Holly. "Other times they left John, and went somewhere else themselves, coming by in the late afternoon or evening to pick him up for the concerts and coffee house gigs. They brought other aging musicians to stay too—Son House, and Skip James."[115]

Max had relatives who designed and manufactured high-quality garments. During a visit, Max was given a beautiful high-class fur-lined coat, the sort opera singers and wealthy artists wear. Unfortunately it did not fit; it was too short in the arms and he put it away in the closet. Winter set in and it was cold in New York. John had arrived and he was feeling the cold so Max took the coat from the closet and handed it to John. He put it on and it fit him perfectly. Max remembers the huge smile on John's face; he wore that coat everywhere.

John had three very busy years with a fairly constant demand for his appearances. He played many coffee houses, of which the most regular spots were the Ontario Place in D.C., the Second Fret in Philadelphia, and the Gaslight in Greenwich Village. He also appeared at the Unicorn in Boston and the Troubadour and the Ash Grove in Los Angeles, as well as larger prestigious venues that were the locations of some of his greatest performances. These included the Oberlin College concert (recorded by Vanguard as the double album *The Best of Mississippi John Hurt*), the University of Chicago, and Carnegie Hall. Carnegie Hall staged a weeklong festival in June 1965; the opening concert included Hurt plus Son House, Muddy Waters, and Chuck Berry.[116] John received a standing ovation from a standing-room-only crowd of 2,000 people who absolutely adored him.[117]

John appeared at the Newport Folk Festivals of 1964 and 1965 (when Bob Dylan caused upheaval in the folk world by playing a Fender Stratocaster). In 1964 Dylan, Peter, Paul and Mary, Judy Collins, Tom Paxton, Skip James, Jean Ritchie, Jesse Fuller, Muddy Waters, and Johnny Cash appeared. Tom Hoskins was present during one of these Newport Festivals when Bill Tydings had conveyed John and Jessie along with Skip James and Fred McDowell and their wives to their accommodation. It was the first time they had all been together and they all started to sing gospel songs. "We were all sitting listening, when along comes Bob Dylan. This guy is fried; he's been up for six days. He goes to the piano—he has no idea what he was doin.' We looked at one another— picked him up by the elbows and carried him out!"[118]

During the period of John's engagements at Carnegie Hall he stayed with Max and Holly Ochs. Holly looked forward to John's visit, but she was concerned that she should be studying for her art history final exam next day. "It was study or fail, and all my life, academic failure had not been an option." Of course, when John returned from the evening concert he wanted to talk. "He felt happy, and expansive, and there was no way I could excuse myself, even if there had been a private place in our tiny apartment. So I sat at his feet and we talked."

Holly recalls the deep emotion and spirituality of the ensuing experience:

I never remembered exactly what he said that night that made the world shift, but it was something very simple—as simple as "God is love." Whatever it was, it woke my soul. I heard him, and when I looked into his kind, loving face, what I saw was God. "Who are you?" I asked wonderingly. But he just smiled. "Tell me more," I said. We talked all night, and in the morning, totally relaxed, freshly baptized into a new world, I told him about the exam, and how I had worried about it, which now seemed endearingly silly. "Miz Holly," he said quietly, "What you need to know ain't in them books."

I took the exam the next morning, cheerfully failing it, and then went to the registrar's office and tranquilly filled out papers for a leave of absence. I had been a student at four colleges, and it was more than enough. John was right. What I needed to know was not in those books. I was through trying to find meaning in my parents' assumptions about

*essentials. I made a private vow that unless the lack of degrees barred
me from something truly important to my life, I would not pursue them
anymore. Since that never happened, I never went back. On Sunday
I took a subway to Harlem and went to church. The congregants were
baffled but accepted me kindly.*

In spite of the apparent popularity of folk music in the early 1960s,
David Evans reported a different angle, recalling that John Hurt was
the people's favorite. "Frankly, there just wasn't that much interest in us
[referring to himself and his friend, Al Wilson, later to become famous
as a member of Canned Heat] or in any of the blues artists really, except
Mississippi John Hurt. He would always draw a good crowd. I remember
many times going to see Son House or Skip James and there'd be fifty
people or less, often quite a bit less. It was depressing that this music
wasn't catching on, wasn't turning people on the way it had turned us
on."[119]

Similarly, as Dick Spottswood reported, "Hurt's delightful demeanor
both onstage and off endeared him to the folk crowd nationwide over the
next three years in greater measure than some of his rougher edged fellow rediscoveries."[120] Of course this popularity seriously irritated some of
these fellow rediscoveries and Dick Spottswood recalled: "He [Hurt] had
a certain magnetism that appealed to people. I know it drove Skip James
crazy because John was a star and he wasn't."

Pat Sky told me that Skip was angry with all of the attention that John
was getting; he didn't consider John a serious blues artist, but John impressed audiences. Dick Waterman wrote to Stephen Calt on October
16, 1966, in which he strongly emphasized the fact that appearances by
Mississippi John Hurt made money whereas Skip James's did not.[121] Stefan
Grossman once took John to meet Reverend Gary Davis at his home
in the Bronx where they all played music together. Later the Reverend
Davis dismissed John Hurt's guitar playing as "old time picking"—which
of course it was.

Whenever John played in Philadelphia, frequently accompanied by
Skip James, he would lodge with his niece Mrs. Lorenzo Meeks. Louisa
Spottswood recalled that John enjoyed his spells in Philly and would often linger awhile after engagements. Louisa had an impression that he
was treated rather better there than at home with Jessie and he had his
hair dyed black and began to dress rather more jauntily. Lorenzo was
one of the family of Hurts from around Greenwood, Mississippi, who
moved to Philly in the 1940s to do domestic work. In the 1960s Lorenzo
did part-time work as an Avon sales lady. In the summer of 1965, Skip

James left his wife Mable and took up with Lorenzo. Lorenzo lived with her stepsister Tee (I. T.) and her daughter and son-in-law at 5634 Pearl Street. In April 1966 Skip and Lorenzo moved to a ground-floor apartment at 5274 Jefferson Street in West Philadelphia.[122]

Tom Hoskins or Archie Edwards would drive John and Skip up to Philly. Sometimes they would all (Jerry Ricks, Tom Hoskins, John, Lorenzo, and Skip) go further north and spend some time relaxing at a cabin by a lake. They would drink and play music and clown around. Jerry recalls that "John was a lot wilder without Jessie, he would sing all the real spicy lyrics to his songs and dance about."

John's popularity increased, especially following articles in the *New York Times*, but the fame did not change him. He had an incredible ability to stay cool, even when, as Jerry Ricks remembered, girls would ask him to sign their T-shirts! Jerry puts this nonchalance down to the fact that unlike others, John was very comfortable with who he was; "He wasn't a professional musician and he didn't quit anything to do this. He had no baggage and no frustrations and he didn't want anything. At big concerts, when introducing a song, he would often twist around the microphone and chat to the people in the front row as if he was sitting in their living room. Maybe that's just how he felt?" He certainly did not appear to recognize audience pressure; in fact he seemed more nervous when recording than when he was in front of an audience.

By mid-1964 John was hugely popular and was greeted by large audiences wherever he played. There was increasing pressure to release his second Piedmont album that had been recorded back in March at the Ontario Place. John was having a good time and enjoying his newfound fame, but trouble was brewing in the background.

4. Management Problems and the Death of Mississippi John Hurt

Developments within Music Research Incorporated

In spite of John's increasing popularity and success, there was unrest at Music Research Inc. (MRI). It appears that the Spottswoods were becoming increasingly dissatisfied with Tom Hoskins's management approach and arguments were occurring over the release of the second Piedmont album, *Worried Blues*.

The MRI share allocation was Dick Spottswood 50 shares, Tom Hoskins 50 shares and ED Denson 25 shares. Dick Spottswood was president and Louisa Spottswood was non-shareholding secretary of the company. At a meeting of the shareholders on August 17, 1964, ED Denson joined the other two as a director of the company.[1] Soon after this a communication difficulty arose and a meeting was held on September 3. The minutes state that Tom Hoskins was now president of the company. Only Tom Hoskins and ED Denson were present at the meeting and the recorded minutes (written by ED Denson in Louisa's absence) indicate some difficulty in communicating with the Spottswoods and state that Louisa Spottswood had indicated that neither she nor Dick would attend the meeting.[2]

A discussion followed that focused on the neglect and absence of the corporate books, and ED Denson suggested, "The Company was suffering severe damages at the hands of the Spottswoods." They then established a chronology of events leading up to the present position. This proposed that, around July 15, the Spottswoods had expressed a wish to "get rid of" Mr. Thomas B. Hoskins. On August 5 the Spottswoods told Hoskins that the corporation needed to take out a loan, but Hoskins was reluctant to do so and asked to see the balance sheet so as to decide whether a loan was necessary. The Spottswoods assured Hoskins that they did need to borrow but did not present the accounts. Louisa Spottswood claimed that the corporation was in debt and owed ten to twelve thousand dollars, but the books had not been updated since December 31, 1963. Hoskins and Denson said that they did not approve the release of the second Piedmont title (*Worried Blues* PLP 13161), indicating that it required either remastering or withdrawal, and it was agreed that no copies would be released until a decision had been agreed.[3]

After returning from the Mariposa Folk Festival around August 13, Hoskins and Denson visited the corporate offices to find that 500 copies of *Worried Blues* had been shipped to reviewers and distributors. According to the minutes of the meeting, Dick Spottswood said it was now too late and nothing could be done about it. The minutes go on to state that on August 17, Louisa Spottswood agreed to present the updated books within two days and that Tom Hoskins ordered that no further financial transactions should take place until the financial status of the corporation was clear. Assets were considered to be around $1,000 with a further $2,000 of income pending. In an effort to conserve funds and prevent further debts accruing, Tom Hoskins proposed that all salaries be suspended. An ensuing negotiation resulted in an agreement that Tom Hoskins and Dick Spottswood would work for nothing until the financial situation was clear.[4]

Further complications occurred throughout August in which Bill Barth, who was managing Skip James, called the Spottswoods crooks and a physical altercation involving Louisa Spottswood and ED Denson ensued. A suggestion to move the offices away from the Spottswoods' home was resisted by the Spottswoods, and on August 26 Denson and Hoskins found the house locked up and the Spottswoods gone. Eventually Denson and Louisa Spottswood met at a restaurant in downtown Washington on September 1. No agreement could be reached on the future of the company and the updated accounts were still unavailable. Mrs. Spottswood promised to present them on September 3. At the meeting on September 3, which the Spottswoods did not attend, a decision was reached that the Spottswoods were unfit to hold office and their positions were declared vacant. Tom Hoskins remained as president, and a vote resulted in the appointment of ED Denson as executive vice president and John A. Fahey as vice president with Denson as secretary and Hoskins as treasurer. The new board then informed the Spottswoods of their decision and requested them to hand over all corporate property, including stocks of records, files, corporate books, etc. They informed their lawyer but stated that they wished to avoid any legal action if possible.[5]

That was not to be, and on October 23, 1964, the assets of the company were sold at auction for $10,000 to Dick Spottswood. These included the contract of March 15, 1963, between John Hurt and MRI, as well as contracts with Skip James, Bukka White, Reverend Robert Wilkins, Jolly Joe's Jug Band, and K. O. Asher Inc. Two ten-inch, forty-four seven-inch, and eight master tapes of Mississippi John Hurt were included as well as the stock of existing Piedmont records.[6] Tom Hoskins was legally prevented from having any contact with John Hurt.

A further shareholders meeting of MRI, which was now without assets, was called by Tom Hoskins on November 18, 1964, to discuss the proposed resolution to declare vacant the directorship of Dick Spottswood. The three directors, Hoskins, Denson, and Spottswood, were present along with Louisa Spottswood, Michael A. Schuchat, counsel for Spottswood, and William J. Powell, general counsel for MRI. A motion to remove Spottswood was upheld and John C. Coffman was appointed to the existing vacancy.[7]

During January 1965 Dick and Louisa Spottswood, trading as Spottswood Music Company Incorporated, negotiated with Herb Gart, John's business manager, alongside Tom Hoskins who was John's personal manager, in order to secure a deal for four Mississippi John Hurt albums with Mercury-Philips Records, which would be worth an immediate advance of $12,500. Gart began searching for and discovering musical talent in 1962 and subsequently was involved in the discovery and management of some big names, including Don McLean and Buffy Sainte-Marie. What happened next is a little unclear, but on April 28, 1965, the Spottswoods informed various companies that they had "no further interest in" various items including master tapes, "which are now the property of Music Research Inc."[8]

All became clear with a letter from William J. Powell, general counsel for MRI, on June 30, 1965, notifying interested parties of the current status of MRI. This letter declared that the suit between Music Research, Inc v. Spottswoods had been settled pursuant to a Settlement Agreement dated April 21, 1965. All property previously sold on October 23, 1964, was returned to MRI, now under the sole direction of Tom Hoskins, with neither party conceding liability or fault.[9] Presumably, as part of the deal, the Spottswoods were repaid their $10,000. Dick and Louisa Spottswood Coughlin later confirmed that, during the summer of 1964, disagreements arose within MRI that led to litigation. The litigation was settled in April 1965, with Tom Hoskins in control of MRI. The Spottswoods continued in the record business, trading as Spottswood Music Company, Inc.

Throughout this period John continued to perform in his usual venues but he was clearly troubled by the arguments and legal battles. On one occasion when John was working in Boston, Fred Bolden recalls his uncle becoming very distressed and telling them of the legal proceedings that were coming up in the near future. "That was the first time I saw him [Uncle John] cry. My mother was outraged." They took John to the Boston City Hospital where he was checked over and returned home with them. Fred does not recall any diagnosis being made.

Later, MRI merged with Takoma Records, which had been run by ED Denson and Gene Rosenthal, who managed Skip James and Bukka White. These performers were added to Piedmont's roster of Robert Wilkins and Mississippi John Hurt. The new company was called Bullfrog Records. On November 30, 1965, John and Herb Gart signed an agreement with Maynard Solomon of Vanguard Recording Society Inc., giving Vanguard sole recording rights to record two LPs. The contract was to last until January 31, 1967. Royalty payments for John's services provided for 5 percent of 90 percent of retail sales with a nonreturnable payment of $2,000 per LP within thirty days of completion of recording.[10] Notably, the contract was for only two LPs and Tom Hoskins, John's personal manager, did not sign it; these were to become important issues in a subsequent lawsuit (see ch. 5).

Enter Dick Waterman

Dick Waterman first saw Mississippi John Hurt at the 1963 Newport Festival. Along with Nick Perls and Phil Spiro he had helped locate Son House, and the three of them were signed as House's managers. Spurred on by his role in finding Son House, Waterman was staying at the Henry Hudson Hotel while attending the New York Folk Festival in 1965, and in the bar of the hotel he established Avalon Productions, a management and booking agency to be located in Cambridge, Massachusetts. He purported to act on behalf of the artists to give them a fair deal and book them the most lucrative gigs. He subsequently represented Bukka White, Skip James, Libba Cotten, and Sleepy John Estes.[11] Waterman appears to have gained a reputation as being tough, and Stephen Calt was very critical of his management of Skip James.[12] However, Mark Greenberg knew a lot of the musicians and told me that Dick took good care of his people and that he never heard a negative word from anyone handled by him. David Evans stated that Waterman would always negotiate good rates for the musicians he represented. Perhaps his negotiating skills helped him gain this tough reputation.

By the middle of 1965 the folk revival was waning; the breakup of the New Christy Minstrels was a sign to many, including country musician John Denver, who said, "I knew that was it, the folk music movement of the sixties had passed into the history books."[13] Much later, Dave Van Ronk, reminiscing on the days of Lightnin' Hopkins, Skip James, and John Hurt, said, "that is one reason that I tend to cock a jaundiced eye at the recurring rumors of another folk revival . . . we simply do not have the deep sources of talent that we had in the 1960s. Unless we can hatch another generation like Gary, Skip, and John, or John Lee and Muddy Waters, the quality will be sadly second-rate—and the world that produced those people is long gone."[14]

John was immersed in his new career and did not wish to become involved in civil rights issues, but it was difficult to avoid the increasing activity and news coverage being provided. Some musicians were actively supporting the civil rights movement. In Mississippi, 44-year-old Fannie Lou Hamer, the daughter of a black sharecropper from Sunflower County, Mississippi, became a significant leader in the civil rights movement. She formed the interracial Mississippi Freedom Democratic Party (MFDP) after she realized that she had a right to vote, went to the courthouse to register, was dismissed from the plantation because she refused to give up her right to register, and there was an attempt to murder her. In Winona, just a stone's throw from Carrollton, she received a brutal beating that left her permanently injured.[15] Fannie Lou Hamer appeared on stage at the 1965 Newport Folk Festival on July 25, two days after Mississippi John Hurt's appearance (see Fig. 4.1).

In the fall of 1965 Mississippi John Hurt was back in Chicago. David Wexler, president of the University of Chicago Folklore Society, booked John for a concert. By this time Dick Waterman had convinced Tom Hoskins that he could find some well-paying gigs for John, and this was one of them. The concert was set for 8:15 on the evening of Friday, October 29, 1965, in Mandel Hall.[16]

During his week in Chicago, John stayed at Mark Greenberg's apartment on Chicago's South Side. After the concert, which was a huge success, John was invited back to a party at Mark's apartment. David Wexler came to pay John his fee. The arrangement was for a percentage of the door receipts plus a fixed fee of $400. The percentage money was paid to John in cash and he was handed a University of Chicago check for $400. John looked carefully at the check and said, "This check, it's good?" David replied, "Yes, its good, this is the way we do it. This is a major

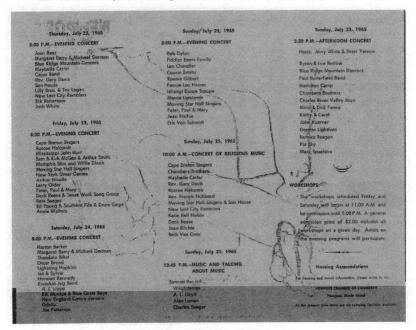

Figure 4.1. Flyer for the 1965 Newport Folk Festival. (Tom Hoskins Archive.)

university—it's a good check." John replied, "Do you have checks?" David said that he did and so John asked if he would take back the University of Chicago check and give him one of his own personal checks. David replied that he could do that, but there really is no difference. John replied, "Well, there is one difference, I got your phone number." David wrote him a personal check. Dick Waterman tells a similar version of the story where he claims that he wrote the check for John.[17]

Mark remembers a party during John's stay, probably on the night of the concert, when a bunch of students and musicians were sitting around chatting, smoking, and drinking in the living room. John was sitting quietly with a smile on his face. Suddenly Son House entered the room clutching a brown bag containing a bottle of spirits. He appeared a little the worse for wear. He stood opposite John and began preaching. Quiet descended on the room, apart from the loud sermon that was being delivered. John listened attentively and began interjecting congregational responses, "That's right" and "yes, that's right." Also during this stay there was a massive power blackout, and Mark remembers sending Dick

Waterman and John Hurt out to buy some candles! Mark remembers that John would sit around playing his guitar all day long.

In December 1965 a second festival, led by former SNCC civil rights activists Sam Block, Willie Peacock, and Willie McGhee, was held in Greenwood, Mississippi. Mississippi John Hurt seemed oblivious to the continuing civil rights struggles in his homeland. However, Fred Bolden remembered some talk of civil rights issues and said that John and Jessie were wholeheartedly in favor of what Dr. King was trying to do, but that they were deathly afraid to participate in such events. He recalled, "No doubt, Aunt Jessie and Uncle John had heard about Cheney, Goodwin, and Schwerner the year before, not to mention the Meredith affair at 'Ole Miss.' I can tell you that Uncle John had a positive attitude about the racial changes taking place in the South. He said to me once, 'Freddie, the chickens is comin' home to roost.' And he laughed."

Return to Mississippi

By 1965 John and Jessie were homesick. They became increasingly ill at ease with life in the unsavory part of Washington and were not keen for the grandchildren to be raised there.[18] John told his grandnephew Fred that he hated the house in D.C. and wanted to move back to Mississippi. Sometime around late 1965 or early 1966, John and the family moved back to Mississippi; Fred Bolden recalled that they had moved to Grenada by the time of John's seventy-fourth birthday on March 8, 1966. They stayed a while with family friend, Ms. Kitty, who had previously lived in Avalon before moving to Grenada. Ms. Kitty helped them find a house to rent at 1 North Levee Street in Grenada. She remembers sitting with John and Jessie talking about the old times in Avalon. The house was simple but comfortable, situated north of the railroad track adjacent to the Yalobusha River. The neighborhood was later demolished and the area is now covered in developing woodland. After John and the family moved to Grenada, John made one final visit to Boston in April 1966 to perform a three-day engagement at Club 47, for which he made $300. He was hired for another gig at the Turks Head on Cape Cod in June or July, but did not show up. Fred called John in Grenada, and John said, "I been real sick, Freddie."

John wrote to Joel Jacobsen from Grenada on March 15, 1966. Jacobsen was the man who made the silent film clips of John with the family at the house in Washington. In the letter John reports that Andrew had been sick, "not serious," while John himself, had "been very sick but lots better now." He also reports that he had not seen Tom Hoskins since Christmas. He finished by saying that he intended to get back to D.C. as soon as he felt able.

Grenada, Mississippi. Mar 3. 15 1966
No 1. N Levee st.
Hellow Mr Jacobson. how are you and family ok. i hope. This leaves
us some is well some is not. Jessie and the Little Girl is ok. Me and the
Little boy is sick. Not seris. i have been very sick but Lots better now.
hope to be ok in a few days. that bad weather did Reach me and family
it was tough a plenty one while but we have spring weather here now.
i dont ever see tom. To ask him anything haven't seen him since Xmas.
dont no where he is but guess i will see him when i gets back up that
way. and i will ask him. about that buisness if i see him. Will be up that
way soon as i feals able to travle. and I hope that wont be to Long. hope
you will make a Great success in your buisness
  John. S. Hurt

Jerry Ricks said that in early 1966, Jim Snow, son the of famous auto-harp player Kilby Snow and a big fan of Mississippi John Hurt, made a handmade guitar for John. I have not been able to trace this instrument, nor have I seen any photographs of it. Another custom guitar came to John through a student of Allan Miller, brother of John Miller, the musician and tutor of the Mississippi John Hurt video lessons,[19] who taught Jack Alderson to play guitar. Jack idolized John Hurt and decided he would make a guitar for him. The guitar had a mother of pearl bar at the twelfth fret which was inscribed "Mississippi John Hurt" (see Figs. 4.4, 4.5).

The Vanguard Recordings

In February 1966 material for three Vanguard studio albums, destined to become *Mississippi John Hurt Today*, *The Immortal Mississippi John Hurt*, and *Last Sessions*—later released together as *The Complete Studio Recordings*—was recorded at the Manhattan Towers Hotel in New York. Additional tracks that went onto the *Last Sessions* album were recorded in July at Vanguard's 23rd Street studio. John played Stefan Grossman's Martin OM-45.

Pat Sky produced these sessions rather by accident and remembers that he was invited to attend the sessions by John, who was staying at his New York apartment at the time. Pat wandered down to the studio

Table 4.1. Guitars that Mississippi John Hurt played	
Period	Guitar
ca. 1905	Black Annie (a Stella?)
ca. 1950	Harmony Stella (photo 1950s)
Early 1963	Gibson J-45 (belonged to Tom Hoskins)
Early 1963	Emory 12-fret slotted peghead (originally belonged to Mike Stewart, then Tom Hoskins)
Early 1963	Gibson/Harmony/homemade 12-string (belonged to Peter Silitch)
Later 1963	Guild F-30 NT Sunburst. Now located at the Denver Folklore Center, Denver, Colorado
1964	Gretsch Resonator (belonged to Archie Edwards)
1966	Martin OM-45 (belonged to Stefan Grossman)
1966	Custom (made by Jim Snow)
1966	Custom (made by Jack Alderson)

around forty minutes after John arrived and found John sitting having a cigarette while people stood around arguing over how the sessions should be managed. Maynard (Mannie) Solomon, head of Vanguard; Herb Gart, who managed Pat Sky; Buffy Saint-Marie and many other artists; and Tom Hoskins were there. Pat approached Mannie and asked, "Would you like to get a really good recording out of John?" He said, "That's what I'm here for." Pat replied, "Well, why don't you make me the producer?" He said, "All right, you're the producer." Pat continues the story, "I immediately ordered everyone out of the studio. When they resisted, I said, 'Just get the hell out of here.' I ran them all out. I got a bottle of whiskey, turned on the tape recorder and we made the records for Vanguard."

Pat Sky played second guitar on "Waiting for You" and "Good Morning Carrie" on the *Last Sessions* album. Jerry Ricks was present during some of these sessions and accompanied John on some of the tracks included on the *Today* album, but he was not acknowledged in the cover notes. Pat Sky had first met John in 1964 or 1965 at the Philadelphia Folk Festival. "We hit it off, partly because I was from the South and understood southern culture." Pat was a performer in his own right and supported John at the Second Fret and the Main Line. Later, on a few occasions, John stayed at Pat's New York apartment. Pat remembers offering John a tour around Manhattan on his motorcycle. After the trip John got off and Pat asked, "What do you think? Did you like it?" John looked pleased and exhilarated, and replied, "It was really great, but I don't ever want to do it again."

"We would eat out around Manhattan a lot and drink together. John was a serious drinker and loved bourbon whiskey. He didn't need much sleep and could sit up until three or four in the morning and be up again at seven." He enjoyed life to the fullest and would say to Pat, "Don't die until you're dead." Pat recalled a discussion they once had about flying. John had recently flown for the first time and did not like it at all. Pat tried to reassure him, saying that it was a pretty safe means of transport and adding, "Anyway, when it's your time to go, it's your time to go." John thought a while and answered, "Yes, but what if you're on the plane and it's the pilot's time to go?"

John did fly on a number of occasions, but was never too keen on it. On one flight to California the movie malfunctioned and a stewardess, who had noticed John and Tom Hoskins boarding with guitars, asked if they would entertain the passengers. They were happy to oblige and so the legendary Mississippi John Hurt played country blues while cruising over the Rocky Mountains. As John put it, "We had a regular hootenanny up there!"[20]

Dick Waterman continued to take an interest in John Hurt and asked Tom Hoskins if he could book him. Hoskins responded saying, "You can book John Hurt if you can get things that will pay highly and with a reasonable schedule. If you can do that you can write and let me know." Hoskins continued:

> But Waterman went behind my back and set up little concerts. I told John, "this isn't working. You go home and don't worry about a thing." I was playing in a band and I went off to North Carolina. I called John at home in Grenada. Jessie answered the phone saying, "John's not here, he's gone with Mr. Waterman." I got in the car and chased him through Ohio and Connecticut [Waterman was managing the Oberlin College and University of Cincinnati gigs]. If I'd have caught him I don't know what I'd have done, but he would not have liked it! He took John when John did not want to go—he couldn't say no. John was sick. [This clearly was the case; see John's letter to Joel Jacobsen above.]

After the event, John said to Hoskins, "Don't ever let anyone come down here and take me again."[21]

Tom Hoskins had taken John up to New York for the Vanguard recording sessions in February. "For this, I got big advances, which I gave to John. He had enough money for ten years or so. He was set. We had recorded everything John did. We didn't need for him to do anything more, but Waterman wouldn't let him do that."[22]

The concert at Oberlin College was booked and arranged by Dick Waterman for April 15. The live performance was recorded for Vanguard by Robert Scherl and was later released as *The Best of Mississippi John Hurt*. (Interestingly, vinyl albums and CDs of this concert wrongly state that the recording was made on April 15, 1965.) This recording was in breach of the MRI management contract, and Tom Hoskins and Gene Rosenthal successfully challenged Vanguard over its release of the material after John's death (see ch. 5).

At the concert, Son House played two sets in the first half, and after the intermission Dick Waterman went on stage to introduce Mississippi John Hurt. Assuming that John was waiting, ready to come on stage, Dick gave a stirring preamble about what a fine musician John was and announced, "Ladies and Gentlemen, Mississippi John Hurt!" But, John did not appear. Dick ad libbed talking about John's origins in Mississippi and what a sweet man he is, but still John did not appear. Dick suddenly spotted John sitting in the front row of the balcony where he had sat and listened to Son House's performance. Dick called out, "John, You have to come down here and play." John rushed down the stairs and onto the stage. His performance was superb, as anyone who has listened to this recording will surely agree.

After the concert, Dick asked what had happened that John was sitting up in the balcony like that. John replied, "Well Dick, I never had anyone say such nice things about me, and I got so that I was likin' it so much that I didn't want to come down and bother you."[23]

Robert Scherl, who produced the recording of the Oberlin concert, reported:

> As brilliant as Son [House] was, no one in the audience could have been prepared for what was to come . . . within several minutes he [Mississippi John Hurt] had the room of four thousand as one single being. I have never seen any entertainer in any field radiate the warmth, humanity, and love that this great man willingly gave to an audience of strangers young enough to be his grandchildren. His singing and guitar playing were never less than brilliant, and his beautiful conversation between songs to the audience made each person feel as though he was speaking intimately and only to them alone. At the finish of the second set, awed silence rose to thunderous applause, which lasted complete with standing ovation for a full five minutes. Hurt returned to perform several more numbers and attempted to leave once more. The audience would not have it. With tears of joy in his eyes he returned once again for several more numbers. Justice was served. After many years of being

*forgotten, all the love and adulation and respect that John Hurt should
have had for so long were at last his and the cup runneth over.*[24]

Enter Gene Bush

In January 1964, Gene Bush's roommate at Emory University in Atlanta, Richard Cheek, returned from his Christmas vacation in Washington, D.C., to say that he had seen a fantastic performance by a little black bluesman named Mississippi John Hurt. Talking to John after the show, Richard mentioned that his college roommate, Gene Bush, was from Laurel, Mississippi. John replied, "Aw they Bushes, they be just like rabbits down in Mississippi." In April, Gene borrowed the album of the 1963 Newport Folk Festival from a neighbor. It was the first time that Gene heard Mississippi John Hurt.

By April 1966 Gene was studying at the University of Cincinnati and had joined the Rabbit Hash Ramblers, a bluegrass band, playing Dobro. Gene had been impressed with Mississippi John Hurt's music, so he was excited to hear that the University of Cincinnati had booked Son House and Mississippi John Hurt to present an afternoon workshop of blues, followed by an evening concert. Gene's band was to play before the workshop. The event was scheduled for the day after the Oberlin College Concert on April 16.

On the day of the concert the Rabbit Hash Ramblers were playing a Flatt and Scruggs number, "All the Good Times Are Past and Gone," on the terrace of the student union building. The melody and some of the lyrics are identical to John's "Nobody Cares for Me." Gene recalls watching a limousine drive up and seeing Dick Waterman, Son House, and Mississippi John Hurt get out and walk across to a bench directly across from the band. Later in the performance Gene took a break on the Dobro: "I looked down to see a little man, knees slightly bent, looking up at me with an incredible warm smile with one tooth in his head. I just about lost it!"

In the evening they attended the concert. Son played in his usual intense style, Gene remarking that whenever Son was playing, he was somewhere else, his eyes rolling into the back of his head. John gave a superb performance, presumably following a similar program to that of the previous night at Oberlin College. He played his newly acquired custom-made guitar. They finished the concert with the two of them duetting on "You Got To Walk That Lonesome Valley." The workshop and concert were reported in the university newspaper the following week, stating:

"At 1:30 there was truly a great blues workshop with Ed 'Son' House and 'Mississippi' John Hurt. This was followed Saturday evening with a Blues concert which earned the two personalities a standing ovation."[25]

After the concert Gene went backstage and was introduced to John. When John realized that Gene was from Mississippi his eyes lit up like a beacon. John asked, "Whereabouts in Mississippi you from?" Gene replied, "Laurel." John said, "Why, my wife's folks are from Hattiesburg. Do you ever get back home?" Gene said that he visited home regularly and so John gave him his address and asked him to come and visit him next time he was down that way. Later, along with Son, John, and Dick, and a few other folk, they retired to Mahogany Hall, a bar and bookstore.

Son House told an amusing tale. A couple of days previously, John and Son had been sitting around picking their guitars when John dozed off to sleep. Son turned around to see that John's cigarette had touched the top of the guitar and had burned his new guitar. He shouted, "Hey John, wake up! You're burning your guitar!" The burn mark, just behind the bridge, can be clearly seen on the video clip of John on the *Rainbow Quest* program with Pete Seeger and in a number of photos.

Dick Waterman accompanied John on several gigs that he had booked in New York City, where he took John to see the Beatles in *A Hard Day's Night*. Waterman also tells of Tommy, the young waiter at the Kettle of Fish, who befriended John. On the night he was leaving the bar to go to Rhode Island and learn to manage his family's funeral business, he came over to say farewell to John. "Goodbye John, I hope to see you again sometime." John replied, "Yeah, but I hope it ain't anytime soon."[26]

Confrontation

By early 1966 Mississippi John Hurt was the most popular of the rediscovered bluesmen, though apparently he was not invited to the three-day Boston Winterfest at which Doc Watson, the New Lost City Ramblers, and Son House appeared.[27] Dick Waterman continued his contact with John. On May 22, 1966, after a concert at the Central High School in Philadelphia, attended by Jerry Ricks (whose birthday it was), the increasing tension between Dick Waterman and Tommy Hoskins came to a head. Lorenzo, Skip James's common-law wife, and her stepsister and cousin T. (I. T.) (John's nieces) decided to intervene, apparently influenced by Waterman. They were convinced that Waterman could offer better deals by including John with Skip James and Son House in a tempting booking package. The two women convinced John that Hoskins was not good for him and he would fare much better with Waterman. The nieces orchestrated the split, and after a confrontation between Waterman and Hoskins and witnessed by Jerry Ricks, John appeared to accept that Waterman would now manage his appearances. Hoskins walked out, but most importantly the original contract with MRI remained in place. Dick Waterman confirmed that he never signed a deal with John.

Unfortunately, John was never the same again. In spite of the undoubted shortcomings of Hoskins, he had been easygoing and had acted as a security blanket for John. Jerry Ricks told me: "Tommy would take care of him. I don't think he had the same vibration with Dick, who was trying to make him something that he wasn't." Jerry Ricks did not see Tommy Hoskins again until they met at a Folk Alliance Conference in Memphis in 2002 or 2003. Tommy walked up and said, "Hey Jerry, do you still hate me?" Jerry replied, "Not in 100 years Tommy, I never hated you." Later Denise Tapp saw Jerry and told him that Tommy had cried when he returned home that day. "He was so pleased that you didn't hate him."

From their new home in Grenada, John and Jessie stayed in contact with their Avalon friends and, in spite of his fame, John continued to play at local gatherings as he always had. Ms. Annie Cook has fond memories of John and Jessie being invited to the christening party of her first grandchild Katherine Lynn Cook, daughter of her son, Virgil Cook Jr., on May 28, 1966. "Everyone had a wonderful time and John played his music for us all." Ms. Cook would also go and listen to him play at his house and told me, "John was one of the gentlest, kindest men I ever knew."

Opinions on John's Management

The substance of the initial recording contract with MRI in 1963, coupled with Tom Hoskins's outward persona as a disorganized hippie with a fondness for alcohol and drugs, caused many people to criticize the effectiveness of his management of John as well as to question his motives and to assume that John was being cheated. For example, Dave Van Ronk expressed the view that "Hoskins had signed John to a contract where he had earned a ridiculous percentage of John's wages, owned his publishing, and controlled all his business, and John actually had to go to court to get out from under his thumb. Naturally, we [presumably a group of friends in the Village] were filled with righteous indignation, and I was cursing Hoskins up hill and down dale."[28]

Whether the conditions of the contract were reasonable, whether the 50 percent could be considered "ridiculous percentage," and whether

Van Ronk was justified in his "righteous indignation" is a matter of opinion, but Hoskins did not own his publishing and John certainly did not go to court to remove himself from Hoskins's control. Indeed, the original MRI contract remained valid long after John's death. Interestingly, John was present during Van Ronk's outburst and following a pause by Van Ronk, John commented, "Well, you know if it weren't for Tom, I'd still be chopping cotton in Mississippi."[29] Of course, that could simply have been a manifestation of the fact that John never spoke ill of anyone, or possibly that he did not agree with the condemnation of Tom Hoskins.

Fred Bolden knew Tom Hoskins and Dick Waterman and appears to provide an objective appraisal of both. He had the following to say about Hoskins.

A lot of guys found Tom too nutty to get along with on a long-term basis, but he adored John Hurt and he spent his management income on the Hurt family. Hoskins I found was an imperfect man, but any mistakes he made were due to his lack of experience fishing in shark-infested waters. I believe my uncle knew this. Tom Hoskins was not a bad person. Man, Tom was like a junkyard dog when I knew him— one who worships his master but sometimes bites the wrong visitors. I learned in life that people are all too happy to believe the worst in most circumstances, and since Tom did nothing to confront the issues and his detractors (in a mature and effective way) misconceptions about Tom still endure.[30]

Of Dick Waterman he said, "Uncle John and Skip [James] highly respected Dick as an honest man who always gave you a square deal right up front." Fred told of his continuing friendship with Waterman and that he paid for Fred to accompany him to blues concerts after John had died.[31]

Pat Sky also felt that exploitative whites were ripping off many of the old bluesmen during this period. With regard to John Hurt, he felt that the contract with MRI was unfair. He told me that, "He made plenty of money, but the managers were siphoning it off." On an occasion at the Gaslight, he recalled suggesting to Sam Hood, the owner, who had normally paid the fee to Tom Hoskins, that he should give the money directly to John. John was handed several hundred dollars and was surprised when he realized how much he had been earning.

Since the Waterman-Hoskins row in Philadelphia, John had been unhappy. Pat Sky recalled that John was depressed by the fighting over his management and would say that he did not know what to do. John Miller and Jerry Ricks also told of John's diminished exuberance and Fred Bolden stated that John had taken ill during a stay with them in Boston in late 1965.

Gene Bush Visits Grenada

On June 29, 1966, about ten weeks after Gene Bush's first meeting with John, Gene and his friend Rick Reidmiller traveled up from Laurel, Mississippi, via Jackson and, around 4:00 p.m., knocked on the door of 1 North Levee Street in Grenada. They were given a warm welcome by John and Jessie and invited in. Andrew (8 years old) was shy, but Ella Mae (11) was happy and cheerful. Gene had taken a banjo and guitar along and they sat with John playing music on the front porch. Around dark, Jessie announced that dinner was ready and they went inside. It was a shotgun house; the first room was a living room, then a dining room, then a kitchen. Off the kitchen in an L shape was a bedroom and bathroom.

Jessie had cooked supper and set the table by the window in the middle room of the house. John, Rick, and Gene sat at the table. Jessie did not eat with them, which was usual practice at that time. The children were not around. The meal was of greens, squash, corn, and cornbread. They did not consume any alcohol. They finished the meal and retired through to the living room. There was a couch and a couple of armchairs. A composite wall hanging of Capitol Hill, the Stars and Stripes, and a picture of John F. Kennedy adorned the wall. They sat and talked. Around 10:00 p.m. a silence descended on the group.

John eventually broke the silence. "Gentlemen, if we were not where we are today, I would ask you to be guests in my house and stay here. But, when in Rome do as the Romans." After a pause, he continued, "Gentlemen, if you were to find your way over here in the morning, we can have breakfast and start over."

After they left, Rick naively asked what all that had been about. Gene told him that John had been concerned for all their safety. It was not acceptable around there for white strangers to be sharing a house with black folk. A ragtag-looking '55 Dodge with two white boys dressed up like protesters was sure to have aroused attention. They slept in their sleeping bags by the Grenada reservoir and after sunup were back at the Hurts' by 8:30 for breakfast. They drank some coffee, shot some pictures, and John and Gene played guitar and banjo. John recounted some of his memories from Mississippi. He mentioned that he sometimes played guitar at the Burning Bush Baptist Church up the street.

Table 4.2. Mississippi John Hurt Appearances

Appearance	Date
Ontario Place, Washington, D.C.	1963-1966
Brick Cellar, Washington, D.C.	1963
Showboat, Washington, D.C.	1963
Newport Folk Festivals	1963, 1964, 1965, 1966
Philadelphia Folk Festival	1963, 1965?
Second Fret, Philadelphia	1963
Main Point, Philadelphia	1963
Tonight Show NBC-TV	1963
Café Yana, Boston	1964
Columbia University, New York	1964
Gaslight Café, New York	1964?
Retort Club, Detroit, Michigan	1964
Ash Grove, Los Angeles	May 7, 1964
Carnegie Hall, New York	1964
Mariposa Folk Festival, Toronto, Canada	1964
New Gate of Cleve, Toronto, Canada	1965
This Hour Has Seven Days, CBC-TV, Toronto, Canada	1965
Town Hall, New York	1965
New York Folk Festival, Carnegie Hall, New York	1965
Massey Hall, Toronto	1965
University of Chicago, Chicago, Illinois	1965
Café a-Go-Go, New York	1965
Some of the People, KUHM Radio, Houston, Texas	1965
Rainbow Quest with Pete Seeger, WNDT-TV, New York	1966
Oberlin College, Oberlin, Ohio (recorded for Vanguard)	1966
University of Cincinnati, Cincinnati, Ohio	1966
Overton Park, Memphis, Tennessee	1966
Vanguard Recordings, New York	1966
Turks Head Coffee Bar, Cape Cod*	1965
Unicorn Coffee Bar, Boston*	?
Club 47, Mount Auburn, Cambridge*	?
WTBS Radio (Now WMBR)*	?
Golden Vanity Café, Boston*	?
Unknown club, Martha's Vineyard*	?
Mainly after Sheldon Harris, *Blues Who's Who*, 1979	
* From Fred Bolden, dates not known.	

John talked of the deal that he had had with W. E. Myer from Virginia back around 1929. The three tunes that John had put Myer's words to all have an old-timey country sound that suited John and sounded a little like Jimmie Rodgers. When Gene commented that "Let the Mermaids Flirt with Me" sounded like Jimmie Rodgers, John grinned, slapped his leg, and said, "I sho' likes Mr. Jimmie Rodgers." John said that he was returning to New York to do some recording and would be staying with Pat Sky (this would have been in July, to record the final tracks for Vanguard). He gave the boys Pat Sky's phone number. Gene and Rick left that afternoon and headed east and up to New York.

On July 12, Gene called Pat Sky. Pat's girlfriend Lucy Brown answered the call. When she realized who was calling she said, "Oh you're the guy that visited John in Grenada, that's all he's talked about since he got here." After they arrived, Pat and John played guitar awhile. Gene sat next to John and showed him the photos he shot in Grenada and asked him if he would like some. John carefully looked through the pictures and then chose one of himself sitting on the porch. Gene asked, "John, is that all you want? You can take more." Following a little persuasion, John grinned and selected another four that he had moved to the top of the pile. Again, as with the offer of the free guitar, John had not wanted to take advantage.

The death of T. C.

Sadly John's son T. C. Hurt died in August 1966, aged 49 years. His funeral was held on August 21. John's presence at the funeral is remembered with great reverence. His granddaughter, Mary Frances, who was only 10 years old at the time and had never attended a funeral before, related the following story to me.

After the funeral service at the St James Church the funeral cortege slowly made its way up the hill toward the Hurt's family cemetery. I remember traveling up that narrow single-track bumpy dirt road in an old Chevy truck with the hearse following behind. Suddenly the truck stopped. After an examination of the engine my brother-in-law Louis, a mechanic, slammed the hood down shaking his head. He shouted, "Daddy John, this truck is flooded and it's not going to start." It was completely impossible to pass on the narrow road and there was utter confusion as people emerged from their cars and stood around talking in the hot sun.

Figure 4.2. John on his front porch at No. 1 North Levee Street, Grenada, Mississippi, June 30, 1966. (Gene Bush, Kingston Springs, Tennessee.)

Amid the confusion, verging on panic, Daddy John emerged from the truck and stared down the hill behind him at the long, stationary column of cars. He gestured to the person walking up the hill toward us to stop and walked around to the back of the truck. He held his finger to his lips in a gesture to silence us. He walked to the center of the road and respectfully removed his hat and cleared his throat before turning his face to the sky. With pleading eyes, he began talking in a fatherly voice. "T. C. son, I know it's you. I want you to know that everything is going to be all right. Now, I got your babies here on this truck and all we want to do is take them up there with you so they can say a proper goodbye. Now, you just let us do that and I will make sure Annie gets this truck back home for the children."

The onlookers stared at one another in silence and disbelief, while Daddy John stood there quietly and with dignity. Finally, a smile rippled over his face like a stone thrown in a pond. He happily put his hat on and tipped it to the sky saying, "Thank you T. C. and much obliged." He hurried back to the front of the truck and firmly commanded Louis, "Hit it!" Louis turned on the ignition, hit the starter, and the truck immediately burst into life. With a wide clown-like grin Daddy John gestured to Louis as if to say, "Told you!"

Figure 4.3. John, Jessie, Ella Mae, and Andrew, No. 1 North Levee Street, Grenada, Mississippi, June 30, 1966. (Gene Bush, Kingston Springs, Tennessee.)

Mary Frances added, "Watching Daddy John play his guitar, I had often thought there was something magical about him as his fingers fluttered softly over the strings. That August day removed any doubt in my mind, and many of my sisters and brothers, that there was something magical and wonderful about this little man!"

In September 1966, just two months before John died in Grenada, Joan Baez and Martin Luther King Jr. participated in a march in Grenada to protest the beatings of black children as schools were desegregated. Ms. Kitty recalls attending the march. "We marched all around town singing songs. We sang 'We Shall Overcome.'" Joan's attempts to enroll five black children resulted in her being banned from entering the school.[32]

Gene Bush Returns

Gene Bush was back in Laurel on September 14, and he made a second trip on his own to Grenada to see John soon after. They picked guitars together and John played some of the songs he had played at the Vanguard sessions in July. They walked together the short distance across the dirt road and through some trees to sit on the bank of the Yalobusha River. They sat on a bank above the river and little was said. In the silence Gene felt some kind of communication, as if they were together in some shared quiet spiritual place. As they watched the river flow by, a train whistle blew in the distance. John remarked, "It's the 3:19 running about ten minutes behind time." John was not wearing a watch and Gene asked, "How do you know that?" John explained that the engineer was telling

Figure 4.4. John with Gene Bush,
No. 1 North Levee Street, Grenada,
Mississippi, June 30, 1966.
(Gene Bush, Kingston Springs,
Tennessee.)

that with his whistle. The train emerged and crossed the trestle bridge over the river on its approach to the Grenada depot.

During the same visit, John asked Gene if he could bring him some squirrels next time he visited. In October, while en route to Oxford to visit his brother C. P. at Ole Miss, Gene dutifully called in and delivered some squirrels. This time he was with his girlfriend, his brother Philip, and Philip's girlfriend. Gene ran into the house with the squirrels in a Styrofoam cooler and handed it to John. John took the parcel from the cooler, discarded the newspaper wrapping to the trashcan, placed the squirrels in the refrigerator, and then placed the cooler under the sink behind a curtain. Gene, looking a little bemused, asked, "John, can I have the cooler back?" John, with a twinkle in his eye, answered, "Oh, I thought that was part of the deal!"

As Gene left the house, Jessie asked Gene when he would be back. Gene said that they were all attending a party at Ole Miss and would be back tomorrow. She answered, "Good, can you bring me some beer?" It was difficult to get beer in Grenada, it being in a dry county. Gene said he would and they left to travel north to Oxford.

Unfortunately, Oxford was also dry and by the time they had attended the party it was close to midnight and they could not get any beer. In the place they were staying Gene noticed a three-quarters full bottle of Old Crow bourbon and, thinking no one would miss it, took it along for Jessie. So on a Sunday in Mississippi, the two young white couples, now joined by Gene's younger brother C. P., plus a partly drunk bottle of Old Crow bourbon made their way south to Grenada in Gene's father's '63 Chrysler station wagon.

Figure 4.5. John on his front porch at No. 1 North Levee Street, Grenada, Mississippi, June 30, 1966, playing the guitar custom-made by Jack Alderson. The burn mark is hidden under John's arm. (Gene Bush, Kingston Springs, Tennessee.)

When the Bush party arrived, John and a friend of his who had just arrived back from church were standing outside the house. Jessie was inside at the middle room table drinking moonshine from a tumbler. Gene went to the car, got the bottle, and handed it to Jessie. Jessie was so pleased she placed the bottle on the table and grabbed Gene and gave him a big hug. When they turned around the bottle had gone! They ran back into the kitchen just in time to see John and friend consuming the final drops of the whisky. Jessie was real mad.

A little later the five visitors sat in the living room and Jessie said, "John, play for the people." So he got his guitar and began playing some hymns. Jessie said, "John that's enough of that, play 'Candy Man.'" So John began playing "Candy Man," but he was not singing it in front of the girls. Jessie shouted, "John, sing the song." After another refusal from John, Jessie began singing to John's guitar:

All you ladies gather 'round, the good sweet Candy Man's in town,
Candy Man, Candy Man,
He's got a stick of candy, it's nine inches long,
He sells it faster than a hog can chew his corn,
Candy Man, Candy Man

Jessie knew all of the words!

Soon, Jessie went off to the kitchen to prepare dinner and returned later to announce, "Gentlemens, dinner is served!" and the party sat down to enjoy a meal of Jessie's squirrel stew. After dinner was over John lit a cigarette. He was a regular smoker and smoked for most of his life. He had a smoker's cough, and his fingers were nicotine stained. Later, after a coughing attack, John took out another cigarette and Gene remarked to John that maybe he should cut down on his smoking. John said that he had been to the doctor, who had said, "John, you gotta quit those Camels." Gene, eyeing the cigarette that John was about to place in his mouth, responded, "But John, you're still smoking," to which John replied, "Well he didn't say nothin' about Pall Malls."

Eventually the party got up to leave and said their goodbyes to John and Jessie. John followed them out to the car and, as the others got into the vehicle, he drew Gene to one side saying, "things aren't going like I would like them, would you be my manager?" Gene was flattered to be asked and said he would think about it and come back in a couple of weeks with an answer. John said, "You know Elvis had other managers before the Colonel." This was the last time Gene saw John.

The Death of Mississippi John Hurt

In October John was out hunting with some of his friends close to the end of St. James Road above Avalon. He felt ill and slumped down at the side of the road. He had suffered a stroke and was taken home to Grenada and later admitted to the Grenada hospital. The stroke left John with a slight twist to his mouth, which affected his speech a little.[33] John died of a myocardial infarction caused by a coronary occlusion on November 2, 1966, while in the Grenada County Hospital. The death certificate stated John's occupation as "Musician." John's brother "Hardy Hurt, Avalon, Miss.," was named as the informant.[34] A response card from Dick Waterman's Avalon Productions informed interested parties of his death simply stating, "John S. Hurt died quietly November 2, 1966. Thank you for your kindness."[35]

Fred Bolden's family received the news of John's death in a phone call from his uncle, Cleveland Hurt Jr. (John's brother Cleveland's son from his marriage to Fannie), who lived on Chicago's South Side. Fred remembers his parents putting him on the next Greyhound bus out of Boston to represent his family at the funeral. Fred wrote a song called "Chicago Bound" to mark his sadness at that time. He described the journey.

Teddy Hurt [a.k.a. Theodore, a.k.a. T. R., John's brother Cleveland's son from his marriage to Lillie] picked us up at Fifty-fourth Street and Prairie Avenue on the South Side and we drove to Mississippi. Also in the car were my Uncle Cleveland, his wife Eula Mae, Aunt Katherine Hurt, and myself. When we got to St. Louis, Teddy's car broke down and we must have been stuck there for about five hours. We arrived into Avalon and stopped off at Stinson's General Store, which looked to me like the only store in town. It had one gas pump and it was a post office as well. Mrs. Stinson was a nice old lady and she asked how my mom was in Boston. Why, she hadn't seen her since 1939. We then drove out to a cotton patch toward a shack sitting out in the middle of the field. It was the home of my cousin, Mary Hurt Wright. This was when we first met and she couldn't have been any more than seven or eight years old.

On the morning of November 13, 1966, Stanley Booth called on musician Furry Lewis at his apartment on Fourth Street in Memphis to take him to Mississippi John Hurt's funeral. Booth provides an account of the funeral in his book, *Rythm Oil*. John had been lying at the Century Funeral Home in Greenwood, Mississippi, for the past eleven days awaiting the finalization of funeral arrangements. They took Interstate 55 as far as Grenada. On the journey they chatted about Hurt's guitar-playing skills and Furry, not keen to accept that anyone was better than him, accepted that Hurt was a wonderful guitar player, but adding, "but he was sho' ugly. I swear 'fore God he was."[36]

In Grenada they avoided attracting attention due to a black and a white man traveling together; Stanley purchased cheeseburgers and root beer from the Burger Broil screen window, and they ate in the car. They got back on the road following Highway 7 through Avalon to Greenwood. They were late finding the funeral home and retraced their steps back to Avalon in search of the funeral procession. They came to a long line of cars leading up to the St. James Baptist Church, close to the place where only months earlier John had performed a small miracle at his son's funeral. The church was full and more people gathered outside; there must have been more than 200 people there.[37]

Sensing that the conspicuous white visitor had come from afar, John's nephew, Theodore Roosevelt Hurt helped them find a place inside the church. Theodore Roosevelt said that Jessie had called him on the night of John's death and he had traveled from Greenwood to Grenada and taken Uncle John's body home from the hospital. Jessie had said, "T. R.,

Uncle John passed this evenin'." Theodore Roosevelt was called T. R. by everyone except Uncle John who called him "Tudderman."

Inside the church the minister abruptly interrupted his sermon, inviting the visitors from out of town to "say a few words." Furry Lewis ad libbed superbly. "This is Furry Lewis talking. We come clean from Memphis to be with you today. I knew John Hurt from the old days. Me and him used to play together on Beale Street [I know of no evidence that John ever played on Beale Street], and seem like I just got kind of filled up inside, and had to come down here to be with you." The congregation responded with a "Tell it!" He finished by saying, "Now John Hurt is gone and we miss him. But you know, we love, but God love best." The congregation again responded with, "That's sayin' it!" Booth added that John Hurt would be long remembered for the music he had given us.³⁸

Fred Bolden remembers his attendance at the funeral. He stayed with his aunt Lorenzo in Greenwood (this is his mother Everlene's sister, referred to as Lorenza in earlier references to the U.S. Census, and not Skip James's wife Lorenzo, who was still in Boston) and visited the funeral home the day before when his older relatives viewed the body. Fred did not go inside. At the church he did look inside the open brown steel casket to see his uncle lying there, dressed in a white shirt with a bow tie and a grey suit. The congregation sang "Milky White Way" and a lady played the piano. He remembers great excitement and grief during the service. "They almost tipped the casket over. I only saw two white friends. That's it! Also, I remember the lady getting up speaking about what dignity Mississippi John Hurt had, etc. Tom wasn't there, nor Mr. Waterman, and to be honest, I expected to see many of my uncle's white friends, but it didn't happen. You know, it's been over forty years. I remember his funeral like yesterday."

There were two couples of white hippies (whose identities remain unknown) conspicuously seated toward the front of the congregation. As they left the church, the congregation sang "Near the Cross, Oh, near the Cross, Be my glory ever, and my weary soul should find, Oh, rest beyond the river." Outside the church John's son Man was sitting in a car crying, "He's gone, he's gone." The man comforting him said, "Hush, boy. Yo' daddy's better off than we are now."³⁹

Mississippi John Hurt was buried in the Hurt family cemetery along St. James Road on November 13, 1966. Fred recalls: "I attended the church service and I went right up to that hill and remained until they had completely buried Uncle John. He was laid out in a brown steel casket. Before they laid him down, they placed the casket into a large wooden box."

Bill Givens was in a jazz club on Divisadero Street in San Francisco when he heard of John's passing. The club was frequented mainly by blacks, and before the evening performance began a scatter of customers was drinking quietly at the bar. A black man came in and ordered a drink.

> *When the beer was poured and sitting in front of him, and the bartender had backed off a step or two, the man said in a neutral tone of voice, as if he were unsure what effect his words would have, but clearly, and a bit loud, as one says something he feels to be of general interest, [he said] Mississippi John Hurt died. Heard it on the radio.*
>
> *I felt the shock of it instantly, a small seismic wave. The black people at the bar all registered the words, which the man had spoken with some visible movement or another, each in his turn, a small gesture of the head, some flexing of the back, a hand brought down smartly on the bar surface. The event had touched them too. I searched their faces, what I could see of them. Those I saw were changed, meaningfully blank, thoughtful, expression turned inward. Those I could not make out, their heads tilted downward, had their attentions fixed on the glass or bottle held tightly in the hand. Whatever was taking place in each one of them was personal. They did not seek each other out with the least furtive glance. A couple of them shook their heads perceptibly. One man was moving his lips silently, perhaps whistling a remembered tune. Another drinker sighed softly several times, a woman. It seemed now quieter than before.*
>
> *Here for a time was a strange memorial to John Hurt. Clearly he was known to his own people, and his death had been taken by them as that of a brother. I thought John would have liked to know that, and I wondered if all the acclaim of the last three years had been mainly such a white man's affair. Presently the jazz musicians filed on stage. John was gone. Shit! I left my beer unfinished on the bar and walked out.*[40]

Gene Bush's mother heard on the radio that the famous blues singer Mississippi John Hurt had died in a hospital in Grenada. Gene drove up to Greenwood on the day scheduled for the funeral. He called the funeral home and spoke to Jessie, who was distraught with grief and dropped the phone. A lady came on and told him that the funeral had been postponed to allow more time for family members to get there. Gene returned home to Laurel and was unable to return to attend the funeral. Almost forty years later on July 5, 2003, Mary Frances Hurt Wright led him, me, and a few other appreciative fans to the secluded Hurt family cemetery and

John's gravesite. This was the day after the first Mississippi John Hurt festival at Valley near Avalon, Mississippi. Gene paid his belated last respects to John. This is where I first met Gene Bush and where I was privileged to play "My Creole Belle" at John's gravesite.

In the weeks following John's death, obituaries appeared in many U.S. newspapers including the *Washington Post* and the *New York Times*,[41] which included photographs of John. The *Washington Post* provided a brief summary of John's life adding, "Although he enjoyed his sudden fame and new wealth, he continued to wear the same clothes he always wore in Avalon—green corduroy shirt, baggy old pants and a battered old brown fedora, his trademark. Even though he wore the hat crunched down to his ears, his face was still etched by the Mississippi sun. He was short (5 feet 4) and stoop shouldered, and his appearance on stage made a memorable impression." The *New York Times* commented: "On stage, he was meditative, shyly announcing each song and saying nothing more, except occasionally to ask his listeners if he should omit the wry little erotica in some of his lyrics. He was always told no." The article continues with a quote from a 1964 article by Robert Shelton in the *Times*. "Phrases of his songs pass from his mouth to the guitar strings and back again in an amiable dialogue. The strings, alternating bass and treble figures, move often with a jogging ragtime flavor, and become a gently philosophical extension of a voice used in similar fashion."

John did not leave a will. On April 21, 1967, Jessie was appointed administratrix of John's estate. He left $2,542.18 in the Grenada Bank, Grenada, Mississippi. The attorney's fees were $200.00. On November 8 the final order of the chancery court of Grenada County ordered that "the remaining funds of the deceased shall go to his two (2) heirs at law, his wife JESSIE LEE HURT, and his son, JOHN WILLIAM HURT."[42] This judgment seemed simple enough, but few could have contemplated the animosity and legal wranglings that were to emerge and continue over the next forty years.

The impact that John Hurt had on those who were fortunate enough to know him will be clear by now. Holly eloquently summarized this:

He was a deeply moral man, but also a deeply tolerant man. His ability to deal gracefully with a world so very different from his own was awe-inspiring. From rural Mississippi to the urban New York of those days was a planetary change. This was a man who had difficulty using a telephone, and whose literacy was based on the Bible. In Greenwich Village it was still the age of the Beat; expressing enthusiasm was uncool. People snapped their fingers instead of applauding performances.

Yet when John took the stage, saying softly, "Got to put the Lord out front," always singing a spiritual before "Candy Man," "Stagolee," and "Avalon Blues," the entire audience opened like flowers and fell in love with his goodness. By the end of his set they would be singing "You Are My Sunshine" with him, their faces as soft as children's, blooming above their black turtlenecks.

Even my atheist father, on a rare evening out with my mother, stopped on the way to the table as though transfixed, looking at John smiling and singing on the stage in his battered old brown hat. "What a good man," he breathed. It was clear that he did not even know he had spoken; the words came from some deep, inner place that had recognized John. That place seemed to be universal. Fiercely as my father would have denied this, perhaps what John touched in everyone was the soul.

I do not know, of course, anything about an afterlife. It is—as I believe it should be to all of us—a Mysterium Tremendum. But, I have always believed that for John there is that old-time heaven, with clouds and angels and harps that I suspect he expected. I can't imagine a God worth worshipping who would disappoint Mississippi John Hurt.

John himself did not attend church a great deal during the sixties, but he was always aware of the presence of his God and would always say his prayers at night. Once, returning to grandnephew Fred's home after a late-night gig he said, "Freddie, don't ever let anyone tell you there ain't no God." At the close of a concert at Boston's Café Yana, when a man shouted out to John "When will we meet again?" John smiled and answered, "Well now, I'll tell you one thing for sure." Raising his hand and pointing skyward, he said, "It might be up there, but I guess none of us know for sure which of us will make it there and which of us won't." Amid the silence that descended, he brought his hand down and tapped his heart with his outstretched finger, "But we are sure to meet in here. If I keep you in my heart, which I surely will, and you keep me in your heart, and I hopes you will, then we will always have the other person anytime we want to look into our heart."[43] John clearly held close an earthly spirituality as well as a heavenly one and this was reinforced by one of his favorite sayings, "Don't die until you're dead."

David Brown boldly wrote that John had died happy.[44] Whether this is true is hard to say; the bickering over his management troubled him and his health was deteriorating. However, John knew that his music was good and that through it he had made an important contribution to people's happiness, though he could probably never have imagined the true

Figure 4.6. John's grave site, Avalon, Mississippi. (Philip R. Ratcliffe.)

breadth and longevity of his story and his music. He had certainly lived life to the fullest in his last three years, had many enjoyable times, and made very many good friends. He gave so much to so many that I am sure that everyone who has been touched by his personality will hope so much that he did die happy.

On December 30, 1966, Jessie wrote to Tom Hoskins to thank him for some gifts that he had sent for Christmas. He had sent a book and a picture of John for Jessie. She wished that Tom could have taken Christmas with them and commented that John was now "resting from worry and labor [and] it is very lonely without him." Dick Spottswood subsequently commented that John "never should have left Mississippi. He was too old to make that transition, and too vulnerable." Jessie commented, "By rights, you know, John went into this when he ought to have been coming out."[45]

On the subject of rediscovering aging bluesmen, Phil Spiro was later to comment, "I'm half inclined to say that if I had to do it all over again, I wouldn't do it." He felt that the young white discoverers and enthusiasts were constantly reminding them of their younger selves through their earlier recordings and not appreciating that in most cases "they were still living on the wrong side of the poverty line." There were constant battles over their management and many wound up feeling they had been cheated.[46]

The suggestion by Adelt that John Hurt was ill treated by his rediscoverers and by white audiences is built upon a statement that Hurt was "suing his rediscoverer, Tom Hoskins."[47] As we have seen Hurt was not suing anyone and he appeared to be delighted by the attention he received from his audiences, and his African American friends Jerry Ricks and Archie Edwards gave no indication that John was unhappy with his situation.

The final word comes from Tom Hoskins. "John Hurt was able to experience many things otherwise impossible. He enjoyed traveling especially to music festivals. He met fans and other musicians who appreciated and respected his music and loved him as a person. The last three and a half years of his life were very satisfying to John Hurt and far removed from being a tenant farmer making twenty eight dollars a month."[48] I think John would have agreed with this analysis.

5. The Legacies of Mississippi John Hurt

Grenada

J essie had loved John deeply and they had rarely been apart. Now she found herself left with young Ella Mae and Andrew in Grenada. Without a will, what was left of the $2,542.18 in John's account at the Grenada Bank, once funeral costs had been paid, was to go to Jessie and Man.[1] What could be more straightforward? The judgment was based on the facts known to the court and provided to them by Jessie and her advisors, which included Tom Hoskins. But it was anything but straightforward, and more than twenty-five years later, this judgment was to be challenged in the same Grenada court. In the intervening period Tom Hoskins attempted to get on with making a living, partly from his Music Research Inc. contract with Mississippi John Hurt, and to ensuring that Jessie and the grandchildren got what was rightfully theirs, including their share of the royalties on John's music.

A month after John's death, on December 4, 1966, Jessie wrote a very businesslike letter to her attorney. She told him that she had heard from Dick Waterman who said that he had been to New York and met with Maynard Solomon of Vanguard Records and Herb Gart, a colleague of Tom Hoskins and John's business manager, and that they had decided to put money into a fund for Jessie and the grandchildren with an intention to pay them an allowance of $200.00 a month. She added that Dick Waterman (in a letter to Jessie of November 26, 1966) had said that they would send her the $700.00 to cover the funeral expenses.[2] A week later on December 11, she wrote anxiously to Maynard Solomon saying that she and the kids were living on social security and asking if he would send her the money that he was holding, adding, "John as gone and I Feels at a lost to see to his business."[3]

That Christmas, Jessie received Christmas presents from Tom Hoskins, including a picture of John, and on December 30 she replied:[4]

Hello Tommy ok I hope the kids and me ar fine we received the package to day it sure was a surprise to us brother (an affectionate name for grandson Andrew) was just ready to try his glove and ball out I told him nope because it would land right in the river Ella Mae she is hurrying for school to begin so she can wear her pretty sweater They ate the santa candy as soon as they open it they are so proud over everything you sent and me to. and this wonderful book I just had to hold back a few tears when I saw John's picture every one that came in had to look through it will take it down and Let his Brothers see it

Many thanks to you for the gifts wish that you could have taken Xmas with us but as it was we did my baking here and we gone down to John brother hardy xmas. eve, John he was not here last xmas. so this xmas. he is resting from worry and Labor it is very lonely here with out him

My Love
Jessie &, the childrens

On January 17, 1967, Jessie had still heard nothing from Vanguard or anyone else about the money she had been told she would receive. She again wrote to Maynard Solomon asking if he would send some money.[5]

Dear Mr Solomon,
please except my asking about the estate settlement of my husband John S Hurt, John passed Nov.2nd 1966 and I were hoping by now that I would be getting some of his money as I was informed that Vanguard ar holding $1,300 for John right now and was going to send me down the $700 for the funeral I do not have any money only my social security once per month. I am not worrying about anyone being dishonest with the money I am worried about my condition. I have not received any of John's money so far please let me no about it
Oblige in advance
Jessie L. hurt

She was clearly becoming a little desperate, but retained her dignity and composure, clearly not wishing to accuse anyone of short-changing her. She sent copies of her letters to Vanguard to Tom Hoskins and on the top of this particular copy Tom had written the words "follow up." Whether he did take any action is not known, but Tom received another copy of a letter that Jessie had sent to Vanguard on February 9, 1967, thanking them for sending some records of John's and copies of some magazines, presumably containing articles about John.[6] She added, "I tried to play one but it is just to much for me to listen to right now it seem just like he were sitting here in the room I just could not stand to listen had to cut it of."

Given that Vanguard sent records and magazines to Jessie, it is tempting to assume that they were sent along with the payment owed, but strangely, Jessie did not mention money at all in her reply. In fact, they had not sent any money; Jessie wrote again to Maynard Solomon on May 15, 1967, almost six months after Dick Waterman had informed her that she would be receiving payment from Vanguard.[7]

Repeating much of what she had previously asked, she added, "I hope and trust in the Lord that you all will be honest with me as I have utmost confidence in you all I will preshate you sending me down the amount you ready have as I am in need please sir let me hear from you[.]"

Remarkably, after so long and in such desperation, Jessie still retained her dignity and composure in spite of being ignored and possibly cheated by people who were in a position to help her and who professed to be her friends. On July 25, 1967, Jessie was still chasing Maynard Solomon for payment.[8] I could find no evidence that she actually received anything until considerably later. Of course the details of intended payment by Vanguard could have been misconstrued during communication between Maynard Solomon, Dick Waterman, and Jessie, but the fact remains that, at best, Vanguard did not communicate effectively with Jessie.

By late 1967 Tom Hoskins was sharing his life with a girl named Ricky. On November 11, Jessie wrote to Ricky and Tom Hoskins.[9] She was clearly very moved by a letter, with a check included, that she had received from them.

Dear Miss. Ricky and Mr. Hoskins I Received your letter oh how glad was I For such a sweet, sweet, Letter it came in a time of need oh yes I remember you well. It is not a day that I do not think about those by gone day when we lived in Washington and I miss. all of you very much thanks you both for the check I thank you so much For your offer and being concerned about the childrens and me. John as gone to never return to me in this life I am living in hope that he and me will meet in a home where we'll never grow old The kids ar doing fine in school
    My Love to you both
    Jessie L. hurt

The house on North Levee Street was in a poor state, and within a month, Jessie moved into a house at 863 Telegraph Street, Grenada.[10] Time rolled by with Jessie struggling to keep a home together for her and the two grandchildren. On April 24, 1968, she wrote to Goldstein, her lawyer, saying that she had received his letter, but that she had not heard from Bill Givens or anyone else.[11]

On October 7, she wrote again to Goldstein mentioning a letter she had received from Hoskins and saying that she had written to Tom Hoskins asking if he would send her some money and adding:

John had been pass ten months before I had heard from Mr. Hoskins
he came down to grenada the next week after I had buried John and gave me a check for $100.00 after I asked for it. Then he told me that he would take care of things for me. Also this past Jan. 28, I got a letter saying that he had a little bit of money that he put into a fund for the children and me and would like to send a check once a month he said this money comes from the reissuing of a John Hurt record out in California he said that it will sell beautifully and that the money would all be mine whatever he get, he also said that it were about a couple of hundred in the fund and expect another check soon said he did not know exactly when as far as exactly how much he said that it should be another couple of hundred
he said maybe about $60.00 or $45.00 once a month would keep me with money and the bank with money. He asked me to write and let him know how much I would like to have so I wrote and told him that I agreed to $45.00 per month
So I have not heard any more about the fund money or the [indecipherable] Money I sure appreciate you helping me

Jessie finished by providing Tom Hoskins's new address, c/o Mr. (Robert) Scherl in Silver Spring, Maryland, and signing herself, "Yours truly Jessie L Hurt."[12]

A photocopy of the final page of a letter and the envelope sent from Tom Hoskins to Jessie was found amongst other papers, but unfortunately the letter is undated and the postmark of the letter indecipherable. However, given the content relative to other correspondence, it was probably sent between November and December of 1968. The letter was sent by special delivery and apparently contained a check for $60. Tom Hoskins wrote apologetically:

". . . but things have not gone to well with me & I really wanted to have some good news for you before I wrote, but of course, I really have no excuse at all.

However, here's $60 to tide you over until I can get some more together as I told you on the phone, I will be sending you $240 in the next few weeks, and I will see what I can do as far as arranging for other money for you and try to set up a regular income that you can count on, like maybe getting Vanguard to pay you every 2 or [so] months instead of every six months.[13]

These are the things I should have done a long time ago but I promise I'll take care of them now.

Please take good care of yourself and the kids, and send me a letter and tell me whats happening. I'll answer every letter.

Love to you, Ella Mae & Brother,

Tommy[14]

The money that Jessie was expecting to receive was to come from the original 1963 and 1964 Piedmont releases and the Vanguard releases, *Mississippi John Hurt Today* in 1966 and *The Immortal Mississippi John Hurt* in 1967. Jessie and Tom Hoskins were not the only people chasing Vanguard for payment. Peter Kuykendall of Wynwood Music Company and Recording Studio had acquired publishing rights to virtually all of John's songs from MRI as payment for his role in the recording of the Piedmont records. The agreement gave Wynwood Music 50 percent of royalties with 50 percent going to MRI. On November 11, 1968, Kuykendall wrote to Maynard Solomon concerning Vanguard's nonpayment with respect to mechanical royalties on six of the tracks recorded on *The Immortal Mississippi John Hurt*.

Kuykendall, who had been instructed by MRI to send their share of the royalties directly to Jessie, emphasized that he needed to let Jessie know what was happening and stated his intention to pass the matter to his attorney if the matter was not resolved.[15] On July 17, 1969, Peter Kuykendall wrote to MRI clearly describing the royalties that he had paid to Jessie from the Origin Jazz Library (OJL) releases over the previous year; $143.36 for six months to June 30, 1968, $49.07 for six months to December 31, 1968 and $45.34 for six months to June 30, 1969. He also stated that he had sent royalties from the Vanguard releases to Jessie.[16]

Although it is impossible to obtain an accurate calculation of the money being generated by all record sales up to this time, it seems clear that although it was not a huge amount, it was sufficient to make a significant difference in the lifestyle of Jessie, Ella Mae, and Andrew had it been

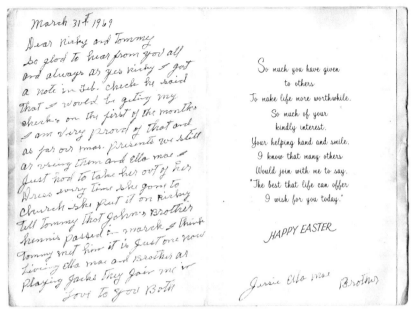

Figure 5.1. Easter card from Jessie Hurt to Tom Hoskins, March 31, 1969. (Tom Hoskins Archive.)

available to them. In any case, the money generated one way or another was about to escalate.

It seems that from around late 1968, after a two-year struggle, Jessie began to receive checks from Vanguard and from Tom Hoskins. Presumably Wynwood Music Co. was passing the Vanguard royalties on to Jessie after taking their own cut and Hoskins was passing royalties from the Piedmont records directly to Jessie. On December 6, 1968, Jessie wrote to Ricky and Tommy saying that their telephone call had "lifted her." She was clearly distressed with Brother (Andrew) having been confined to his bed with a bad cold or flu.[17] She kept him in the house as he recovered and reported that "Ella Mae is now catching it." The weather was cold and wet. She had received checks from Music Research Inc. dated October 4, and December 2, and she enquired whether the check covered one or two months.[18]

Tom was still with Ricky in March 1969, and he was clearly still taking care, at least intermittently, of Jessie, Ella Mae, and Brother. He continued to do so for many more years to come. On March 31 Jessie sent an Easter greeting card to Ricky and Tommy with a message saying that she was due to receive checks on the first of the month (see Fig. 5.1).[19] She thanked them for Ella Mae's Christmas present of a new dress and reported the death of John's brother Hennis, who died on February 9, 1969, saying, "it is just one now living," presumably referring to Hardy, the remaining sibling of John's who died two years later on February 1, 1971, aged 89 years.[20]

Between 1969 and 1971 Jessie moved from Telegraph Street to an apartment at Washington Gardens, an apartment complex that reflected a new social initiative in Grenada County. It had limited space and was created to cater for those on low income. Jessie's income was clearly sparse at that time, suggesting that she was receiving little money from anyone. She remained friendly with Ms. Kitty, who had helped her and John find the house on North Levee Street. In early 1971 Tom Hoskins advised Jessie about leaving a will to look after the grandchildren, and on May 8, 1971, she wrote to him from Washington Gardens.

> *Dear Mr Hoskins*
> *please excuse me for so long about writing Very glad to get a letter from you as you asked about having a will made out to Brother and Ella Mae that is what I should have did Long before now and to will this prevent royalties being sent to us? as you spoke about my son you may include him with a small amount I want Brother and Ella Mae to have a Legal right of John money the biggest part and about the money I have in the bank is very small I am very careful about spending as the childrens Grow older it takes more I keeps our insurance paid I pay $51.0 for rent water heat and light that include in the rent I pay My phone bill some time it be as much as $12.00 Clothes some time. high price food a week The cheopist of food down here ar high I do not spend any more than I hofter I just can not afford it becouse everything is on me. You may send the will on down as soon as you can oh yes as you said about the children going to camp just don't bother about it because you has been very nice we ar having plenty of rain I tried to get you twice on the phone I sure miss Ricky she were such a nice person very nice*
> *Yours truly*
> *Jessie*[21]

But they did go to camp, as evidenced by a further letter from Jessie on January 4, 1972, in which she adds that she is now in a nice warm house.

The January 4 letter[22] indicated that Tom Hoskins had again sent gifts for Jessie and the grandchildren. It appears that he also asked Jessie about making a will to benefit Ella Mae and Andrew, because she responds by saying that she had not heard from Hoskins since last April and understood that he was drafting a will: ". . . you promise me that you would send a will to me for me to see and for me to take it to a Grenada lawyer and have him look at it and explain it to me."

Tom Hoskins clearly took seriously his moral obligation to look after Jessie's interests, as evidenced by the letters sent to him by Jessie and recovered from his possessions following his death in 2002. Although his contact with her appears to have been somewhat sporadic, Tom did help get a will organized. Jessie did leave a will.

Vanguard Records

In 1965, in an attempt to gain more exposure and sales for John's music and establish him as a major artist, Music Research Inc. instructed Herb Gart to act on its behalf in negotiating a contract with a major record company. Subsequently, Gart was authorized by Tom Hoskins to enter into a two-record contract with the Vanguard Record Company. This agreement resulted in the New York sessions in 1966 that were directed and produced by Maynard Solomon and Pat Sky (see ch. 4).

Although Vanguard had been contracted to produce and release only two albums,[23] they subsequently released a third LP, claiming that Herb Gart had authorized this and that Vanguard had gained rights to release more of Hurt's music. Robert Scherl produced this third album from recordings of the Oberlin concert in 1966. Vanguard later released a fourth album, *Mississippi John Hurt Last Sessions*, from the studio material they had recorded in New York in 1966 (see Table 5.1). All studio recordings were later reissued as *Mississippi John Hurt: The Complete Studio Recordings*.

Table 5.1. Vanguard Records releases by Mississippi John Hurt 1966–72.			
Title	Record Number	Recording Location and Date	Release Date
Mississippi John Hurt Today	VSD 79220	Manhattan Towers Hotel, New York, February 1966	1966
The Immortal Mississippi John Hurt	VSD 79248	Manhattan Towers Hotel, New York, February 1966	1967
The Best of Mississippi John Hurt	VSD 19/20	Oberlin College, Oberlin, Ohio, April 15, 1966	1971
Mississippi John Hurt Last Sessions	VSD 79327	Manhattan Towers Hotel, February 1966 and Vanguard Studios, New York, July 1966	1972

Vanguard and Adelphi Records

In 1969 or 1970 Hoskins discussed an agreement with Gene Rosenthal of Adelphi Records about releasing a "definitive Mississippi John Hurt album"; a double LP with extensive notes, photographs, background material, etc., to be called *Memorial Anthology*. The material for this had been recorded primarily at the Ontario Place in 1964 by Rosenthal and was to include a recorded interview of John talking to Pete Seeger. Adelphi paid a $700 advance to MRI and a contract was drawn up on June 8, 1970.[24]

In addition to the Ontario Place recordings, Rosenthal was considering using recordings of Mississippi John Hurt performances made at the Retort Coffeehouse in Detroit in 1964 for *Memorial Anthology*. On September 10, 1970, he wrote to W. Wright Gedge, the owner of the Wright Gedge Stereo Recording Company, Gross Pointe, Michigan, who had made the recordings, asking permission.[25] Gedge replied in the affirmative, saying that he had sent off the required master tapes under separate cover.[26] According to the credits on the released *Memorial Anthology*, these Detroit recordings were not used, although some tracks recorded at the Blues House in Washington were added to those recorded at the Ontario Place. Presumably the Detroit recordings, and possibly other recordings of John's performances, still exist.

However, the plans for a *Memorial Anthology* were about to be thwarted. The unauthorized release of the third and fourth Vanguard albums in 1971 and 1972 was considered by Rosenthal to seriously jeopardize the potential success of his planned *Memorial Anthology*. He delayed work on the project and accused Tom Hoskins of agreeing to the Vanguard releases without telling him. He claimed that the Vanguard releases interfered with his contract with MRI and that they would damage potential sales of *Memorial Anthology*. Tom Hoskins informed Rosenthal that the third and fourth releases by Vanguard in 1971 and 1972 were unauthorized and not part of his MRI contract with Vanguard. Presumably he was aware that the Oberlin concert had been recorded, as he had been staying with Robert Scherl, the producer of the recording, in Silver Spring, Maryland, in 1968.[27]

Hoskins convinced Rosenthal that he had no knowledge of Vanguard's activities and the two of them set out to sue Vanguard in 1973, arguing that Vanguard had caused problems for the Adelphi–MRI contract and that Vanguard had fraudulently obtained Hurt's and Gart's signatures. Hoskins and Rosenthal agreed to split the costs of pursuing the Vanguard suit and to share any revenue from it.

The court dismissed Adelphi's claims but upheld the MRI claim against Vanguard. The case was concluded on November 10, 1975, resulting in a payment of $297,000 to Tom Hoskins in 1976.[28] Legal costs swallowed almost a third of this, but Hoskins was left with around $214,000 of which, true to his word, he handed $107,000 to Gene Rosenthal. Hoskins quickly spent his share on a home, several cars, motorcycles, records, and stereo equipment and paid his income taxes.[29] The MRI contract did not specify that John would receive any income from successful lawsuits over his recordings and apparently none of this money, which could have made a huge difference to her quality of life in her later years, went to Jessie and family.

Origin Jazz Library Records

In a further attempt to increase recognition and sales of John's music, Tom Hoskins decided to lease permission for rereleases of the original Piedmont albums to the Origin Jazz Library run by Bill Givens. In a letter to Jessie's attorney, George Goldstein, of May 21, 1968, Bill Givens clearly set out that he had concluded a contract with MRI in November 1967 to do this and released the LPs in February 1968.[30] He added that business had been very good for a small operation, having shipped out more than a thousand copies of each release. Givens's letter was clearly a response to a question he had received from Goldstein asking about payments to Jessie. He went on to say:

> *I made them a substantial advance and agreed to pay them royalties that are quite generous. It is stipulated in my contract with them that they will assume the responsibility of forwarding to Mrs. Hurt whatever is due to her according to their contractual arrangements with her late husband. I have been given to understand that they are exceeding the minimum requirements of their responsibility to her by a wide margin. I would appreciate it if you would contact Jesse Hurt, at whose table I had the pleasure of dining many times when I lived in Washington, and assure her than the money she has been receiving from Music Research these last few months is in consideration of royalties on the two recordings.[31]*

Six years later, in a letter to Tom Hoskins dated July 17, 1974, Bill Givens presented figures for the payment of royalties from the sales of the OJL rereleases of the original Piedmont albums. Total payments from OJL since December 15, 1972, amounted to $2,524.50. Givens added that the albums were holding steady at about 30 percent of his total business with no particular falling off. He did suggest: "However, with the business outlook as bleak as everyone keeps saying, maybe you should be thinking about taking the 2 Hurts back and getting them out yourself. If you put some new covers on them, a lot of people will buy them all over again."[32]

A letter of October 20, 1974, appears to confirm that MRI did take them back and states, rather bluntly, that the right to reissue the two Piedmont albums is hereby terminated.[33] Oddly, a sales letter from MRI, dated February 15, 1973, advised record distributors that the lease agreement with OJL had already been terminated. Inexplicably, OJL actually continued to sell these records until 1992 and royalties on them amounted to about $48,000 over the twenty-five years of OJL sales, all of which was paid to Tom Hoskins.[34]

Rebel Records

In 1971 it became apparent to Tom Hoskins that a Canadian LP of Mississippi John Hurt was being marketed illegally and without authorization. It took Hoskins, with help from Gene Rosenthal, until 1975 to locate the perpetrator, John Irvine of Rebel Records in Toronto, Canada.[35] The Rebel LP, recorded in 1964–65, was titled, *Mississippi John Hurt Volume One of a Legacy* and was released between 1969 and 1971.[36] Hoskins and Rosenthal visited Irvine and were apparently shown a contract between him and Peter Kuykendall (Wynwood Music Company and Recording Studio) that purported to pass master tapes of John Hurt's music recorded by Kuykendall to Irvine.[37] A further dispute ensued between Wynwood (Kuykendall) and Hoskins over the ownership of the tapes and the associated copyright. The whereabouts of these tapes is currently unknown.]

After Rebel Records had been informed that their use of the original masters was illegal, they immediately withdrew the records from sale. A Canadian bank immediately seized the master recordings and Hoskins, unable to recover them, obtained a copy of the Rebel LP, remastered from that, and produced and released his own version of the *Legacy* album on Piedmont in 1975[38] (later reissued on CD by Rounder).

Rounder Records

Rounder Records became involved in producing and marketing Mississippi John Hurt records in 1990, when they leased the masters of the original Piedmont albums from Tom Hoskins, and in 1991, when they released them on CD. Tom Hoskins had Rounder send all royalties to him while Wynwood continued to pay their royalties to John William Man Hurt and Ella Mae after Jessie's death.

Collectables Records

In 1994 Tom Hoskins signed an agreement with Collectables Records of Philadelphia, Pennsylvania, to release a CD of John Hurt's music. The company issued the CD *Satisfying Blues* on April 24, 1995. By 2001 he had received $3,164 in royalties from them.[39]

Jessie Dies in Grenada

After two years of delays and confusion over royalty payments following John's death, Jessie began receiving payments from MRI (including royalties from OJL), Vanguard, and Wynwood and may have been relatively comfortable in her apartment in Washington Gardens, though she was not well off. She began to suffer from high blood pressure and diabetes; she died at the Grenada County Hospital on July 20, 1982, aged between 79 and 91 years old.[40] She was buried close to John and other members of the Hurt family at the St. James cemetery above Avalon. She left barely sufficient money to pay for the funeral expenses and insufficient to purchase a grave marker. Her grave remains unmarked to this day.

Jessie's son, John W. (Man) Hurt informed the registrar of her death, providing his mailing address as 714 South Street, Grenada.[41] This is the home of Ms. Kitty (Mrs. Lillian Mitchell), who had remained friendly with John and Jessie since they all lived in Avalon, provided board, and helped John and Jessie find the house on North Levee Street when they returned to Grenada in 1966. It seems that Man was lodging with Ms. Kitty at the time of Jessie's death. Ella Mae also lived in Grenada and married before moving away. Ms. Kitty told me that after Jessie's death, "a man from New York came and asked her for John's hat and took it away."

In a will dated December 29, 1972, Jessie left the residue of her estate, after funeral expenses and debts had been paid, in trust for the benefit of her son, John William (Man) Hurt, and her grandchildren, Ella Mae Hurt and Andrew Lee Hurt. The trustees, named as Thomas Bird Hoskins, Mahlon Kline Lea, and Leland McMahon Talbot, were empowered to provide an income to the beneficiaries as they saw fit. The trust was to terminate when Andrew, the youngest grandchild reached an age of 25 years. In the event that Andrew was 25 years old before Jessie's death the trust was not to be created and her property was to be distributed, 10 percent to John William (Man) and 90 percent to be shared equally by the grandchildren. Tom Hoskins was appointed as executor of her will.[42] Andrew was 23 and Ella Mae 27 when Jessie died. The trust was established.

Life Goes On for Tom Hoskins

With the successful conclusion of the Vanguard suit, at the close of the 1970s Tom Hoskins got on with his rather impromptu life style, hoping that he could settle down to a continuing income from his earlier labors. Hoskins befriended artist Bill Storck, whose brother had built a cabin on Bill's property in the woods near a small lake in Maryland. Tom lived in the cabin for several months around 1984–85. Bill takes up the story:

> *I first met Fang at Bill Tydings' garage. I was a John Hurt fan and was playing John Hurt music on my guitar. Tom heard me and we struck up a friendship. We met around 1983 and we spent a lot of time together until I got married in 1987. He lived on the edge—a simple life; living out of the back of his car. Tom was charming, humorous, very intelligent and generous, but he could be very demanding. Eventually, his drinking got out of hand and I had to ask him to leave.*

Tom Hoskins loved the outdoors and he loved to fish. His sister Suzanne told of his close attraction to watery environments; how he liked to be around lakes and rivers and riparian wildlife. He once had a job as fisheries warden on Chesapeake Bay. He was also an avid collector of anything interesting to him and had a nose for finding things. Joe Lee tells of an amazing discovery by Hoskins of 5,000 hours of recordings of bluegrass and country musicians from the 1950s and 1960s that included priceless material of Flatt and Scruggs, Johnny Cash, and the Stanley Brothers. Joe Lee encouraged Hoskins to deposit the tapes with

Figure 5.2. Tom Hoskins. (Suzanne Hoskins Brown.)

the Library of Congress, but they are still owned by Leon Kagarise, who recorded them in Maryland in the 1950s and 1960s.[43]

He became interested in exploring the links between African and African American music and eventually found sponsorship for two trips to Africa to search for African musicians. However, according to sister Suzanne, he was upstaged by Paul Simon's 1986 album *Graceland*. Bill Storck continues: "When Tom returned from Africa, he stayed with Bill Tydings and his wife to be, Trudy. Bill told him the rules; no smoking in the house. Tom chain smoked Camel and drank. He agreed, then immediately broke all the rules. He pushed at the boundaries. By 1987 Bill Tydings had also asked Fang to find other accommodation."

Suzanne's husband Joe liked Tommy and always looked forward to his visits, though the two of them could hardly have been more different. Joe recalled a trip he took with Tom in 1996 or 1997. "It was the trip of my life. I think Tommy was using me; I had a credit card and Tommy did not. We needed to rent cars." They traveled by Amtrak and rented cars along the way. They called in to see Tommy's friend and musician Delta X (Stephan Michelson) in Portland, Oregon.

"We bought records, which were all conveyed over to Mike Stewart's house in North Carolina. Tommy carried a hiking bottle filled with vodka. At one point Tommy was smoking marijuana in a non-smoking compartment and people were complaining, but Tommy was oblivious. An announcement came on the public address system, 'we have ways of detecting cigarette smoke. Smoking marijuana is a federal offence, and if we find you, we will have federal marshals meet the train.'" Next day a black waitress said to Joe, "can't you take care of that boy?"

Tommy was still sending money to Ella Mae, who had moved to Tacoma, Washington, and on the same trip they called in to see her. Joe remembers a man coming into the room: "he didn't want us in there. I felt very uncomfortable."

Adelphi Records: *Memorial Anthology*

In January 1994, twenty years after the initial delay provoked by the Vanguard releases in 1971–72, Adelphi Records (Gene Rosenthal's company) released *Memorial Anthology* with an introduction by Gene Rosenthal. The double CD was subtitled *Previously Unreleased Recordings from the Blues Vault*. Unfortunately, Rosenthal did not mention his intention to do this to Tom Hoskins and Hoskins asked for the return of his tapes. Rosenthal refused, saying that Hoskins owed him money, including the original advance of $700 that he had given to Hoskins back in 1970. Disagreements about the income and allocation of profits between Hoskins and Rosenthal led to hostilities that resulted, at one stage, in police intervention.[44] Hoskins was ordered not to meet with Rosenthal again. Once again, Tom Hoskins was drawn into fighting his battles in a court of law.

In addition, Gene Rosenthal had apparently taken possession of the original Rebel masters that had been seized by a bank in Canada. When Bill Tydings visited Rosenthal in 1977 to collect Hoskins's tapes, Rosenthal had not given over all of the material that he had, saying that some had been lost.[45] However, nearly twenty years later in 1995, Gene Rosenthal claimed to have possession of the "most desirable master" for the Rebel recording, which, as part of the settlement of the litigation between Hoskins and Rosenthal, he gave back to Hoskins.[46] Thus, in 1997 Hoskins was able to authorize Rounder Records to release a CD version of the album called *Mississippi John Hurt: Legend*.[47] Hoskins received a $2,500 advance from Rounder.[48]

Rosenthal also illegally withheld the Library of Congress master tapes, which belonged to Hoskins under the 1963 contract. The court decided that Hoskins could have made at least $90,000 over the previous fifteen years had he had access to this and the Rebel material and that Rosenthal was responsible for this loss. Rosenthal also owed Hoskins at least $11,874 from the original Piedmont deal that ended in 1978. Tom's friend Joe Lee lent him the money to finance the litigation against Rosenthal's illegal use of the *Memorial Anthology* material and his retention of other tapes belonging to Hoskins. A bitter court battle ensued.

Settlement between Hoskins and Rosenthal was reached in 1995, giving Hoskins virtually all that he wanted. It was accepted that the 1970 agreement to produce the *Memorial Anthology* did not survive the Vanguard litigation and that the initial advance of $700 had been paid back by Hoskins as part of the accountings related to the Vanguard case in 1975. Furthermore, it was agreed and accepted that Rosenthal had illegally issued *Memorial Anthology* in 1993 and had made no attempt to contact Hoskins prior to its release. Rosenthal also had no right to use the photographs on the *Anthology* cover without permission under the original 1963 MRI agreement. The settlement agreement[49] required Hoskins to grant Adelphi rights in perpetuity to continue manufacturing and distributing *Memorial Anthology*, for which Hoskins would receive agreed royalties including an advance of $2,000 to be paid by June 30, 1996. Rosenthal was also required to pay Hoskins a further $12,000 immediately, to include payment of outstanding royalties earned on sales of *Memorial Anthology* through December 31, 1994.

The Library of Congress Recordings

The Library of Congress recordings that Dick Spottswood had masterminded soon after John's rediscovery in July 1963 were intended to record the majority of his music for posterity.[50] Following the subsequent recording and commercial release of much of John's repertoire between 1963 and 1966, the Library of Congress tapes were judged to represent versions recorded at a time before John had regained his full virtuosity.[51] Consequently, little commercial interest was shown in them for nearly twenty years, and they remained within the Library of Congress collections. Eventually their importance was recognized, and they were released on the Flyright and Heritage labels in the United Kingdom in 1980, 1982, and 1988[52]—not in the United States.

In 1990 Rounder Records approached Man Hurt (who was still lodging with Ms. Kitty in Grenada at this time) to obtain his permission to approach the Library of Congress with a view to releasing the music in the United States.[53] Man agreed to the proposal; however, the project did not go ahead and no Rounder release occurred. It would be another fourteen years—over forty years after they were first recorded—before Fuel 2000 Records eventually released the recordings for worldwide consumption on two double CDs.[54]

The Hurts and the Hoskins

Tom Hoskins did not have much chance to celebrate his victory over Rosenthal or his income from his original MRI contract. In 1993, eleven years after Jessie's death, it was discovered that John and Gertrude had never legally divorced and therefore Gertrude and her family had a legal claim on the estate.[55] Added to this was the question of the rights to income from recordings and music. It was to take another ten years or so to sort out.

Gertrude Hurt's descendants decided to seek a ruling on their legitimate rights to an inheritance from the Mississippi John Hurt estate. On March 11, 1993, Irene Smith, one of John and Gertrude's granddaughters, led a plaintiffs' complaint on behalf of Gertrude and her family against defendants Tom Hoskins and Bill Nowlin of the Rounder Record Group seeking a determination on three issues:

1. that Gertrude's side of the family are the rightful heirs.
2. that the management agreement (MRI) of March 15, 1963, was unconscionable and should be cancelled because "the terms of the contract are so outrageous, abusive, [and] fraudulent" that they "constitute total robbery by the defendant Thomas Hoskins."
3. that a mandatory injunction be raised to compel Hoskins, Nowlin. and Rounder to pay royalties to plaintiffs.[56]

Tom Hoskins was hardly aware of Gertrude and her side of the family, nor is there any evidence that Jessie ever mentioned them to him. This seems understandable given that, although Jessie knew Gertrude, it was widely accepted that John and Gertrude had parted long ago and Jessie had been his wife for over thirty-five years.

Most of John's East Coast acquaintances had no knowledge of Gertrude and her side of the family, but John's grandnephew, Fred Bolden, said that his mother knew Gertrude very well and grew up with her cousins, John and Gertrude's children T. C. and Ida Mae. The Spottswoods and, presumably, Tom Hoskins had heard of her, but she had not featured in John's life since they had known him. As far as most people in the East were concerned, Jessie was John's wife. Indeed, even some of John's acquaintances in the Valley area were not aware of Gertrude, although T. C. and his family were well known. Billy Campbell and Josephine Jackson, who have lived in the Valley community all of their lives, explained that people traveled very little in those days and there was little interchange even between the Delta folk in Avalon and the hill folk around Valley. In spite of this, however, T. C.'s children would frequently visit John (Daddy John) and Jessie in the Valley area and Gertrude (Mama Dear), who lived close to them on Delta land in Avalon. Gertrude and her sister Jennie Simms were photographed together along with Jessie, John, and the grandchildren outside John's house in 1963 when Tom Hoskins first visited (see ch. 3), and it seems likely that she was among the folks singing along inside the house when Hoskins made those first recordings.

Gertrude described Jessie as a "loose" woman who traveled from southern Mississippi to a logging camp near Avalon in the hopes of finding a man.[57] Jessie later confirmed to John's grandnephew Fred Bolden that she had been searching for a husband. Gertrude also claimed that Jessie was already pregnant with Man Hurt when she met John, but this is not possible as John "married" Jessie on December 4, 1927, and Man was not born until 1932. Gertrude said that John never married Jessie, but a record of the marriage of John Hurt to Jessie Nelson in 1927 was located in the Leflore County courthouse.[58] Jessie had previously been married, changing her name from Cole to Nelson (see ch. 1). However, John was apparently never divorced from Gertrude, and so his marriage to Jessie was bigamous and invalid. John had told Tom Hoskins that he had talked to his white boss at the time about his split with Gertrude and he said that he would "take care of it." Apparently he failed to do that, perhaps thinking that it was not important for a poor black sharecropper.

Gertrude and her children with John, Ida Mae and T. C., had always lived around Avalon, except for the brief period that Gertrude, Will Conley, Ida Mae, and T. C. spent in Bolivar County during the 1920s. It had apparently not entered anyone's head that they might expect an inheritance from John. After all, poor black sharecroppers were not in the habit of leaving much to anyone anyhow.

Gertrude's children and grandchildren all knew Jessie and remained close to her even after John's death. Irene Smith (Mary Frances's sister) said, "We knew Miss Jessie wasn't our real grandmother, but we treated her like a grandmother." She added that Gertrude sometimes looked after Man Hurt, but Man gave a contradictory account, saying that the only father and mother he ever knew were John and Jessie and that the Hurts were only interested in getting the royalties.[59] Mary Frances found this account by Man particularly distressing, telling me that her Uncle Man and her mother were childhood friends and that Man was responsible for introducing her mother, Annie Dora Richardson, to her father T. C. Man was the only Uncle that T. C.'s children had on the paternal side of the family and they had close contact with Man as children. Mary Frances and her siblings deeply loved and respected Ms. Jessie, and Mary Frances remembered that Jessie sent gifts of clothing for her mother and gifts for the children, including a pair of roller skates for Mary Frances, from Washington, D.C.

Mary Frances's brother Lonnie, who spent many years working in Indianapolis but returned to Avalon, said that as a young man his grandfather was the most influential person in his life. *Memphis Flyer* reporter Heather Heilman reported:

> As he looked at the house where his grandfather lived and thought about the conflict that divided his family, he began to weep. "Money would be good, but it's not about money. It's about this family." Lonnie said that Man had recently visited them in 1999. "He was down here two months ago, sat down, and had dinner at our table." Lonnie continued, "If you could have known my grandfather you'd understand. My grandfather was a very, very special person. I'm not talking just because of his music or the money he made, I'm talking as a person. When I was a kid he would talk to me. He encouraged me to make something of myself, without ever yelling at me. He taught me not to be bitter about the way things are. He's part of me." He added, "The family's sacrifices were humanity's gain."[60]

The court case proceeded. Hoskins's legal team presented affidavits from four people described as "experts from the record industry" (Stephen C. LaVere, ED Denson, Stefan Grossman, and Charles Kingman Mitchell)[61] who stated that they felt that the terms of the original Music Research Inc. contract were "well within industry standards and very fair to John Hurt," and that there was no proof that the terms were outrageous, abusive, and fraudulent.[62] A court ruling on February 16, 1994, vindicated Hoskins, Nowlin, and Rounder.[63]

It took a further five years to settle the issue of inheritance. On May 17, 1999, in the Chancery Court of Grenada County, Mississippi, it was ruled that the only rightful heirs of John S. Hurt, deceased, are his wife, Gertrude Conley Hurt, the heirs of his deceased daughter, Idella Hurt Johnson (Ida Mae), who are Dorothy Miller and Jesse Johnson; and the heirs of his deceased son, T. C. Conley Hurt, which include, petitioners Irene Smith, Willie Ed Conley Hurt, T. C. Conley Hurt Jr., Lonnie Conley Hurt, Ulysses Conley Hurt, Sterling Conley Hurt, Mary Frances Conley Hurt Wright, Mary Ann Conley Hurt West, Rebecca Conley

Hurt, Henry Lee Conley Hurt, Annie Conley Hurt White, and Bobbie Conley Hurt Lawrence.[64] But this did not address Tom Hoskins's rights relevant to his continuing interest in John's music, and a further challenge on behalf of Gertrude's side of the family by Irene Smith against Hoskins was raised.

On January 24, 2000, Tom Hoskins, who was then residing at 185 Piedmont Road, Rutherfordton, North Carolina, answered under oath several questions raised by the Hurts. This was aimed at establishing the rights to John's recordings under the terms of the initial Music Research contract. Hoskins described his rediscovery of Mississippi John Hurt and his subsequent relationship with John and Jessie. This included providing transport for them, taking care of medical needs, shopping for clothes and groceries, registering the children in school, and paying for them to attend a YMCA summer camp in Dowington, Pennsylvania, for three or four years.[65]

Hoskins went on to describe how he had intended to make a profit from his promotion of Mississippi John Hurt, but that Hurt was unable to generate enough income during his lifetime to make this possible.

While the fees for his appearances were very respectable, he was not able to work as often as a younger performer might have been. Additionally, someone had to travel with him which added expenses for food, tickets, etc. The terms of the Hurt–Music Research contract were never enforced by Music Research or myself. From 1965, nearly all gross revenue from all sources was paid to John Hurt and later to his widow, Jessie until her death around 1980. My relationship with the Hurts had become one of family. I had promised John that if he died before Jessie, I would do what I could to see to the welfare of Jessie, Andrew Lee and Ella Mae. This I did to the best of my ability.

Far from being "robbed" by Music Research and myself as is alleged in this lawsuit, John Hurt was able to experience many things otherwise impossible. He enjoyed traveling especially to music festivals. He met fans and other musicians who appreciated and respected his music and loved him as a person. The last three and a half years of his life were very satisfying to John Hurt and far removed from being a tenant farmer making twenty-eight dollars a month. It is my hope to now begin to derive some financial return from my investment in John Hurt's recordings as called for in the Hurt–Music Research agreement. As I have no children or close relatives, I intend to leave my interest in the recordings to the two Hurt grandchildren, Andrew Lee and Ella Mae Hurt.[66]

Vanguard paid royalties to John until his death and then to Jessie until she died. After 1981, Vanguard and Lawrence Welk Music Company, to whom Vanguard subsequently sold the contract, paid royalties to Tom Hoskins, who in turn paid a percentage to John William and Ella Mae.

Tom Hoskins was required to provide accounts covering his dealings with the various record companies; these were presented on March 4, 2001, and accepted by the court based on credible evidence on October 25, 2004.[67] The court summarized the income as shown in Table 5.2.

In 1992 Wynwood was still sending money to John William "Man" Hurt and his daughter Ella Mae. Andrew could not be traced at this time, but had apparently been living in Fort Smith, Arkansas, around 1985.[68] According to the original Music Research contract, the company, now owned by Tom Hoskins, was entitled to half of Vanguard and Wynwood Royalties. However, Hoskins, under oath in the Chancery Court of Grenada County, Mississippi, gave the following account of what actually took place.

> John and his common law wife, Jesse [sic], who was named sole heir by this Court on November 8, 1967, had two young grandchildren to raise and their only income was his occasional live performances and record royalties. In 1965, I gained control of Music Research and made the decision to advance all royalties to John's family, as they needed it more than I did. They were in their early 70s, raising two young grandchildren and I was a young man of 25, single and able to support myself by other means. My thinking was, "They get money now when they need it and I'll get mine later when I'm older."

Hoskins went on to state: "I did not take any of the Vanguard money until 1994 and have never taken any of the Wynwood money to this day."[69] The court found that these facts had been established by credible evidence. Tom Hoskins had named Ella Mae his heir.[70]

The Welk Music Group purchased Vanguard in 1986. On June 30, 1994, their royalties manager, Mardelle Cordero, sent a check for $26,712.92 to Tom Hoskins's lawyer as payment of royalties for the period 1986–93. Apparently this payment is included in the $33,000 paid by Vanguard to Tom Hoskins (see Table 5.2).

In March 1998 Rounder Records passed on to Tom Hoskins a letter that they had received from a Paul Van Gelder of Carmel, California, who said he had some audiotapes and a film reel (shot by Jacobsen) of Mississippi John Hurt and the Reverend Robert Wilkins. Hoskins contacted Van Gelder, saying that the material was stolen from his Maryland

Table 5.2. Summary of Income and Its Distribution

Period	Record or Publishing Company	John Hurt, Jessie et al.	MRI/Tom Hoskins
1966-1972	Vanguard	$19,117.42 (estimated)	
1966-1972	Wynwood	$13,109.10 (estimated)	
1967-1992	Origin Jazz Library	$48,000.00 (estimated)	
1973-1983	Vanguard	$41,021.66 (estimated)	
1973-1992	Wynwood	$40,026.00 (estimated)	
1984-1997	Vanguard	$9,500.00 (actual)	
1993-2000	Wynwood	$63,000.00 (estimated)	
1984-1999	Vanguard		$33,000 (estimated)
1993-1999	Rounder		$33,820.69* (actual)
	Adelphi		$16,715.45 (actual)
	Collectables		$3,164.00 (actual)
Totals		**$233,774.18**	**$86,700.14**

* Includes $4,247.35 withheld at the time, pending conclusion of litigation.

apartment in 1965 and asked for the return. There is no known record of whether this material was returned and it has not been possible to trace Van Gelder.

The Death of Tom Hoskins

In 2002, just six months before he died, Tom turned up at Bill Storck's house seeking a safe place to store several boxes containing papers and records, "He turned up in an old Volvo crammed with all his possessions. He handed me a box of tapes and an envelope, saying, 'this is the Rosetta stone. It is priceless. Do not lose this.'" Around three years later, in 2005, Bill handed me that same package and the tapes and asked if I would convey them to Tom's sister Suzanne, which I did. The package contained the original letters that had been written by John in 1963–66, and by Jessie in 1966–71, and sent to Tom. The tapes included the original re-cordings made by Tom in John's house in Avalon in March 1963 when he rediscovered Mississippi John Hurt.

On January 27, 2002, almost two years to the day after court proceed-ings had been initiated by the Hurt family, exhausted by the continual battles over the legacy of Mississippi John Hurt, lonely and with failing eyesight, Tom Hoskins died. He was 61 years old. His life ebbed away in a trailer park in Tallahassee, Florida, where he was found in a comatose state, his liver failing. By the time his sister Suzanne and her husband Joe got down there he was in a very poor state and died soon after in the hospital. The CD player and space heater that Suzanne and Joe had bought for him and his prized Emory guitar that John had played when he first visited Washington, and which he played at the Newport Folk Festival in 1963, were gone. Bill Storck told me, "Fang had placed so much value on that guitar, especially as John had played it."

Suzanne inherited Tom's estate, which largely consisted of several cardboard boxes of papers, records, and tapes. More significantly, her inheritance also involved substituting for her brother and shouldering the burden of the ongoing court case. Bill told me that Tom would have been furious that Suzanne had to spend so much money on litigation with the Hurt family.

Closure of the Hurt and Hoskins Litigation

The case rumbled on and eventually, on October 25, 2004, the Chancery Court in Grenada County, Mississippi, calculated that the estate of Tom Hoskins was entitled to half of the $233,774.18 that Jessie and family had received since John died, less the amount that he had already received. This appeared to leave $30,186.95 owed to Hoskins by the heirs. The court ruled that the estate of Tom Hoskins owns all rights in and to any music recorded by John Hurt during the terms of the management agreement (March 15, 1963–March 15, 1973), including record copyrights, as well as the physical tapes on which the recordings are embedded, along with a continuing entitlement to receive royalties from the Vanguard, Rounder, Adelphi, and Collectables record contracts and the Wynwood publishing agreement. The court dismissed the plaintiffs' (Gertrude's family) complaint and ordered that they should pay the costs of the court.[71]

Subsequently, a "Release and Settlement Agreement" was made between the Hurt estate (Gertrude's family, with Mary Francis Hurt Wright as executrix) and the Hoskins estate (with Suzanne Brown as executrix). The two sides agreed that all royalty payments, including those currently held in escrow, from Vanguard, Rounder, Adelphi, and Collectables would be divided equally between the Hurt heirs and the Hoskins estate. Agreement was also reached that the Mississippi John Hurt materials, including copyright and all extensions and renewals thereof, are owned by the Hoskins estate.[72]

On the subject of further recordings of Mississippi John Hurt, agreement was reached that each of the parties would cooperate in good faith to negotiate an agreement with Jay Warner, who manages the publishing rights for many artists, for the distribution and use of recordings of musical performances and spoken words of Mississippi John Hurt and tapes, CDs, and other recording formats, with all net revenues being disbursed equally between them. This agreement expired in August 2008. Similarly, agreement was reached that the parties would cooperate for the purpose of enhancing the Mississippi John Hurt Museum, including the loan of items for display.

John clearly enjoyed much of his rediscovery time, playing his music to appreciative and adoring audiences, making many good friends and generally enjoying life. He was never rich, but John did not desire money; and although his performing career did not generate huge amounts of money, relative to what John and his family had been used to before 1963 there was enough to make a considerable difference to their lifestyle. While they reaped some benefits from this, after John's death Jessie and the grandchildren suffered considerable hardship almost entirely due to negligence on the part of several people, including some of those indirectly involved. Although incompetence, rather than premeditated malice, played a large part in this neglect, it has left an inexcusable legacy of hardship to the remaining Hurt family members.

Back in Avalon

John's many friends and relatives around Valley missed John and Jessie. After John died Jessie made the trip from Grenada from time to time to visit John's brothers Hennis and Hardy until their deaths in 1969 and 1971. Today Avalon is a shadow of what it once was. It no longer qualifies as a town, being a quiet, hardly noticeable cluster of houses off Highway 7. The Stinson's Store had been the focus of the Avalon community since the Stinsons opened the store in 1908. Locals Larry and Mary Smith and Leagh Watson told me that Mrs. Stinson continued to run the store after the death of her husband in 1957 until around 1970, when it closed. In the mid-1970s it reopened and was run by Elaine and Bud Leishman for about two years after which they sold it to Buddy Cook who continued to run it for a further two years until around 1980, when it closed for good.

Figure 5.3. The author at the Valley Store, July 2003. (Neil Harpe.)

On a very windy day in the early 1980s it burned, and only the concrete base and metal supports remain today. The sharecropper's shacks and the other stores are long gone. The railroad station building, covered in creepers, finally collapsed in 2008. Only the abandoned Avalon cotton gin remains from the old days, along with a scatter of houses located along the old Highway 7. Up the hill at Valley, there are hardly any dwellings along St. James Road, and the Hurt cemetery is all that remains there of a bygone age.

The Morelands sold the Valley Store in 1968 to Lahoma and Joyce Matthews, who owned it briefly before selling it to Larry Smith, the present owner, in 1969. The store finally closed down in 1994.[73]

Gertrude's granddaughter Dorothy had always lived with Gertrude since her mother's murder. After the death of T. C. in 1966, without a man to work on the plantation, Gertrude and Mary Frances's family houses were no longer available to them and they were forced to move. Gertrude and Dorothy found a small apartment in Greenwood. The living conditions were poor. In 1996, when Gertrude was 105 years old, the water heater in the building exploded and the building was engulfed in flames. Gertrude was rescued from her room by her grandson Leggeso Kimble.[74]

Figure 5.4. John's house on its original site, 2001. (Mary Frances Hurt Wright.)

Mary's mother Annie Richardson inherited land from her parents that had been in the Hurt family since she married T. C., and she was able to build a house there after T. C.'s death. Many of John's living descendants are living a meager lifestyle today, as they always have. It is to be hoped that, following the relatively recent settlements, and the release of funds, this will change for the better.

John's last employer in Valley, Albert Reginald Perkins, died on July 29, 1996, after being attacked by a bull. Longest lived of John's generation was his first wife, Gertrude, who died three months after Tom Hoskins on April 26, 2002. Her close family and the temporary grave marker indicate that she was born June 25, 1890, and aged 111 years at her death. However, early census data (see ch. 1) indicate that she was born in 1898, listed at 2 years old in 1900, and 12 in 1910. This would make her 103 when she died.

The Valley store and John's house are pretty much the only inanimate connections left to the thriving community that once nurtured the famous songster. But the memories live on among the older folk, and they are passing them along to the younger ones.

Rescuing John's House

By the end of the twentieth century John's old house was decaying. Nobody had lived in it since John, Jessie, Ella Mae, and Andrew left for

Washington in 1963. Perkins used it to store hay until his death in 1996. In 1995 Mary Frances was having recurring visions of her Daddy John's house sitting and decaying in that field. By the end of 1997 the frustration led her to make a lone trip to Mississippi. She told none of her relatives in Carroll County and Greenwood that she was coming, not even her mother. She took the train to Greenwood and rented a car. Stopping nowhere, she drove to Daddy John's old house.

Nothing about the house had changed since her previous visit a few months earlier. She stood gazing at the house with her back to the road when a car stopped behind her. It was fairly common for people to come and take pictures of the house or pose on the porch or by the old well and she did not turn around. In frustration and with little thought she uttered the words, "God, I wish I knew who owned this house." The person behind her asked what that old house meant to her and what she would do with it if she knew. She replied, "My grandfather used to live here a long time ago." The man asked again, "What would you do if you knew who owned the house?" Out of the blue she replied, "I would make it a museum."

The man responded immediately, "I am the owner of this house and you can buy it from me." In shock she turned around, asking if he knew her or her grandfather. The stranger responded, "I do not know you or your grandfather, but God told me you would be here today." He said that he had sold all the land around there except the house and the land that surrounded it. Someone from up north had offered him $5,000 some years ago, but his daughter had talked him out of it, thinking that it may be of more value for the family of the person who once lived there. Then he said, "I will sell it to you now for the same price." To Mary it might well have been a million dollars. She didn't have even $500 at that time. She said nothing of her financial situation and promised him she would have the money the next day.

She jumped into the car and immediately drove to the Peoples Bank and Trust in North Carrollton and asked to speak with the president. His name was Pate and a clerk showed her into his office. She told him her story and how she had promised to have $5,000 available for the purchase next day. She rambled on and on about her vision of saving Daddy John's house until she noticed that Pate was simply leaning back in his chair and staring at her in disbelief. When she stopped talking he took advantage of the silence to ask, "What is it you are trying to buy?" She replied more calmly, telling him where the house was located and that it was no longer a house, but a barn. To Mary's surprise he answered, "You mean the old John Hurt house? Sure, you can pick up your check tomorrow."

The next day, as soon as the check was placed into her hands, she went immediately to the store on the corner across the street from the bank where Dave Murphy, the owner of Daddy John's house, was waiting. As soon as she saw Murphy's face she sensed a problem. He took her aside and told her that the owners of the surrounding land did not want a museum there, as it would disrupt their privacy. Someone might even burn it down. Continuing, he added, "but if you could move the house, you can have it free of charge." She thought, "Move a house?!" Utterly devastated, she returned to her mother's house to wait until her train left for Chicago the following evening. When she arrived, her mother's telephone was ringing. She answered it. It was a friend that normally checked on her mother after her dialysis treatments. Sensing the despair in Mary's voice, she asked, "Why are you so upset?" Mary told of her dilemma. The lady replied, "Moving houses is no big deal. People do that kind of thing all the time. In fact my parents moved a house and I know that the company is still in business."

A few minutes later she called back with the telephone number of the company located in Kosciusko, Mississippi. Mary called them and described the situation with Daddy John's house. The man explained that he could move the house using hydraulic jacks, but that it would be very expensive. Fearing another setback she asked how much? He replied, $5000.00. She immediately asked him to repeat the figure to be sure that she had heard him properly. He replied that a house that age would require special care and it was the best deal he could do and that she could take it or leave it. Of course, it was a perfect deal.

With the house moved to Mary's land close by, she needed help, and it came along in the form of Art Browning. Art had grown up in Avalon and was aware of John, but never met him. He left Avalon to live in Jackson, Mississippi in 1960. Later, he heard about John's rediscovery and became a big Hurt fan. He decided to move back to Avalon in 1995 and often passed by John's old house along from the Valley Store.

Art was passing by one day, and as he glanced over to the big magnolia tree that shaded the front porch of John's old house, he stopped short, hardly believing his eyes. The house was gone! He made inquiries and soon learned that John's granddaughter had succeeded in moving the house down the road to her place. When he arrived at the newly located old house, he saw a young lady sweeping dust and hay from the place; he asked what she was doing. She replied that she was cleaning her granddaddy's house up and that she was going to turn it into a museum. Seeing the scale of the task ahead, he promptly offered to help: "A museum? You're going to need things to put in it." And so he began scouring the countryside and asking the locals for artifacts that might enhance the new museum. Items of furniture, record sleeves, photographs, and press cuttings were donated, and the museum took shape.

Mary had previously met Floyd Bailey, who also offered to help, and was the first one to open the door of the dilapidated house. "There were wasps and yellow jackets in there, and I was stung several times," he said.

The Mississippi John Hurt Foundation

In spite of her recent activity, Mary was still bewildered about the recognition given to her Daddy John and realized that there was more to do. She established the Mississippi John Hurt Blues Foundation in 1999. The foundation is a nonprofit foundation with the following objectives:

- To preserve the family and musical history of Mississippi John Hurt.
- To expose disadvantaged urban and rural children to folk/blues music by providing educational opportunities and hands-on experience.
- To nurture aspiring musicians in the field of folk/blues by providing performance opportunities and scholarship assistance.
- To promote appreciation of African American culture as it relates to the foundation of music by providing students with in-depth study.

The foundation seeks corporate and individual support to fund these objectives.

Neil Harpe, an artist and musician from Annapolis, Maryland, and a big fan and exponent of Hurt's music, had painted some very fine pictures of blues musicians and he had recently finished a picture of Mississippi John Hurt and placed it on his website. In 2002 he received a telephone call enquiring about the picture. A lady's voice said, "You have a picture of my grandfather on your website and I'd like to buy it." Neil answered, "I'm afraid you must be mistaken, that is a picture of the musician, Mississippi John Hurt." Her response floored Neil: "Yes, I know, he's my grandfather." A long discussion followed. Neil, in common with other people who knew of John Hurt during his rediscovery period, knew nothing about this side of the family. The picture was acquired for the museum and now occupies a central position on entering the building.

As word of the foundation and the Museum spread, Mary began to accumulate pieces of furniture and memorabilia about John. Floyd Bailey and Art Browning continue to support Mary to this day. Art is the curator of the museum and Bailey is always on hand to help with all manner of organizational and maintenance jobs needed to keep things going. Mary organized a dedication ceremony and music festival to open the museum on July 4, 2002.

John Sebastian, who named his sixties rock band the Lovin' Spoonful after lyrics in John's "Coffee Blues," was the special guest, and musicians Mike Baytop, Eleanor Ellis, and Neil Harpe traveled from Annapolis to attend. Mary decided that she would hold an annual festival each July 4, and in 2003 the first Mississippi John Hurt Festival was held.

Increasing Recognition in Mississippi

After the second festival on July 7, 2004, Mississippi John Hurt was honored by the Mississippi Department of Archives and History with a state historic marker on Highway 7 at Avalon. The marker reads:

> *John S Hurt (1893–1966) was a pioneer blues and folk guitarist. Self-taught, Hurt rarely left his home at Avalon, where he worked as a farmer. Although he recorded several songs in 1928, including "Avalon Blues" and "Frankie," he lived in relative obscurity before he was "rediscovered" in the blues revival of the 1960s.*

A small dedication ceremony was held at the marker site at which Art Browning, the museum curator; Steve Cheseborough, a local Greenwood musician and writer; and this author Phil Ratcliffe performed. Local dignitaries and Mary Frances Hurt Wright made speeches. Mary Frances said: "This sign marks an important period in my life, because it confirms the historical and heroic attempt my grandfather made toward a completion of life. It confirms what an individual can do if he or she believes in himself and is willing to sacrifice enough to accomplish his dreams. I hope people, as I have, use my grandfather as an example to continue to endeavor and persevere in whatever their dreams may be."

Interestingly, Mary views her grandfather's achievements as a person as being greater than his achievements as a musician. This is perhaps to be expected from a family member, but it does support the view expressed in this book that John Hurt's persona was every bit as significant as Mississippi John Hurt the musician.

A further tribute was made on February 25, 2008, when a crowd of around one hundred gathered at the Valley Store in the hill country above Avalon for the dedication of a second historic marker (see Fig. 5.5). Apart

Figure 5.5. Mary Frances Hurt Wright at the Mississippi John Hurt Historic Marker, Valley Store, Valley. Mississippi Blues Commission, 2008. (Philip R. Ratcliffe.)

from John's house that now houses the museum, the store is just about the only remaining building that John actually frequented. The store is special because it served as the center of the small Valley community for nearly a century. The crowd gathered to witness the unveiling of a Mississippi Blues Trail marker provided by the Mississippi Blues Commission honoring Mississippi John Hurt. Wanda Clark, director of the Blues Trail Project, emceed the event and paid tribute to Hurt, saying that her father had visited the store and knew John. Gene Bush paid tribute by telling of the day he sat with John overlooking the Yalobusha River near the house on North Levee Street in Grenada (see ch. 4). They had sat for nearly two hours in silence. Gene said, "He had a quietness about him that spoke volumes."

On my way to attend this event, I stopped off in Atlanta to pick up Tom Hoskins's sister Suzanne. At the dedication ceremony I was invited to pay my own tribute to John and to speak of my progress in writing this biography. Most significantly, I was able to bring together Mary Frances and Suzanne who, in spite of past differences, share a common desire to increase the recognition of Mississippi John Hurt (see Fig. 5.6).

The marker reads:

> *World-renowned master of the acoustic guitar John Hurt, an important figure in the 1960s folk blues revival, spent most of his life doing farm work around Avalon in Carroll County and performing for parties and*

Figure 5.6. The author with Mary Frances Hurt Wright and Suzanne Hoskins Brown at the Valley Store historic marker dedication ceremony, February 2008. (Annie Ratcliffe.)

local gatherings. Hurt (1893–1966) only began to earn a living from music after he left Mississippi in 1963 to play at folk festivals, colleges, and coffeehouses. His first recordings, 78 rpm discs released in 1928– 29, are regarded as classics of the blues genre.

On the reverse side of the marker there is an abundance of information summarizing the story of John's life.

Tributes to Mississippi John Hurt

Many artists have drawn inspiration from the music of Mississippi John Hurt and many have honored this by recording his songs and by composing others about him. John had asked his close friend Archie Edwards to continue his music: "Brother Arch, whatever you do, teach my music to other people. Don't make no difference what color they are, teach it to them. Because I don't want to die and you don't want to die. Teach them my music and teach them your music."[75]

Archie felt uncomfortable carrying this responsibility, due to his modesty in worrying that people would think he was trying to cash in on John Hurt's name and reputation. As a consequence Archie did not play guitar seriously again for two years after John's death, when he returned and wrote "The Road is Rough and Rocky," openly displaying his sadness for John's passing and his friendship with him.

> *The road is rough and rocky but it won't be rocky long,*
> *John Hurt was my best friend but now he's dead and gone.*[76]

Patrick Sky displays a photograph of himself with Mississippi John Hurt on his 1975 LP *Two Steps Forward One Step Back* on which he covers John's "Frankie and Albert," "Payday," and "Candy Man."[77] In 1999 Bill Morrissey released his tribute, the CD *Songs of Mississippi John Hurt.* Another tribute CD, *Tribute to the Music of Mississippi John Hurt*, published in July 2001, included contributions from a variety of big names including Taj Mahal, Bill Morrissey, John Hiatt, Geoff Muldaur, Alvin Youngblood Hart, Steve and Justin Earle, and Lucinda Williams. The 1972 LP by Taj Mahal, *Recycling the Blues and Other Related Stuff*,[78] carries a photo of Taj and Mississippi John Hurt taken at a Newport Folk Festival on the cover, implying a connection between the two, but he does not play any John Hurt songs on the record.

Lost Jim (Jim Ohlmschmidt) has recorded three CDs of John's music: *Lost Jim Sings & Plays Mississippi John Hurt, Payday: Lost Jim Plays & Sings Mississippi John Hurt Vol. 2*, and *Got the Blues, Can't Be Satisfied: Lost Jim Sings Mississippi John Hurt Vol. 3*.[79] Stefan Grossman commented, "Jim really captures the feel, sound and atmosphere of John's music. The guitar playing is spot on and the vocals are great—very warm and evocative."

Tunes composed about Mississippi John Hurt are included in Table 5.3, which culminates with the very fine tribute by Lost Jim in which he strings together snippets of melodies from several of John's tunes into a self-composed song, "Dear Old Daddy John" about the story of John's life. Appendix 4 provides a discography of Mississippi John Hurt's music based on the excellent web-based, illustrated discography by Stefan Wirz.[80]

Stefan Grossman has played an important role in introducing a lot of aspiring musicians to Mississippi John Hurt's music and, thereby, his persona. As a young man in New York in the 1960s, Stefan was obsessed with learning how to play guitar in the way of the old blues musicians. He met and learned from Mississippi John Hurt and Reverend Gary Davis. Since those days, in addition to becoming a leading exponent of finger style guitar, he has established himself through his Stefan Grossman Guitar Workshop as one of the primary teachers of the genre. Guitar workshop

Table 5.3. Tunes composed about Mississippi John Hurt

Title	Artist	Album
Requiem for John Hurt	John Fahey	*John Fahey: Requia and Other Compositions for Guitar*, Vanguard VRS-9259 (SVRL-19033 UK), 1968
John Hurt	Hollins and Star	*Sidewalks Talking*, Ovation OV 14-07, 1970
Sam Lay & Mississippi John	Sam Lay	*Sam Lay in Bluesland*, Blue Thumb BTS-14, 1970
Funeral Song for John Hurt	John Fahey	*John Fahey and His Orchestra: Of Rivers and Religion*, Reprise CHR 1006, 1972; *John Fahey: Live in Tasmania*, Takoma TAK 7089, 1981
Did You Hear John Hurt	Tom Paxton	*Tom Paxton: New Songs From the Briarpatch*, Vanguard VSD-79395, 1977
Mississippi John	Wizz Jones	*Wizz Jones: Magical Flight*, PLR 009 (UK), 1977; Folk Freak FF 4003, 1978; Scenes of SCOFCD 1006, 1999
Did You Hear John Hurt	Dave Van Ronk	*Dave Van Ronk: Somebody Else, Not Me*, Philo PH 1065, 1979; *The Greenwich Village Folk Festival 1989-90*, Gadfly 222 (CD Gadfly 100591), 1990; *Dave Van Ronk: . . . and the tin pan bended and the story ended . . .* , Smithsonian Folkways CD SFW 40156, 2004
Did You Hear John Hurt	Doc and Merle Watson	*Sittin' Here Pickin' the Blues*, Rounder CD 1166-11617-2, 2004
John Hurt	Doc and Merle Watson	*Red Rocking Chair*, Flying Fish 17252, 1981
John Hurt Medley	Chris Smither	*Chris Smither: It Ain't Easy*, Adelphi AD 1031 and GCD 1031, 1984
Ode To Mississippi John Hurt	Stefan Grossman	*Stefan Grossman: Love, Devils and Blues*, Shanachie 97001, 1988
John Hurt	Dave Van Ronk	*Dave Van Ronk: A Chrestomathy*, Gazell GPCD 2007/8, 1992
Did You Hear John Hurt	Tom Paxton & Dave Van Ronk	*Christine Lavin Presents: Follow That Road*, Rounder/Philo CD 1164, 1994
Mississippi John	Happy and Artie Traum	*The Test of Time*, Roaring Stream RS 201, 1994
John Hurt Medley	Shinobu Sato	*Shinobu Sato: Little Signs of Autumn*, Waterbug CD 3, 1994
John Hurt Medley	Terry Robb's Acoustic Blues Trio	*Terry Robb: Acoustic Blues Trio*, Burnside CD 19, 1995

John Hurt in the 21st Century	Peter Lang	*Peter Lang: Guitar*, Horus HM 1036, 2003
Did You Hear John Hurt?	Eve Goldberg	*Eve Goldberg: Crossing the Water*, Borealis BCD 150, 2003
Tribute to Mississippi John Hurt	Chris Smither	*Honeysuckle Dog*, Okra-Tone CD 4971, 2004
Did You Hear John Hurt?'	Tom Paxton, Bob Gibson & Anne Hills	*Tom Paxton, Bob Gibson & Anne Hills: Best Of Friends*, Appleseed CD 1077, 2004
Mississippi John Hurt (Instrumental)	Taj Mahal	*Blues Masters: Taj Mahal*, Digital Musicworks International, 2005
Daddy John (Instrumental)	Lost Jim	*Payday: Lost Jim Plays & Sings Mississippi John Hurt, Vol 2* JPG Records, 2006
Dear Old Daddy John	Lost Jim	*Got The Blues, Can't Be Satisfied: Lost Jim Sings Mississippi John Hurt*, CD to be released

lessons on CD by Grossman[81] and DVDs by John Miller[82] along with the accompanying booklets provide an effective way for guitarists to become familiar with Hurt's music and have played a significant role in introducing Hurt's music to a large number of people.

On April 12, 2006, the New York Guitar Festival presented "Blues Fallin' Down Like Rain": four evenings celebrating the music of Mississippi John Hurt, Skip James, Charlie Patton, and Elizabeth Cotten. The performers included Jorma Kaukonen, John Hammond, Rory Block, Stefan Grossman, Taj Mahal, Mike Seeger, Alvin Youngblood Hart, Jen Chapin, and Charlie Sexton.

Later that year, on November 18, the Friends of Old Time Music (FOTM) presented their conference, "Folk Music in the City," at the Proshansky Auditorium CUNY Graduate Center, 365 Fifth Avenue at 34th Street. At Town Hall that evening, they presented the Friends of Old Time Music Tribute Concert with Doc Watson and the New Lost City Ramblers. Among an eminent gathering of guest speakers that included Ron Cohen, John Cohen, Izzy Young, Kate Rinzler, Peter Siegel, Ray Allen, Mike Seeger, Richard Kurin, Henrietta Yurchenco, Doc Watson, Bill Malone, and Jean Ritchie, Mary Frances Hurt Wright spoke about her grandfather, Mississippi John Hurt. It was almost forty years after he had appeared as a guest performer there.

Mississippi John Hurt is recognized all over the world as one of the greatest of the early southern folk musicians, and more and more people are enjoying his music. John's legacy to humanity as a wonderful warm

Figure 5.7. The author (a.k.a. Dr. Phil; Delta Dan) with Gene Bush at the Mississippi John Hurt Festival, 2009. (Jim Steeby.)

person whose personal philosophy transcends false boundaries of race and class is also increasingly recognized with every new generation. I hope that this book will continue to spread this message and be recognized as a fitting tribute to that wonderful little man in the fedora from Avalon, Mississippi.

A Final Word

On July 2, 2003, accompanied by Neil Harpe, I arrived at the first Mississippi John Hurt festival among the hills in Valley above Avalon, Mississippi. The sun was shining and it was hot and humid. The scene was relaxed. People were wandering around making ready for the gospel and blues festivals to be held over the next two days. I immediately spotted the old shotgun house in which John and Jessie had lived. As we got out of the car we were greeted with a warm welcome from an elegant lady with a big smile.

"Hi and welcome, I am Mary Frances," she said. I could hardly believe that I was here in Avalon talking to Mississippi John Hurt's granddaughter. The next two days were a whirl of excitement, friendship, love, and emotion. I spent hours talking to local people who had known John. I scribbled a few notes, played some of John's tunes, and drank a beer or two under the shade of the trees in the humid heat of midsummer Mississippi. Without being aware of it, I had begun to catalogue the story of Mississippi John Hurt. Now I have come full circle. I hope that you have enjoyed his story.

Appendix I

Interviews, Correspondence, and Personal Communications

All digital sound recordings and copies of correspondence and emails are held in the Philip R. Ratcliffe Archive, Dunoon, Scotland, UK.

Fred Bolden recorded interview, Boston, 2006 and subsequent email messages.

Cindy Bennett, recorded interview, Avalon, Mississippi, 2004.

Suzanne Hoskins Brown and Joe Brown, recorded interview, Smyrna, Georgia, 2006 and subsequent discussions and correspondence.

Art Browning, recorded interview, Avalon, Mississippi, 2006 and subsequent discussions.

Gene Bush, recorded interview, Kingston Springs, Tennessee, 2006 and subsequent discussions and correspondence.

Charles Campbell, recorded interview, Valley, Mississippi, 2004.

Fred Clarke, recorded interview, Avalon, Mississippi, 2004.

Annie Cook, recorded interview, Avalon, Mississippi, 2004 and subsequent discussions.

Louisa Spottswood Coughlin, recorded interview, 2007 and subsequent correspondence.

David Evans, personal communications, 2009 and 2010.

Mark Greenberg, recorded interview, Montpelier, Vermont, 2006.

Stefan Grossman, recorded interview, Pateley Bridge, UK, 2006, and subsequent discussions.

Holly Ann Ehrich Ochs MacNamee Henderson, emailed notes, 2007 and subsequent correspondence.

Tony Howe, emailed notes, 2006 and subsequent correspondence.

Bonnie Hurt, recorded interview, Greenwood, Mississippi, 2007.

Josephine Jackson and Billy Campbell, recorded interview, Carrollton, Mississippi, 2009.

Ron Johnson, emailed notes, 2006 and subsequent correspondence.

Joe Lee, recorded interview, Rockville, Maryland, 2007.

Tom Lucas, emailed notes, 2007 and subsequent correspondence.

Dorothy Miller, recorded interview, Greenwood, Mississippi, 2007.

John Miller, recorded interview, Northampton, England, UK, 2006 and subsequent discussions.

Lillian Mitchell (Ms. Kitty), recorded interview, Grenada, Mississippi, 2007.

Fannie Mohead, recorded interview, Valley, Mississippi, 2007.

Max Ochs, recorded interviews, Annapolis, Maryland, 2004, 2005, 2006 and subsequent correspondence.

Jerry Ricks, recorded interview, University of Northampton, England, 2006 and subsequent correspondence.

Howard Rye, correspondence, 2010.

Peter Silitch, recorded interview, West Virginia, 2005, 2006.

Pat Sky, recorded interview, Chapel Hill, North Carolina, 2006.

Larry Smith, recorded interview, Avalon, Mississippi, 2008, 2009.

Larry and Mary Smith and Leagh Watson, emailed notes, 2009.

Dick Spottswood, recorded interview, Annapolis, Maryland, 2004 and subsequent correspondence.

Mike Stewart (Backward Sam Firk), recorded interview, Mill Springs, South Carolina, 2006 and subsequent correspondence.

Bill Storck, recorded interviews, Annapolis, Maryland, 2005 and 2006.

Denise Tapp, emailed notes, 2006 and subsequent correspondence.

Bill Tydings, recorded interview, Annapolis, Maryland, 2006 and subsequent correspondence.

Dick Waterman, recorded interview, Batesville, Mississippi, 2005 and subsequent correspondence.

Mary Frances Hurt Wright, recorded interviews, Avalon, Mississippi, 2004, 2005, 2006, 2007 and subsequent correspondence.

Appendix II

Contract between Music Research Incorporated and Mississippi John Hurt, 1963

MANAGEMENT AGREEMENT

MADE this 15th day of March, 1963, by and between MUSIC RESEARCH, INCORPORATED, of 1741 K Street, Northwest, Washington 6, District of Columbia, hereinafter referred to as the "Manager," and JOHN S. HURT, also known as Mississippi John Hurt, of Avalon, Mississippi, hereinafter referred to as "Artist,"

WITNESSETH

WHEREAS, Manager has the knowledge and skill to effectively promote the professional welfare of Artist to the mutual profit of both Manager and Artist, and Manager desires to undertake such promotion, and

WHEREAS, Manager is willing to expend time, effort and money for the development of the career and profession of the Artist, and,

WHEREAS, Artist desires to obtain the counsel advice, guidance and management of Manager in the entertainment industry, having full faith in the ability of Manager to effectively promote his career;

NOW THEREFORE, in consideration of the mutual promises herein contained, and for other good and valuable considerations herein specified, the parties hereto mutually agree and covenant as follows:

1. Artist hereby employs Manager to render its service to Artist in Artist's capacity as entertainer, performer, singer, musician, instrumentalist, and artist, as Artist's sole and exclusive personal representative, manager and advisor in the entertainment industry and in music research, including but not limited to appearances in vaudeville, motion pictures,

legitimate theatres, television, radio broadcasting, recording, for phonograph records, electrical transcriptions, appearances at hotels, restaurants, clubs, schools, colleges, night clubs, bars, cabarets, coffee houses, and all other appearances in any way connected with or related to the entertainment industry or music research in the United States, its territories and possessions and in all foreign countries throughout the world. The aforesaid enumeration shall not be deemed a limitation upon the services Artist shall render for Manager, but merely a partial enumeration by way of illustration.

2. Manager agrees that it will perform such services as personal representative, manager, and advisor as in its discretion are required to advance the best interests of Artist in Artist's capacity of entertainer, performer, singer, instrumentalist, musician and artist.

3. Artist does not hereby engage or require Manager to procure or provide engagements for Artist or to act as a booking agent in his behalf, but Artist does hereby grant to Manager the exclusive right to arrange for such services from others on behalf of Artist and/or to provide such services itself in its sole discretion.

4. Artist acknowledges that Manager is engaged in a similar capacity or will be engaged in a similar capacity for others, and Artist agrees that Manager is not obligated to devote his time and attention exclusively to Artist. It is agreed that Manager may engage in active roles for other Artists, record companies, publishing companies or other entertainment interests, in any capacity whatsoever. Manager may assign this contract to any other individual provided however that the terms hereof are not altered except for substitution of another party or parties for Manager.

5. Artist agrees to refer to Manager all verbal or written proposals, communications, or requests for Artist's appearances and services, and Artist agrees that Manager may publicly represent itself as acting for artist in the capacity herein set forth. For this purpose Manager shall have the rights to use Artist's photograph and his name for advertising materials, and to authorize others to use Artist's name and photograph in such manner as Manager may deem advisable, "name" being any professional or legal name of Artist individually or as a member of a group or as a group.

6. Artist represents that and warrants that he has the exclusive and legal right to use the trade or professional name set forth herein, and Artist hereby transfers, assigns and conveys all right, title and interest in and to the use of said name to Manager. Artist may use said name professionally, only as Manager, within its sole discretion and control shall permit, direct or allow. Artist agrees and warrants that Artist shall not, nor permit

anyone else to, use said name except with permission of Manager and under and subject to the terms and conditions and provisions set forth by Manager. Artist shall not adopt any other name except with Manager's permission.

7. Artist hereby appoints Manager his true and lawful attorney-in-fact during the term of this agreement, or renewal thereof, to sign and make on Artist's behalf all agreements in connection with all engagements and arrangements contemplated herein whereby Artist's name, likeness, services or talents are mentioned, referred to or utilized, and to collect for and on behalf of Artist all proceeds, monies or other compensation within the scope of this agreement or renewal thereof. Artist agrees to perform all engagements and to make all appearances in accordance with all agreements entered into by Manager on Artist's behalf.

8. Artist hereby represents and warrants that he has no outstanding agreements nor has he made any other arrangements, oral or written, which shall in any manner interfere with or prevent him from carrying out the terms and conditions of this agreement. Artist further agrees that he will not, during the term hereof, engage any other person, firm or corporation to act in the capacity of personal manager, representative or advisor. This agreement shall supercede any former agreements that may exist between Manager and Artist regarding the subject matter of this agreement.

9. As compensation for Manager's services herein, Artist agrees to pay Manager a sum equal to Fifty percent (50 percent) of all gross compensation received by Artist from all sources as the result of Artist's professional activities enumerated but not limited to those in paragraph "1." herein, and from any and all agreements entered into during the term hereof, or from any and all extensions, renewals or substitutions hereof, regardless of whether the terms of said agreements or said extensions, renewals or substitutions extend beyond the term of this agreement.

10. Artist agrees that he will pay to Manager the compensation as agreed in Paragraph "9." herein immediately upon receipt by Artist of any monies received for his services as aforesaid. Artist hereby further agrees to reimburse Manager with respect to any and all expenses Manager may incur on Artist's behalf, but only to the extent of royalties received by Artist. It is further agreed that Manager shall have the right to deduct from royalties paid to him by others for Artist such amounts as are due by Manager by the terms of this agreement, and pay the balance thereof to Artist.

11. Artist further covenants and agrees that he will faithfully and conscientiously and to the best of his ability give such auditions and submit

to such tests as will, from time to time, be arranged for Artist by Manager using such material in connection therewith as Manager may direct Artist to use, and where engagements are obtained for Artist with respect to his activities hereunder, Artist will fulfill and perform such engagements to the very best of his ability.

12. Artist hereby specifically authorizes and empowers Manager, whenever Manager may deem the same necessary in order to further promote and advance Artist's career hereunder, to employ the services of a booking agent or agents for such purpose, and Artist agrees to pay one-half of the cost of such services.

13. Artist agrees that Manager shall have the exclusive right to make recordings of Artist's music and performances during the term of this agreement, or in Manager's discretion to contact with others for making recordings of Artist's music and performances on behalf of Artist. In all cases of Manager producing recordings of Artist's music and performances on records bearing the label of Manager, or the trademark of Manager, or on tape or other media bearing said label or trademark of Manager, Manager shall bear the expense of producing such recordings and Artist shall be compensated at the rate of fifteen cents ($.15) per record sold where said record contains only the art of Artist and two cents ($.02) per selection or "track" where said record contains the art of others as well as the art of the Artist, per such record sold, Manager to bear all expenses of sales of such records as well as all expenses of production of such records. The terms, "record," and "records," shall be construed to include the terms, "tape," and "tapes," as well as any other recording media. This method of compensation to Artist with regard to recordings produced on Manager's label or under Manager's trademark is an exception to the method of compensation provided for in Paragraph "9." herein for all other services rendered to Artist by Manager. In all cases where Manager elects to contract to other recording companies or individuals on behalf of Artist, the method of compensation shall be that provided for in Paragraph "9."

14. With regard to any musical composition or lyrics or both which Artist represents to Manager to be Artist's original art, such musical composition or lyrics having been composed or written or created by Artist at any time in the past but not copyrighted or which shall be composed or written during the terms of this contract, Artist agrees to permit Manager to take out and procure a copyright or copyrights thereon in the name of Manager in the United States or elsewhere, and such copyrights shall become the absolute property of Manager forever. Artist further agrees to indemnify Manager against all damage in consequence of any such

copyrighted material and other material used by Artist containing any infringement of copyright or libelous matters.

15. The terms of this agreement shall be for a period of five (5) years from the date hereof. If at the end of this term of the contract, Artist shall have earned a gross aggregate sum in excess of five hundred Dollars, ($500.00) during the said contract period as a result of Artist's professional activities as set forth in Paragraph "1." herein, then, and in such event, this agreement shall be automatically extended and renewed for an additional term under the same provisions and terms hereof, such additional term to be also of five (5) years duration, except if Manager shall give notice prior to said renewal or extension that it does not desire to renew or extend the same.

16. If any part of this agreement should be held invalid by a competent authority, the remainder shall nevertheless remain valid and binding on the parties hereto.

IN WITNESS WHEROF, the undersigned as parties hereto have hereunto set in their hands and seals on the date first hereinabove written.

JOHN S. HURT, Artist   SEAL
MUSIC RESEARCH, INCORPORATED
By: Richard K. Spottswood, Pres.
   Manager
By: Thos B. Hoskins, Vice Pres.
   Manager

ATTEST
Louisa C. H. Spottswood
Secretary

Appendix III

Vanguard Contract, July 11, 1963

Vanguard Recording Soc., Inc.
154 West 14th Street
New York 11, N.Y.

Gentlemen:

In return for good and valuable consideration paid by you I hereby give you the exclusive right to record all musical selections and performances to be given by me at the Newport Folk Festival at Newport, Rhode Island on July 26, 27 and 28 and any postponed dates, together with the right to use my name, likeness and biographical material for advertising, trade and other purposes, and to manufacture, sell and distribute phonograph records and any other reproductions of all or parts of such performances. This release will also extend to any person or corporation to whom you may assign, in the usual course of business, your rights to manufacture or sell any album or other reproduction made of the above performances.

You agree that I may be permitted to record selections used by you hereunder for any other person, firm or corporation, without restriction by you.

I agree that each record shall be subject to your approval as satisfactory for manufacture and sale, and that all recordings and the performances therein shall be entirely your property. I hereby warrant and represent that I am free to give you this right and that no prior agreement or performance interfere therewith.

For each solo performance released by you, you shall pay me the sum of Fifty Dollars ($50.00) or at the rate of A. F. M. union scale if applicable, whichever is higher, on or before the date of release. Accompaniments by me for other solo performers shall be paid at the rate of A. F. M. union scale, on or before the date of release.

> Very truly yours,
> Mississippi John Hurt
> Date July 11 1963

ABOVE AGREED TO:
Maynard Solomon, Vanguard Recording Soc., Inc.

> SEE RIDER ATTACHED

[The Rider attached to the document reads as follows]

RIDER TO AGREEMENT BETWEEN MISSISSIPPI JOHN HURT AND VANGUARD RECORDING SOC., INC. FOR NEWPORT FOLK FESTIVAL

Vanguard agrees to pay copyright royalties on any of John Hurt's compositions recorded and released hereunder at the statutory rate of two cents (2c) per selection per record sold.

Appendix IV

Mississippi John Hurt Discography

78 rpm recordings

Frankie (400221-B)
Nobody's Dirty Business (400223-B)
Recorded and issued in 1928. OKeh
8560.

Monday Morning Blues (400219-B)
Shiverlie Blues (400220-B)
Casey Jones (400222-B)
Blessed Be The Name (400224-B)
Meeting On The Old Camp Ground
(400225-B)
Sliding Delta (400226-B)
Big Leg Blues (401474-B)
Window Light Blues (401482-B)
OKeh unissued.

Stack O'Lee Blues (401481-B)
Candy Man Blues (401483-B)
Recorded 1928 and issued in 1929.
OKeh 8654.

Blessed Be The Name (401485-B)
Praying On The Old Camp Ground
(401486-B)
Recorded 1928 and issued in 1929.
OKeh 8666.
Blue Harvest Blues (401487-A)
Spike Driver Blues (401488-B)

Recorded 1928 and issued in 1929.
OKeh 8692.

Louis Collins (401472-A)
Got The Blues Can't Be Satisfied
(401484-B)
Recorded 1928 and issued in 1929.
OKeh 8724.

Ain't No Tellin' (401471-A)
Avalon Blues (401473-B)
Recorded 1928 and issued in 1929.
OKeh 8759.

LP/CD compilations

**Anthology Of American Folk Music.
Vol. 1 of 2 LP set—Ballads.**
Frankie [OKeh 8560]
1952, Folkways FP-251. 1997,
Rereleased as 6 CD box set by
Smithsonian Folkways.

**Anthology Of American Folk Music.
Vol. 3 of 2 LP set—Songs.**
Spike Driver Blues [OKeh 8692]
1952, Folkways FP-253. 1997,
Rereleased as 6 CD box set by
Smithsonian Folkways.

The Mississippi Blues 1927–1940.
Got The Blues, Can't Be Satisfied
[OKeh 8724]
Louis Collins [OKeh 8724]
1963, Origin Jazz Library OJL-5.

Mississippi John Hurt - Folk Songs And Blues.
Avalon Blues
Richland Women Blues
Spike Driver Blues
Salty Dog
Cow Hooking Blues
Spanish Fangdang
Casey Jones
Louis Collins
Candy Man Blues
My Creole Bell
Liza Jane (God's Unchanging Hands)
Joe Turner Blues
1963, Piedmont PLP 13157, Gryphon GLP 13157. Reissued (*Volume I of the Original Recordings Folksongs and Blues*) OJL 8053. Reissued on CD, (*Avalon Blues 1963*)**,** Rounder CD 1081 (1991) and Vivid Sound VSCD–130 (Japan 2001).

Newport Folk Festival 1963 The Evening Concerts Vol. 1.
See, See Rider
Stagolee
Spike Driver Blues
Coffee Blues
1963, Vanguard VRS-9148 (mono), VSD-79148 (stereo), VTC 1688 (tape stereo), Fontana FL.6041 (UK mono), 1964, Vanguard/Orizzonte ORL 8197 (It stereo). Reissued on CD, Vanguard VCD 77002 (1997 US), Vanguard VCD 770002-2.

Blues At Newport
Candy Man
Trouble, I've Had It All My Days
Frankie

1964, Vanguard VRS-9145 (mono), VSD-79145 (stereo).

Mississippi John Hurt - Worried Blues
Lazy Blues
Farther Along
Sliding Delta
Nobody Cares For Me
Cow Hooking Blues No. 2
Talking Casey
Weeping And Wailing
Worried Blues
Oh Mary, Don't You Weep
I Been Cryin' Since You Been Gone ˙
1964, Piedmont PLP 13161, Chesapeake CLP 13161. Reissued (*Mississippi John Hurt, 1964 Volume II of the Original Recordings Worried Blues*), 1968. OJL 8054. Reissued on CD (*Worried Blues 1963*), Rounder CD 1082 (1991), Vivid Sound VSCD-131.

Friends of Old Time Music
Monday Morning Blues
Pallet On The Floor
1964, Folkways FA 2390, Disc D-113 (1965).

Blues at Newport 1964—Part 2
Sliding Delta
Bye And Bye I Will See Jesus
Talking Casey
1965, Vanguard VRS 9181 (mono), VSD 79181 (stereo). Reissued on 2 CDs (*The Blues at Newport 1964 parts 1* and *2*), King/Vanguard KICP 2118/9 (Japan 1991).

Traditional Music at Newport 1964—Part 2
Coffee Blues
1965, Vanguard VRS 9183 (mono), VSD 79183 (stereo).

Blues Rediscoveries
Ain't No Tellin' [OKeh 8759]
Avalon Blues [OKeh 8759]
1966, RBF 11.

The Party Blues
Candy Man Blues [OKeh 8654]
1966, Melodeon MLP 7324.

Mississippi John Hurt Today!
Pay Day
I'm Satisfied
Candy Man
Make Me A Pallet On The Floor
Talking Casey
Corrinna, Corrinna
Coffee Blues
Louis Collins
Hot Time In The Old Town Tonight
If You Don't Want Me Baby
Spike Driver's Blues
Beulah Land

Plus tracks from KICP 2034 (Vanguard
    VSD 79248)
Since I've Laid My Burden Down
Moaning The Blues
Richland Woman Blues
Hop Joint
Monday Morning Blues
Keep On Knocking
Stagolee
Nearer My God To Thee
1966, Vanguard VSD 79220,
    (*Mississippi John Hurt*) (UK)
    Vanguard SVRL 19032, (*Mississippi
    John Hurt*) Fontana TFL 6079,
    Reissued on CD 1987, Vanguard
    CD 79220-2, (*Today*) with additional
    tracks KICP-2034 (Japan), Pure
    Pleasure 9220.

**Mississippi Blues Vol. 1
    (1927–1942)**
Blue Harvest Blues [OKeh 8692]
1967, Roots RL 302.

They Sang The Blues (1927–1929)
Nobody's Dirty Business
1967, Historical ASC-17, Historical
    ASC-5829-17, Historical HLP-17.

**The Immortal Mississippi John
    Hurt**
Since I've Laid My Burden Down
Moaning The Blues
Buck Dance
Lazy Blues
Richland Women Blues
Tender Virgins
Hop Joint
Monday Morning Blues
I've Got The Blues
I Can't Get Satisfied
Keep On Knocking
Chicken
Stagolee
Nearer My God To Thee
1967, Vanguard VSD 79248 (US),
    SVRL 19005 (UK), Reissued on CD
    Vanguard CD 79248-2.

Mississippi Moaners 1927–1942
Big Leg Blues [OKeh unissued]
1968, Yazoo L 1009, Yazoo CD 1009
    (1991).

Classic Guitar Blues
Frankie [OKeh 8560]
Spike Driver Blues [OKeh 8692]
1968, Confidential CLP 002 (France).

**The Mississippi Blues No. 3:
    Transition, 1926–1937**
Stack O Lee Blues [OKeh 8654]
1969, Origin Jazz Library OJL-17.

**Mississippi John Hurt
    (1963–1964)**
Candy Man
Trouble, I've Had It All My Day
Frankie
Monday Morning Blues
Pallet On The Floor

Coffee Blues
See See Rider
Stagolee
Spike Driver Blues
Sliding Delta
Bye And Bye I Will See Jesus
Talking Casey
1969, Private PR 5 (Austria).

The Story Of The Blues
Stack O' Lee Blues [OKeh 8654]
1969, CBS 22135.

The Best Of Mississippi John Hurt
Here I Am, Oh Lord, Send Me
I Shall Not Be Moved
Nearer My Good To Thee
Baby What's Wrong With You
Ain't Nobody's Business
Salty Dog Blues
Coffee Blues
Avalon, My Home Town
Make Me A Pallet On The Floor
Since I've Laid This Burden Down
Sliding Delta
Monday Morning Blues
Richland Women Blues
Candy Man
Stagolee
My Creole Belle
C. C. Rider
Spanish Fandango
Talking Casey
Chicken
You Are My Sunshine
1970, Vanguard VSD 19/20, Vanguard
    VMS 73103 (sides A and B only
    mid-line series), Reissued on 2 CDs
    Vanguard CD 19/20-2 (1987).

**Mississippi John Hurt The
    Original 1928 Recordings**
Frankie [OKeh 8560]
Nobody's Dirty Business [OKeh 8560]
Ain't No Tellin [OKeh 8759]
Louis Collins [OKeh 8724]
Avalon Blues [OKeh 8759]

Big Leg Blues [OKeh unissued]
Stack O Lee Blues [OKeh 8654]
Candy Man Blues [OKeh 8654]
Got The Blues Cant Be Satisfied [OKeh
    8724]
Blessed Be The Name [OKeh 8666]
Praying On The Old Camp Ground
    [OKeh 8666]
Blue Harvest Blues [OKeh 8692]
Spike Driver Blues [OKeh 8692]
notes by Les Astrella
1971, Spokane SPL 1001, Biograph
    BLP C4 (1972), Yazoo L 1065
    (1979).

**Mississippi John Hurt Last
    Sessions**
Poor Boy, Long Ways From Home
Boys You're Welcome
Joe Turner Blues
First Missed Him
Funky Butt
Spider, Spider
Waiting For You
Shortnin' Bread
Trouble, I've Had It All My Days
Let The Mermaids Flirt With Me
Good Morning, Carrie
Nobody Cares For Me
All Night Long
Hey, Honey, Right Away
You've Got To Die
Goodnight Irene
1972, Vanguard VSD 79327, Reissued
    on CD Vanguard CD 79327-2.

The Great Blues Men
Moanin' The Blues
1972, Vanguard VSD 25/26, Vanguard/
    King GW-203/4 (Japan 1972).
    Reissued on CD Vanguard CD 25/26
    (1988).

**Bukka White Sings Sic 'em Dogs
    On Me 1927 to 1939**
Stack O'Lee Blues [OKeh 8654]
1972, Herwin H 201.

Mississippi John Hurt 1928 His First Recordings Stack O' Lee Blues

Frankie [OKeh 8560]
Nobody's Dirty Business [OKeh 8560]
Ain't No Tellin [OKeh 8759]
Louis Collins [OKeh 8724]
Avalon Blues [OKeh 8759]
Big Leg Blues [OKeh unissued]
Stack O Lee Blues [OKeh 8654]
Candy Man Blues [OKeh 8654]
Got The Blues Cant Be Satisfied [OKeh 8724]
Blessed Be The Name [OKeh 8666]
Praying On The Old Camp Ground [OKeh 8666]
Blue Harvest Blues [OKeh 8692]
Spike Driver Blues [OKeh 8692]
1972, Biograph BLP C4, Yazoo LP 1065 (1979).

Mississippi John Hurt Volume One Of A Legacy

Trouble I've Had It All My Days
Pera Lee
See See Rider
Louis Collins
Coffee Blues
Nobody's Dirty Business
Do Lord Remember Me
Monday Morning Blues (05:17) [extended version]
Let The Mermaids Flirt With Me
Pay Day
Stack-O-Lee (07:21) [extended version]
Casey Jones
Frankie And Albert (05:01) [extended version]
1975, Rebel CLPS 1068 (Canada), Piedmont CLPS 1068 (US 1975). Reissued on CD Rounder CD 1100 (1997).

Great Bluesmen Newport

Sliding Delta
Trouble, I've Had It All My Day

1976, Vanguard VSD 77/78, King/ Vanguard LAX-155 (Japan 1976). Reissued on CD, Vanguard CD 77/78 (*Great Bluesmen At Newport 1959–1965*) (1991).

The Great Bluesmen Vol. II

Candy Man
1978, PYE Golden Hour, GH 879.

Mississippi John Hurt 1928 Sessions

Got The Blues Cant Be Satisfied [OKeh 8724]
Louis Collins [OKeh 8724]
Blue Harvest Blues [OKeh 8692]
Avalon Blues [OKeh 8759]
Blessed Be The Name [OKeh 8666]
Nobody's Dirty Business [OKeh 8560]
Frankie [OKeh 8560]
Ain't No Tellin [OKeh 8759]
Big Leg Blues [OKeh unissued]
Stack O Lee Blues [OKeh 8654]
Praying On The Old Camp Ground [OKeh 8666]
Spike Driver Blues [OKeh 8692]
Candy Man Blues [OKeh 8654]
Spokane SPL 1001 (1971?), Biograph BLP C4 (1972), Yazoo L 1065. Reissued on CD Yazoo 1065 (1990).

Mississippi John Hurt Monday Morning Blues

(The Library Of Congress Recordings Volume One)
Nobody's Dirty Business
Monday Morning Blues take 2
Hey Baby Right Away
Spanish Fangdang
Pay Day
Keep On Knocking
Talking Casey Jones
Let The Mermaids Flirt With Me
Got The Blues That Can't Be Satisfied
Stocktime
Candy Man
Pera-Lee

Trouble I've Had All My Days
Waiting For You
1980, Flyright FLYLP 553.

Mississippi John Hurt Avalon Blues
(The Library Of Congress Recordings Volume Two)
Avalon Blues
Joe Turner
Good Morning Miss Carrie
Richlands Women Blues
Frankie (and Albert)
If You Don't Want Me (two versions)
Louis Collins
Stackolee
Rubber Dolly
Coffee Blues
Slidin' Delta
Keep On Knockin'
Corrina, Corrina
Funky Butt
1982, Heritage HT-301.

Mississippi John Hurt Satisfied
Candy Man
My Creole Belle
Make Me A Pallet On The Floor
Shake That Thing
I'm Satisfied
Salty Dog
Nobody's Business But Mine
The Angels Laid Him Away
Casey Jones
Baby What's Wrong With You
Lonesome Blues
1982, Quicksilver Intermedia QS 5007.
Reissued on CD Prestige Elite
CD 37 (Prestige Raw Blues series)
(2002).

Mississippi John Hurt The Candy Man
Richland Women Blues
Trouble, I've Had It All My Days
C-h-i-c-k-e-n
Coffee Blues

Monday Morning Blues
Frankie And Albert
Talking Casey
Here I Am, Oh Lord, Send Me
Hard Time In The Old Town Tonight
Spike Driver's Blues
1982, Quicksilver Intermedia QS 5042,
Blue Moon BMLP 1.030 (1986),
Prestige Elite CD 37 (Prestige Raw
Blues Series) (2002).

Mississippi John Hurt Shake That Thing
Candy Man
My Creole Belle
Make Me A Pallet On The Floor
Shake That Thing
I'm Satisfied
Salty Dog
Nobody's Business But Mine
The Angels Laid Him Away
Casey Jones (Ramblin' Mind)
Baby, What's Wrong With You?
Lonesome Blues
1986, Quicksilver Intermedia QS 5042,
Blue Moon BMLP 1.030, Prestige
Elite CD 37 (Prestige Raw Blues
Series) (2002).

Mississippi John Hurt Sacred And Secular
(The Library Of Congress Recordings Volume Three)
Pallet On The Floor
Stackolee
I'm Satisfied
Ain't Nobody But You Babe [I Don't Love Nobody]
C. C. Rider
Waiting For A Train
Funky Butt
Shortnin' Bread
Mary Don't You Weep
Farther Along
Do Lord Remember Me
Over In The Glory Land

Glory Glory Hallelujah [Since I've Laid
My Burden Down]
What A Friend We Have In Jesus
Weeping And Wailing
Where Shall I Be
1988, Heritage HT-320.

Country Blues Live
I Shall Not Be Moved
Avalon Blues
I Hate To See That Evening Sun Go
Down
Payday
Casey Jones
Spanish Flang Dang
Welcome
1988 Document CD DLP 525, Limited
Edition.

Checkin' Out The Blues
I'm Satisfied
Monday Morning Blues
1988 Style LP STYRL007, Style CD
STYRD007.

Mississippi John Hurt Avalon Blues
Avalon Blues
Richlands Women Blues
Frankie And Albert
Louis Collins
Stackolee
Coffee Blues
Slidin' Delta
Corrine Corrina
Nobody's Dirty Business
Monday Morning Blues
Hey Baby Right Away
Spanish Flangdang
Pay Day
Talking Casey Blues
Let The Mermaids Flirt With Me
Got The Blues That Can't Be Satisfied
Stocktime
Candy Man
Pera-Lee
Trouble I've Had All My Days
1989, Flyright FLYCD 06, Flyright
FLYCD 06 (2000).

The Greatest Songsters (1927–1929)
Frankie
Nobody's Dirty Business
Ain't No Tellin'
Louis Collins
Avalon Blues
Big Leg Blues
Stack O'Lee Blues
Candy Man Blues
Got The Blues Can't Be Satisfied
Blessed Be The Name
Praying On The Old Camp Ground
Blue Harvest Blues
Spike Driver Blues
1990, Document DOCD 5003, P-Vine
PCD 2259 (2003).

Mississippi John Hurt: The Songster
Long, Lonesome Blues
Richlands Women Blues
Trouble, I've Had It All My Days
C-H-I-C-K-E-N
Coffee Blues
Monday Morning Blues
Frankie
Talkin' Casey
Here I Am, Oh Lord, Send Me
Candy Man Blues
My Creole Belle
Ain't No Tellin'
Shake That Thing
I'm Satisfied
Salty Dog
Nobody's Dirty Business
Louis Collins
Casey Jones
Baby, What's Wrong With You
Hot Times in The Old Town Tonight
Spike Driver Blues
1991, King Bee KNB 1002 (US).

Blues At Newport
Candy Man
Coffee Blues
Stagolee
1991, Vanguard CD 70115-2.

Mississippi John Hurt In Concert
Nobody's Business But Mine
Angels Laid Him Away
Baby What's Wrong With You
Casey Jones
Candy Man
Lonesome Blues
My Creole Belle
Make Me A Pallet On The Floor
Trouble I Had All My Days
Chicken
Coffee Blues
Shake That Thing
Monday Morning Blues
Frankie And Albert
Salty Dog
Spike Driver Blues
Here Am I, Oh Lord, Send Me
Talking Casey
Hot Time In The Old Town Tonight
I'm Satisfied
Richland Women Blues
1991, Blue Moon CD 083, Magnum CD 21 (1995).

Mississippi John Hurt Memorial Anthology
Slidin' Delta
Salty Dog
Louis Collins
Staggerlee
Monday Mornin' Blues
Comin' Home
Candyman Blues
A Hot Time In The Old Town Tonight
K. C. Jones Blues
Make Me A Pallet On Your Floor
You Can't Come In
Joe Turner
Spanish Flangdang
Lonesome Am I
I Shall Not Be Moved
C. C. Rider
Trouble Blues
Lovin' Spoonful
Richland Woman Blues
Frankie & Albert (Johnny)
Creole Belle

Chicken
Pete Seeger/John Hurt Interview
Let The Mermaids Flirt With Me
Nobody's Dirty Business
Stop Time (Buck Dance)
Worried Blues
Avalon Blues
1993, Genes GCD 9906/7.

Blues With A Feeling
Here I Am Lord Send Me
Pallet On Your Floor
1993, Vanguard VCD2-77005.

Mississippi John Hurt Satisfying Blues
C-H-I-C-K-E-N Blues
Monday Morning Blues
Candy Man
Lonesome Blues
Nobody's Business But Mine
Angels Laid Him Away
Baby What's Wrong With You
Richland Women Blues
Frankie And Albert
Salty Dog
Spike Driver's Blues
Hot Time In The Old Town Tonight
My Creole Belle
Make Me A Pallet On Your Floor
Coffee Blues
1995, Collectables VCL 5529.

Mississippi John Hurt Avalon Blues: The Complete 1928 OKeh Recordings
Frankie [OKeh 8560]
Nobody's Dirty Business [OKeh 8560]
Ain't No Tellin [OKeh 8759]
Louis Collins [OKeh 8724]
Avalon Blues [OKeh 8759]
Big Leg Blues [OKeh unissued]
Stack O Lee Blues [OKeh 8654]
Candy Man Blues [OKeh 8654]
Got The Blues Can't Be Satisfied [OKeh 8724]
Blessed Be The Name [OKeh 8666]

Praying On The Old Camp Ground
[OKeh 8666]
Blue Harvest Blues [OKeh 8692]
Spike Driver Blues [OKeh 8692]
1996, Columbia/Sony CK64986.

Vanguard Blues Sampler
Corrina, Corrina
1996, Vanguard CD 74002-2.

**Mississippi John Hurt Coffee
  Blues**
Frankie & Albert
Talkin' Casey
Trouble I Had All My Day
Coffee Blues
Hard Time In Old Town Tonight
Chicken Blues
Here I Am, Oh Lord Send Me
Spike Driver Blues
Richland Woman Blues
Monday Morning Blues
1986, IMP/Blues Collector 309.

Mississippi John Hurt Legend
Trouble, I've Had It All My Days
Pera Lee
See See Rider
Louis Collins
Coffee Blues
Nobody's Dirty Business
Do Lord Remember Me
Monday Morning Blues (05:17)
Let The Mermaids Flirt With Me
Pay Day
Stack-O-Lee (07:21)
Casey Jones
Frankie And Albert (05:01)
Stockwell (previously unissued)
1997, Rebel CLPS 1068 (Ca 1975),
  Piedmont CLPS 1068 (US 1975).
  Reissued on CD Rounder CD 1100.

**Mississippi John Hurt Satisfied
  . . . Live**
Candy Man

My Creole Belle
Make Me A Pallet On The Floor
Shake That Thing
I'm Satisfied
Salty Dog
Nobody's Business But Mine
Angels Laid Him Away
Casey Jones (Talkin' Casey)
Baby, What's Wrong With You?
Lonesome Blues
1997, Beacon 51577, Boomerang BEA-
  51577.

Blues With A Feeling Vol. 2
Here I Am Lord Send Me
Pallet On Your Floor
1997, Vanguard VCD 73134.

**Mississippi John Hurt
  Rediscovered**
Coffee Blues
I'm Satisfied
Make Me A Pallet On Your Floor
Monday Morning Blues
Since I've Laid My Burden Down
Stocktime (Buck Dance)
Hot Time In The Old Town Tonight
Richland Women Blues
Keep On Knocking
Stagolee
Hop Joint
Funky Butt
It Ain't Nobody's Business
Salty Dog Blues
Candy Man
You Are My Sunshine
I've Got The Blues And I Can't Be
  Satisfied
Nearer My God To Thee
Shortnin' Bread
Avalon, My Home Town
First Shot Missed Home
Let The Mermaids Flirt With Me
Talking Casey
Goodnight Irene
1998, Vanguard CD 79519.

Mississippi John Hurt The Complete Studio Recordings

Pay Day
I'm Satisfied
Candy Man
Make Me A Pallet On The Floor
Talking Casey
Corrinna, Corrinna
Coffee Blues
Louis Collins
Hot Time In The Old Town
If You Don't Want Me Baby
Spike Driver Blues
Beulah Land
Since I've Laid My Burden Down
Moanin' The Blues
Stocktime (Buck Dance)
Lazy Blues
Richland Woman Blues
Wise And Foolish Virgins (Tender Virgins)
Hop Joint
Monday Morning Blues
I've Got The Blues And I Can't Be Satisfied
Keep On Knocking
The Chicken
Stagolee
Nearer My God To Thee
Poor Boy, Long Ways From Home
Boys You're Welcome
Joe Turner Blues
First Shot Missed Him
Farther Along
Funky Butt
Spider, Spider
Waiting For You
Shortnin' Bread
Trouble, I've Had It All My Days
Let The Mermaids Flirt With Me
Good Morning, Carrie
Nobody Cares For Me
All Night Long
Hey, Honey, Right Away
You've Got To Die
Goodnight Irene
1998, 3 CD set, Vanguard CD 70181-3.

The Best Of Mississippi John Hurt Ain't No Tellin'

Richland Woman Blues
Trouble I Had All My Days
Chicken
Coffee Blues
Monday Morning Blues
Frankie And Albert
Talking Casey
Here Am I, Oh Lord, Send Me
Hot Time In The Old Town Tonight
Spike Driver Blues
Candy Man
My Creole Belle
Make Me A Pallet On The Floor
Shake That Thing
I'm Satisfied
Salty Dog
Nobody's Business But Mine
The Angels Laid Him Away
Casey Jones
Baby, What's Wrong With You?
Lonesome Blues
1998, Aim CD 10.

The Early Blues Roots of Bob Dylan Under The Influence, Vol. 4

Frankie And Albert
Candy Man
2000, Catfish CD 168.

Mississippi John Hurt Live!

Nobody's Business But Mine
Angels Laid Him Away
Baby What's Wrong With You
Casey Jones
Candy Man
Lonesome Blues
My Creole Belle
Make Me A Pallet On The Floor
Trouble I Had All My Days
Chicken
Coffee Blues
Shake That Thing
Monday Morning Blues

Frankie And Albert
Salty Dog
Spike Driver Blues
Here Am I, Oh Lord, Send Me
Talking Casey
Hot Time In The Old Town Tonight
I'm Satisfied
Richland Women Blues
2001, Allegro 120007.

Mississippi John Hurt Revisited
I'm Satisfied
Nobody's Business But Mine
Rich Women Blues
Baby What's Wrong With You
Talking Casey
Candy Man
Here Am I, Oh Lord, Send Me
Casey Jones
Spike Driver Blues
Lonesome Blues
Salty Dog
My Creole Belle
Make Me A Pallet On The Floor
Shake That Thing
Trouble I Had All My Days
Coffee Blues
The Angels Laid Him Away
C-H-I-C-K-E-N
2001, Varese CD 061149.

Mississippi John Hurt
Nobody's Business But Mine
Angels Laid Him Away
Baby What's Wrong With You
Casey Jones
Candy Man
Lonesome Blues
My Creole Belle
Make Me A Pallet On The Floor
Trouble I Had All My Days
Chicken
Coffee Blues
Shake That Thing
Monday Morning Blues
Frankie And Albert
Salty Dog

Spike Driver Blues
Here Am I, Oh Lord, Send Me
Talking Casey
Hot Time In The Old Town Tonight
I'm Satisfied
Richland Women Blues
2001, Dressed To Kill 890.

Mississippi John Hurt Live
Here Am I, Oh Lord, Send Me
I Shall Not Be Moved
Nearer My God To Thee
Baby, What's Wrong With You?
Ain't Nobody's Business
Salty Dog
Coffee Blues
Avalon My Home Town
Make Me A Pallet On The Floor
Since I've Laid My Burden Down
Sliding Delta
Monday Morning Blues
Richland Woman Blues
Candy Man
Stagolee
My Creole Belle
C. C. Rider
Spanish Fandango
Talking Casey
Chicken
You Are My Sunshine
Hop Joint
Trouble I Had All My Days
Spike Driver Blues
2002, Vanguard SKU 79702.

**Mississippi John Hurt Ain't
Nobody's Business**
Nobody's Business But Mine
The Angels Laid Him Away
Baby What's Wrong With You
Casey Jones
Candy Man
Lonesome Blues
My Creole Belle
Make Me A Pallet On Your Floor
Trouble I Had All My Days
C-H-I-C-K-E-N Blues

Coffee Blues
Shake That Thing
Monday Morning Blues
Frankie And Albert
Salty Dog
Spike Drivers Blues
Here Am I, Lord, Send Me
Talking Casey
Hot Time In The Old Town Tonight
I'm Satisfied
Richland Women Blues
2002, Quicksilver Intermedia QS 5007
& QS 5042 (1982), Prestige Elite CD
37 (Prestige Raw Blues series).

Best Of Mississippi John Hurt
Unknown track listing
2002, Classic World CD 2032.

Mississippi John Hurt Frankie & Albert
Hot Time In Old Town Tonight
Candy Man
Baby, What's Wrong With You
Frankie And Albert
Louis Collins
Richland Woman Blues
I'm Satisfied
My Creole Bell
C-H-I-C-K-E-N Blues
Shake That Thing
Spike Driver Blues
Salty Dog
Casey Jones
Talkin' Casey
Coffee Blues
Monday Morning Blues
Trouble I Had All My Days
Nobody's Business But My Own
Make Me A Pallet On Your Floor
Lonesome Blues
Here I Am/Oh Lord Send Me
2003, Tomato Music CD 2070.

Mississippi John Hurt Live At Newport
Unknown track listing
2003, Universe 071 (I). ·

Mississippi John Hurt Today
Pay Day
I'm Satisfied
Candy Man
Make Me A Pallet On The Floor
Talking Casey
Corrinna, Corrinna
Coffee Blues
Louis Collins
Hot Time In The Old Town Tonight
If You Don't Want Me Baby
Spike Driver's Blues
Beulah Land
2003, Universe 073 (I).

Mississippi John Hurt Live Vol. 1
Here I Am, Oh Lord, Send Me
I Shall Not Be Moved
Nearer My Good To Thee
Baby What's Wrong With You
Ain't Nobody's Business
Salty Dog Blues
Coffee Blues
Avalon, My Home Town
Make Me A Pallet On The Floor
Since I've Laid This Burden Down
Sliding Delta
Monday Morning Blues
2003, Universe 082 (I).

Mississippi John Hurt Live Vol. 2
Unknown track listing
2003, Universe 088 (I).

Mississippi John Hurt King Of The Blues Vol. 4
Frankie
Nobody's Dirty Business
Ain't No Tellin'
Louis Collins
Avalon Blues
Big Leg Blues
Stack O Lee Blues
Candy Man Blues
Got The Blues Can't Be Satisfied
Blessed Be The Name
Praying On The Old Camp Ground

Blue Harvest Blues
Spike Driver Blues
2003, The Reissue Project, Document
   Records, Vienna, Austria, Document
   DOCD 5003 (1990), P-Vine PCD
   2259.

Mississippi John Hurt D.C. Blues:
   Library of Congress Recordings
Avalon Blues
Richlands Women Blues
Frankie And Albert
Trouble I've Had All My Days
Pera-Lee
Candy Man
Stockwell
Got The Blues That Can't Be Satisfied
Let The Mermaids Flirt With Me
Talking Casey Jones
Pay Day
Louis Collins
Stackolee
Coffee Blues
Slidin' Delta
Corrina, Corrina
Hey Baby Right Away
Pallet On The Floor
Waiting For A Train
Funky Butt
Spanish Flandang
Monday Morning Blues
Shortenin' Bread
Oh Mary Don't You Weep
Farther Along
Do Lord Remember Me
Over In The Glory Land
Glory Glory Hallelujah [Since I've Laid
   My Burden Down]
What A Friend We Have In Jesus
Where Shall I Be
Weeping And Waiting
Joe Turner
If You Don't Want Me
Rubber Dolly
Keep Me Knockin' (You Can't Come In)
2004, Fuel 2000 2 CD set CD 061407.

Mississippi John Hurt Candy
   Man Blues The Complete 1928
   Sessions
Frankie
Louis Collins
Nobody's Dirty Business
Ain't No Tellin'
Stack O' Lee
Avalon Blues
Big Leg Blues
Praying On The Old Camp Ground
Candy Man Blues
Blessed Be Thy Name
Blue Harvest Blues
Spike Driver Blues
Got The Blues (Can't Be Satisfied)
2004, Snapper SBLUECD 010.

Mississippi John Hurt / Bukka
   White Shake' Em on Down
Candy Man Blues
Blessed Be the Name
Nobody's Dirty Business
Louis Collins
Praying on the Old Camp Ground
Spike Driver Blues
Avalon Blues
Ain't No Tellin'
Blue Harvest Blues
Frankie
Big Leg Blues
Stack O' Lee Blues
Got the Blues (Can't Be Satisfied)
2004, History CD 1941.

Mississippi John Hurt D.C. Blues:
   Library of Congress Recordings
   Vol. 2
Monday Morning Blues
Nobody's Dirty Business
If You Don't Want Me
Spike Driver (John Henry)
Salty Dog
My Creole Belle
Casey Jones
Waiting For You (I Forgive You Before
   I Go)

Stackolee [Alternate Version]
Walking The Floor Over You
Camp Meeting Tonight On The Camp
  Ground
Blessed Be the Name Of The Lord
When The Roll Is Called Up Yonder
Blind Man Sit In The Way And Cried
Glory To His Name
I'll Fly Away
Ten Virgins (When The Bridegroom
  Comes)
Avalon Blues
Cow Hooking Blues
I'm Satisfied
Ain't Nobody But You Babe
Shortnin' Bread
Redwing
Four O'Clock Blues
See See Rider
I Got Mine
Good Morning Miss Carrie
Alabama Bound
Looking This Way
God's Unchanging Hand
Poor Boy A Long Way From Home
Frankie, No. 2
Chicken Song
You Are My Sunshine
Will The Circle Be Unbroken
You Got To Get Ready
2005, Fuel 2000 2 CD set CD 061495.

**Mississippi John Hurt Lonesome
  Blues**
Baby, What's Wrong With You
Candy Man
Frankie And Albert
Monday Mornin' Blues
Make Me A Pallet On Your Floor
Talking Casey
Trouble I Had All My Days
Casey Jones Talkin' Casey
My Creole Belle
Lonesome Blues
Shake That Thing
Coffee Blues
I'm Satisfied
Hot Time In The Old Town Tonight

Here I Am, Oh Lord Send Me
Nobody's Business But Mine
C-H-I-C-K-E-N Blues
Spike Drivers Blues
Salty Dog
The Angels Laid Him Away
2005, BLITZ MCPS HHMMCD 325.

**The Best of Mississippi John Hurt
  Columbia Original Masters**
Frankie [OKeh 8560]
Nobodys Dirty Business [OKeh 8560]
Ain't No Tellin [OKeh 8759]
Louis Collins [OKeh 8724]
Avalon Blues [OKeh 8759]
Big Leg Blues [OKeh unissued]
Stack O Lee Blues [OKeh 8654]
Candy Man Blues [OKeh 8654]
Got The Blues (Can't Be Satisfied)
  [OKeh 8724]
Blessed Be The Name [OKeh 8666]
Praying On The Old Camp Ground
  [OKeh 8666]
Blue Harvest Blues [OKeh 8692]
Spike Driver Blues [OKeh 8692]
2008, Sony BMG CD 15.

Mississippi John Hurt Tribute Albums

**Bill Morrissey: Songs Of
  Mississippi John Hurt**
If You Don't Want Me
Avalon Blues
Shake That Thing
Louis Collins
First Shot Missed Him
Big Leg Blues
Hey, Honey, Right Away
Joe Turner Blues
I'm Satisfied
Beulah Land
Funky Butt
Coffee Blues
Monday Morning Blues
Good Morning, Carrie
Hot Times In The Old Town
1999, Philo CD 711216.

Notes

Foreword

1. Mary Frances Hurt Wright is Mississippi John Hurt's granddaughter. She and her side of the family called her grandfather "Daddy John."

Introduction

1. Martin C. Strong, *The Essential Rock Discography* (Edinburgh: Cannongate, 2006), p. 320. Lonnie Donegan's "Rock Island Line" was first released in 1955 on 10-inch LP, *New Orleans Joys* by the Chris Barber Jazz Band, Decca LF 1198, 1955. Subsequently released as a single, it sold three million copies, stayed in the UK charts for twenty-two weeks, and was the first record by a British performer that made the American top ten.

2. John and Alan Lomax, *American Ballads and Folk Songs* (New York: Macmillan, 1934); Jerry Silverman, *Folk Blues*, (New York: Macmillan, 1958).

3. *The Mississippi Blues, No. 3: Transition, 1926–1937*, Origin Jazz Library OJL-17, 1969.

4. *Ibid.*, notes by Dave Evans.

5. Harry Smith, *Anthology of American Folk Music*, Three volume, six-LP set, FP 251, FP 252, FP 253 (New York: Folkways Records, 1952). Reissued on six-CD box set, CD SFW 40090/A28746-51 (Washington: Smithsonian Folkways, 1997).

6. Jim O'Neal, "I Once Was Lost But Now I'm Found" in *Nothing But The Blues*, ed. Lawrence Cohn (New York: Abbeville, 1993), p. 359.

7. Ted Gioia, *Delta Blues: The Life and Times of the Mississippi Masters Who Revolutionized American Music* (New York: Norton, 2008), pp. 357–58.

8. Bill Wyman with Richard Havers, *Bill Wyman's Blues Odyssey* (London: Dorling Kindersley, 2001), p. 144.

9. Larry Hoffman, notes to *Mississippi John Hurt Memorial Anthology*, CD GCD 9906/7, Blues Vault Series, Genes, 1993.

10. Ken Ficara, review of *I'd Rather Be the Devil: Skip James and the Blues*, by Stephen Calt (New York: Da Capo, 1994), www.panix.com, 2006.

Chapter 1

1. Passenger and Immigration Lists Index, 1500s–1900s, U.S. Immigration Records. Ancestry.com.

2. Clyde Adrian Woods, *Development Arrested: The Cotton and Blues Empire of the Mississippi Delta* (London and New York: Verso, 1998), p. 43.

3. Ron Johnson, personal communication, 2006. Ron Johnson is conducting personal research on the Hurt families in the United States.

4. Westley F. Busbee Jr., *Mississippi: A History* (Wheeling, IL: Harlan Davidson, 2005), p. 18.

5. Frank E. Smith, *The Yazoo River* (Jackson: University Press of Mississippi, 1954), pp. 54–55.

6. Hugh Brogan, *Longman History of the United States of America* (London, Guild, 1985), pp. 67–68; Sylvia S. Kasprycki, "Southeast," in *The Cultures of Native North Americans*, ed. Christian F. Feest (Cologne, Germany: Koneman, 2000), p. 158.

7. Elmo Howell, *Mississippi Backroads: Notes on Literature and History* (Memphis: Langford, 1998), p. 63.

8. *Ibid.*, pp. 60–63.

9. *Ibid.*, p. 63.

10. U.S. Federal Census, 1880, Carroll County, Mississippi, Enumeration District 19, p. 22, Line 10, Dwelling 198, Family 198, Enumerated June 16–17, 1880. Ancestry.com.

11. Lewis W. Jones, "The Mississippi Delta," in *Lost Delta Found: Rediscovering the Fisk University–Library of Congress Coahoma Study, 1941–42/John W. Work, Lewis Wade Jones, and Samuel C. Adams*, ed. Robert Gordon and Bruce Nemerov (Nashville: Vanderbilt University Press, 2005), p. 43.

12. U.S. Federal Census, 1870, Russell County, Alabama, p. 9, Line 16, Dwelling 65, Family 69, Enumerated August 17, 1870. Ancestry.com.

13. U.S. Federal Census, Slave Schedule, 1860, Russell County, Alabama. Ancestry.com.

14. Charles S. Johnson, *Shadow of the Plantation* (Chicago: University of Chicago Press, 1934), p. 8.

15. U.S. Federal Census, Slave Schedule, 1860, Southern Division, Russell County, Alabama, p. 77, Line 3, Enumerated July 13, 1860. Ancestry.com.

16. U.S. Federal Census, 1860, Russell County, Alabama, p. 60, Line 3, Dwelling 453, Family 436, Enumerated July 13, 1860. Ancestry.com.

17. U.S. Federal Census, 1850, Muscogee County, Georgia, p. 80, Line 34, Dwelling 190, Family 195, Enumerated December 12, 1850. Ancestry.com.

18. Paul Ruffins and Fath Davis Ruffins, "Ten Myths, Half-truths and Misunderstandings about Black History," in *Black Issues in Higher Education* (Chicago: Cox, Matthews, 1997), p. 5.

19. Marriage Bond of Mary Jane McCain and Isom Hurt, 1867, Marriage Records, Old Records Room of the Courthouse, Carrollton, Mississippi.

20. Schools Superintendents Record for Carroll County, 1880, Old Records Room of the Courthouse, Carrollton, Mississippi.

21. U.S. Federal Slave Schedule, 1860, Carroll County, Police District 2, p. 16, Line 40, Enumerated September 8, 1860. Ancestry.com.

22. U.S. Federal Census, 1870 Carroll County, Mississippi, Sub-Division 27, Township 20, p. 8, Line 39, Dwelling 54, Family 54, Enumerated August 17, 1870. Ancestry.com.

23. U.S. Federal Census, 1860, Carroll County, Mississippi, District 2, p. 18, Line 7, Dwelling 126, Family 126, Enumerated September 10, 1860. Ancestry.com.

24. U.S. Federal Census, 1850, Tallahatchie County, Mississippi, p. [?], Line 29, Dwelling 361, Family 361, Enumerated November 13, 1850. Ancestry.com

25. Suzi Parker and Jake Tapper, "McCain's Ancestors Owned Slaves," *Politics 2000*, February 15, 2000. www.Salon.com.

26. Petition by N. H. McCain to apprentice Mary Jane, Minutes of Carroll County Probate Court, p. 589, February 20, 1866. Old Records Room of the Courthouse, Carrollton, Mississippi.

27. Johnson, *Shadow of the Plantation*, pp. 66–88.

28. Louisa Spottswood Coughlin, Letter to Philip R. Ratcliffe: "When liner notes were written for his first Piedmont album, he told us he was 69. A year or so later he told me with some embarrassment that he was actually 71 when rediscovered." His rediscovery on March 3 was just five days before his birthday on March 8. Assuming that he considered himself 71 in 1963, this would make 1892 his birth year.

29. Molly Caldwell Crosby, *The American Plague: The Untold Story of Yellow Fever, the Epidemic That Shaped Our History* (New York: Berkeley, 2006), p. 74.

30. *Ibid.*, pp. 11–14.

31. Howell, *Mississippi Back Roads*, pp. 129–30.

32. Johnson, *Shadow of the Plantation*, pp. 19–20.

33. Paul A. Cimbala, "Black Musicians from Slavery to Freedom: An Exploration of an African-American Folk Elite and Cultural Continuity in the Nineteenth-Century Rural South," *Journal of Negro History* 80 (1995): pp. 15–29.

34. *Ibid.*

35. Stewart Brumfield and Ellett Lawrence II, *Leflore County Mississippi Centennial 1871–1971* (Leflore County Commemorative Book Committee, 1971), p. 5.

36. Dorothy Scarborough, *On the Trail of Negro Folk-Songs* (Cambridge, MA: Harvard University Press, 1925), p. 267.

37. Avalon, Early County Settlements of Carroll County, Mississippi, Carroll County, Mississippi Genealogical and Historical Web Project www.thesgenweb.org/ms/carroll/history/townlist.htm.

38. Johnson, *Shadow of the Plantation*, p. 11.

39. Description of U.S. Federal Census Records. Ancestry.com.

40. U.S. Federal Census, 1900, Carroll County, Enumeration District 15, p. 14, Line 10, Dwelling 228, Family 228, Enumerated June 18, 1900. Ancestry.com.

41. List of Educable Children, 1900, Old Records Room of the Courthouse, Carrollton, Mississippi.

42. Marriage of Sam Hurt to Lizzie Johnson on December 20, 1893, and Marriage of Jim Hurt to Georgia Miers on December 25, 1894, Marriage Records, Old Records Room of the Courthouse, Carrollton, Mississippi.

43. Mississippi John Hurt, recording by Tom Hoskins, unpublished tape recording of interview and music with Mississippi John Hurt and family, Avalon, Carroll County, Mississippi, March 1963. Tom Hoskins Archive.

44. List of Educable Children 1892, 1896, 1900, Old Records Room of the Courthouse, Carrollton, Mississippi.

45. U.S. Federal Census, 1900, Carroll County, Beat 2, District 15.

46. Gertrude Hurt Conley, video interview by Mary Frances Hurt Wright. Philip R. Ratcliffe Archive.

47. U.S. Federal Census, 1900, Carroll County, Mississippi, Enumeration District 15, p. 13, Line 23, Dwelling 219, Family 219, Enumerated June 16, 1900. Ancestry.com.

48. Land Records, Old Records Room of the Courthouse, Carrollton, Mississippi. Personal communication from Susie James and Giles Fuller.

49. Mississippi John Hurt interview by Tom Hoskins and Nick Perls at Ontario Place, Washington D.C., October 13, 1963, Stefan Grossman's Guitar Workshop. www.Guitarvideos.com.

50. Marriage of Harvey Hoskins (Recorded as Henry in 1900 U.S. Federal Census) to Ida Lang on May 11, 1887, Marriage Records, Old Records Room of the Courthouse, Carrollton, Mississippi.

51. Gertrude Hurt Conley, video interview by Mary Frances Hurt Wright.

52. *Sears Roebuck Catalogue 1902*, Facsimile (New York: Crown, 1969); *Sears Roebuck Catalogue 1908, No. 117*, Facsimile (Chicago: Gun Digest, 1969).

53. Marriage of Junious Hurt to Loucretia Betterton on August 7, 1903, Marriage Records, Old Records Room of the Courthouse, Carrollton, Mississippi.

54. Mississippi John Hurt interview by Tom Hoskins and Nick Perls.

55. *Ibid.*

56. Johnson, *Shadow of the Plantation*, pp. xxi, 32.

57. Record of sale of land belonging to Mary Jane Hurt to F. Sabin, February 26, 1906, at Hamrick, Carroll County, Mississippi, Land Records, Old Records Room of the Courthouse, Carrollton, Mississippi. John told Tom Hoskins that his mother still owned some land when he was 27 years old (1919) (Mississippi John Hurt interview by Tom Hoskins and Nick Perls).

58. U.S. Federal Census, 1900, Carroll County, Mississippi, Enumeration District 15, p. 8, Line 67, Dwelling 119, Family 118, Enumerated June 8, 1900. Ancestry.com.

59. Mississippi John Hurt, recording by Tom Hoskins, Avalon, March 1963.

60. George W. Kay, "Mississippi John Hurt," an interview by George W. Kay and Dick Spottswood, *Jazz Journal* 17, no. 2 (February 1964).

61. Mississippi John Hurt, *Pete Seeger's Rainbow Quest*, DVD (Shanachie SH-DV 607, 2005).

62. U.S. Census, 1910, Carroll County, Mississippi, Enumeration District 38, p. 15, Line 35, Dwelling 257, Family 257, Enumerated May 11, 1910.Ancestry.com.

63. Mississippi John Hurt, *Pete Seeger's Rainbow Quest*.

64. Kay, "Mississippi John Hurt."

65. Tom Hoskins, recording with Mississippi John Hurt, Avalon, March 1963.

66. Mississippi John Hurt, handwritten "Life Story" letter given to Tom Hoskins 1963. Complete text provided in chapter 3 and reproduced in part as Figure 3.8.

67. The hurricane, with winds gusting to 135 mph, struck Galveston, Texas, on September 8, 1900. It was considered the deadliest natural disaster in U.S. history. More than 3,600 homes were wrecked by the fifteen-foot storm surge and almost a quarter of the city's 38,000 residents died. Sin-Killer Griffin and his congregation at Darrington State Farm, Sandy Point, Texas, recorded one of the most emotional performances of a disaster ballad about the event on *Negro Religious Songs and Services*, Library of Congress Archive of Folk Culture (Rounder CD 1514, 1999).

68. Lynn Abbott and Doug Seroff, *Ragged But Right: Black Traveling Shows, "Coon Songs," and the Dark Pathway to Blues and Jazz*, (Jackson: University Pres of Mississippi, 2007), p. 12.

69. Adam Gussow, *Seems Like Murder Here: Southern Violence and the Blues Tradition* (Chicago: University of Chicago Press, 2002), p. 51.

70. *Sears Roebuck Catalogue 1897*, Facsimile (New York: Chelsea House, 1968). Sears listed guitars in their catalogue beginning in 1894 and in that year offered eight guitars ranging in price from $4.50 to $26.00. These included Kenwood, Columbian, Windsor, and Washburn makes or models. By 1897 they offered twelve models that included Our Spanish Guitar ($3.95), Our Columbian Standard American Guitar ($5.20), Our "Euterpe" Guitar ($5.75), and The Troubadour ($8.65) as well as some Washburns.

71. Neil Harpe, *Stella Guitars: The Guitars of the Oscar Schmidt Company* (Annapolis, MD: Neil Harpe, private publication, 2003), p. 79.

72. Lawrence Cohn, Notes to *Avalon Blues: The Complete 1928 OKeh Recordings* (Sony CD CK 64986/ DIDP 089710, 2008).

73. Harpe, *Stella Guitars*, p. 79.

74. "Two Women Lynched by Mississippi Mob," *New York Times*, August 2, 1901, p. 1.

75. *Ibid.*

76. "Will Prosecute Lynchers," *New York Times*, August 4, 1901, p. 1.

77. Gussow, *Seems Like Murder Here*, p. 45.

78. Woods, *Development Arrested*, p. 84.

79. Nell Irvin Painter, *Exodusters: Black Migration to Kansas after Reconstruction* (Lawrence: University of Kansas Press, 1986), p. 154.

80. William T. Martin Riches, *The Civil Rights Movement Struggle and Resistance,* 2nd ed., (Basingstoke, England: Palgrave Macmillan, 2004), p. 6; Busbee, Mississippi: A History, p. 178.

81. Tony Howe, "Growth of the Lumber Industry (1840 to 1930)," *Mississippi History Now* (Online publication of Mississippi Historical Society), 2001.

82. Mississippi John Hurt interview by Tom Hoskins and Nick Perls.

83. Abbott and Seroff, *Ragged But Right*, p. 89.

84. Bruce Bastin, notes to *Mississippi John Hurt, Avalon Blues, Volume 2*, LP (Heritage HT 301, 1982); Gussow, *Seems Like Murder Here*, p. 178; Scarborough, *On the Trail of Negro Folk-Songs*, p. 89.

85. Cohn, notes to *Avalon Blues*.

86. David Evans, "Charley Patton, the Conscience of the Delta," in *The Voice of the Delta—Charley Patton and The Mississippi Delta Blues Traditions Influences, and Comparisons: An International Symposium*, ed. Robert Sacre (Leige, Belgium: Presses Universitaires de Liege, 1987), pp. 109–217.

87. David Evans, *Big Road Blues: Tradition and Creativity in the Blues* (Berkeley: University of California Press, 1982), p. 9.

88. Paul Oliver, "Lookin' for the Bully, An Enquiry into a Song and its Story," in *Nobody Knows Where The Blues Come From*, ed. Robert Springer (Jackson: University Press of Mississippi, 2006), p. 108.

89. Richard D. Barnet, Bruce Nemerov and Mayo R. Taylor, *The Story Behind the Song: 150 Songs That Chronicle the 20th Century* (Westport, CT: Greenwood, 2004), p. 27.

90. Abbott and Seroff, *Ragged But Right*, p. 28.

91. John Anderson, "He Done Me Wrong," *Archive of African American Music* 8 (November 2006): pp. 4–5.

92. Cecil Brown, *Stagolee Shot Billy*, (Cambridge, MA: Harvard University Press, 2003), pp. 21–37.

93. Mississippi John Hurt interview by Tom Hoskins and Nick Perls; Mississippi John Hurt, spoken introduction to "Stack O'Lee Blues," on *Mississippi John Hurt, Legend* (Rounder CD 1100, 1997).

94. Mississippi John Hurt interview by Tom Hoskins and Nick Perls.

95. *Mississippi String Bands Vol 1.* (County Records CD 3513, 1998); Mississippi John Hurt, *Last Sessions* (Vanguard VSD 79327, 1972). The Mississippi Possum Hunters recording of "The Last Shot Got Him" is not attributed to a source, while on Hurt's recording, "First Shot Missed Him," the tune is credited as Public Domain.

96. Mississippi John Hurt, Original tape recordings of first Piedmont sessions, 1963. Courtesy of Peter Silitch, recording engineer.

97. Mississippi John Hurt, recollections about writing "Louis Collins," 78 RPMs. www.archive.org.

98. Lewis Collins newspaper articles from the *McDowell Recorder*, June 13, 25, 27, 1924, and *Welch Daily News*, June 10, August 17, November 8, 17, 1924, West Virginia Division of Culture and History. www.wvculture.org.

99. Elijah Wald, *Escaping the Delta: Robert Johnson and the Invention of the Blues* (New York: Harper Collins, 2004), p. 178.

100. Evans, *Big Road Blues*, p. 58.

101. Evans, *Big Road Blues*, p. 40.

102. Woods, *Development Arrested*, pp. 81–83.

103. Gussow, *Seems Like Murder Here*, p. 23.

104. Julius E. Thompson, *Lynchings in Mississippi: A History, 1865:1965* (Jefferson, NC. McFarland, 2001), pp. 65, 84, 98, 122, 143, 161.

105. Evans, *Big Road Blues*, p. 18.

106. Peter K. Siegel, notes to *Friends of Old Time Music: The Folk Arrival 1961–1965*, 3-CD set (Smithsonian Folkways SFW CD 40160, 2006); Jon Hartley Fox, notes to *Mississippi John Hurt, Legend* (Rounder CD 1100, 1997).

107. Cohn, notes to *Avalon Blues*.

108. Alberta Hunter, *Down Hearted Blues* 78 (Paramount 12005, 1922).

109. Norfolk Jazz Quartet, *Norfolk Jazz and Jubilee Quartets: Complete Recorded Works in Chronological Order, Volume 1 1921–1923*)Document DOCD-5381, 1995).

110. Daniel Fleck, *Mississippi John Hurt: A Repertorial Study* (master's thesis, University of Memphis, 2009).

111. Andrew M. Cohen, "The Hands of Blues Guitarists," in *Ramblin' On My Mind*, ed. David Evans (Urbana: University of Illinois Press, 2008), pp. 152–78.

112. Abbott and Seroff, *Ragged But Right*, pp. 210–57.

113. Robert M. W. Dixon, John Godrich, and Howard Rye, *Blues and Gospel Records 1890–1943 Fourth Edition* (Oxford, England: Clarendon, 1997), p. 418.

114. Newman I. White, *American Negro Folk-Songs* (Cambridge, MA: Harvard University Press, 1928).

115. Newman I. White, "The White Man in the Woodpile: Some Influences on Negro Secular Folk-Songs," *American Speech* 4 (October 1928–August 1929), pp. 207–15; cited in Paul Oliver, *Songsters and Saints: Vocal Traditions on Race Records* (Cambridge, England: Cambridge University Press, 1984), p. 47.

116. Oliver, *Songsters and Saints*, p. 77.

117. Abbott and Seroff, *Ragged But Right*, p. 210.

118. Oliver, *Songsters and Saints*, p. 81.

119. Fleck, *Mississippi John Hurt: A Repertorial Study*, p. 12.

120. Lawrence Cohn, notes to *Avalon Blues*.

121. Mississippi John Hurt interview by Tom Hoskins and Nick Perls.

122. Comparing the 1910 and 1920 censuses, no Hurts lived close to the Evans in 1910, but Felix Evans lived next door to John and family in 1920. U.S. Federal Census, 1910, Carroll County, Mississippi, Enumeration District 29, p. 14, Line 99, Dwelling 286, Family 297, Enumerated May 3, 1910; 1920, Carroll County, Mississippi, Enumeration District 28, p. 6, Line 76, Dwelling 137, Family 129, Enumerated February 2, 1920. Ancestry.com.

123. U.S. Federal Census, 1900, Carroll County, Mississippi, Beat 20, Enumeration District 15, Sheet 7. Enumerated June 8, 1900. Ancestry.com.

124. Gertrude Hurt Conley, video interview with Mary Frances Hurt Wright.

125. U.S. Federal Census, 1880, Carroll County, Mississippi, Enumeration District 19, p. 32, Line 30, Dwelling 292, Family 292, Enumerated June 22, 1880; 1900, Carroll County, Mississippi, Enumeration District 210, p. 10, Line 43, Dwelling 179, Family 185, Enumerated June 18, 1900; 1900, Carroll County, Mississippi, Enumeration District 15, p. 15, Line 69, Dwelling 261, Family 261, Enumerated June 19, 1900; 1900, Carroll County, Mississippi, Enumeration District 15, p. 13, Line 29, Dwelling 219, Family 219, Enumerated June 16, 1900; 1910, Carroll County, Enumeration District 38, p. 18, Line 38, Dwelling 258, Family 258, Enumerated May 11, 1910. Ancestry.com.

126. Gertrude Hurt Conley, video interview.

127. Carroll County, Mississippi, Beat 2, District 5. Comparison of U.S. Federal Census data for 1900 and 1910. Ancestry.com.

128. U.S. Federal Census, 1910, Carroll County, Mississippi, Enumeration District 29, p. 10, Line 50, Dwelling 194, Family 203, Enumerated April 27, 1910; 1910, Carroll County, Mississippi, Enumeration District 300, p. 8, Line 56, Dwelling 143, Family 143, Enumerated April 30, 1910. Ancestry.com.

129. Susie James, personal communication relating personal research on Ida Hoskins marriage to Hardy Hurt, 2006.

130. Chancery Court record book 5, p. 183, Record of the granting of divorce decree number 2568 in the case of Cleveland Hurt vs. Lillie Hurt, 15 June 1915, Old Records Room of the Courthouse, Carrollton, Mississippi.

131. Susie James, Personal communication relating personal research concerning Hennis Hurt's marriage to Lillie Meeks, 2006.

132. U.S. Federal Census, 1930, Carroll County, Mississippi, Enumeration District 8-2, p. 3, Line 39, Enumerated April 4, 1930. Ancestry.com.

133. U.S. Federal Census, 1910, Carroll County, Mississippi, Enumeration District 29, p. 8, Line 56, Dwelling 154, Family 161, Enumerated April 27, 1910; 1910, Carroll County, Mississippi, Enumeration District 38, p. 18, Lines 35–37, Dwelling 257, Family 257, Enumerated May 11, 1910. Ancestry.com.

134. U.S. Federal Census, 1910, Carroll County, Mississippi, Enumeration District 29, p. 15, Line 17, Dwelling 288, Family 299, Enumerated May 4, 1910. Ancestry.com.

135. Mississippi John Hurt interview by Tom Hoskins and Nick Perls.

136. Sale of Valley Store and adjoining land to C J Kerr on November 18, 1912, Land Records, Old Records Room of the Courthouse, Carrollton, Mississippi.

137. U.S. Federal Census, 1930 Ancestry.com.

138. Mississippi John Hurt interview by Tom Hoskins and Nick Perls.

139. Land Records, Books 25/12, 25/145, 25/520, Old Records Room of the Courthouse, Carrollton, Mississippi.

140. Johnson, *Shadow of the Plantation*. p. 112.

141. Bradley G. Bond, *Mississippi: A Documentary History* (Jackson: University Press of Mississippi, 2003), pp. 182–84; Woods, *Development Arrested*, pp. 92–95, 121–44; Johnson, *Shadow of the Plantation*, p. 112.

142. Gertrude Hurt Conley, video interview; Marriage license for the marriage of John Hurt and Gertrude Hoskins, July 14, 1916. Affidavit witnessed and signed by Felix Evans, John's neighbor; Marriage Record of marriage of John Hurt to Gertrude Hoskins on August 20, 1916, by Reverend G. W. Miller, Old Records Room of the Courthouse, Carrollton, Mississippi.

143. Paul C. Edie, *The Victor-Victrola Age: An Overview of the Phonographs of the Victor Talking Machine Company*. www.Victor-victrola.com, 2006–2008.

144. Mark A. Humphrey, "Holy Blues, The Gospel Tradition," in *Nothing But the Blues*, ed. Lawrence Cohn,/ (New York: Abbeville, 1993), p. 113.

145. Gayle Dean Wardlow, *Chasin' That Devil Music* (San Francisco: Backbeat, 1998), p. 144.

146. Draft registration card for John Hurt, U.S. Draft Records. Ancestry.com.

147. John Hurt, Certificate of Death, State of Mississippi, State File No. 19067. Mississippi State Department of Health and Vital Records.

148. Sheldon Harris, *Blues Who's Who* (New Rochelle, NY: Arlington House, 1979), pp. 257–59, lists Piedmont 13157 and George W. Kay, "Mississippi John Hurt," an interview by George W. Kay and Dick Spottswood, as its primary sources for this information. Similar information is provided at the National Park Service, Lower Mississippi Delta Region Trail of the Hellhound website, which may have been derived from Harris's book. However, the information about John playing around Jackson ca. 1912 is not provided in the George Kay article or the notes to Piedmont 13157.

149. Abbott and Seroff, *Ragged But Right*, p. 215, 216.

150. Cohn, notes to *Avalon Blues*.

151. Johnson, *Shadow of the Plantation*, pp. 71–75.

152. Book 5, p. 202. Record of the granting of divorce decree number 2591 in the case of Daisy Hurt vs. Paul Hurt, January 11, 1916, Old Records Room of the Courthouse, Carrollton, Mississippi.

153. Stewart E. Tolnay and E. M. Beck, *A Festival of Violence: An Analysis of Southern Lynchings 1882–1930* (Urbana: University of Illinois Press [1995]), p. 72.

154. Mississippi John Hurt interview by Tom Hoskins and Nick Perls. The transcription of the interview reads "Warren," but John almost certainly was referring to Ward Hambrick.

155. *Ibid.*

156. *Ibid.*

157. *Ibid.* These seemingly meaningless words were a result of the written transcription of the original interview and may not accurately portray John's actual words.

158. *Ibid.*

159. *Ibid.*

160. U.S. Federal Census, 1920, Carroll County, Mississippi, Enumeration District 28, p. 12, Line 50, Dwelling 252, Family 254, Enumerated February 7, 1920, Ancestry.com; U.S. death records, Edmund West, comp. Family Data Collection—Deaths [online]. Provo, UT: The Generations Network, Inc., 2001.

161. Mississippi John Hurt interview by Tom Hoskins and Nick Perls.

162. U.S. Federal Census, 1920, Carroll County, Mississippi, Enumeration District 28. Ancestry.com.

163. *Ibid.* The Hurts were living in Township 20, Beat 2, Enumeration District 28. The family numbers allocated in the census indicate the close proximity of the families; Ella and Ned Moore (123); Cleveland, Fannie and family (122); Hardy and Ida (127); John, Gertrude, and family (130).

164. Edna Stinson was recorded as Ellsea in the U.S. Federal Census, 1920. Her mother was Italian.

165. Mississippi John Hurt interview by Tom Hoskins and Nick Perls.

166. U.S. Federal Census, 1920, Carroll County, Mississippi, Enumeration District 28. Ancestry.com.

167. This assumption is based on the fact that the Stinsons are known to have occupied the store on what is now Highway 7 in the Delta, and the ferryman and the fisherman almost certainly were occupied on the Potacocowa Creek to the west of Highway 7 and the railroad. The remaining families included railroad workers and plantation managers who are presumed to be living close to the railway track and depot and the Avalon cotton gin close to the Stinson's Store. Two brothers who shared the same house, Clifton Muller and M. M. Muller, were employed as plantation manager and ginner, respectively. In the original census records, alongside the occupation of ginner, under the heading referring to the place of work are the words "Avalon Gin."

168. U.S. Federal Census, 1920, Carroll County, Mississippi, Enumeration District 28, p. 6, Line 59, Dwelling 131, Family 123, Enumerated February 2, 1920. Ancestry.com.

169. Susie James, personal communication relating to personal research confirming Hennis Hurt's role as a trustee of Joliff school, 2005.

170. Johnson, *Shadow of the Plantation*, pp. 64–66, 67.

171. "Greetings from Greenwood, Mississippi." www.Aboutgreenwoodms.com.

172. Busbee Jr., *Mississippi: A History*, pp. 186–87.

173. Mississippi John Hurt interview by Tom Hoskins and Nick Perls.

174. *Ibid.*

175. *Ibid.*

176. The photograph of the turkey hunt and bear comes from a commemorative book, *Carroll County . . . Looking Back Through The Years* (Winona, Mississippi: The Conservative, 1998), p. 127. Lee Mattox is the grandson of the family depicted in the bear picture and provided the following information: "The picture was taken near Avalon between 1913 and 1915. Dr. Charles C. Mattox, Lee's grandfather, killed the bear while turkey hunting for the family's Thanksgiving dinner. The dogs in the picture ran up on the bear and were injured in an ensuing attack by the bear. My grandfather had to shoot the bear to prevent it from killing his dogs. My father, who was born in 1919, was the youngest child and had not been born when this picture was taken. The infant being held by the nanny in the picture was his sister, who would have been 5 years or so older than him, which led to dating the picture between 1913 and 1915."

177. Nolan Porterfield, *The Life and Times of America's Blue Yodeler, Jimmie Rodgers* (Urbana: University of Illinois Press, 1992), p. 48–50.

178. Alan Mirken, *1927 Edition of The Sears, Roebuck Catalogue, The Roaring Twenties*, (New York: Bounty, 1970), p. 691; Paul C. Edie, personal communication relating to the availability of low-cost Victrola phonographs following the introduction of the new Orthophonic machines in 1925; Dorothy Dickins, *A Nutrition Investigation of Negro Tenants in the Yazoo-Mississippi Delta*, cited in *Early Downhome Blues: A Musical and Cultural Analysis,* 2nd ed., by Jeff Todd Titon (Chapel Hill: University of North Carolina Press, 1994), p. 11; Johnson, *Shadow of the Plantation*, p. 184. Information based on a sample of 612 black families in Macon, Alabama, in 1930–31; Edie, *The Victor-Victrola Age.*

179. Mirken, *The 1927 Edition of The Sears, Roebuck Catalogue*, p. 675.

180. David Evans, "High Water Everywhere: Blues and Gospel Commentary on the 1927 Mississippi River Flood," in *Nobody Knows Where The Blues Come From*, p. 33.

181. Titon, *Early Downhome Blues*, p. 201.

182. Mississippi Fred McDowell cited in Jeff Todd Titon, *Early Downhome Blues*, p. 282–83.

183. John M. Barry, *Rising Tide: The Great Mississippi Flood and How It Changed America* (New York: Touchstone, 1997), p. 133; David Evans, "Rubin Lacy," in *Blues Unlimited* (January 1967), reproduced in *Nothing But The Blues*, ed. Mike Leadbitter (London: Hanover, 1971), p. 242.

184. Bond, *Mississippi, A Documentary History*, p. 148.

185. Guido Van Rijn, "Coolidge's Blues," in *Nobody Knows Where The Blues Come From*, p. 152.

186. Heather Heilman, "Lawsuit Blues: The Curious Battle over the Legacy of Mississippi John Hurt," *Memphis Flyer*, October 21–27, 1999, pp. 18–22.

187. Wardlow, *Chasin' That Devil Music*. p. 142.

188. Johnson, *Shadow of the Plantation*, pp. 71–72.

189. U.S. Federal Census, 1930, Bolivar County, Mississippi, Enumeration District 6-41, p. 15, Line 13, Dwelling 319, Family 324, Enumerated April 22, 1930. Ancestry.com.

190. U.S. Federal Census 1910, Hattiesburg, Ward 4, Forest County, Mississippi, Enumeration District 141, p. 10, Line 87, Dwelling 245, Family 256, Enumerated May 20, 1910; 1920, Hattiesburg, Ward 4, Forest County, Mississippi, Enumeration District 14, p. 17, Line 86, Dwelling 304, Family 371, Enumerated January 14, 1920. Ancestry.com.

191. Mississippi John Hurt interview by Tom Hoskins and Nick Perls.

192. Kay, "Mississippi John Hurt."

193. U.S. Federal Census, 1920, Carroll County, Mississippi, Enumeration District 29, p. 10, Line 38, Dwelling 194, Family 187, Enumerated January 16, 1920. Ancestry.com.

194. Mississippi John Hurt interview by Tom Hoskins and Nick Perls; Wald, *Escaping the Delta*, p. 48.

195. Barry, *Rising Tide*, p. 14–15.

196. *Ibid.*, pp. 194, 285.

197. *Ibid.*, pp. 201–6, 275–76.

198. *Ibid.*, pp. 305, 308–17.

199. *Ibid.*, pp. 313–14.

200. *Ibid.*, pp. 308–17; Evans, *High Water Everywhere*, pp. 50–52.

201. Barry, *Rising Tide*, pp. 278, 286.

202. Evans, *High Water Everywhere*, pp. 60–61.

203. Smith, *The Yazoo River*, p. 212.

204. Barry, *Rising Tide*, pp. 304–6, 363.

205. U.S. Federal Census, 1930, Bolivar County, Mississippi, Enumeration District 6-41, p. 15, Line 13, Dwelling 319, Family 324, Enumerated April 22, 1930. Ancestry.com.

206. Tom Hoskins, recording with Mississippi John Hurt, Avalon, March 1963; Harry Bollick, notes provided to author from personal research on Carroll County fiddle and string band music. Philip R Ratcliffe Archive; Porterfield, *The Life and Times of Jimmie Rodgers*, p. 433.

207. A complete list of Narmour and Smith's recordings is presented in Tony Russell, *Country Music Records: A Discography, 1921–1942*, (Oxford, England: Oxford University Press, 2004, 2008), pp. 649_50; Henry Young, cited by Harry Bollick, notes provided to author from personal research on Carroll County fiddle and string band music; Narmour and Smith, "Avalon Quickstep," *Mississippi String Bands, Vol. One* (County Records CD 3513, 1998); Harry Bollick and Friends, *Carroll County, Mississippi* (New Timey CD, 2005).

208. Jas Obrecht, "Mississippi John Hurt," Excerpt from a book in progress, *Early Blues*, Mindspring.com, 1995. I have been unable to determine Obrecht's source of this important information.

209. Tom Hoskins, recording with Mississippi John Hurt, Avalon, March 1963; Mississippi John Hurt interview by Tom Hoskins and Nick Perls.

210. Pete Seeger/John Hurt Interview, *Mississippi John Hurt: The Memorial Anthology* (Blues Vault GCD 9906/7, 1994).

211. Advertisement in *Memphis Commercial Appeal*, February 10, 1928, Benjamin L Hooks Public Library and Information Center, Memphis.

212. Tony Russell, "Country Music on Location: 'Field Recording' before Bristol," *Popular Music* 26/1: pp. 23–31 (Cambridge, England: Cambridge University Press, 2007);"McCall Comes Tumbling Down," *Memphis Commercial Appeal*, June 23, 1975, Benjamin L Hooks Public Library and Information Center, Memphis.

213. Dixon, Godrich, and Rye, pp. 418–19.

214. Cohn, notes to *Avalon Blues*.

215. Dixon, Godrich, and Rye, p. 418.

216. Ibid., p. 755.

217. Russell, *Country Music Records A Discography, 1921-1942*, p. 63.

218. Ibid., p. 649.

219. Richard Spottswood and David A. Jason, "Discoveries Concerning Recorded Ragtime," *Jazz Journal*, Vol 21 No. 2 (February 1968), p. 7. Dixon, Godrich, and Rye, *Blues and Gospel Records 1890-1943 Fourth Edition*, p. 368.

220. Of the other records advertised along with "Frankie"/"Nobody's Dirty Business," Victoria Spivey's "Jelly Look What You Have Done"/"Red Lantern Blues" (OKeh 8550) was also advertised in the *Baltimore Afro-American* on April 21, 1928, and the *Chicago Defender* and *Pittsburgh Courier* on April 28, 1928. Louis Armstrong's "Struttin' With Some Barbecue"/"Once In a While" (OKeh 8566) was also advertised in the *Baltimore Afro-American* and *Pittsburgh Courier* on May 26, 1928. These titles were actually by Louis Armstrong and his Hot Five.

221. Laurie Wright, *OKeh Race Records: The 8000 Race Series* (Chigwell, England: L Wright, private publication, 2001), pp. 134–36; Robert M. W. Dixon and John Godrich, *Recording the Blues* (New York: Stein and Day, 1970), p. 64; Dixon, Godrich, and Rye, p. xxvii.

222. Letter to Mississippi John Hurt from T. G. Rockwell, November 8, 1928, reproduced in Dick Spottswood, "Mississippi John Hurt," *Blues Unlimited* (August 1963) and in *Nothing But the Blues*, ed. Mike Leadbitter (London: Hanover, 1971), pp. 245–46; The letter was reproduced in part in the notes to the original Piedmont release, *Presenting Mississippi John Hurt: Folk Songs and Blues*, 1963 and the re-release on Piedmont PLP-13157. These omit the reference to the request for John to meet Polk in Memphis to collect his ticket and expense money for the trip to New York.

223. Pete Seeger interview, *Memorial Anthology* CD; H. C. Spier cited in, Wardlow, *Chasin' That Devil Music*, p. 147;149 Dixon, Godrich, and Rye, p. 709, 151; Dixon and Godrich, *Recording the Blues*, pp. 27–28.

224. Tom Hoskins, recording with Mississippi John Hurt, Avalon, March 1963.

225. Mississippi John Hurt interview by Tom Hoskins and Nick Perls.

226. Dixon, Godrich and Rye, *Blues and Gospel Records 1890-1943 Fourth Edition*, p. 899.

227. OKeh 40000 Series Numerical Listing, http://www.78discography.com.

228. Tom Hoskins, recording with Mississippi John Hurt, Avalon, March 1963; Mississippi John Hurt interview by Tom Hoskins and Nick Perls.

229. Dixon, Godrich, and Rye, pp. 368, 755.

230. Mississippi John Hurt interview by Tom Hoskins and Nick Perls.

231. *Ibid.*

232. *Ibid.*

233. Dixon, Godrich, and Rye, p. 810.

234. *Mississippi John Hurt 1928 Sessions*, LP, L 1065, 1968, issued on CD (Yazoo CD 1065, 1990) and *Avalon Blues: The Complete 1928 OKeh Recordings* (Sony Roots N' Blues Series CK 64986, 1996)

235. Peter Silitch, original recordings of first Piedmont sessions, 1963.

236. Tom Hoskins, recording with Mississippi John Hurt, Avalon, March 1963.

237. Wald, *Escaping the Delta*, pp. 52–66.

238. Cohn, notes to *Avalon Blues*.

239. "Mississippi" was probably added at the suggestion of Rockwell, who appeared to like to add geographical prefixes to his artists (e.g., Texas Alexander, Mississippi Sheiks, Georgia Bill).

Chapter 2

1. Wright, *OKeh Race Records: The 8000 Race Series*, p. 160. These newspapers, along with the *Pittsburgh Courier*, were the usual national advertising outlets for race records.

2. *Ibid.*, pp. 162, 168, 174–76, 181–82.

3. Elijah Wald, *Escaping the Delta* (New York: Amistad, 2004), p. 80.

4. Dixon, Godrich, and Rye, *Blues and Gospel Records 1890–1943*, p. 418.

5. Russell, *Country Music Records*, pp. 649–50.

6. Dixon, Godrich, and Rye, *Blues and Gospel Records 1890-1943*, pp. 151–53, 642–45, 972–74.

7. Greil Marcus, notes to Dock Boggs, *Country Blues—Complete Early Recordings (1927–29)* (Revenant CD 205, 1998); Russell, *Country Music Records*, p. 116. Dock Boggs and Emry Arthur were the only artists to be recorded on The Lonesome Ace label.

8. Letter to Dock Boggs from W. E. Myer, Richlands, Virginia, June 10th, 1930, reproduced in notes to Dock Boggs, *Country Blues—Complete Early Recordings.*

9. Kay, "Mississippi John Hurt," pp. 24–26.

10. *Ibid.*; Alex van der Tuuk, *Paramount's Rise and Fall: A History of the Wisconsin Chair Company and Its Recording Activities* (Denver: Mainspring, 2003), p. 175.

11. *Ibid.*, pp. xvi, 175. The New York Recording Laboratories of Port Washington, Wisconsin, initiated the Paramount label in 1917. Having previously recorded in Chicago and New York City, recording was transferred to Grafton, Wisconsin, in late 1929.

12. Kay, "Mississippi John Hurt"; Christopher Milne, "Dock Boggs—A Biography" chris@colfaxcg.com.

13. Stewart Brumfield and Ellett Lawrence II, *Leflore County Mississippi Centennial 1871–1971* (Leflore County Commemorative Book Committee, 1971), p. 21.

14. Dixon and Godrich, *Recording the Blues*, pp. 64–77.

15. William E. Leuchtenburg, *Franklin D. Roosevelt and the New Deal* (New York: Harper and Row, 1963), pp. 124–26.

16. Mississippi John Hurt interview by Tom Hoskins and Nick Perls.

17. Smith, *The Yazoo River*, p. 309.

18. Jones, "The Mississippi Delta," p. 37.

19. Mississippi John Hurt interview by Tom Hoskins and Nick Perls.

20. Busbee, *Mississippi: A History*, pp. 184–216.

21. Robert K. D. Peterson, "Charley Patton and His Mississippi Boweavil Blues," *American Entomologist* (Fall 2007): pp. 142–44.

22. Mississippi John Hurt interview by Tom Hoskins and Nick Perls.

23. *Ibid*.

24. Burton Cotton Gin and Museum, Burton, Texas. www.cottonginmuseum.org.

25. James C. Cobb, *The Most Southern Place On Earth* (New York: Oxford University Press, 1992), pp. 50–60.

26. Woods, *Development Arrested*, p. 48.

27. Donald Holley, *The Mechanical Cotton Picker*, EH.Net Encyclopedia, ed. Robert Whaples, June 16, 2003. eh.net/encyclopedia/article/holley.cottonpicker.

28. Mississippi John Hurt interview by Tom Hoskins and Nick Perls.

29. The lyrics reflect the theme of Memphis Minnie's three hit tunes issued in 1930 and 1932 (Dixon and Godrich, *Recording the Blues*, p. 70): "Bumble Bee," Vocalion 1476, 1930; "Bumble Bee No. 2," Vocalion 1556, 1931; "New Bumble Bee," Vocalion 1618, 1931. But these actual words do not occur in any of the Memphis Minnie tunes. These lyrics are closer to those of "I'm a King Bee" by Slim Harpo (Excello 2113, 1957), a recording made years later.

30. Susie James, "Who Turned Around John Hurt's Tombstone?" *Greenwood Commonwealth*, August 2, 2000.

31. Susie James, "Narmour and Smith, A Carroll County Story," *Greenwood Commonwealth*, November 21, 1997.

32. *Ibid*.

33. Donna Ladd, "Our Boy Trent," *Jackson Free Press*, December 9, 2002. An article about Senator Trent Lott.

34. Statement of Principles, Council of Conservative Citizens. www.cofcc.org.

35. Susie James, "Narmour and Smith, A Carroll County Story." Beating straws is a way of playing the fiddle where one person fingers the notes while another beats straws on the strings.

36. Harry Bollick, notes from a 2003 interview with Donald (Sonny) Smith, son of Shell Smith.

37. Gene Clardy and Stan Clements recorded four titles for Vocalion in Memphis on February 18, 1930; Russell, *Country Music Records*, pp. 212–13.

38. Susie James, notes on a story on Charles Campbell in 2000.

39. Mississippi John Hurt interview by Tom Hoskins and Nick Perls.

40. *Ibid*.

41. John Work III, "Untitled Manuscript," in *Lost Delta Found*, pp. 80, 120.

42. Samuel C. Adams Jr., "Changing Negro Life in the Delta," in *Lost Delta Found*, p. 236.

43. Work, "Untitled Manuscript," p. 81.

44. Anne Smith, notes of an interview by Harry Bollick.

45. Work, "Untitled Manuscript," p. 84.

46. Palmer, *Deep Blues*, p. 104.

47. Robert Petaway, "Catfish Blues," recorded March 28, 1941, in Chicago (Bluebird B8838); Tommy McClennan, "Deep Blue Sea Blues," recorded September 15, 1941, in Chicago (Bluebird B9005).

48. Palmer, *Deep Blues*, p. 104.

49. Peter Guralnick, *Searching for Robert Johnson*, (New York: Plume, 1998), pp. 17, 36–39.

50. Palmer, *Deep Blues*, p. 129.

51. David Honeyboy Edwards, *The World Don't Owe Me Nothing: The Life and Times of Delta Bluesman Honeyboy Edwards* (Chicago: Chicago Review Press, 1997), pp. 99–100.

52. Guralnick, *Searching for Robert Johnson*, pp. 51–52.

53. Steve Cheseborough, *Blues Travelin: The Holy Sites of Delta Blues* (Jackson: University Press of Mississippi, 2001), p. 116.

54. Gioia, *Delta Blues*, p. 284.

55. Scott Barretta, *Mack Allen Smith,* Mississippi Arts Commission, 2002–2008. www.arts.state.ms.us.

56. Mack Allen Smith page, Rockabilly Hall of Fame. www.rockabillyhall.com.

57. Dardanelle Hadley, *Dardanelle Down Home—The Way Things Used to Be*, CD/cassette (Hadley Music, 1994). Stories about her past were recorded during a radio show she did in Senatobia for WJNC. WKNO in Memphis then picked them up and in 1996 the vignettes ran on PRM. By the 1940s and 1950s Dardanelle had become famous playing with the Lionel Hampton Orchestra and Nat Cole. She played regular slots in Tokyo and in New York and on cruise liners, including the Queen Elizabeth II.

58. Harris, *Blues Who's Who*, p. 227.

59. Dixon and Godrich, *Recording the Blues*, p. 99; Wardlow, *Chasin' That Devil Music*, p. 138.

60. Gordon and Nemerov, p. 15.

61. *Ibid.*, pp. 9, 15.

62. Palmer, *Deep Blues*, pp. 15–16.

63. Mississippi John Hurt interview by Tom Hoskins and Nick Perls.

64. Gayle Dean Wardlow, "Got Four, Five Puppies, One Little Shaggy Hound," *Blues Unlimited* 142 (1982): 4–11, and in *Chasin' That Devil Music*, p. 58.

65. Dixon, Godrich, and Rye, *Blues and Gospel Records 1890-1943*, p. 97.

66. David Evans, "Rubin Lacy" in *Nothing But the Blues*, p. 242; Wardlow, "Got Four, Five Puppies, One Little Shaggy Hound," pp. 45–46.

67. *Ibid.*, p. 56.

68. U.S. Federal Census, 1930, Carroll County, Mississippi, Enumeration District 2, p. 19, Line 21, Dwelling 391, Family 320, Enumerated April 29, 1930. Ancestry.com.

69. *Ibid.*, Lines 16–34, Dwellings 387–393, Families 318–322.

70. Record of sale by Hennis Hurt to Mrs. Edna Stinson for $687.04 on December 7, 1931. Old Records Room of the Courthouse, Carrollton, Mississippi.

71. U.S. Federal Census, 1920, Carroll County, Mississippi, Enumeration District 28, p. 20, Line 22, Dwelling 424, Family 413, Enumerated February 18, 1920. Ancestry.com.

72. Hadley, *Dardanelle Down Home*. Dardanelle Hadley was born Marcia Marie Mullen, but was later called Dardanelle by her father. As Dardanelle Hadley, she

became a famous jazz pianist and vocalist. Her reminiscences provide valuable information about Avalon.

73. *Ibid.*; Draft registration cards for Hurt brothers John (1485), Junious (1486) and Paul (1487), World War I Draft Registration Cards 1917–1918. Ancestry.com.

74. Hadley, *Dardanelle Down Home*.

75. U.S. Federal Census, 1930, Carroll County, Mississippi, Enumeration District 2.

76. Hadley, *Dardanelle Down Home*. The description of the Stubblefields' store, owned by George C. Stubblefield and his wife Mannie, confirm its location in Avalon (rather than the hill country) and helps identify the location of neighboring properties and families (see Table 2.1). Given Hadley's reference to Mrs. Stubblefield, it seems that Stubblefield may have died prior to the period that she is referring to, suggesting sometime after 1930. The Stubblefields were recorded as being 50 years of age in the 1930 census, reinforcing the view that Hadley's description referred to later in the 1930s.

When Dardanelle Hadley attended Greenwood Junior High school, she boarded with the Moore family in Greenwood during the week, and spent the weekends at home in Avalon. Her music teacher, Gladys Bacon, is listed in the 1930 U.S. Census as a 31-year-old music teacher in Greenwood. Curiously, her father Marcius Mullen is recorded as being employed as a state highway patrolman and his brother Clifton could not be traced anywhere in the census records for 1930. Dardanelle made no reference to her father being a law officer, but did remember her Uncle Clifton, who drove a buggy around the plantation and dressed like a "dandy." Perhaps some of her memories come from before 1930 and fortunes on the plantation changed leading up to the Depression, with her father becoming a law officer and Uncle Clifton leaving the United States or dying?

77. U.S. Federal Census, 1930, Carroll County, Mississippi, Enumeration District 3, p. 11, Line 7, Dwelling 219, Family 223, Enumerated April 24, 1930; 1930, Carroll County, Mississippi, Enumeration District 3, p. 14, Lines 54–57, Dwelling 299–300, Family 303–304, Enumerated April 30, 1930. Ancestry.com.

78. Note from Lee F. Liddell about his father. Mississippi John Hurt Museum, Avalon, Mississippi.

79. John William Hurt, Birth Certificate Registration 8254, March 20, 1932, Mississippi State Department of Health.

80. U.S. Federal Census, 1930, Bolivar County, Mississippi, Enumeration District 6–41, p. 15, Lines 13–17, Dwelling 319, Family 324, Enumerated April 22, 1930. Ancestry.com.

81. Black Donley School List 1935, Old Records Room of the Courthouse, Carrollton, Mississippi.

82. Adams, "Changing Negro Life in the Delta," p. 229.

83. *Ibid.*, pp. 229–30.

84. *Ibid.*, p. 231.

85. Palmer, *Deep Blues*, pp. 118, 119.

86. *Ibid.*, pp. 119–20.

87. Adams, "Changing Negro Life in the Delta," pp. 232–34.

88. Palmer, *Deep Blues*, p. 144.

89. *Sears Roebuck and Company Catalogue Spring and Summer, 1940* (Los Angeles, Sears Roebuck, 1940).

90. Land Records, Books 28/245, 31/266, Old Records Room of the Courthouse, Carrollton, Mississippi.

91. Giles Fuller, personal communication via Susie James.

92. Note from Lee F. Liddell about his father, Mississippi John Hurt Museum.

93. Mississippi John Hurt interview by Tom Hoskins and Nick Perls.

94. Lawrence Hoffman, "John William Hurt: And Daddy Would Play All Night Long," Unidentified newspaper article, 1993. Tom Hoskins Archive.

95. Ibid.

96. Notes from Harry Bollick.

97. Olin Goss, interview by Susie James.

98. Barry Lee Pearson, notes from an interview with John William "Man" Hurt, 1993.

99. Mississippi John Hurt interview by Tom Hoskins and Nick Perls. In the transcribed interview the snake is described as a "cortswood," which is probably a misinterpretation of *coach whip*;
U.S. Federal Census, 1930, Carroll County, Mississippi, Enumeration District 1, p. 2, Line 52, Dwelling 10, Family 11, Enumerated April 4, 1930. Ancestry.com. A. J. W. Watts is recorded as a one-year-old child, which could have been the young Joe. Presumably he would have been at least fifteen (he was married and had a cabin) when the incident with the snake happened, placing the incident anytime between 1945 and 1960.

100. Ray B. Browne, *A Night with the Hants and Other Alabama Folk Experiences* (Madison: University of Wisconsin Press, 1976), p. 121.

101. Mississippi John Hurt interview by Tom Hoskins and Nick Perls.

102. Ernest W. Baughman, *Type and Motif Index of the Folktales of England and North America* (The Hague, Netherlands: Mouton, 1966), pp. 85–89.

103. Memphis Minnie, "Stinging Snake Blues," *Memphis Minnie and Kansas Joe: Complete Recorded Works 1929–1934, Vol. 4: 1933–1934* (Document Records DOCD-5031, 1991).

104. Roger Conant and Joseph T. Collins, *A Field Guide to Reptiles and Amphibians, Eastern and Central North America* (New York: Houghton Mifflin, 1998); "Chasing the Story of the Hoop Snake," *Newsletter of the Colorado Herpetological Society* 28, no. 4 (2001).

105. Susie James, notes on a story she did on Charles Campbell in 2000.

106. *Ibid*.

107. A Hines Moore (aged 45) was recorded in the 1920 U.S. Federal Census lodging with Hennis and Lillie Hurt. In 1930 a Hinds Moore (50) lived with Ned and Ella Moore and was recorded as being a cousin of Ned. It seems likely that this was the same man that was found dead in the gravel pit in 1947, though the ages indicate a birth year of 1875, 1880, or 1861.

108. Jerry Yocom and Jack Hairston, "Missing Negro Found in Treacherous Gullies of Avalon Gravel Pit," *Morning Star*, Greenwood, Mississippi, Sunday, January 4, 1948, p. 1.

109. Lucille Hurt, wife of Hennis Hurt, cited in Tom Miller, "Lifetime of Living with Music," *Greenwood Commonwealth*, November 23, 1997, p. 2A.

110. Arnie Watson, cited in Miller, "Lifetime of Living with Music."

111. Susie James, "A Hurt Homecoming," *Greenwood Commonwealth*, August 15, 2000.

112. Mississippi John Hurt and family, unpublished tape recording of interview and music, Avalon, Carroll County, Mississippi, March 1963. Tom Hoskins Archive.

113. *Ibid.*; Anonymous, "Son Questions Story about Hurt," *Greenwood Commonwealth*, February 26, 1998.

114. U.S. Federal Census, 1930, Sunflower County, Mississippi, Enumeration District 26, p. 2, Line 43, Dwelling 36, Family 39, Enumerated April 2, 1930. Ancestry.com.

115. Olin Goss, interview by Susie James.

116. Susie James, "A Hurt Homecoming."

117. Smith, *The Yazoo River*, p. 182.

118. Busbee, *Mississippi: A History*, pp. 268, 270.

119. Bond, *Mississippi: A Documentary History*, pp. 196–98.

120. C. Vann Woodward, *The Strange Career of Jim Crow* (New York: Oxford University Press, 1966), pp. 116–17.

121. "Text Books in Mississippi," *Opportunity: Journal of Negro Life* 18 (April 1940): pp. 99–100, cited in Bond, *Mississippi: A Documentary History*, pp. 195–96.

122. Woodward, *The Strange Career of Jim Crow*, pp. 127, 136.

123. Thompson, *Lynchings in Mississippi*, p. 141.

124. Devery Scott Anderson, 2004. EmmettTillMurder.com.

125. Harry Bollick, notes to Philip R. Ratcliffe; Philip C. Kolin, "The Legacy of Emmett Till," *Southern Quarterly* (Summer 2008): pp. 1–3.

126. William T. Martin Riches, *The Civil Rights Movement: Struggle and Resistance,* 2nd ed. (Basingstoke, UK: Palgrave Macmillan, 2004), p. 65.

127. *Ibid.*, p. 66.

128. Heilman, "Lawsuit Blues," pp. 19–24.

129. *The Story of Greenwood, Mississippi*, recorded and produced by Guy Carawan for the Student Non-Violent Coordinating Committee (SNCC), 1965 (Smithsonian Folkways FD 5593, 2006).

130. *Ibid.*

131. John Lomax and Alan Lomax, *American Ballads and Folk Songs* (New York: Macmillan, 1934).

132. Harry Smith, *Anthology of American Folk Music.*

133. Nat Hentoff, notes for *The Freewheelin' Bob Dylan* (Columbia CD 32390, 1962).

Chapter 3

1. John Edwards of Sydney, Australia, died age 26 in 1960. He was one of the foremost collectors of American country music. His record collection of over 2,500 rare records, correspondence, discographies, and writings is held in the Southern Folklife Collection, Manuscripts Department Library of the University of North Carolina, Chapel Hill, North Carolina. The collection was purchased from University of California, Los Angeles, in 1983 and has since been added to.

2. Kay, "Mississippi John Hurt," pp. 24–26.

3. Letter from Tom Hoskins to Alex Haley, February 12, 1982. Tom Hoskins Archive.

4. Nervous Norvus (Jimmy Drake), with Red Blanchard & the Smogrollers, "The Fang"/"The Bullfrog Hop" (both written by Jimmy Drake), Dot 15500, September 1956. The complete recorded works of Nervous Norvus was issued on *Stone Age Woo: The Zorch Sounds of Nervous Norvus* (Norton B0002AAPIA, 2004).

5. Letter from Tom Hoskins to Alex Haley.

6. *Ibid.*

7. Letter from Leland M. Talbot to David Segal, *Washington Post*, June 27, 2001.

8. *Ibid.*

9. Letter from Tom Hoskins to Alex Haley, February 12, 1982.

10. David Brown, "From Avalon to Eternity," *Greenwood Commonwealth*, December 12, 1976, and reproduced within notes to the reissue of the original Piedmont LPs, *Mississippi John Hurt: Avalon Blues* (Rounder CD 1081, 1991) and *Mississippi John Hurt: Worried Blues* (Rounder CD 1082, 1991); Tom Hoskins, handwritten corrections to "From Avalon to Eternity." Tom Hoskins Archive; letter from Tom Hoskins to Alex Haley, February 12, 1982.

11. Mississippi John Hurt and family, Avalon, Carroll County, Mississippi, March 1963.

12. Deposition of Thomas Bird Hoskins; Civil Action No. 122898, in the Circuit Court for Montgomery County, Thomas B. Hoskins v. Eugene R. Rosenthal d/b/a Adelphi Studios and d/b/a Adelphi Records and d/b/a Genes Compact Disc Company and Adelphi Records, Inc., January 11, 1995, p. 44. Tom Hoskins states that the name of the girl was Janet Rodd, that she accompanied him to Avalon, and that he never saw her again and did not know of her whereabouts. It has proved impossible to trace Janet Rodd.

13. Denise Tapp, "Untitled essay on Tom Hoskins" accompanying *Fang 1941-2002*, CD (private publication, Joe Lee, undated).

14. Kay, "Mississippi John Hurt," pp. 24–26.

15. Tapp, "Untitled essay on Tom Hoskins."

16. "Chuck Berry," Wikipedia. The commonly used reference to the Mann Act refers to the White Slave Traffic Act of 1910.

17. An interesting example of how events can become distorted emerges from Robert Gilpin, "The Way It Ought to Sound: John Smith Hurt and the Blues of the Mississippi," *Journal of Mississippi History* 63: p. 1. 2001, who tells of a cream-colored Buick containing Hoskins and Stewart, that "rolled south down Highway 61" in the spring of 1963 as a preliminary to the rediscovery of Hurt. The supporting reference is cited as Ed Ward's liner notes to the Vanguard album *Mississippi John Hurt: Rediscovered* (Vanguard CD 79519-2, 1998). However, Ward's account does not mention what make of car they traveled in. It is also unlikely that they would have traveled along Highway 61 unless using a roundabout route. Making reference to 61, the route taken by many bluesmen traveling between the Delta and Memphis and Chicago and referred to as the "Blues Highway," would add color to the story.

18. Letter from Joe Lee to *Washington City Paper*, December 9, 2005; Tapp, "Untitled essay on Tom Hoskins."

19. Mississippi John Hurt and family, Avalon, Carroll County, Mississippi, March 1963.

20. Ward, notes to *Mississippi John Hurt: Rediscovered*.

21. Kay, "Mississippi John Hurt," pp. 24–26.

22. All attempts to trace Janet Rodd have so far failed.

23. Kay, "Mississippi John Hurt," pp. 24–26.

24. Interview by Pete Seeger, *Mississippi John Hurt: Memorial Anthology*.

25. "Mississippi John," *Newsweek*, February 17, 1964, pp. 87–88.

26. Mississippi John Hurt and family, Avalon, Carroll County, Mississippi, March 1963.

27. Bill Givens unpublished draft liner notes for OJL 8053 and 8054. Tom Hoskins Archive.

28. A 50:50 split would have been familiar to John as it was the basis for many sharecropping agreements.

29. Deposition of Thomas Bird Hoskins; Civil Action No. 81-0946, in the United States District Court for the District of Columbia. Adelphi Records Inc. v. Polygram Records v. Mark Wenner, 1982, p. 6.

30. Mississippi John Hurt, *Folk Songs and Blues* (Piedmont PLP 13157). The original tapes from these sessions have survived. Peter Silitch Archive.

31. Dick Spottswood, Unpublished typescript, 1964. Tom Hoskins Archive.

32. *The Story of Greenwood, Mississippi* (Smithsonian Folkways FD 5593, 2006).

33. Letter from Mississippi John Hurt to Tom Hoskins, April 22, 1963. Tom Hoskins Archive.

34. Dick Spottswood, notes to *Presenting Mississippi John Hurt: Folksongs and Blues*.

35. Tom Hoskins, undated recorded interview with unknown interviewer. Tom Hoskins Archive.

36. *Ibid*.

37. Riches, *The Civil Rights Movement*, pp. 69–70.

38. Letter from Mississippi John Hurt to Tom Hoskins, May 4, 1963. Tom Hoskins Archive.

39. Kay, "Mississippi John Hurt," pp. 24–26.

40. Barney Josephson with Terry Trilling-Josephson, *Café Society: The Wrong Place for the Right People* (Urbana: University of Illinois Press, 2009), pp. xi, 3.

41. Elijah Wald, *Josh White: Society Blues* (New York: Routledge, 2002), pp. 102–4. Josh White became a resident artist at Café Society in 1940, heralding an era of presenting American folk music coupled with civil rights awareness to white intellectuals. He remained a regular there through the early 1940s.

42. Barry Lee Pearson, *Virginia Piedmont Blues: The Lives and Art of Two Virginia Bluesmen* (Philadelphia: University of Pennsylvania Press, 1990), p. 35.

43. *Ibid*., p. 54.

44. Archie Edwards, transcript of an interview with Barry Lee Pearson. Philip R. Ratcliffe Archive.

45. *Ibid*.

46. Pearson, *Virginia Piedmont Blues*, pp. 81, 265

47. Archie Edwards, transcript of an interview with Barry Lee Pearson.

48. Pearson, *Virginia Piedmont Blues*, p. 75.

49. Ronald D. Cohen, *Rainbow Quest: The Folk Music Revival & American Society 1940–1970*, (Amherst and Boston: University of Massachusetts Press, 2002), p. 204.

50. Brown, "From Avalon to Eternity."

51. Riches, *The Civil Rights Movement*, p. 73. The assassin was Byron De La Beckwith, a member of the Ku Klux Klan who was arrested, tried, and acquitted by an all-white jury. In 1994 the case was reopened and a retrial led to a murder conviction. Throughout the summer of 1963, SNCC, CORE, and SCLC continued their efforts to register black voters, and white supremacists continued to thwart these efforts.

52. Cohen, *Rainbow Quest*, pp. 204–5.

53. Mississippi John Hurt, *D.C. Blues: The Library of Congress Recordings, Vols. 1 and 2* (Fuel 2000 Records CD302 061 407 2, 2004; CD302 061 495 2, 2005).

54. Mississippi John Hurt, *Worried Blues* (Piedmont PLP 13161, 1963).

55. Kay, "Mississippi John Hurt," pp. 24–26.

56. Bruce Bastin, notes to Mississippi John Hurt, *Avalon Blues, Vol. 2* (LP, Heritage HT 301,1981).

57. Mississippi John Hurt, *D.C. Blues, Vol. 1.*

58. Bill Dahl, notes to *D.C. Blues.*

59. *Newport Folk Festival 1963: The Evening Concerts, Vol. 1* (LP, Vanguard VRS-9148 [mono]/VSD-79148 [stereo], 1963).

60. *Blues at Newport* (LP, Vanguard VRS 9145 [mono]/ VSD 79145 [stereo], 1964).

61. Eric Von Schmidt and Jim Rooney, *Baby Let Me Follow You Down: The Illustrated Story of the Cambridge Folk Years*, 2nd ed. (Amherst and Boston: University of Massachusetts Press, 1994), pp. 190–91, 193–94.

62. Stephen Calt, *I'd Rather Be the Devil*, p. 251. John Fahey was a musician with an interest in ethnomusicology. He received an MA degree in folklore and mythology from UCLA.

63. *Newport Folk Festival 1963: The Evening Concerts, Vol. 1.*

64. John gave this account to Gene Bush in Grenada in 1966.

65. Riches, *The Civil Rights Movement*, pp. 71–72.

66. *Ibid.*, p. 72.

69. Heilman, "Lawsuit Blues."

68. Letter from Mississippi John Hurt to Tom Hoskins, May 4, 1963. Tom Hoskins Archive.

69. Sean Ambrose, "Goodbye Avalon," *Mississippi Magazine* (1964). Tom Hoskins Archive (Photocopy, no date or page numbers).

70. Mississippi John Hurt interview by Tom Hoskins and Nick Perls.

71. Bill Givens, unpublished draft notes for OJL 8053 and 8054. Tom Hoskins Archive.

72. Cohen, *Rainbow Quest*, p. 205.

73. Dick Spottswood, notes to *Worried Blues.*

74. Eric Park, unpublished draft notes for OJL 8053 and 8054. Tom Hoskins Archive.

75. Ed Ward, notes to *Mississippi John Hurt Rediscovered.*

76. Von Schmidt and Rooney, *Baby Let Me Follow You Down.* pp. 193–99.

77. David Evans, interview, www.bluesnet.hub.org, and personal communication to author.

78. Fred Bolden, contribution to Blindman's Blues Forum, January 6, 2005.

79. David Evans, "Bessie Smith's 'Back-Water Blues': The Story Behind the Song," *Popular Music* 26:1 (2006): pp. 97–116. "Back-Water Blues" was composed

by Bessie Smith and recorded on February 17, 1927, before the great flood of the lower Mississippi River that year. The song was about a flood of the Cumberland River that flooded Nashville, Tennessee, on December 25, 1926.

80. Dave Van Ronk, *The Mayor of MacDougal Street* (New York: Da Capo, 2005), p. 188.

81. *Ibid.*, p. 188.

82. Calt, *I'd Rather Be the Devil*, p. 233.

83. *Ibid.*, pp. 294–96.

84. Ambrose, "Goodbye Avalon."

85. Siegel, notes to *Friends of Old Time Music.*

86. *Ibid.*

87. *Ibid.*

88. Van Ronk, *The Mayor of MacDougal Street*, p. 189.

89. *Ibid.*

90. Spottswood, notes to *Worried Blues.*

91. Happy Traum, "Mississippi John Hurt and the Fingerstyle Tradition" article from unknown magazine, 1974. Tom Hoskins Archive.

92. Kay, "Mississippi John Hurt," pp. 24–26.

93. Spottswood, notes to *Worried Blues.*

94. Tom Hoskins, undated recorded interview with unknown interviewer. Tom Hoskins Archive.

95. Archie Edwards, transcript of an interview with Barry Lee Pearson. Philip R. Ratcliffe Archive.

96. Mississippi John Hurt and Skip James with ED Denson, radio interview with Phil Spiro, Boston, Massachusetts. Philip R Ratcliffe Archive.

97. Fred Bolden, contribution to Blindman's Blues Forum, July 18, 2005.

98. William Bradford Huie, *Three Lives for Mississippi* (New York: WWC, 1965). This event occurred on the same day that Nick Perls, Phil Spiro, and Dick Waterman left Mississippi on the hunt for Son House, see Von Schmidt and Rooney, *Baby Let Me Follow You Down*, p. 193; and a few days before a Pete Seeger concert in Meridian, see Cohen, *Rainbow Quest*, p. 208.

99. Woodward, *The Strange Career of Jim Crow*, p. 185.

100. Michael J. Klarman, *From Jim Crow to Civil Rights: The Supreme Court and the Struggle for Racial Equality* (New York: Oxford University Press, 2004), p. 407.

101. Riches, *The Civil Rights Movement*, p. 87–88.

102. Bill Givens, unpublished draft liner notes for OJL 8053 and 8054.

103. Dick Waterman, "John Hurt: Patriarch Hippie," *Sing Out* 17, no. 1 (February/March 1967): pp. 4–7.

104. *The Guitar of Mississippi John Hurt, Vol. 1, Taught by John Miller*, Stefan Grossman's Guitar Workshop (Video/DVD OV12056, 2002).

105. "A Three-Day Look at the Blues," *Chicago Daily News*, January 23, 1965. Tom Hoskins Archive.

106. Van Ronk, *The Mayor of MacDougal Street*, p. 190.

107. Waterman, "John Hurt: Patriarch Hippie."

108. John Milward, notes to Mississippi John Hurt, *The Complete Studio Recordings* (Vanguard CD181/83-2, 2000).

109. Debra Ruben, Second Fret website, www.secondfret.com, 1996–2008.

110. Mississippi John Hurt, *Last Sessions* (LP, Vanguard VSD 79327, 1972).

111. Tom Hoskins, undated recorded interview with unknown interviewer. Tom Hoskins Archive.

112. Max Ochs, as told to E. G. Dubovsky, *With Mississippi John Hurt* (Berkeley, California: Arkady, 2004), pp. 11–13.

113. *Ibid.*

114. Dick Spottswood, additional notes to Mississippi John Hurt, *Memorial Anthology.*

115. It has not been possible to determine the identity of the alleged dishonest agents.

116. Cohen, *Rainbow Quest*, p. 234.

117. Givens, unpublished draft notes for OJL 8053 and 8054.

118. Hoskins, undated recorded interview with unknown interviewer.

119. David Evans, interview, www.bluesnet.hub.org.

120. Bill Dahl, notes to *D.C. Blues.*

121. Calt, *I'd Rather Be the Devil*, pp. 304–6.

122. *Ibid.*, pp. 294–96.

Chapter 4

1. Music Research, Incorporated. Minutes of Shareholders Meeting, August 17, 1964. Tom Hoskins Archive.

2. Music Research, Incorporated. Board of Directors Meeting, September 3, 1964. Tom Hoskins Archive.

3. *Ibid.*

4. *Ibid.*

5. *Ibid.*

6. Bill of Sale of assets of Music Research Inc., dated October 23, 1964. Tom Hoskins Archive.

7. Music Research, Incorporated. Minutes of Shareholders Meeting, November 18, 1964. Tom Hoskins Archive.

8. Letter April 28, 1965, from Spottswoods to Audio Matrix, Inc., Bronx, New York; Dulce Tone Company, Long Island City, Queens, New York; Plastylite Corporation, Plainfield, New Jersey; Globe Productions, Inc, Bronx, New York. Tom Hoskins Archive.

9. Letter June 30, 1965, from W. J. Powell to "All Interested Parties." Re: Record of the Chancery Court of Arlington County Re: Music Research Inc., Complainant vs. Richard K. Spottswood and Louisa C. H. Spottswood, Defendants, 14 June, 1965. Plus inventory of properties to be transferred to Music Research Inc. Tom Hoskins Archive.

10. Agreement dated November 30, 1965, between Vanguard Recording and Mississippi John Hurt. Signed by Mississippi John Hurt, Herb Gart, Hurt's business manager, and Maynard Solomon of Vanguard Recording Society. Tom Hoskins Archive.

11. Von Schmidt and Rooney, *Baby Let Me Follow You Down*, p. 198.

12. Calt, *I'd Rather Be the Devil*, pp. 298–310, 330–31, 348–49.

13. Cohen, *Rainbow Quest*, p. 230.

14. Van Ronk, *The Mayor of MacDougal Street*, p. 191.

15. Bond, *Mississippi: A Documentary History*, pp. 271–74.

16. "Concerts and Recitals," *Chicago Tribune*, Sunday, October 24, 1965, p. 8.

17. Dick Waterman, notes to *The Immortal Mississippi John Hurt* (Vanguard VRS-9248 [mono]/VSD-79248 [stereo], CD VMD 79248, 1967).

18. Tom Hoskins, undated recorded interview with unknown interviewer.

19. *The Guitar of Mississippi John Hurt, Vols. 1 and 2, Taught by John Miller*.

20. David Brown, "From Avalon to Eternity"; Mississippi John Hurt, Interview by Pete Seeger.

21. Tom Hoskins, undated recorded interview with unknown interviewer.

22. *Ibid*.

23. Dick Waterman, notes to *The Immortal Mississippi John Hurt*.

24. R. Scherl, Notes to Mississippi John Hurt, *The Candy Man* (Intermedia Records, 1982).

25. Nancy Sonsotta, "Spring Arts Festival: First For Campus," University of Cincinnati *News Record*, April 21, 1966, p. 12.

26. Dick Waterman, *Between Midnight and Day: The Last Unpublished Blues Archive* (New York: Thunder's Mouth, 2003), p. 18.

27. Cohen, *Rainbow Quest*, p. 252.

28. Van Ronk, *The Mayor of MacDougal Street*, p. 188.

29. *Ibid*., p. 189.

30. Fred Bolden, contribution to Blindman's Blues Forum, February 19, 2005.

31. *Ibid*.

32. Joan Baez official web site. www.joanbaez.com.

33. Hoffman, "John William Hurt."

34. John Hurt, Certificate of Death.

35. Lawrence Cohn, "Mississippi John Hurt 1892–1966," *Saturday Review*, February 1967, p. 10, cited in R. Gilpin, "John Smith Hurt and the Blues," *Journal of Mississippi History* 63, no. 1 (Spring 2001).

36. Stanley Booth, *Rythm Oil: A Journey Through the Music of the American South* (Cambridge, MA: Da Capo, 2000), pp. 37–45.

37. *Ibid*., p. 41.

38. *Ibid*., p. 44–45.

39. *Ibid*., p. 45.

40. Givens unpublished draft liner notes for OJL 8053 and 8054.

41. William A. Shumann, "Singer Mississippi John Hurt Dies at 74," obituary, *Washington Post*, November 5, 1966. Tom Hoskins Archive; Anonymous, "Mississippi John Hurt, 74 Dies: A Singer of Wry Country Blues," obituary, *New York Times*, November 11, 1964. Tom Hoskins Archive.

42. Estate of John Hurt, deceased, Final Order (No. 11,266) of the Chancery Court of Grenada County, on November 8, 1967.

43. Waterman, notes to *The Immortal Mississippi John Hurt*.

44. Brown, "From Avalon to Eternity."

45. *Ibid*.

46. Von Schmidt and Rooney, *Baby Let Me Follow You Down*, pp. 198–99.

47. Ulrich Adelt, *Blues Music in the Sixties A Story in Black and White*. (New Brunswick, Rutgers University Press, 2010), p. 47.

48. Answer to plaintiffs' first set of interrogatories, Answer to interrogatory No. 2, from Thomas B. Hoskins. Irene Smith et al. vs. Thomas B. Hoskins: In The Chancery Court of Grenada County, Mississippi, January 24, 2005.

Chapter 5

1. Estate of John Hurt, deceased, Final Order.
2. Copy of letter from Jessie Hurt to unknown attorney (probably George E. Goldstein), December 4, 1966. Tom Hoskins Archive.
3. Copy of letter from Jessie Hurt to Maynard Solomon of Vanguard Records, December 11, 1966. Tom Hoskins Archive.
4. Letter from Jessie Hurt to Tom Hoskins, December 30, 1966. Tom Hoskins Archive.
5. Copy of letter from Jessie Hurt to Maynard Solomon of Vanguard Records, January 17, 1967. Tom Hoskins Archive.
6. Copy of letter from Jessie Hurt to Maynard Solomon of Vanguard Records, February 9, 1967. Tom Hoskins Archive.
7. Copy of letter from Jessie Hurt to Maynard Solomon of Vanguard Records, May 15, 1967. Tom Hoskins Archive.
8. Copy of letter from Jessie Hurt to Maynard Solomon of Vanguard Records, July 25, 1967. Tom Hoskins Archive.
9. Letter from Jessie Hurt to Tom Hoskins, November 11, 1967. Tom Hoskins Archive.
10. Envelopes from Jessie Hurt sent from No. 1 North Levee Street, November 11, 1967, and from 863 Telegraph Street, Grenada, Mississippi, December 3, 1967. Tom Hoskins Archive.
11. Copy of letter from Jessie Hurt to George E. Goldstein of Goldstein and Goldstein, Philadelphia, April 24, 1968. Tom Hoskins Archive.
12. Copy of letter from Jessie Hurt to George E. Goldstein of Goldstein and Goldstein, Philadelphia, October 7, 1968. Tom Hoskins Archive.
13. It was and remains standard practice for record companies to prepare accounts and make payments every six months.
14. Copy of letter (part) and envelope from Tom Hoskins to Jessie Hurt ca. November–December 1968. Tom Hoskins Archive.
15. Copy of letter from Peter V. Kuykendall of Wynwood Music Co. to Maynard Solomon of Vanguard Records, New York, November 11, 1968. Tom Hoskins Archive.
16. Copy of letter from Peter V. Kuykendall of Wynwood Music Co. to Leland Talbot III of Music Research Inc., Annapolis, Maryland, July 17, 1969. Tom Hoskins Archive.
17. A severe epidemic of influenza struck the United States in late 1968.
18. Letter from Jessie Hurt to Tom Hoskins, December 6, 1968. Tom Hoskins Archive.
19. Easter card from Jessie Hurt to Tom Hoskins, March 31, 1969. Tom Hoskins Archive.
20. Grave marker for Hardy Hurt, St. James Cemetery, Avalon, Mississippi.
21. Letter from Jessie Hurt to Tom Hoskins, May 8, 1971. Tom Hoskins Archive.

22. Letter from Jessie Hurt to Tom Hoskins, January 4, 1972. Tom Hoskins Archive.

23. Agreement of November 30, 1965, between Vanguard Record and Mississippi John Hurt.

24. Copy of Agreement between Adelphi Studios and Music Research Incorporated, June 8, 1970. Tom Hoskins Archive.

25. Copy of letter from Eugene Rosenthal of Adelphi Studios to W. Wright Gedge of Wright Gedge Stereo Recording Company, Grosse Point, Michigan, September 10, 1970. Tom Hoskins Archive.

26. Copy of letter from W. Wright Gedge of Wright Gedge Stereo Recording Company, Grosse Point, Michigan, to Eugene Rosenthal of Adelphi Studios, September 18, 1970. Tom Hoskins Archive.

27. Copy of letter from Jessie Hurt to George E. Goldstein of Goldstein and Goldstein, Philadelphia, October 7, 1968, in which Jessie provides Goldstein with Tom Hoskins's address c/o Robert Scherl. Tom Hoskins Archive

28. United States Court of Appeals, Second Circuit, No. 67 Docket 76-7160: Music Research, Inc., and Adelphi Records, Inc. v. Vanguard Recording Company, Inc., Argued November 10, 1976. Decided December 30, 1976. Tom Hoskins Archive.

29. Deposition of Thomas Bird Hoskins; Civil Action No. 81-0946, in the United States District Court for the District of Columbia. Adelphi Records Inc. v. Polygram Records v. Mark Wenner, September 19, 1982, p. 16. Tom Hoskins Archive.

30. Mississippi John Hurt, *Volume I of the Original Piedmont Recordings Folksongs and Blues* (PLP-13157, 1963) and *Volume II of the Original Piedmont Recordings Worried Blues* (PLP-13161, 1964).

31. Copy of letter from Bill Givens of Origin Jazz Library to George E. Goldstein of Goldstein and Goldstein, Philadelphia, May 21, 1968. Tom Hoskins Archive.

32. Copy of letter from Bill Givens of Origin Jazz Library, Berkeley, California to Tom Hoskins of Music Research Inc., Maryland, July 17, 1974. Tom Hoskins Archive.

33. Copy letter from Tom Hoskins of Music Research Inc., Maryland to Bill Givens of Origin Jazz Library, Berkeley, California, October 20, 1974. Tom Hoskins Archive.

34. Findings of Fact and Conclusions of Law, In the Chancery Court of Grenada County, Mississippi; Irene Smith, et al., Plaintiffs versus Thomas Hoskins Estate, Suzanne Brown Executrix, Cause No. 92-8-277, October 26, 2004, p. 17. Tom Hoskins Archive.

35. Deposition of Thomas Bird Hoskins; Civil Action No. 122898, in the Circuit court for Montgomery County, Thomas B. Hoskins v. Eugene R. Rosenthal t/a Adelphi Studios and t/a Adelphi Records and t/a Genes Compact Disc Company and Adelphi Records, Inc., January 11, 1995, pp. 81, 103. Tom Hoskins Archive.

36. An advertisement from "Loose Blues News," November 1995, for recently found factory fresh copies of the Rebel Records release of *Mississippi John Hurt Volume One of a Legacy*, Rebel Records CLPS 1068, priced at $12.99 was posted on Toronto Blues Society website, www.torontobluessociety.com. Subsequent correspondence with Rebel Records suggests that the LP was released between 1969 and 1971.

37. Written anonymous account (part) of a summary of legal difficulties that had beset MRI 1963–1975. Tom Hoskins Archive.

38. Mississippi John Hurt, *Volume One of a Legacy* (LP, Piedmont-Legacy CLPS-1068, 1975), produced by Music Research, Inc., producers of Piedmont and Bullfrog Records.

39. Accounting of Thomas Hoskins, Irene Smith, et al., versus Thomas Hoskins, et al. Cause No. 92-8-277 in the Chancery Court of Grenada County, Mississippi, March 4, 2001. Tom Hoskins Archive.

40. Certificate of Death, Jessie L. Hurt, State of Mississippi Department of Health File Number: 123-82-11523. The death certificate gives the birth date as September 11, 1903 and her age as 73. The arithmetic is incorrect; if she was born in 1903 her age would be 79. Other sources suggest that Jessie was born in 1891, 1894 or 1895, which would make her actual age 91, 88, or 87.

41. *Ibid.*

42. Copy of Last Will and Testament of Jessie Lee Hurt, December 29, 1972. Tom Hoskins Archive.

43. Joe Lee, *Fang 1941-2002* (CD, Private undated publication, Joe Lee); "Leon Kagarise's Music Collection," National Public Radio, June 2, 2003. npr.org/templates/story/story.php?storyId=1280910.

44. Deposition of Thomas Bird Hoskins; Civil Action No. 81-0946, in the United States District Court for the District of Columbia. Adelphi Records Inc. v. Polygram Records v. Mark Wenner, September 10, 1982, pp. 131–35. Tom Hoskins Archive.

45. Deposition of Thomas Bird Hoskins; Civil Action No. 122898, in the Circuit Court for Montgomery County, Thomas B. Hoskins v Eugene R. Rosenthal t/a Adelphi Studios and t/a Adelphi Records and t/a Genes Compact Disc Company and Adelphi Records, Inc., January 11, 1995, pp. 105–10.

46. Letter from his attorney Charles F. Morgan to Thomas B. Hoskins, January 20, 1995.

47. Jon Hartley Fox, notes to *Mississippi John Hurt Legend* (Rounder CD 1100, 1997).

48. Contract between William G. Nowlin Jr. of Rounder Records and Thomas B. Hoskins, April 14, 1991, licensing Rounder's use of the *John Hurt Legacy* LP. Tom Hoskins Archive.

49. Letter and attached draft licensing agreement re: Hoskins v. Eugene R. Rosenthal, et al. Montgomery County Court Case No. 122898, June 30, 1995. Tom Hoskins Archive.

50. Dick Spottswood, notes to Mississippi John Hurt, *D.C. Blues* Library of Congress Recordings Volume 2 (double CD, Fuel 2000 302 061 495 2, 2005).

51. Dick Spottswood, in Kay, "Mississippi John Hurt."

52. UK issues of the Library of Congress recordings of Mississippi John Hurt: *Monday Morning Blues*, Library of Congress Recordings Volume 1 (Flyright FLYLP 553, 1980); *Avalon Blues*, Library of Congress Recordings Volume 2 (Heritage HT-301, 1982); *Sacred and Secular*, Library of Congress Recordings Volume 3 (Heritage HT-320, 1988).

53. Copy of letter to John William Hurt, March 2, 1990, from Bill Nowlin of Rounder Records. Tom Hoskins Archive.

54. *D.C. Blues*, Library of Congress Recordings Volume 1 and Volume 2.

55. Order to determine rightful heirs of John S. Hurt deceased, Chancery Court of Grenada County, Mississippi, No. 92-8-277, May 17, 1999.

56. United States District Court for the Northern District of Mississippi, March 11, 1993, Case Number 3:92CV167-B-O. Tom Hoskins Archive.

57. Heilman, "Lawsuit Blues."

58. *Ibid*.

59. Letter from John William "Man" Hurt in *Greenwood Commonwealth*, cited in Heilman, "Lawsuit Blues," p. 21.

60. Heilman, "Lawsuit Blues," p. 21.

61. LaVere, Denson, and Grossman were involved with small independent record labels. Mitchell was Hoskins's lawyer and familiar with the recording industry.

62. United States District Court for the Northern District of Mississippi, March 11, 1993, Case Number 3:92CV167-B-O. Tom Hoskins Archive.

63. Findings of Fact, Conclusions of Law and Order Granting Summary Judgment, February 16, 1994, In the Chancery Court of Grenada County, State of Mississippi. Tom Hoskins Archive.

64. Order to determine rightful heirs of John S. Hurt deceased, Chancery Court of Grenada County, Mississippi, No. 92-8-277, May 17, 1999. Tom Hoskins Archive.

65. Answer to Plaintiffs' First Set of Interrogatories, Irene Smith, et al., versus Thomas Hoskins, et al. Cause No. 92-8-277 in the Chancery Court of Grenada County, Mississippi, January 24, 2000. Tom Hoskins Archive.

66. *Ibid*.

67. Accounting of Thomas Hoskins, Irene Smith, et al., versus Thomas Hoskins, et al. Cause No. 92-8-277. Tom Hoskins Archive; Findings of Fact and Conclusion of Law, re: Irene Smith et al. versus Thomas Hoskins Estate, Suzanne Brown, Executrix. Cause No. 92-8-277, In the Chancery Court of Grenada County, Mississippi, Ordered, October 25, 2004; Filed October 26, 2004. Tom Hoskins Archive.

68. Letter from the Library of Congress, Washington D.C., to Mr. Delaney (probably of Rounder Records), April 13, 1985. Tom Hoskins Archive.

69. Accounting of Thomas Hoskins, Irene Smith, et al., versus Thomas Hoskins, et al. Cause No. 92-8-277.

70. Findings of Fact and Conclusion of Law, re- Irene Smith et al. versus Thomas Hoskins Estate, Suzanne Brown, Executrix. Cause No. 92-8-277; Heilman, "Lawsuit Blues," p. 24.

71. Findings of Fact and Conclusion of Law, re: Irene Smith et al. versus Thomas Hoskins Estate, Suzanne Brown, Executrix. Cause No. 92-8-277.

72. Release and Settlement Agreement relating to the Findings of Fact and Conclusion of Law, re: Irene Smith et al. versus Thomas Hoskins Estate, Suzanne Brown, Executrix. Cause No. 92-8-277, In the Chancery Court of Grenada County, Mississippi. Ordered, October 25, 2004; Filed October 26, 2004. Tom Hoskins Archive.

73. Land Records, Old Records Room of the Courthouse, Carrollton, Mississippi, and interview of Records administrator, Debbie McLean.

74. A. Renee Williams, "105-year-old woman rescued from blaze," Press cutting from unknown source, Mississippi John Hurt Museum, Valley, Carrollton, Mississippi.

75. "Archie Edwards, A Biography," by Richard Burton, Archie Edwards Blues Heritage Foundation, 2007.

76. Archie Edwards, "The Road Is Rough And Rocky" (45, SRI NR 4328-2, 1977).

77. Patrick Sky, *Two Steps Forward One Step Back* (Leviathan SLIF 2000, 1975); Bill Morrissey, *Songs of Mississippi John Hurt* (Philo/Rounder CD 11671-1216-2, 1999; *Avalon Blues: A Tribute to the Music of Mississippi John Hurt* (Vanguard CD 7958-2, 2001).

78. Taj Mahal, *Recycling the Blues and Other Related Stuff* (Pure Pleasure Records/Columbia, LPUREPL 1605 [AL 31605], 1972).

79. *Lost Jim Sings & Plays Mississippi John Hurt* (Alabama Jubilee Music, 2005); *Payday: Lost Jim Plays & Sings Mississippi John Hurt, Vol. 2* (JPG Records, 2006); *Got The Blues, Can't Be Satisfied: Lost Jim Sings Mississippi John Hurt*, to be released.

80. Stefan Wirz, Mississippi John Hurt discography (www.wirz.de>.

81. *The Music of Mississippi John Hurt*, including two CDs and written music, words, and tablature of a selection of tunes, Stefan Grossman's Masters of Country Blues Guitar, Warner Bros. Publications, Miami Florida, 1993; *Shake That Thing: The Guitar of Mississippi John Hurt Volume 1*, Stefan Grossman, including three CDs and written music and tablature of a selection of tunes, Mel Bay Publications, Pacific, Montana, 2003; *Avalon Blues, The Guitar of Mississippi John Hurt Volume 2*, Stefan Grossman, including three CDs and written music and tablature of a selection of tunes, Mel Bay Publications, Pacific, Montana, 2003.

82. *The Guitar of Mississippi John Hurt Volume One, Taught by John Miller*, DVD OV12056; *Volume Two*, DVD OV12067, Stefan Grossman Guitar Workshop, Sparta, New Jersey, 2002.

Index

Page numbers in **bold** refer to illustrations.

Edwards, Archie, 27, 203; John and, 142–44, 148, 162, 173, 235–36; at the National Institutes of Health, 162; "The Road Is Rough and Rocky," 236
Edwards, David "Honeyboy," 82, 95–96
Edwards, John, 121
Elder Richard Bryant's Sanctified Singers, 60
Elliot, Ramblin' Jack, 146, 166
Ellis, Eleanor, 233
Estes, Sleepy John, 123, 177
Evans, David, 25, 26, 55, 172, 177–78
Evans, Felix, 32, 37, 39, 40
Evers, Medgar, 144–45, 284n51

Fahey, John, 146, 147, 175
Fang. *See* Hoskins, Tom
Fiddlin' Bob Larkin and His Music Makers, 60
Firk, Backward Sam. *See* Stewart, Mike
Fisher, Sandy, 136
Flames, The, 79
Flatt and Scruggs, 185, 216
Fleck, Daniel, 27, 29
Flyright Records, 219
Folk Alliance Conference, 187
Fox, Jon Hartley, 26
Fretted instruments, 147
Friends of Old Time Music (FOTM), 238
Fuel 2000 Records, 219
Fuller, Blind Boy, 27, 81, 82
Fuller, Jessie, 156, 158, 171

Gahr, David, 157
Galveston hurricane (1900), 17, 268n67
Gart, Herb, 176, 177, 182, 211
Gart, John, 177
Gaslight Café, 154, 160, 166, 167, 170, 188
Gedge, W. Wright, 212
Gene Autry's Deluxe Collection of Over 80 Songs, 97
Georgia Sea Island Singers, 146
Gerakis, John, 155
Gillum, Jazz, "Key to the Highway," 95
Givens, Bill, 165, 199, 213–14

Golden Gate Jubilee Singers, 82–83
Goldstein, George, 213
Goldwater, Barry, 164
Goodman, Andrew, 163–64
Gordner, D. M., 7
Goss, Olin, 100, 107, 108–9
Great Depression, 70–72
Great Mississippi River Flood (1927), 54–56
Green, Silas, 35
Greenberg, Mark, 120, 177, 178–80
Greenwood, Miss., 94, 116
Greenwood *Commonwealth*, 52
Greenwood Voter Registration Project, 116
Grenada, Miss., 94
Grossman, Stefan: Friends of Old Time Music and, 144, 158; John and, 120, 136, 144, 147, 158–59, 161, 172, 236; New York Guitar Festival and, 238; Stefan Grossman Guitar Workshop and, 236, 238
guitar, 10, 50, 97
Gunning, Sarah, 166
Gussow, Adam, *Seems Like Murder Here*, 25
Guthrie, Woody, 117

Hadley, Dardanelle, 79–80, 85–87, 279n76
Hairston, Jack, 104
Haley, Alex, 123
Hambrick, Flowers, 32
Hambrick, J. J., 14, 32
Hambrick, J. W., 32
Hambrick, Minnie Lee, 14, 32
Hambrick, Norma, 32
Hambrick, Ward, 32, 36–37
Hamer, Fannie Lou, 116, 178
Hammond, John, 238
Hamp, Charles W.: "Avalon Town," 63; "My Kinda Love," 63; "Sitting on the Stairs," 63; "The Spell of the Blues," 63
Handy, W. C., 51; "The Hooking Cow Blues," 26
Hanks, George, 74